Adaptive Thinking

EVOLUTION AND COGNITION

General Editor: Stephen Stich, Rutgers University

Published in the series

Simple Heuristics That Make Us Smart
   Gerd Gigerenzer, Peter Todd, and
   the ABC Research Group
Adaptive Thinking: Rationality in the Real World
   Gerd Gigerenzer

Adaptive Thinking

Rationality in the Real World

Gerd Gigerenzer

UNIVERSITY PRESS

2000

OXFORD
UNIVERSITY PRESS

Oxford   New York
Athens   Auckland   Bangkok   Bogotá   Buenos Aires   Calcutta
Cape Town   Chennai   Dar es Salaam   Delhi   Florence   Hong Kong   Istanbul
Karachi   Kuala Lumpur   Madrid   Melbourne   Mexico City   Mumbai
Nairobi   Paris   São Paulo   Shanghai   Singapore   Taipei   Tokyo   Toronto   Warsaw

and associated companies in
Berlin   Ibadan

Published by Oxford University Press, Inc.
198 Madison Avenue, New York, New York 10016

Oxford is a registered trademark of Oxford University Press

Library of Congress Cataloging-in-Publication Data
Gigerenzer, Gerd.
    Adaptive thinking : rationality in the real world / Gerd Gigerenzer.
        p.   cm.—(Evolution and cognition)
    Includes bibliographical references and index.
    ISBN 0-19-513622-5
        1. Reasoning.   2. Thought and thinking.   3. Logic.   I. Title.   II. Series.
    BC177.G53   2000
    128'.33—dc21   99-052833

9 8 7 6 5 4 3 2 1

Printed in the United States of America
on acid-free paper

For Raine and Thalia

PREFACE

Some years ago, I had lunch with a motley group of colleagues at Stanford, mostly psychologists and economists, who were interested in decision making in an uncertain world. We chewed our way through our sandwiches and through the latest embellishments of the prisoner's dilemma, trading stories of this or that paradox or stubborn irrationality. Finally, one economist concluded the discussion with the following dictum: "Look," he said with conviction, "either reasoning is *rational* or it's *psychological*."

This supposed opposition between the rational and the psychological has haunted me ever since. For the economists and psychologists seated at the picnic table with me that afternoon, it meant a division of labor. The heavenly laws of logic and probability rule the realm of sound reasoning; psychology is assumed to be irrelevant. Only if mistakes are made are psychologists called in to explain how wrong-wired human minds deviate from these laws. Chernobyl, U.S. foreign policy, and human disasters of many kinds have been associated with failures in logical thinking. Adopting this opposition, many textbooks present first the laws of logic and probability as the standard by which to measure human thinking, then data about how people actually think. The discrepancy between the two makes people appear to be irrational.

Adaptive Thinking offers a different story. I view the mind in relation to its environment rather than in opposition to the laws of logic or probability. In a complex and uncertain world, psychology is indispensable for sound reasoning; it is rationality's fuel rather than its brake. This book is about rethinking rationality as adaptive thinking: to understand how minds cope with specific environments, ecological and social. The chapters in this book elaborate the idea that human thinking—from scientific creativity to simply understanding what a positive HIV test means—"happens" partly outside of the mind. For instance, new laboratory instruments can inspire scientists to create new metaphors and theories, and new ways of representing uncertainties can either cloud or facilitate physicians' understanding of risks. In this sense, *in*sight can come from *out*side the mind.

The chapters provide both research programs and case studies. For instance, the program of *ecological rationality* studies the mind in relation to its environment, past and present. *Bounded rationality* stresses that sound reasoning can be achieved by simple heuristics that do not follow the prescriptions of logic and probability. *Social rationality* is a form of ecological rationality in which the environment consists of conspecifics and that highlights the importance of domain-specific behavior and cognition in social environments.

Adaptive Thinking is a collection of what I consider the most important of my papers on rationality, reasoning and rituals in the 1990s. I have rewritten, updated, and shortened them to bring out the coherent story they tell as a whole. The papers were originally addressed to different scientific communities. This book affords readers the opportunity, for the first time, to see how the various theoretical endeavors and practical applications fit together.

Berlin   G. G.
July 1999

ACKNOWLEDGMENTS

People

My special thanks go to Daniel G. Goldstein, who coauthored the articles on which Chapters 2 and 8 are based, and Ulrich Hoffrage, who coauthored the articles on which Chapters 5, 6, and 7 are based. I have been extraordinarily lucky to have had Dan and Ulrich first as students and now as colleagues—I could have not wished for better companions. I would also like to thank Axel Ebert and Heinz Kleinbölting, who coauthored the articles on which Chapters 5 and 7, respectively, are based.

The chapters in this book have profited from the comments and ideas of many people: Hal R. Arkes, Peter Ayton, Paul B. Baltes, Peter Barker, Robert Boyd, Valerie M. Chase, Michael Cole, Leda Cosmides, Denise D. Cummins, Jean Czerlinski, Arnold Davidson, Frans de Waal, Juan Delius, Raphael Diepgen, Berna Eden, Ward Edwards, Ruma Falk, Christian Fiebach, Klaus Fiedler, Baruch Fischhoff, Jennifer Freyd, Vittorio Girotto, William Goldstein, Daniel G. Goldstein, Joel Goldstein, Adam S. Goodie, Howard E. Gruber, Kennneth R. Hammond, John Hartigan, Reid Hastie, Wolfgang Hell, Ralph Hertwig, Miles Hewstone, Johannes Hönekopp, Ulrich Hoffrage, Janellen Huttenlocher, Jerome Kagan, Winfried Kain, Gideon Keren, Horst Kilcher, David Klahr, Gernot Kleiter, Jonathan J. Koehler, Andreas Krebs, Elke M. Kurz, Paolo Legrenzi, Sarah Lichtenstein, R. Duncan Luce, Albert Madansky, James S. Magnuson, Brendan Maher, Ken Manktelow, Laura Martignon, David McNeill, Barbara Mellers, Arthur Miller, Geoffrey F. Miller, John Monahan, David J. Murray, David Over, Silvia Papai, John Payne, Jörg Quarder, Terry Regier, Frank Renkewitz, Werner Schubö, Peter Sedlmeier, Anna Senkevitch, Simon Shaffer, Herbert A. Simon, Dan Sperber, Ursula M. Staudinger, Nancy Stein, Stephen M. Stigler, Andreas Stoltze, Wolfgang Stroebe, Gerhard Strube, Patrick Suppes, Zeno Swijtink, Peter M. Todd, John Tooby, Tom Trabasso, Amos Tversky, Elke Weber, Andy Whiten, William Wimsatt, Norton Wise, Werner Wittmann, and Alf Zimmer.

I am also very grateful to Donna Alexander, Valerie M. Chase, Dagmar Fecht, Felix Guettler, Madeline Hoyt, Amy Johnson, Ulrich Kuhnert, Kathleen Much, and Anita Todd for their support in the preparation of the manuscript.

Last but not least, I wish to thank Steve Stich and Peter Ohlin, who helped bring this book into being.

There is one person to whom I owe so much that "thank you" is not the right term: Lorraine Daston, who is my wife, emotional support, and intellectual companion in the world of ideas.

Institutions

The research reported in this book was supported by fellowships and grants from the Center for Advanced Study in the Behavioral Sciences, Stanford; the Center for Interdisciplinary Research, Bielefeld, Germany; Deutsche Forschungsgemeinschaft, Germany; Fonds zur Förderung der Wissenschaften, Austria; the National Science Foundation; the Spencer Foundation; and the University of Chicago School Mathematics Project Fund for Research in Mathematics Education. I am particularly grateful to the Max Planck Society, which has provided outstanding research support since 1995.

Publishers

Chapter 1 is an edited version of G. Gigerenzer (1991), From tools to theories: A heuristic of discovery in cognitive psychology, *Psychological Review, 98,* 254–267, reprinted with permission of the American Psychological Association. Chapter 2 is a shortened and updated version of G. Gigerenzer and D. G. Goldstein (1996), Mind as computer: The birth of a metaphor, *Creativity Research Journal, 9,* 131–144, reprinted with permission of Lawrence Erlbaum Associates. Chapter 3 is based on G. Gigerenzer (in press), Ideas in exile: The struggles of an upright man, in K. R. Hammond and T. R. Stewart (eds.), *The essential Brunswik: Beginnings, explications, applications* (New York: Oxford University Press), reprinted with permission. Chapter 4 is an edited and shortened version of G. Gigerenzer (1998), Ecological intelligence: An adaptation for frequencies, in D. D. Cummins and C. Allen (eds.), *The evolution of mind* (pp. 9–29) (New York: Oxford University Press), reprinted with permission. Chapter 5 is an edited version of G. Gigerenzer, U. Hoffrage, and A. Ebert (1998), AIDS counseling for low-risk clients, *AIDS CARE, 10,* 197–211, reprinted with permission of Carfax Publishers. Chapter 6 is based on parts of G. Gigerenzer and U. Hoffrage (1995), How to improve Bayesian reasoning without instruction: Frequency formats, *Psychological Review, 102,* 684–704, and G. Gigerenzer and U. Hoffrage (1999), Overcoming difficulties in Bayesian reasoning: A reply to Lewis & Keren and Mellers & McGraw, *Psychological Review, 106,* 425–430, reprinted with permission of the American Psychological Association. Chapter 7 is a shortened version of G. Gigerenzer, U. Hoffrage, and H. Kleinbölting (1991), Probabilistic mental models: A Brunswikian theory of confidence, *Psychological Review, 98*, 506–528, reprinted with permission of the American Psychological Association. Chapter 8 is an updated version of G. Gigerenzer and D. G. Goldstein (1996), Reasoning the fast and frugal way: Models of bounded rationality, *Psychological Review*, 103, 650–669, reprinted with permission of the American Psychological Association. Chapters 9 and 10 are based on G. Gigerenzer (1996), Rationality: Why social context matters, in P. B. Baltes, and U. M. Staudinger (eds.), *Interactive minds: Life-span perspectives on the social foundation of cognition* (pp. 319–346) (Cambridge: Cambridge University Press), reprinted with permission. Chapter 11 is a shortened version of G. Gigerenzer (1997), The modularity of social intelligence, in A. Whiten & R. W. Byrne (eds.), *Machiavellian intelligence II* (pp. 264–288) (Cambridge: Cambridge University Press), reprinted with permission. Chapter 12 is based on G. Gigerenzer (1991), How to make cognitive illusions disappear. Beyond "heuristics and biases," in W. Stroebe & M. Hewstone (eds.), *European Review of Social Psychology, 2*, 83–115, reprinted with permission of John Wiley & Sons. Chapter 13 is a slightly shortened version of G. Gigerenzer (1993), The Superego, the Ego, and the Id in statistical reasoning, in G. Keren & C. Lewis (eds.), *A handbook for data analysis in the behavioral sciences: Methodological issues* (pp. 311–339). Hillsdale, NJ: Lawrence Erlbaum Associates, reprinted with permission. Chapter 14 is an edited version of G. Gigerenzer (1998), Surrogates for theories, *Theory and Psychology, 8*, 195–204, reprinted with permission of Sage Publications.

CONTENTS

WHERE DO NEW IDEAS
COME FROM?

I wrote "From Tools to Theories" in one of the cabinlike offices at the Center for Advanced Study in Palo Alto in 1990. That was in the good old days when the offices had no telephones, e-mail, or other communication facilitators to interrupt one's thoughts. In the meantime, the Center, like you and I, has surrendered to technology. Chapter 1 is about the impact of new technologies on creative thinking—an impact of a productive rather than a disruptive kind. New tools can suggest new scientific ideas and metaphors about nature, society, and the mind. When this happens, we can trace discoveries back to the changing technological environment in which they evolved rather than attributing them to some mystical process inside a scientist's head. In this sense, new *in*sights can come from *out*side the mind.

Two influential tools fueled the cognitive revolution: new statistical techniques and the computer. Both started as tools for data processing and ended up as theories of mind. The power of tools to inspire new theories derives from changes both in the technological environment (new tools) and in the social environment in which a scientist works (the community of tool users). The social environment is influential in several ways. First, it affects the pragmatic use of a tool (of which there are many), which then leaves its mark on the new theories of mind. Second, entrenchment of the tool in the research community is an important precondition for its final acceptance as a model of mind. Finally, new social organizations can inspire the creation of tools in the first place, as evidenced by the invention of the machine computer. Babbage's computer was modeled after a new social organization of work, namely, the division of labor in large-scale manufacturing. The social origin of the computer illustrates how a metaphor can cut both ways: First computers were modeled after minds, and later minds were modeled after computers.

Computers and statistics have both been used to fulfill the timeless longing to replace judgment by the application of content-blind, mechanical rules. Such mechanization has become an ideal in many professions, including copyediting. For instance, the copyeditor at *Psychological Review* who worked on "From Tools to Theories" had the rule that a single author speaking in the first person should not use "we" but "I." One sentence in my original manuscript read: "Good ideas are hard to come by, and we should be grateful for those few we have, whatever their lineage." I lost this argument; every time I reinstated the "we," the copyeditor took it out again, until it eventually was replaced by "one."

The three chapters in this section elaborate and extend ideas developed in two earlier books, *Cognition as Intuitive Statistics* (1987, with D. J. Murray) and *Measurement and Modeling in Psychology* (1981, published in German). "From Tools To Theories" won the American Association for the Advancement of Science (AAAS) Prize for Behavioral Science Research in 1991. It shows how statistical methods have turned into metaphors of mind. The tools-to-theories heuristic, one of several heuristics of discovery, can explain the emergence of a broad range of theories and shed light on their limitations and potentials.

From Tools to Theories

A Heuristic of Discovery

Scientific inquiry can be viewed as "an ocean, continuous everywhere and without a break or division" (Leibniz, 1690/1951, p. 73). Hans Reichenbach (1938) nonetheless divided this ocean into two great seas, the context of discovery and the context of justification. Philosophers, logicians, and mathematicians claimed justification as a part of their territory and dismissed the context of discovery as none of their business, or even as "irrelevant to the logical analysis of scientific knowledge" (Popper, 1935/1959, p. 31). Their sun shines over one part of the ocean and has been enlightening about matters of justification, but the other part of the ocean still remains in a mystical darkness where imagination and intuition reign, or so it is claimed. Popper, Braithenaite, and others ceded the dark part of the ocean to psychology and, perhaps, sociology, but few psychologists have fished in these waters. Most did not dare or care.

The discovery versus justification distinction has oversimplified the understanding of scientific inquiry. For instance, in the debate over whether the context of discovery is relevant to understanding science, both sides in the controversy have construed the question as whether the *earlier* stage of discovery should be added to the *later* justification stage (Nickles, 1980). Conceiving the two-context distinction as a temporal distinction (first discovery, then justification), however, can be misleading because justification procedures (checking and testing) and discovery processes (having new ideas) take place during all temporal stages of inquiry. In fact, the original distinction drawn by Reichenbach in 1938 did not include this temporal simplification; his was not even a strict dichotomy (see Curd, 1980). I believe that the prevailing interpretation of the two contexts as conceptually distinct events that are in one and only one temporal sequence has misled many into trying to understand discovery without taking account of justification.

In this chapter, I argue that discovery can be understood by heuristics (not a logic) of discovery. I propose a heuristic of discovery that makes use of methods of justification, thereby attempting to bridge the artificial distinction be-

3

tween the two. Furthermore, I attempt to demonstrate that this discovery heuristic may be of interest not only for an a posteriori understanding of theory development but also for understanding limitations of present-day theories and research programs and for the further development of alternatives and new possibilities. The discovery heuristic that I call the *tools-to-theories heuristic* (see Gigerenzer & Murray, 1987) postulates a close connection between the light and the dark parts of Leibniz's ocean: Scientists' tools for justification provide the metaphors and concepts for their theories.

The power of tools to shape, or even to become, theoretical concepts is an issue largely ignored in both the history and philosophy of science. Inductivist accounts of discovery, from Bacon to Reichenbach and the Vienna Circle, focus on the role of data but do not consider *how* the data are generated or processed. Nor do the numerous anecdotes about discoveries—Newton watching an apple fall in his mother's orchard while pondering the mystery of gravitation; Galton taking shelter from a rainstorm during a country outing when discovering correlation and regression toward mediocrity; and the stories about Fechner, Kekulé, Poincaré, and others that link discovery to the three B's: beds, bicycles, and bathrooms. What unites these anecdotes is the focus on the vivid but prosaic circumstances; they report the setting in which a discovery occurs, rather than analyzing the process of discovery.

The question Is there a logic of discovery? and Popper's (1935/1959) conjecture that there is none have misled many into assuming that the issue is whether there exists a logic of discovery or only idiosyncratic personal and accidental reasons that explain the "flash of insight" of a particular scientist (Nickles, 1980). I do not think that formal logic and individual personality are the only alternatives, nor do I believe that either of these is a central issue for understanding discovery.

The process of discovery can be shown, according to my argument, to possess more structure than thunderbolt guesses but less definite structure than a monolithic logic of discovery, of the sort Hanson (1958) searched for, or a general inductive hypothesis-generation logic (e.g., Reichenbach, 1938). The present approach lies between these two extremes; it looks for structure beyond the insight of a genius but does not claim that the tools-to-theories heuristic is (or should be) the only account of scientific discovery. The tools-to-theories heuristic applies neither to all theories in science nor to all cognitive theories; it applies to a specific group of cognitive theories developed during the last three or four decades, after the so-called cognitive revolution.

Nevertheless, similar heuristics have promoted discovery in physics, physiology, and other areas. For instance, it has been argued that once the mechanical clock became the indispensable tool for astronomical research, the universe itself came to be understood as a kind of mechanical clock, and God as a divine watchmaker. Lenoir (1986) showed how Faraday's instruments for recording electric currents shaped the understanding of electrophysiological processes by promoting concepts such as "muscle current" and "nerve current."

Thus, this discovery heuristic boasts some generality both within cognitive psychology and within science, but this generality is not unrestricted. Because there has been little research in how tools of justification influence theory development, the tools-to-theories heuristic may be more broadly applicable than I am able to show in this chapter. If my view of heuristics of discovery as a heterogeneous bundle of search strategies is correct, however, this implies that generalizability is, in principle, bounded.

What follows has been inspired by Herbert Simon's notion of heuristics of discovery but goes beyond his attempt to model discovery with programs such as BACON that attempt to induce scientific laws from *data* (discussed later). My focus is on the role of the tools that process and produce data, not the data themselves, in the discovery and acceptance of theories.

How Methods of Justification Shape Theoretical Concepts

My general thesis is twofold:

1. *Discovery*. New scientific tools, once entrenched in a scientist's daily practice, suggest new theoretical metaphors and concepts.
2. *Acceptance*. Once proposed by an individual scientist (or a group), the new theoretical metaphors and concepts are more likely to be accepted by the scientific community if their members are also users of the new tools.

By *tools* I mean both analytical and physical methods that are used to evaluate given theories. Analytical tools can be either empirical or nonempirical. Examples of analytical methods of the empirical kind are tools for data processing, such as statistics; examples of the nonempirical kind are normative criteria for the evaluation of hypotheses, such as logical consistency. Examples of physical tools of justification are measurement instruments, such as clocks. In this chapter, I focus on analytical rather than physical tools of justification, and among these, on techniques of statistical inference and hypothesis testing. My topic is theories of mind and how social scientists discovered them after the emergence of new tools for data analysis rather than of new data.

In this context, the tools-to-theories heuristic consists in the discovery of new theories by changing the conception of the mind through the analogy of the statistical tool. The result can vary in depth from opening new general perspectives, albeit mainly metaphorical, to sharp discontinuity in specific cognitive theories caused by the direct transfer of scientists' tools into theories of mind.

A brief history follows. In American psychology, the study of cognitive processes was suppressed in the early 20th century by the allied forces of operationalism and behaviorism. The operationalism and the inductivism of the Vienna Circle, as well as the replacement of the Wundtian experiment by experimentation with treatment groups (Danziger, 1990), paved the way for the institutionalization of inferential statistics in American experimental psychology between 1940 and 1955 (Gigerenzer, 1987a; Toulmin & Leary, 1985). In experimental psychology, inferential statistics became almost synonymous with scientific method. Inferential statistics, in turn, provided a large part of the new concepts for mental processes that have fueled the so-called cognitive revolution since the 1960s. Theories of cognition were cleansed of terms such as restructuring and insight, and the new mind has come to be portrayed as drawing random samples from nervous fibers, computing probabilities, calculating analyses of variance (ANOVA), setting decision criteria, and performing utility analyses.

After the institutionalization of inferential statistics, a broad range of cognitive processes, conscious and unconscious, elementary and complex, were reinterpreted as involving "intuitive statistics." For instance, Tanner and Swets (1954) assumed in their theory of signal detectability that the mind "decides" whether there is a stimulus or only noise, just as a statistician of the Neyman-Pearson school decides between two hypotheses. In his causal attribution theory, Harold H. Kelley (1967) postulated that the mind attributes a cause to an effect in the same way as behavioral scientists have come to do, namely by performing an ANOVA and testing null hypotheses. These two influential theories show the breadth of the new conception of the "mind as an intuitive statistician." They also exemplify cognitive theories that were suggested not by new data but by new tools of data analysis.

In what follows, I present evidence for three points. First, the discovery of theories based on the conception of the mind as an intuitive statistician caused discontinuity in theory rather than being merely a new, fashionable language: It radically changed the kind of phenomena reported, the kind of explanations looked for, and even the kind of data that were generated. This first point illustrates the profound power of the tools-to-theories heuristic to generate quite innovative theories. Second, I provide evidence for the "blindness" or inability of researchers to discover and accept the conception of the mind as an intuitive statistician before they became familiar with inferential statistics as part of their daily routine. The discontinuity in cognitive theory is closely linked to the preceding discontinuity in method, that is, to the institutionalization of inferential statistics in psychology. Third, I show how the tools-to-theories heuristic can help to define the limits and possibilities of current cognitive theories that investigate the mind as an intuitive statistician.

Discontinuity in Cognitive Theory Development

What has been called the "cognitive revolution" is more than the overthrow of behaviorism by mentalist concepts. These concepts have been continuously part of scientific psychology since its emergence in the late 19th century, even coexisting with American behaviorism during its heyday (Lovie, 1983). The cognitive revolution did more than revive the mental; it has changed what the mental means, often dramatically. One source of this change is the tools-to-theories heuristic, with its new analogy of the mind as an intuitive statistician. To show the discontinuity within cognitive theories, I briefly discuss two areas in which an entire statistical technique, not only a few statistical concepts, became a model of mental processes: (a) stimulus detection and discrimination and (b) causal attribution.

What intensity must a 440-Hz tone have to be perceived? How much heavier than a standard stimulus of 100 g must a comparison stimulus be in order for a perceiver to notice a difference? How can the elementary cognitive processes involved in those tasks, known today as *stimulus detection* and *stimulus discrimination*, be explained? Since Herbart (1834), such processes have been explained by using a threshold metaphor: Detection occurs only if the effect an object has on the nervous system exceeds an absolute threshold, and discrimination between two objects occurs if the excitation from one exceeds that from another by an amount greater than a differential threshold. E. H. Weber and G. T. Fechner's laws refer to the concept of fixed thresholds; Titchener (1896) saw in differential thresholds the long-sought-after elements of mind (he counted approximately 44,000); and classic textbooks, such as Brown and Thomson's (1921) and Guilford's (1954), document methods and research.

Around 1955, the psychophysics of absolute and differential thresholds was revolutionized by the new analogy between the mind and the statistician. W. P. Tanner and others proposed a "theory of signal detectability" (TSD), which assumes that the Neyman-Pearson technique of hypothesis testing describes the processes involved in detection and discrimination. Recall that in Neyman-Pearson statistics, two sampling distributions (hypotheses H_0 and H_1) and a decision criterion (which is a likelihood ratio) are defined, and then the data observed are transformed into a likelihood ratio and compared with the decision criterion. Depending on which side of the criterion the data fall, the decision "reject H_0 and accept H_1" or "accept H_0 and reject H_1" is made. In straight analogy, TSD assumes that the mind calculates two sampling distributions for noise and signal plus noise (in the detection situation) and sets a decision criterion after weighing the cost of the two possible decision errors (Type I and Type II errors in Neyman-Pearson theory, now called *false alarms* and *misses*). The sensory input is transduced into a form that allows the brain to calculate its likelihood ratio, and depending on whether this ratio is smaller or larger than the criterion, the subject says "no, there is no signal" or "yes, there is a signal." Tanner (1965) explicitly referred to his new model of the mind as a "Neyman-Pearson" detector, and, in unpublished work, his flow-charts included a drawing of a homunculus statistician performing the unconscious statistics in the brain (Gigerenzer & Murray, 1987, pp. 49–53).

The new analogy between mind and statistician replaced the century-old concept of a fixed threshold by the twin notions of observer's attitudes and observer's sensitivity. Just as the Neyman-Pearson technique distinguishes between a subjective part (e.g., selection of a criterion dependent on cost–benefit considerations) and a mathematical part, detection and discrimination became understood as involving both subjective processes, such as attitudes and cost–benefit considerations, and sensory processes. Swets, Tanner, and Birdsall

(1964, p. 52) considered this link between attitudes and sensory processes to be the main thrust of their theory. The analogy between technique and mind made new research questions thinkable, such as How can the mind's decision criterion be manipulated? A new kind of data even emerged: Two types of error were generated in the experiments, false alarms and misses, just as the statistical theory distinguishes two types of error.

As far as I can tell, the idea of generating these two kinds of data was not common before the institutionalization of inferential statistics. The discovery of TSD was not motivated by new data; rather, the new theory motivated a new kind of data. In fact, in their seminal article, Tanner and Swets (1954, p. 401) explicitly admitted that their theory "appears to be inconsistent with the large quantity of existing data on this subject" and proceeded to criticize the "form of these data."

The Neyman-Pearsonian technique of hypothesis testing was subsequently transformed into a theory of a broad range of cognitive processes, ranging from recognition in memory (e.g., Murdock, 1982; Wickelgren & Norman, 1966) to eyewitness testimony (e.g., Birnbaum, 1983) to discrimination between random and nonrandom patterns (e.g., Lopes, 1982).

My second example concerns theories of causal reasoning. In Europe, Albert Michotte (1946/1963), Jean Piaget (1930), the gestalt psychologists, and others had investigated how certain temporospatial relationships between two or more visual objects, such as moving dots, produced phenomenal causality. For instance, the participants were made to perceive that one dot launches, pushes, or chases another. After the institutionalization of inferential statistics, Harold H. Kelley (1967) proposed in his "attribution theory" that the long-sought laws of causal reasoning are in fact the tools of the behavioral scientist: R. A. Fisher's ANOVA. Just as the experimenter has come to infer a causal relationship between two variables from calculating an ANOVA and performing an F test, the person-in-the-street infers the cause of an effect by unconsciously doing the same calculations. By the time Kelley discovered the new metaphor for causal inference, about 70% of all experimental articles already used ANOVA (Edgington, 1974).

The theory was accepted quickly in social psychology; Kelley and Michaela (1980) reported there were more than 900 references in one decade. The vision of the Fisherian mind radically changed the understanding of causal reasoning, the problems posed to participants, and the explanations looked for. I list a few discontinuities that reveal the "fingerprints" of the tool. (a) ANOVA needs repetitions or numbers as data in order to estimate variances and covariances. Consequently, the information presented to the participants in studies of causal attribution consists of information about the frequency of events (e.g., McArthur, 1972), which played no role in either Michotte's or Piaget's work. (b) Whereas Michotte's work still reflects the broad Aristotelian conception of four causes (see Gavin, 1972), and Piaget (1930) distinguished 17 kinds of causality in children's minds, the Fisherian mind concentrates on the one kind of causes for which ANOVA is used as a tool (similar to Aristotle's "material cause"). (c) In Michotte's view, causal perception is direct and spontaneous and needs no inference, as a consequence of largely innate laws that determine the organization of the perceptual field. ANOVA, in contrast, is used in psychology as a technique for inductive inferences from data to hypotheses, and the focus in Kelley's attribution theory is consequently on the data-driven, inductive side of causal perception.

The latter point illustrates that the specific use of a tool, that is, its practical context rather than its mathematical structure, can also shape theoretical conceptions of mind. To elaborate on this point, assume that Harold Kelley had lived one-and-a-half centuries earlier than he did. In the early 19th century, significance tests (similar to those in ANOVA) were already being used by astronomers (Swijtink, 1987), but they used their tests to reject data, so-called outliers, and not to reject hypotheses. At least provisionally, the astronomers assumed that the theory was correct and mistrusted the data, whereas the ANOVA mind, following the current statistical textbooks, assumes the data to be correct and mistrusts the theories. So, to a nineteenth-century Kelley, the mind's causal attribution would have seemed expectation driven rather than data driven: The statistician homunculus in the mind would have tested the data and not the hypothesis.

As is well documented, most of causal attribution research after Kelley took the theoretical stand that attribution is a "lay version of experimental design and analysis" (Jones & McGillis, 1976, p. 411), and elaboration of the theory was in part concerned with the *kind* of intuitive statistics in the brain. For instance, Ajzen and Fishbein (1975) argued that the homunculus statistician is Bayesian rather than Fisherian.

These two areas—detection and discrimination, and causal reasoning—may be sufficient to illustrate some of the fundamental innovations in the explanatory framework, in the research questions posed, and in the kind of data generated. The spectrum of theories that model cognition after statistical inference ranges from auditive and visual perception to recognition in memory and from speech perception to thinking and reasoning. It reaches from the elementary, physiological end to the global, conscious end of the continuum called *cognitive*. I give one example for each end. (a) Luce (1977) viewed the central nervous system (CNS) as a statistician who draws a random sample from all activated fibers, estimates parameters of the pulse rate, aggregates this estimate into a single number, and uses a decision criterion to arrive at the final perception. This conception has led to new and interesting questions; for instance, How does the CNS aggregate numbers? and What is the shape of the internal distributions? (b) The 18th-century mathematicians Laplace and Condorcet used their "probability of causes" to model how scientists reason (Daston, 1988). Recently, Massaro (1987) proposed the same statistical formula as an algorithm of pattern recognition, as "a general algorithm, regardless of the modality and particular nature of the patterns" (p. 16).

The degree to which cognitive theories were shaped by the statistical tool varies from theory to theory. On the one hand, there is largely metaphorical use of statistical inference. An example is Gregory's (1974) hypothesis-testing view of perception, in which he reconceptualized Helmholtz's "unconscious inferences" as Fisherian significance testing: "We may account for the stability of perceptual forms by suggesting that there is something akin to statistical significance which must be exceeded by the rival interpretation and the rival hypothesis before they are allowed to supersede the present perceptual hypothesis" (p. 528). In his theory of how perception works, Gregory also explained other perceptual phenomena, using Bayesian and Neyman-Pearsonian statistics as analogies, thus reflecting the actual heterogeneous practice in the social sciences. Here, a new perspective, but no quantitative model, is generated. On the other hand, there are cognitive theories that propose quantitative models of statistical inference that profoundly transform qualitative concepts and research practice. Examples are the various TSDs of cognition mentioned earlier and the theory of adaptive memory as statistical optimization by Anderson and Milson (1989).

To summarize: The tools-to-theories heuristic can account for the discovery and acceptance of a group of cognitive theories in apparently unrelated subfields of psychology, all of them sharing the view that cognitive processes can be modeled by statistical hypothesis testing. Among these are several highly innovative and influential theories that have radically changed our understanding of what *cognitive* means.

Before the Institutionalization of Inferential Statistics

There is an important test case for the present hypotheses (a) that familiarity with the statistical tool is crucial to the discovery of corresponding theories of mind and (b) that the institutionalization of the tool within a scientific community is crucial for the broad acceptance of those theories. That test case is the era before the institutionalization of inferential statistics. Theories that conceive of the mind as an intuitive statistician should have a very small likelihood of being discovered and even less likelihood of being accepted. The two strongest tests are cases in which (a) someone proposed a similar conceptual analogy and (b) someone proposed a similar probabilistic (formal) model. The chances of theories of the first kind being accepted should be small, and the chances of a probabilistic model being interpreted as "intuitive statistics" should be similarly small. I know of only one case each, which I analyze after defining first what I mean by the phrase "institutionalization of inferential statistics."

Statistical inference has been known for a long time but not used as theories of mind. In 1710, John Arbuthnot proved the existence of God using a significance test; as mentioned earlier, astronomers used significance tests in the 19th century; G. T. Fechner's (1897) statistical text *Kollektivmasslehre* included tests of hypotheses; W. S. Gosset (using the pseudonym Student) published the *t* test in 1908; and Fisher's significance testing techniques, such as ANOVA, as well as Neyman-Pearsonian hypothesis-testing methods, have been available since the 1920s (see Gigerenzer et al., 1989). Bayes's rule has been known since 1763. Nonetheless, there was little interest in these techniques in experimental psychology before 1940 (Rucci & Tweney, 1980).

The statisticians' conquest of new territory in psychology started in the 1940s. By 1942, Maurice Kendall could comment on the statisticians' expansion: "They have already overrun every branch of science with a rapidity of conquest rivalled only by Attila, Mohammed, and the Colorado beetle" (p. 69). By the early 1950s, half of the psychology departments in leading American universities offered courses on Fisherian methods and had made inferential statistics a graduate program requirement. By 1955, more than 80% of the experimental articles in leading journals used inferential statistics to justify conclusions from the data (Sterling, 1959). Editors of major journals made significance testing a requirement for articles submitted and used the level of significance as a yardstick for evaluating the quality of an article (e.g., Melton, 1962).

I therefore use 1955 as a rough date for the institutionalization of the tool in curricula, textbooks, and editorials. What became institutionalized as the logic of statistical inference was a mixture of ideas from two opposing camps, those of R. A. Fisher on the one hand and Jerzy Neyman and Egon S. Pearson (the son of Karl Pearson) on the other (see Chapter 13).

Discovery and Rejection of the Analogy

The analogy between the mind and the statistician was first proposed before the institutionalization of inferential statistics, in the early 1940s, by Egon Brunswik at Berkeley (e.g., Brunswik, 1943). As Leary (1987) has shown, Brunswik's probabilistic functionalism was based on a very unusual blending of scientific traditions, including the probabilistic world view of Hans Reichenbach and members of the Vienna Circle and Karl Pearson's correlational statistics.

The important point here is that in the late 1930s, Brunswik changed his techniques for measuring perceptual constancies, from calculating (nonstatistical) "Brunswik ratios" to calculating Pearson correlations, such as functional and ecological validities. In the 1940s, he also began to think of the organism as "an intuitive statistician," but it took him several years to spell out the analogy in a clear and consistent way.

The analogy is this: The perceptual system infers its environment from uncertain cues by (unconsciously) calculating correlation and regression statistics, just as the Brunswikian researcher does when (consciously) calculating the degree of adaptation of a perceptual system to a given environment. Brunswik's intuitive statistician was a statistician of the Karl Pearson school, like the Brunswikian researcher. Brunswik's intuitive statistician was not well adapted to the psychological science of the time, however, and the analogy was poorly understood and generally rejected.

Brunswik's analogy came too early to be comprehended and accepted by his colleagues of the experimental community; it came before the institutionalization of statistics as the indispensable method of scientific inference, and it came with the "wrong" statistical model, correlational statistics. Correlation was an indispensable method not in experimental psychology but rather in its rival discipline, known as the Galton-Pearson program, or, as Lee Cronbach (1957) put it, the "Holy Roman Empire" of "correlational psychology" (p. 671).

The schism between the two scientific communities had been repeatedly taken up in presidential addresses before the American Psychological Association (Cronbach, 1957; Dashiell, 1939) and had deeply affected the values and the mutual esteem of psychologists (Thorndike, 1954). Brunswik could not persuade his colleagues from the experimental community to consider the statistical tool of the competing community as a model of how the mind works. Ernest Hilgard (1955), in his rejection of Brunswik's perspective, did not mince words: "Correlation is an instrument of the devil" (p. 228).

Brunswik, who coined the metaphor of "man as intuitive statistician," did not survive to see the success of his analogy. It was accepted only after statistical inference became institutionalized in experimental psychology and with the new institutionalized tools rather than (Karl) Pearsonian statistics serving as models of mind. Only in the mid-1960s, however, did interest in Brunswikian models of mind emerge (e.g., Hammond, Stewart, Brehmer, & Steinmann, 1975).

The tendency to accept the statistical tools of one's own scientific community (here, the experimental psychologists) rather than those of a competing community as models of mind is not restricted to Brunswik's case. For example, Fritz Heider (1958, pp. 123, 297), whom Harold Kelley credited for having inspired his ANOVA theory, had repeatedly suggested factor analysis—another indispensable tool of the correlational discipline—as a model of causal reasoning. Heider's proposal met with the same neglect by the American experimental community as did Brunswik's correlational model. Kelley replaced the statistical tool that Heider suggested by ANOVA, the tool of the experimental community. It seems to be more than a mere accident that both Brunswik and Heider came from a similar, German-speaking tradition, where no comparable division into two communities with competing methodological imperatives existed.

Probabilistic Models without the Intuitive Statistician

My preceding point is that the statistical tool was accepted as a plausible analogy of cognitive processes only after its institutionalization in experimental psychology. My second point is that although some probabilistic models of cognitive processes were advanced before the institutionalization of inferential statistics, they were not interpreted using the metaphor of the mind as intuitive statistician. The distinction I draw is between probabilistic models that use the metaphor and ones that do not. The latter kind is illustrated by models that use probability distributions for perceptual judgment, assuming that variability is caused by lack of experimental control, measurement error, or other factors that can be summarized as experimenter's ignorance. Ideally, if the experimenter had complete control and knowledge (such as Laplace's superintelligence), all probabilistic terms could be eliminated from the theory. This does not hold for a probabilistic model that is based on the metaphor. Here, the probabilistic terms model the ignorance of the mind rather than that of the experimenter. That is, they model how the homunculus statistician in the brain comes to terms with a fundamentally uncertain world. Even if the experimenter had complete knowledge, the theories would remain probabilistic because it is the mind that is ignorant and needs statistics.

The key example is represented in L. L. Thurstone, who in 1927 formulated a model for perceptual judgment that was formally equivalent to the present-day TSD. But neither Thurstone nor his followers recognized the possibility of interpreting the formal structure of their model in terms of the intuitive statistician. Like TSD, Thurstone's model had two overlapping normal distributions, which represented the internal values of two stimuli and which specified the corresponding likelihood ratios, but it never occurred to Thurstone to include in his model the conscious activities of a statistician, such as the weighing of the costs of the two errors and the setting of a decision criterion. Thus neither Thurstone nor his followers took the—with hindsight—small step to develop the "law of comparative judgment" into TSD. When Duncan Luce (1977) reviewed Thurstone's model 50 years later, he found it hard to believe that nothing in Thurstone's writings showed the least awareness of this small but crucial step. Thurstone's perceptual model remained a mechanical, albeit probabilistic, stimulus–response theory without a homunculus statistician in the brain. The small conceptual step was never taken, and TSD entered psychology by an independent route.

To summarize: There are several kinds of evidence for a close link between the institutionalization of inferential statistics in the 1950s and the subsequent broad acceptance of the metaphor of the mind as an intuitive statistician: (a) the general failure to accept, and even to understand, Brunswik's intuitive statistician before the institutionalization of the tool and (b) the case of Thurstone, who proposed a probabilistic model that was formally equivalent to one important present-day theory of intuitive statistics but was never interpreted in this way; the analogy was not yet seen. Brunswik's case illustrates that tools may act on two levels: First, new tools may suggest new cognitive theories to a scientist. Second, the degree to which these tools are institutionalized within the scientific community to which the scientist belongs can prepare (or hinder) the acceptance of the new theory. This close link between tools for justification on the one hand and discovery and acceptance on the other reveals the artificiality of the discovery–justification distinction. Discovery does not come first and justification afterward. Discovery is *inspired by* justification.

How Heuristics of Discovery May Help in Understanding Limitations and Possibilities of Current Research Programs

In this section I argue that the preceding analysis of discovery is of interest not only for a psychology of scientific discovery and creativity (e.g., Gardner,

1988; Gruber, 1981; Tweney, Doherty, & Mynatt, 1981) but also for the evaluation and further development of current cognitive theories. The general point is that institutionalized tools like statistics do not come as pure mathematical (or physical) systems but with a practical context attached. Features of this context in which a tool has been used may be smuggled Trojan-horse fashion into the new cognitive theories and research programs. One example was mentioned earlier: The formal tools of significance testing have been used in psychology as tools for rejecting *hypotheses*, with the assumption that the data are correct, whereas in other fields and at other times the same tools were used as tools for rejecting *data* (outliers), with the assumption that the hypotheses were correct. The latter use of statistics is practically extinct in experimental psychology (although the problem of outliers routinely emerges) and therefore also absent in theories that liken cognitive processes to significance testing. In cases like these, analysis of discovery may help to reveal blind spots associated with the tool and, as a consequence, new possibilities for cognitive theorizing.

I illustrate this potential in more detail using examples from the "judgment under uncertainty" program of Daniel Kahneman, Amos Tversky, and others (see Kahneman & Tversky, 1982). This stimulating research program emerged from the earlier research on human information processing by Ward Edwards and his coworkers. In Edwards's work, the dual role of statistics as a tool and a model of mind is again evident: Edwards, Lindman, and Savage (1963) proposed Bayesian statistics for scientific hypothesis evaluation and considered the mind as a reasonably good, albeit conservative, Bayesian statistician (e.g., Edwards, 1966). The judgment-under-uncertainty program also investigates reasoning as intuitive statistics but focuses on so-called errors in probabilistic reasoning. In most of the theories based on the metaphor of the intuitive statistician, statistics or probability theory is used both as normative and as descriptive of a cognitive process (e.g., both as the optimal and the actual mechanism for speech perception and human memory; see Massaro, 1987, and Anderson & Milson, 1989, respectively). This is not the case in the judgment-under-uncertainty program; here, statistics and probability theory are used only in the normative function, whereas actual human reasoning has been described as "biased," "fallacious," or "indefensible" (on the rhetoric, see Lopes, 1991).

In the following, I first point out three features of the practical *use* of the statistical tool (as opposed to the mathematics). Then I show that these features reemerge in the judgment-under-uncertainty program, resulting in severe limitations on that program. Finally, I suggest how this hidden legacy of the tool could be eliminated to provide new impulses and possibilities for the research program.

The first feature is an assumption that can be called "There is only one statistics." Textbooks on statistics for psychologists (usually written by nonmathematicians) generally teach statistical inference as if there existed only one logic of inference. Since the 1950s and 1960s, almost all texts teach a mishmash of R. A. Fisher's ideas tangled with those of Jerzy Neyman and Egon

S. Pearson, but without acknowledgment. The fact that Fisherians and Neyman-Pearsonians could never agree on a logic of statistical inference is not mentioned in the textbooks, nor are the controversial issues that divide them. Even alternative statistical logics for scientific inference are rarely discussed. For instance, Fisher (1955) argued that concepts such as Type II error, power, the setting of a level of significance before the experiment and its interpretation as a long-run frequency of errors in repeated experiments are concepts inappropriate for scientific inference—at best they could be applied to technology (his pejorative example was Stalin's). Neyman, for his part, declared that some of Fisher's significance tests are "worse than useless" (because their power is less than their size; see Hacking, 1965, p. 99). I know of no textbook written by psychologists for psychologists that mentions and explains this and other controversies about the logic of inference. Instead, readers are presented with an intellectually incoherent mix of Fisherian and Neyman-Pearsonian ideas, but a mix presented as a seamless, uncontroversial whole: *the* logic of scientific inference (for more details, see Chapter 13).

The second assumption that became associated with the tool during its institutionalization is "There is only one meaning of probability." For instance, Fisher and Neyman-Pearson had different interpretations of what a level of significance means. Fisher's was an epistemic interpretation, that is, that the level of significance indicates the confidence that can be placed in the *particular* hypothesis under test, whereas Neyman's was a strictly frequentist and behavioristic interpretation, which claimed that a level of significance does not refer to a particular hypothesis but to the relative frequency of wrongly rejecting the null hypothesis if it is true in the long run. Although the textbooks teach both Fisherian and Neyman-Pearsonian ideas, these alternative views of what a probability (such as a level of significance) could mean are generally neglected—not to speak of the many other meanings that have been proposed for the formal concept of probability.

Third and last, the daily practice of psychologists assumes that statistical inference can be applied mechanically without checking the underlying assumptions of the model. The importance of checking whether the assumptions of a particular statistical model hold in a given application has been repeatedly emphasized, particularly by statisticians. The general tendency in psychological practice (and other social sciences) has been to apply the test anyhow, as a kind of ritual of justification required by journals but poorly understood by authors and readers alike.

These features of the practical context, in which the statistical tool has been used, reemerge at the theoretical level in current cognitive psychology, just as the tools-to-theories heuristic would lead one to expect.

Example 1: There Is Only One Statistics, Which Is Normative

Tversky and Kahneman (1974) described their judgment-under-uncertainty program as a two-step procedure. First, participants are confronted with a reasoning problem, and their answers are compared with the so-called normative or correct answer, supplied by statistics and probability theory. Second, the *deviation* between the participant's answer and the so-called normative answer, also called a *bias of reasoning*, is attributed to some heuristic of reasoning.

One implicit assumption at the heart of this research program says that statistical theory provides exactly one answer to the real-world problems presented to the participants. If this were not true, the deviation between participants' judgments and the "normative" answer would be an inappropriate *explanandum*, because there are as many different deviations as there are statistical answers. Consider the following problem:

> A cab was involved in a hit-and-run accident at night. Two companies, the Green and the Blue, operate in the city. You are given the following data:
>
> (i) 85% of the cabs in the city are Green and 15% are Blue. (ii) A witness identified the cab as a Blue cab. The court tested his ability to identify cabs under the appropriate visibility conditions. When presented with a sample of cabs (half of which were Blue and half of which were Green), the witness made correct identifications in 80% of the cases and erred in 20% of the cases.
>
> Question: What is the probability that the cab involved in the accident was Blue rather than Green? (Tversky & Kahneman, 1980, p. 62)

The authors inserted the values specified in this problem into Bayes's rule and calculated a probability of .41 as the "correct" answer, and, despite criticism, they have never retreated from that claim. They saw in the difference between this value and the participants' median answer of .80 an instance of a reasoning error, known as *neglect of base rates*. But alternative statistical solutions to the problem exist.

Tversky and Kahneman's reasoning is based on one among many possible Bayesian views—which the statistician I. J. Good (1971), not all too seriously, once counted up to 46,656. For instance, using the classical principle of indifference to determine the Bayesian prior probabilities can be as defensible as Tversky and Kahneman's use of base rates of "cabs in the city" for the relevant priors, but it leads to a probability of .80 instead of .41 (Levi, 1983). Or, if Neyman-Pearson theory is applied to the cab problem, solutions range between .28 and .82, depending on the psychological theory about the witness's criterion shift—the shift from witness testimony at the time of the accident to witness testimony at the time of the court's test (Birnbaum, 1983; Gigerenzer & Murray, 1987, pp. 167–174).

There may be more arguable answers to the cab problem, depending on what statistical or philosophical theory of inference one uses and what assumptions one makes. Indeed, the range of possible statistical solutions is about the range of participants' actual answers. The point is that none of these statistical solutions is the *only* correct answer to the problem, and therefore it makes little sense to use the deviation between a participant's judgment and *one* of these statistical answers as the psychological *explanandum*.

Statistics is an indispensable tool for scientific inference, but, as Neyman and Pearson (1928, p. 176) pointed out, in "many cases there is probably no single best method of solution." Rather, several such theories are legitimate, just as "Euclidean and non-Euclidean geometrics are equally legitimate" (Neyman, 1937, p. 336). My point is this: The idée fixe that statistics speaks with one voice has reappeared in research on intuitive statistics. The highly interesting judgment-under-uncertainty program could progress beyond the present point if (a) participants' judgments rather than deviations between judgments and a so-called normative solution are considered as the data to be explained and if (b) various statistical models are proposed as competing hypotheses of problem-solving strategies rather than one model being proposed as *the* general norm for rational reasoning. The willingness of many researchers to accept the claim that statistics speaks with one voice is the legacy of the institutionalized tool, not of statistics per se.

Note the resulting double standard: Many researchers on intuitive statistics argue that their participants should draw inferences from data to hypotheses by using Bayes's rule, although they themselves do not. Rather, the researchers use the institutionalized mixture of Fisherian and Neyman-Pearsonian statistics to draw their inferences from data to hypotheses.

Example 2: There Is Only One Interpretation of Probability

Just as there are alternative logics of inference, there are alternative interpretations of probability that have been part of the mathematical theory since its inception in the mid-17th century (Daston, 1988; Hacking, 1975). Again, both the institutionalized tool and the recent cognitive research on probabilistic reasoning exhibit the same blind spot concerning the existence of alternative interpretations of probability. For instance, Lichtenstein, Fischhoff, and Phillips (1982) have reported and summarized research on a phenomenon called *overconfidence*. Briefly, participants were given questions such as "Absinthe is (a) a precious stone or (b) a liqueur"; they chose what they believed was the correct answer and then were asked for a confidence rating in their answer, for example, 90% certain. When people said they were 100% certain about individual answers, they had in the long run only about 80% correct answers; when they were 90% certain, they had in the long run only 75% correct answers; and so on. This discrepancy was called overconfidence bias and was explained by general heuristics in memory search, such as confirmation biases, or general motivational tendencies, such as a so-called illusion of validity.

My point is that two different interpretations of probability are compared: degrees of belief in single events (i.e., that *this* answer is correct) and relative frequencies of correct answers in the long run. Although 18th-century mathematicians, like many of today's cognitive psychologists, would have had no problem in equating the two, most mathematicians and philosophers since then have. For instance, according to the frequentist point of view, the term *probability*, when it refers to a single event, "has no meaning at all" (Mises, 1928/1957, p. 11) because probability theory is about relative frequencies in the long run. Thus, for a frequentist, probability theory does not apply to single-event confidences, and therefore no confidence judgment can violate probability theory. To call a discrepancy between confidence and relative frequency a *bias* in probabilistic reasoning would mean comparing apples and oranges. Moreover, even subjectivists would not generally think of a discrepancy between confidence and relative frequency as a bias (see Kadane & Lichtenstein, 1982, for a discussion of conditions). For a subjectivist such as Bruno de Finetti, probability *is* about single events, but rationality is identified with the internal consistency of probability judgments. As de Finetti (1931/1989, p. 174) emphasized: "However an individual evaluates the probability of a particular event, no experience can prove him right, or wrong; nor in general, could any conceivable criterion give any objective sense to the distinction one would like to draw, here, between right and wrong."

Nonetheless, the literature on overconfidence is largely silent on even the possibility of this conceptual problem (but see Keren, 1987). The question about research strategy is whether to use the deviation between degrees of belief and relative frequencies (again considered as a bias) as the *explanandum* or to accept the existence of several meanings of probability and to investigate the kind of conceptual distinctions that untutored people make. Almost all research has been done within the former research strategy. And, indeed, if the issue were a general tendency to overestimate one's knowledge, as the term *overconfidence* suggests—for instance, as a result of general strategies of memory search or motivational tendencies—then asking people for degrees of belief or for frequencies should not matter.

But it does. In a series of experiments (Gigerenzer, Hoffrage, & Kleinbölting, 1991; see also May, 1987), participants were given several hundred questions of the absinthe type and were asked for confidence judgments after every question was answered (as usual). In addition, after each 50 (or 10, 5, and 2) questions, they were asked *how many* of those questions they believed they had answered correctly; that is, frequency judgments were requested. This design allowed comparison both between their confidence in their individual answers and true relative frequencies of correct answers, and between judgments of relative frequencies and true relative frequencies. Comparing frequency judgments with the true frequency of correct answers showed that overestimation or overconfidence disappeared in 80% to 90% of the participants, depending on experimental conditions. Frequency judgments were precise or even showed underestimation. Ironically, after each frequency judgment, participants went on to give confidence judgments (degrees of belief) that exhibited what has been called overconfidence.

As in the preceding example, a so-called bias of reasoning disappears if a controversial norm is dropped and replaced by several descriptive alternatives, statistical models, and meanings of probability, respectively. Thus probabilities for single events and relative frequencies seem to refer to different meanings of confidence in the minds of the participants. This result is inconsistent with previous explanations of the alleged bias by deeper cognitive deficiencies (e.g., confirmation biases) and has led to the theory of probabilistic mental models, which describes mechanisms that generate different confidence and frequency judgments (see Chapter 7). Untutored intuition seems to be capable of making conceptual distinctions of the sort statisticians and philosophers make (e.g., Cohen, 1986; Lopes, 1981; Teigen, 1983). And it suggests that the important research questions to be investigated are How are different meanings of probability cued in everyday language? and How does this affect judgment?, rather than How can the alleged bias of overconfidence be explained by some general deficits in memory, cognition, or personality?

The same conceptual distinction can help to explain other kinds of judgments under uncertainty. For instance, Tversky and Kahneman (1982a, 1983) used a personality sketch of a character named Linda that suggested she was a feminist. Participants were asked which is more probable: (a) that Linda is a bank teller or (b) that Linda is a bank teller and active in the feminist movement. Most participants chose Alternative b, which Tversky and Kahneman (1982a) called a "fallacious" belief, to be explained by their hypothesis that people use a limited number of heuristics—in the present case, representativeness (the similarity between the description of Linda and the alternatives a and b). Participants' judgments were called a *conjunction fallacy* because the probability of a conjunction of events (bank teller and active in the feminist movement) cannot be greater than the probability of one of its components.

As in the example just given, this normative interpretation neglects two facts. First, in everyday language, words like *probable* legitimately have several meanings, just as "if . . . then" and "or" constructions do. The particular meaning seems to be automatically cued by content and context. Second, statisticians similarly have alternative views of what probability is about. In the context of some subjectivist theories, choosing Alternative b truly violates the rules of probability; but for a frequentist, judgments of single events such as in the Linda problem have nothing to do with probability theory: As the statistician G. A. Barnard (1979, p. 171) objected, they should be treated in the context of psychoanalysis, not probability.

Again, the normative evaluation explicit in the term *conjunction fallacy* is far from being uncontroversial, and progress in understanding reasoning may be expected by focusing on people's judgments as *explanandum* rather than on their deviations from a so-called norm. As in the previous example, if problems of the Linda type are rephrased as involving frequency judgments (e.g., "How many out of 100 cases that fit the description of Linda are [a] bank tellers and [b] bank tellers and active in the feminist movement?"), then the so-called conjunction fallacy decreases from 77% to 27%, as Fiedler (1988) showed. "Which alternative is more probable?" is not the same as "Which alternative is more frequent?" in the Linda context. Tversky and Kahneman (1983) found similar results, but they maintained their normative claims and treated the disappearance of the phenomenon merely as an exception to the rule (p. 293).

Example 3: Commitment to Assumptions versus Neglect of Them

It is a commonplace that the validity of a statistical inference is to be measured against the validity of the assumptions of the statistical model for a given situation. In the actual context of justification, however, in psychology and probably beyond, there is little emphasis on pointing out and checking crucial assumptions. The same neglect is a drawback in some Bayesian-type probability revision studies. Kahneman and Tversky's (1973) famous engineer–lawyer study is a case in point (see also Mueser, Cowan, & Mueser, 1999). In the study, a group of students was told that a panel of psychologists had made personality descriptions of 30 engineers and 70 lawyers, that they (the students) would be given 5 of these descriptions, chosen at random, and that their task was to estimate for each description the probability that the person described was an engineer. A second group received the same instruction and the same descriptions but was given inverted base rates, that is, 70 engineers and 30 lawyers. Kahneman and Tversky found that the mean probabilities were about the same in the two groups and concluded that base rates were ignored. They explained this alleged bias in reasoning by postulating that people use a general heuristic, called *representativeness*, which means that people generally judge the posterior probability simply by the similarity between a description and their stereotype of an engineer.

Neither Kahneman and Tversky's (1973) study nor any of the follow-up studies checked whether the participants were committed to or were aware of a crucial assumption that must hold in order to make the given base rates relevant: the assumption that the descriptions have been randomly drawn from the population. If not, the base rates are irrelevant. There have been studies, such as Kahneman and Tversky's (1973) "Tom W." study, in which participants were not even told whether the descriptions were randomly sampled. In the engineer–lawyer study, participants were so informed (in only one word), but the information was false. Whether a single word is sufficient to direct the attention of participants toward this crucial information is an important question in itself, because researchers cannot assume that in everyday life, people are familiar with situations in which profession guessing is about randomly selected people. Thus many of the participants may not have been committed to the crucial assumption of random selection.

In a controlled replication (Gigerenzer, Hell, & Blank, 1988), a simple method was used to make participants aware of this crucial assumption: Participants themselves drew each description (blindly) out of an urn and gave their probability judgments. This condition made base-rate neglect largely disappear; once the participants were committed to the crucial assumption of random sampling, their judgments were closer to Bayesian predictions than to base rate neglect. This finding indicates that theories of intuitive statistics have to deal with how the mind analyzes the structure of a problem (or environment) and how it infers the presence or absence of crucial statistical assumptions—just as the practicing statistician has to first check the structure of a problem in order to decide whether a particular statistical model can be applied. Checking structural assumptions precedes statistical calculations (see also Cohen, 1982; Einhorn & Hogarth, 1981; Ginossar & Trope, 1987).

My intention here is not to criticize this or that specific experiment, but rather to draw attention to the hidden legacy that tools bequeath to theories. The general theme is that some features of the practical context in which a tool has been used (to be distinguished from its mathematics) have reemerged and been accepted in a research program that investigates intuitive statistics, impeding progress. Specifically, the key problem is a simplistic conception of normativeness that confounds one view about probability with the criterion for rationality.

Although I have dwelt on the dangerous legacy that tools hand on to theories, I do not mean to imply that a theory that originates in a tool is ipso facto a bad theory. The history of science, not just the history of psychology, is replete with examples to the contrary. Good ideas are hard to come by, and one should be grateful for those few that one has, whatever their lineage. But knowing that lineage can help to refine and criticize the new ideas. In those cases in which the tools-to-theories heuristic operates, this means taking a long, hard look at the tools—and the statistical tools of social scientists are overdue for such a skeptical inspection.

Discussion

New technologies have been a steady source of metaphors of mind: "In my childhood we were always assured that the brain was a telephone switchboard. ('What else could it be?')," recalled John Searle (1984, p. 44). The tools-to-theories heuristic is more specific than general technology metaphors. Scientists' tools, not just any tools, are used to understand the mind. Holograms are not social scientists' tools, but computers are, and part of their differential acceptance as metaphors of mind by the psychological community may be a result of psychologists' differential familiarity with these devices in research practice.

The computer, serial and parallel, would be another case study for the tools-to-theories heuristic—a case study that is in some aspects different. For instance, John von Neumann (1958) and others explicitly suggested the analogy between the serial computer and the brain. But the main use of computers in psychological science was first in the context of justification: for processing data; making statistical calculations; and as an ideal, endlessly patient experimental subject. Recently, the computer metaphor and the statistics metaphors of mind have converged, both in artificial intelligence and in the shift toward massively parallel computers simulating the interaction between neurons.

Herbert A. Simon's Heuristics of Discovery and the Tools-to-Theories Heuristic

Herbert A. Simon (1973) and his coworkers (e.g., Langley, Simon, Bradshaw, & Zytkow, 1987) explicitly reconsidered the possibility of a logic of discovery. For example, a series of programs called BACON has "rediscovered" quantitative empirical laws, such as Kepler's third law of planetary motion. How does BACON discover a law? Basically, BACON starts from data and analyzes them by applying a group of heuristics until a simple quantitative law can be fitted to the data. Kepler's law, for instance, can be rediscovered by using heuristics such as "If the values of two numerical terms increase together, then consider their ratio" (Langley et al., 1987, p. 66). Such heuristics are implemented as production rules.

What is the relation between heuristics used in programs like BACON and the tools-to-theories heuristics? First, the research on BACON was concerned mainly with the ways in which laws could be induced from data. BACON's heuristics work on extant data, whereas the tools-to-theories heuristic works on extant tools for data generation and processing and describes an aspect of discovery (and acceptance) that goes beyond data. As I argued earlier, new data can be a consequence of the tools-to-theories heuristic, rather than the starting point to which it is applied. Second, what can be discovered seems to have little overlap. For Langley et al. (1987), discoveries are of two major kinds: quantitative laws such as Kepler's law and qualitative laws such as taxonomies using clustering methods. In fact, the heuristics of discovery proposed in that work are similar to the statistical methods of exploratory data analysis (Tukey, 1977). It is this kind of intuitive statistics that serves as the analogy to discovery in Simon's approach. In contrast, the tools-to-theories heuristic can discover new conceptual analogies, new research programs, and new data. It cannot—at least not directly—derive quantitative laws by summarizing data, as BACON's heuristics can.

The second issue, What can be discovered?, is related to the first, that is, to Simon's approach to discovery as induction from *data*, as "recording in a parsimonious fashion, sets of empirical data" (Simon, 1973, p. 475). More recently, Simon and Kulkarni (1988) went beyond that data-centered view of discovery and made a first step toward characterizing the heuristics used by scientists for planning and guiding experimental research. Although Simon and Kulkarni did not explore the potential of scientists' tools for suggesting theoretical concepts (and their particular case study may not invite this), the tools-to-theories heuristic can complement this recent, broader program to understand discovery. Both Simon's heuristics and the tools-to-theories heuristic go beyond the inductive probability approach to discovery (such as Reichenbach's). The approaches are complementary in their focus on aspects of discovery, but both emphasize the possibility of understanding discovery by reference to heuristics of creative reasoning, which go beyond the merely personal and accidental.

The Tools-to-Theories Heuristic beyond
Cognitive Psychology

The examples of discovery I give in this chapter are modest instances compared with the classical literature in the history of science treating the contribution of a Copernicus or a Darwin. But in the narrower context of recent
cognitive psychology, the theories I have discussed count as among the most
influential. In this more prosaic context of discovery, the tools-to-theories heuristic can account for a group of significant theoretical innovations. And, as I
have argued, this discovery heuristic can both open and foreclose new avenues
of research, depending on the interpretations attached to the statistical tool.
My focus is on analytical tools of justification, and I have not dealt with physical tools of experimentation and data processing. Physical tools, once familiar
and considered indispensable, also may become the stuff of theories. This
holds not only for the hardware (like the software) of the computer, but also
for theory innovation beyond recent cognitive psychology. Smith (1986) argued
that Edward C. Tolman's use of the maze as an experimental apparatus transformed Tolman's conception of purpose and cognition into spatial characteristics, such as cognitive maps. Similarly, he argued that Clark L. Hull's fasci-
nation with conditioning machines has shaped Hull's thinking of behavior as
if it were machine design. With the exception of Danziger's (1985, 1987) work
on changing methodological practices in psychology and their impact on the
kind of knowledge produced, however, there seems to exist no systematic research program on the power of familiar tools to shape new theories in psychology.

But the history of science beyond psychology provides some striking instances of scientists' tools, both analytical and physical, that ended up as theories of nature. Hackmann (1979), Lenoir (1986), and Wise (1988) have explored how scientific instruments shaped the theoretical concepts of, among
others, Emil DuBois-Reymond and William Thomson (Lord Kelvin).

The case of Adolphe Quetelet illustrates nicely how the tools-to-theories
heuristic can combine with an interdisciplinary exchange of theories. The statistical error law (normal distribution) was used by astronomers to handle observational errors around the true position of a star. Quetelet (1842/1969), who
began as an astronomer, transformed the astronomer's tool for taming error into
a theory about society: The true position of a star turned into *l'homme moyen*,
or the ideal average person within a society, and observational errors turned
into the distribution of actual persons (with respect to any variable) around
l'homme moyen—actual persons now being viewed as nature's errors. Quetelet's social error theory was in turn seminal in the development of statistical
mechanics; Ludwig Boltzmann and James Clerk Maxwell in the 1860s and
1870s reasoned that gas molecules might behave as Quetelet's humans do;
erratic and unpredictable as individuals, but regular and predictable when
considered as a collective (Porter, 1986). By this strange route of discovery—
from astronomer's tool to a theory of society, and from a theory of society to

a theory of a collective of gas molecules—the deterministic Newtonian view of the world was finally overthrown and replaced by a statistical view of nature (see Gigerenzer et al., 1989). Thus there seems to exist a broader, interdisciplinary framework for the tools-to-theories heuristic proposed here, which has yet to be explored.

Discovery Reconsidered

Let me conclude with some reflections on how the present view stands in relation to major themes in scientific discovery.

Data-to-Theories Reconsidered   Should psychologists continue to tell their students that new theories originate from new data, if only because "little is known about how theories come to be created," as J. R. Anderson remarked in the introduction to his *Cognitive Psychology* (1980, p. 17)? Holton (1988) noted the tendency among physicists to reconstruct discovery with hindsight as originating from new data, even if this is not the case. His most prominent example is Einstein's special theory of relativity, which was and still is celebrated as an empirical generalization from Michelson's experimental data by such eminent figures as R. A. Millikan and H. Reichenbach, as well as by the textbook writers. As Holton demonstrated with firsthand documents, the role of Michelson's data in the discovery of Einstein's theory was slight, a conclusion shared by Einstein himself.

Similarly, with respect to more modest discoveries, I argue that a group of recent cognitive theories did not originate from new data, but in fact often created new kinds of data. Tanner and Swets (1954) are even explicit that their theory was inconsistent with the extant data. Numerical probability judgments have become the stock-in-trade data of research on inductive thinking since Edwards's (1966) work, whereas this kind of dependent variable was still unknown in Humphrey's (1951) review of research on thinking.

The strongest claim for an inductive view of discovery came from the Vienna Circle's emphasis on sensory data (reduced to the concept of "pointer readings"). Carnap (1928/1969), Reichenbach (1938), and others focused on what they called the *rational reconstruction* of actual discovery rather than on actual discovery itself, in order to screen out the merely irrational and psychological. For instance, Reichenbach reconstructed Einstein's special theory of relativity as being "suggested by closest adherence to experimental facts," a claim that Einstein rejected, as mentioned earlier (see Holton, 1988, p. 296). It seems fair to say that all attempts to logically reconstruct discovery in science have failed in practice (Blackwell, 1983, p. 111). The strongest theoretical disclaimer concerning the possibility of a logic of discovery came from Popper, Hempel, and other proponents of the hypothetico-deductive account, resulting in the judgment that discovery, not being logical, occurs irrationally. Theories are simply "guesses guided by the unscientific" (Popper, 1959, p. 278). In contrast, I have dealt with guesses that are guided by the scientific, by tools of justification. Induction from data and irrational guesses are not exhaustive of scientific discovery, and the tools-to-theories heuristic explores the field beyond.

Scientists' Practice Reconsidered   The tools-to-theories heuristic is about scientists' practice, that is, the analytical and physical tools used in the conduct of experiments. This practice has a long tradition of neglect. The very philosophers who called themselves logical empiricists had, ironically, little interest in the empirical practice of scientists. Against their reduction of observation to pointer reading, Kuhn (1970) emphasized the theory ladenness of observation. Referring to perceptual experiments and gestalt switches, he said: "Scientists see new and different things when looking with familiar instruments in places they have looked before" (p. 111). Both the logical empiricists and Kuhn were highly influential on psychology (see Toulmin & Leary, 1985), but neither's view has emphasized the role of tools and experimental conduct. Their role in the development of science has been grossly underestimated until recently (Danziger, 1985; Lenoir, 1988).

Through the lens of theory, it has been said, growth of knowledge can be understood. But there is a recent move away from a theory-dominated account of science that pays attention to what really happens in the laboratories. Hacking (1983) argued that experimentation has a life of its own and that not all observation is theory laden. Galison (1987) analyzed modern experimental practice, such as in high-energy physics, focusing on the role of the fine-grained web of instruments, beliefs, and practice that determine when a fact is considered to be established and when experiments end. Both Hacking and Galison emphasized the role of the familiarity experimenters have with their tools, and the importance and relative autonomy of experimental practice in the quest for knowledge. This is the broader context in which the present tools-to-theories heuristic stands: the conjecture that theory is inseparable from instrumental practices.

In conclusion, my argument is that discovery in recent cognitive psychology can be understood beyond mere inductive generalizations or lucky guesses. More than that, I argue that for a considerable group of cognitive theories, neither induction from data nor lucky guesses played an important role. Rather, these innovations in theory can be accounted for by the tools-to-theories heuristic. So can conceptual problems and possibilities in current theories. Scientists' tools are not neutral. In the present case, the mind has been re-created in their image.

2

Mind as Computer

The Social Origin of a Metaphor

Have philosophers of science spent too little time inside the laboratories to be drawn in by the glamour of technology? Tools, after all, fascinate scientists. New tools can directly, rather than through new data, inspire new theories. This chapter extends the thesis of a *tools-to-theories heuristic* from statistical tools to the computer.[1] Recall that the thesis is twofold:

1. *Discovery.* New scientific tools, once entrenched in a scientist's daily practice, suggest new theoretical metaphors and concepts.
2. *Acceptance.* Once proposed by an individual scientist (or a group), the new theoretical metaphors and concepts are more likely to be accepted by the scientific community if their members are also users of the new tools.

This chapter is divided into two parts. In the first part, we argue that a conceptual divorce between intelligence and calculation circa 1800, motivated by a new social organization of work, made mechanical computation (and ultimately the computer) conceivable. The tools-to-theories heuristic comes into play in the second part. When computers finally became standard laboratory tools in the 20th century, the computer was proposed, and with some delay accepted, as a model of mind. Thus we travel in a full circle from mind to computer and back.

The work on which this chapter is based was coauthored with D. G. Goldstein.

1. Although we are only dealing with theories of mind, this does not imply that the tools-to-theories heuristic is not applicable in the analysis of other scientific domains. Schaffer (1992) provided several examples from the history of electromagnetism, in which theories stemmed from tools. For instance, in 1600, the court physician William Gilbert described the Earth as a vast spherical magnet. This new idea stemmed from the tool he had invented (a magnet, the small *terrella*) and subsequently used as an analogy to understand the world. This projection had consequences. Gilbert inferred that, because his *terrella* rotated, so did the Earth. The tool proved Copernicanism.

From Mind to Computer

> "Well, Babbage, what are you dreaming about?" to which I replied, "I am thinking that all these tables (pointing to the logarithms) might be calculated by machinery." (Charles Babbage, 1812/1994, p. 31)

The president of the Astronomical Society of London, Henry Colebrooke (1825), summed up the significance of Babbage's work: "Mr. Babbage's invention puts an engine in place of the computer" (p. 510). This seems a strange statement about the man who is now praised for having invented the computer. But, at Babbage's time, the computer was a human being—in this case, someone who was hired for exhaustive calculations of astronomical and navigational tables.

How did Babbage (1791–1871) ever arrive at the idea of putting a mechanical computer in place of a human one? A divorce between intelligence and calculation, as Daston (1994) argued, made it possible for Babbage to conceive this idea.

In the Enlightenment, calculation was not considered a rote, mechanical thought process. In contrast, philosophers of the time held that intelligence and even moral sentiment were in their essence forms of calculation. Calculation was the opposite of the habitual and the mechanical, remote from the realm of menial labor. For Condillac, d'Alembert, Condorcet, and other Enlightenment philosophers, the healthy mind worked by constantly taking apart ideas and sensations into their minimal elements, then comparing and rearranging these elements into novel combinations and permutations. Thought was a combinatorial calculus, and great thinkers were proficient calculators. In the eulogies of great mathematicians, for instance, prodigious mental reckoning was a favorite topic—Gauss's brilliant arithmetic was perhaps the last of these stock legends. Calculation was the essence of moral sentiment, too. Even self-interest and greed (as opposed to dangerous passions), by their nature of being calculations, were at least predictable and thereby thought to reinforce the orderliness of society (Daston, 1988, 1994).

The Computer as a Factory of Workers

By the turn of the nineteenth century, calculation was shifting from the company of *hommes éclairés* and savants to that of the unskilled work force. Extraordinary mental arithmetic became associated with the idiot savant and the sideshow attraction. Calculation became seen as dull, repetitive work, best performed by patient minds that lacked imagination. Women ultimately staffed the "bureaux de calculs" in major astronomical and statistical projects (despite their earlier being accused of vivid imaginations and mental restlessness; see Daston, 1992). Talent and genius ceased to be virtuoso combinatorics and permutations and turned into romantic, unanalyzable creations. Thereby, the stage became set for the neoromanticism in twentieth-century philosophy of science that declared creativity as mystical and the context of discovery as "irrelevant to the logical analysis of scientific knowledge" (Popper, 1959, p. 31).

Daston (1994) and Schaffer (1994) argued that one force in this transformation was the introduction of large-scale division of labor in manufacturing, as evidenced in the automatic system of the English machine-tool industry and in the French government's large-scale manufacturing of logarithmic and trigonometric tables for the new decimal system in the 1790s. French engineer Gaspard Riche de Prony organized the French government's titanic project for the calculation of 10,000 sine values to the unprecedented precision of 25 decimal places and some 200,000 logarithms to 14 or 15 decimal places during the French Revolution. Inspired by Adam Smith's praise of the division of labor, Prony organized the project in a hierarchy of tasks. At the top was a handful of excellent mathematicians, including Adrien Legendre and Lazare Carnot, who devised the formulae; in the middle were 7 or 8 persons trained in analysis; at the bottom were 70 or 80 unskilled persons who knew only the rudiments of arithmetic and who performed millions of additions and subtractions. These "manufacturing" methods, as Prony called them, pushed calculation away from intelligence and toward work. The terms *work* and *mechanical* have been linked in both England and France since the middle of the nineteenth century. Work concerned the body but not the mind; in large-scale manufacturing, each worker did only one thing his or her whole life.

After it was shown that elaborate calculation could be carried out by an assemblage of unskilled workers, each knowing very little about the large computation, it became possible for Babbage to conceive of replacing these workers with machinery. Babbage's view of the computer bore a great resemblance to a factory of unskilled human workers. When Babbage talked about the parts of his "Analytical Engine," the arithmetic computation and the storage of numbers, he called these the "mill" and the "store," respectively (Babbage, 1812/1994, p. 23). The metaphor came from the textile industry, in which yarns were brought from the store to the mill, were woven into fabric, and were then sent back to the store. In the Analytical Engine, numbers were brought from the store to the arithmetic mill for processing, and the results were returned to the store. Commenting on this resemblance, Lady Lovelace said, "We may say most aptly that the Analytical Engine weaves algebraic patterns just as the Jaquard loom weaves flowers and leaves" (Babbage, 1812/1994, p. 27).[2] In his chapter on the "division of mental labor," Babbage explicitly referred to the French government's program for the computation of new decimal tables as the inspiration and foundation of a general science of machine intelligence.

Let us summarize the argument. During the Enlightenment, calculation was the distinctive activity of the scientist and the genius and the very essence of

---

2. The Jaquard loom, a general-purpose device loaded with a set of punched cards, could be used to weave infinite varieties of patterns. Factories in England were equipped with hundreds of these machines, and Babbage was one of the "factory tourists" of the 1830s and 1840s.

the mental life. New ideas and insights were assumed to be the product of the novel combinations and permutations of ideas and sensations. In the first decades of the nineteenth century, numerical calculation was separated from the rest of intelligence and demoted to one of the lowest operations of the human mind. After calculation became the repetitive task of an army of unskilled workers, Babbage could envision mechanical computers replacing human computers. Pools of human computers and Babbage's mechanical computer manufactured numbers in the same way as the factories of the day manufactured their goods.[3]

The Computer as a Brain

Babbage's dream that all tables of logarithms could be calculated by a machine, however, did not turn into a reality during his lifetime. He never completed any of the three machines he had started to build. Modern computers, such as the ENIAC and the EDVAC at the University of Pennsylvania, came about during and after World War II. Did the fathers of computer science see the mind as a computer? We argue that the contemporary analogy stating that the mind is a computer was not yet established before the "cognitive revolution" of the 1960s. As far as we can tell, two groups were willing to draw a parallel between the human and the computer, but neither used the computer as a theory of mind. One group, which tentatively compared the nervous system and the computer, is represented by Hungarian mathematician John von Neumann (1903–1957). The other group, which investigated the idea that machines might be capable of thought, is represented by English mathematician and logician Alan Turing (1912–1954).

Von Neumann, known as the father of the modern computer, wrote about the possibility of an analogy between the computer and the human nervous system. It seems that von Neumann's reading of Warren McCulloch and Walter Pitts's (1943) paper, "A Logical Calculus of the Ideas Immanent in Nervous Activity," triggered his interest in information processing in the human brain soon after the paper was published (Asted, 1990). McCulloch and Pitts's paper starts with the statement that, because of the all-or-none character of the nervous system, neural events can be represented by means of propositional logic. The McCulloch-Pitts model did not deal with the structure of neurons, which were treated as "black boxes." The model was largely concerned with the mathematical rules governing the input and output of signals. In a 1945 report on EDVAC (the Electronic Discrete Variable Computer), von Neumann described the computer as being built from McCulloch and Pitts's idealized neurons rather than from vacuum tubes, electromechanical relays, or mechan-

---

3. Calculation became dissociated and opposed not only to the human intellect but also to moral impulse. Madame de Staël, for instance, used the term *calcul* only in connection with the "egoism and vanity" of those opportunists who exploited the French Revolution for their own advantage and selfishness (Daston, 1994).

ical switches. Understanding the computer in terms of the human nervous system appeared strange to many, including the chief engineers of the ENIAC project, Eckert and Mauchly (Aspray, 1990, p. 173). But, von Neumann hoped that his theory of natural and artificial automata would improve understanding of the design both of computers and of the human nervous system. His last work (for the Silliman lectures), neither finished nor delivered due to illness, was largely concerned with pointing out similarities between the nervous system and the computer—between the neuron and the vacuum tube—but added cautionary notes on their differences (von Neumann, 1958).

What was the reception of von Neumann's tentative analogy between the nervous system and the computer? His intellectual biographer, Aspray (1990, p. 181), concluded that psychologists and physiologists were less than enthusiastic about the McCulloch-Pitts model; Seymor Papert spoke of "a hostile or indifferent world" (McCulloch, 1965, p. xvii), and McCulloch himself admitted the initial lack of interest in their work (p. 9).

The Computer as a Mind

> I believe that at the end of the century the use of words and general educated opinion will have altered so much that one will be able to speak of machines thinking without expecting to be contradicted. (Alan Turing, 1950, p. 442)

Von Neumann and others looked for a parallel between the machine and the human on the level of hardware. Turing (1950), in contrast, thought the observation that both the modern digital computer and the human nervous system are electrical was based on a "very superficial similarity" (p. 439). He pointed out that the first digital computer, Babbage's Analytical Engine, was purely mechanical (as opposed to electrical) and that the important similarities to the mind are in function rather than in hardware. Turing discussed the question of whether machines can think rather than the question of whether the mind is like a computer. Thus he was looking in a direction *opposite* that in which psychologists were looking after the cognitive revolution, and consequently he did not propose any theories of mind. For example, the famous Turing test is about whether a machine can imitate a human mind but not vice versa. Turing argued that it would be impossible for a human to imitate a computer, as evidenced by the human's inability to perform complex numerical calculations quickly. Turing also discussed the question of whether a computer could be said to have free will, a property of humans. Many years later, cognitive psychologists, under the assumptions that the mind is a computer and that computers lack free will, pondered the question of whether humans could be said to have free will. A similar story to this is that Turing (1947/1969) contemplated teaching machines to be intelligent using the same principles used to teach children. The analogy of the computer as a mind was reversed again after the cognitive revolution, as McCorduck (1979) pointed out, when Massachusetts Institute of Technology (MIT) psychologists tried to teach children with the very methods that had worked for computers.

Turing anticipated much of the new conceptual language and even the very problems Allen Newell and Herbert Simon later attempted to address, as we see in the second part of this chapter. With amazing prophecy, Turing suggested that many intellectual issues can be translated into the form "Find a number *n* such that . . ."; that is, he suggested that searching is the key concept for problem solving and that Whitehead and Russell's (1935) *Principia Mathematica* might be a good start for demonstrating the power of the machine (McCorduck, 1979, p. 57).

Not only did Turing's life end early and under tragic circumstances, but his work had practically no influence on artificial intelligence in Britain until the mid-1960s (McCorduck, 1979, p. 68). Neither von Neumann nor his friends were persuaded to look beyond similarities between cells and diodes to functional similarities between humans and computers.

To summarize, we have looked at two groups who compared humans and computers before the cognitive revolution. One of these groups, represented by von Neumann, spoke tentatively about the computer as a brain but warned about taking the analogy too far. The other group, represented by Turing, asked whether the computer has features of the human mind but not vice versa— that is, this group did not attempt to design theories of mind through the analogy of the tool.

Before the second half of the century, the mind was not yet a computer. However, a new incarnation of the Enlightenment view of intelligence as a combinatorial calculus was on the horizon.

From Computer to Mind

> The computer is a member of an important family of artifacts called symbol systems, or more explicitly, physical symbol systems . . . The hypothesis is that a physical symbol system . . . has the necessary and sufficient means for general intelligent action. (Herbert Simon, 1969, p. 26)

What has been called in retrospect the *cognitive revolution* in American psychology of the 1960s is more than an overthrow of behaviorism by mentalist concepts. The cognitive revolution did more than revive the mental; it changed its meaning. One source of this change is the projection of new tools (i.e., statistics and computers) into the mind. We refer to this heuristic of discovery as the *tools-to-theories heuristic*. The two new classes of theories that emerged and that partially overlap pictured the new mind as an "intuitive statistician" or a "computer program."

In this section, we see how a tools-to-theories explanation accounts for the new conception of the mind as a computer, focusing on the discovery and acceptance of Simon and Newell's brand of information-processing psychology. We try to reconstruct the discovery of Newell and Simon's (1972) information-processing model of mind and its (delayed) acceptance by the psychological community in terms of the tools-to-theories heuristic.

Discovery

Babbage's mechanical computer was preceded by human computers. Similarly, Newell and Simon's first computer program, the "Logic Theorist" (LT), was preceded by a human computer. Before the LT was up and running, Newell and Simon reconstructed their computer program out of human components (Simon's wife, children, and several graduate students) in order to see if it would work. Newell wrote up the subroutines of the LT program on index cards:

> To each member of the group, we gave one of the cards, so that each person became, in effect, a component of the LT computer program—a subroutine that performed some special function, or a component of its memory. It was the task of each participant to execute his or her subroutine, or to provide the contents of his or her memory, whenever called by the routine at the next level above that was then in control.
>
> So we were able to simulate the behavior of the LT with a computer constructed of human components. . . . The actors were no more responsible . . . than the slave boy in Plato's Meno, but they were successful in proving the theorems given them. (Simon, 1991, p. 207)

The parallels to Prony's *bureaux de calculs* and the large-scale manufacturing of the new factories of the early nineteenth century are striking. At essence is a division of labor, in which the work is done by a hierarchy of humans—each requiring little skill and repeating the same routine again and again. Complex processes are achieved by an army of workers who never see but a little piece of the larger picture.[4]

However, between Prony's human computer and Simon's human computer is an important difference. Prony's human computer and Babbage's mechanical computer (modeled after it) performed numerical calculations. Simon's human computer did not. Simon's humans matched symbols, applied rules to symbols, and searched through lists of symbols—in short, performed what is now generally known as symbol manipulation.

The reader will recall from the first part of this chapter that the divorce between intelligence and numerical calculation made it possible for Babbage to replace the human computer with a mechanical one. In the twentieth century, intelligence and calculation are still divorced. Given this divorce and the early conception of the computer as a fancy number cruncher, it is no wonder that the computer never suggested itself as a theory of mind. We argue that an

---

4. The Manhattan Project at Los Alamos, where the atomic bomb was constructed, housed another human computer. Although the project could draw on the best technology available, in the early 1940s mechanical calculators (e.g., the typewriter-sized Marchant calculator) could only add, subtract, multiply, and, with some difficulty, divide. Richard Feynman and Nicholas Metropolis arranged a pool of people (mostly scientists' wives, who were getting paid three-eighths of the scientists' salary), each of whom repetitively performed a small calculation (e.g., cubing a number) and passed the result on to another person, who incorporated it into yet another computation (Gleick, 1992).

important precondition for the view of mind as a computer is the realization that computers are symbol-manipulation devices in addition to being numerical calculators. Newell and Simon were among the first to realize this. In interviews with Pamela McCorduck (1979), Newell recalled, "I've never used a computer to do any numerical processing in my life" (p. 129). Newell's first use of the computer at RAND Corporation—a prehistoric card-programmed calculator hooked up to a line printer—was printing symbols representing airplanes for each sweep of a radar antenna.

The symbol-manipulating nature of the computer was important to Simon because it corresponded to some of his earlier views on the nature of intelligence:

> The metaphor I'd been using, of a mind as something that took some premises and ground them up and processed them into conclusions, began to transform itself into a notion that a mind was something which took some program inputs and data and had some processes which operated on the data and produced output. (cited in McCorduck, 1979, p. 127)

It is interesting to note that 20 years after seeing the computer as a symbol-manipulating device, Newell and Simon came forth with the explicit hypothesis that a physical symbol system is necessary and sufficient for intelligence.

The Logic Theorist generated proofs for theorems in symbolic logic—specifically, the first 25 or so theorems in Whitehead and Russell's (1935) *Principia Mathematica*. It even managed to find a proof more elegant than the corresponding one in the *Principia Mathematica*.

In the summer of 1958, psychology was given a double dose of the new school of information-processing psychology. One dose was the publication of Newell, Shaw, and Simon's (1958) *Psychological Review* article, "Elements of a Theory of Human Problem Solving"; the other dose was the Research Training Institute on the Simulation of Cognitive Processes at the RAND Corporation, which we discuss later.

The *Psychological Review* article is an interesting document of the transition between the view that the LT is a tool for proving theorems in logic (the artificial intelligence view) and an emerging view that the LT is a model of human reasoning (the information-processing view). In fact, Newell et al. (1958) went back and forth between both views, explaining that "the program of LT was not fashioned directly as a theory of human behavior; it was constructed in order to get a program that would prove theorems in logic" (p. 154); later, they wrote that the LT "provides an explanation for the processes used by humans to solve problems in symbolic logic" (p. 163). The evidence provided for projecting the machine into the mind is mainly rhetorical. For instance, Newell et al. spent several pages arguing for the resemblance between the methods of LT and concepts (e.g., "set," "insight," "hierarchy") described in the earlier psychological literature on human problem solving.

In all fairness, despite Newell et al.'s claim, the resemblance to these earlier concepts as they were used in the work of Karl Duncker, Wolfgang Köhler, and others is slight. New discoveries, by definition, clash with what has come before, but it is often a useful strategy to hide the amount of novelty and to claim historical continuity. When Tanner and Swets (1954) proposed (in the *Psychological Review* four years earlier) that another scientific tool (i.e., the Neyman-Pearsonian techniques of hypothesis testing) would model the cognitive processes of stimulus detection and discrimination, their signal-detection model also clashed with earlier notions, such as the notion of a sensory threshold. Tanner and Swets, however, chose not to conceal this schism between the old and the new theories, explicitly stating that their new theory "appears to be inconsistent with the large quantity of existing data on this subject" (p. 401). As we argued before, there is a different historical continuity in which Newell and Simon's ideas stand—the earlier Enlightenment view of intelligence as a combinatorial calculus.

Conceptual Change

Newell et al. (1958) tried to emphasize the historical continuity of what was to become their new information-processing model of problem solving, as did Miller, Galanter, and Pribram (1960) in their *Plans and the Structure of Behavior* when they linked their version of Newell and Simon's theory to many great names such as William James, Frederic Bartlett, and Edward Tolman. We believe that these early claims for historical continuity served as protection: George Miller, who was accused by Newell and Simon of having stolen their ideas and gotten them all wrong, said, "I had to put the scholarship into the book, so they would no longer claim that those were their ideas. As far as I was concerned they were old familiar ideas" (Baars, 1986, p. 213). In contrast to this rhetoric, here we emphasize the discontinuity introduced by the transformation of the new tool into a theory of mind.

The New Mind

What was later called the "new mental chemistry" pictured the mind as a computer program:

> The atoms of this mental chemistry are symbols, which are combinable into larger and more complex associational structures called lists and list structures. The fundamental "reactions" of the mental chemistry employ elementary information processes that operate upon symbols and symbol structures: copying symbols, storing symbols, retrieving symbols, inputting and outputting symbols, and comparing symbols. (Simon, 1979, p. 363)

This atomic view is certainly a major conceptual change in the views about problem solving compared to the theories of Köhler, Wertheimer, and Duncker, but it bears much resemblance to the combinatorial view of intelligence of the Enlightenment philosophers.[5]

The different physical levels of a computer lead to Newell's cognitive hierarchy, which separates the knowledge level, symbol level, and register-transfer levels of cognition. The seriality of 1971-style computers is actually embedded in Newell's cognitive theory (Arbib, 1993).

One of the major concepts in computer programming that made its way into the new models of the mind is the decomposition of complexity into simpler units, such as the decomposition of a program into a hierarchy of simpler subroutines or into a set of production rules. On this analogy, the most complex processes in psychology, such as scientific discovery, can be explained through simple subprocesses. Thus the possibility of the logic of scientific discovery, the existence of which Karl Popper so vehemently disclaimed, has returned in the analogy between computer and mind (Langley, Simon, Bradshaw, & Zytkow, 1987).

The first general statement of Newell and Simon's new vision of mind appeared in their 1972 book, *Human Problem Solving*. Newell and Simon argued for the idea that higher level cognition proceeds much like the behavior of a production system—a formalism from computer science (and before that symbolic logic) that had never before been used in psychological modeling. Newell and Simon (1972) wrote of the influence of programming concepts on their models:

> Throughout the book we have made use of a wide range of organizational techniques known to the programming world: explicit flow control, subroutines, recursion, iteration statements, local naming, production systems, interpreters, and so on. . . . We confess to a strong premonition that the actual organization of human programs closely resembles the production system organization. (p. 803)

Here we do not attempt to probe the depths of how Newell and Simon's ideas of information processing changed theories of mind; the commonplace usage of computer terminology in the cognitive psychological literature since 1972 is a reflection of this. How natural it seems for present-day psychologists to speak of cognition in terms of *encoding, storage, retrieval, executive processes, algorithms,* and *computational cost.*

---

5. In fact, the new view was directly inspired by 19th-century mathematician George Boole (1854/1958), who, in the very spirit of the Enlightenment mathematicians such as the Bernoullis and Laplace, set out to derive the laws of logic, algebra, and probability from what he believed to be the laws of human thought. Boole's algebra culminated in Whitehead and Russell's (1935) *Principia Mathematica*, describing the relation between mathematics and logic, and in Claude Shannon's seminal work (his master's thesis at MIT in 1940), which used Boolean algebra to describe the behavior of relay and switching circuits (McCorduck, 1979, p. 41).

New Experiments, New Data

The tools-to-theories heuristic implies that new theories need not be a consequence of new experiments and new data. Instead, new tools can transform the kinds of experiments performed and data collected. This consequence of the tools-to-theories heuristic is also known to have happened when statistical tools turned into theories of mind (and around the same time).

One such case is the revolution of psychophysics through a new tool called *Neyman-Pearsonian hypothesis testing* (see Chapter 1). The new theory of mind inspired by this tool is known as *signal-detection theory*. The Neyman-Pearson technique deals with two kinds of errors, Type I and Type II (or false alarms and misses). When Tanner and Swets (1954) projected the tool into the mind, stimulus detection and discrimination—earlier understood in terms of "thresholds"—then became seen as a decision between two competing hypotheses based on a criterion that balances the probability of two kinds of errors. Consequently, the avalanche of experiments on auditory and visual detection and discrimination that followed their proposal kept track of both kinds of error in participants' judgments. The important point is that earlier experiments, such as the classical works of Fechner and Thurstone, paid attention to only one kind of error (Gigerenzer, 1994b). What happened is that the new statistical tool inspired a new theory of mind, which in turn changed the kind of data generated in research. In this way, Tanner and Swets were able, in good conscience, to discard the years of contradicting results that preceded them.

A similar story is to be told with the conceptual change brought about by Newell and Simon—it mandated a new type of experiment that in turn involved new kinds of subjects, data, and justification. In academic psychology of the day, the standard experimental design, modeled after the statistical methods of Ronald Fisher, involved many subjects and randomized treatment groups. The 1958 *Psychological Review* article used the same terminology of *design of the experiment* and *subject* but radically changed their meanings. There were no longer groups of human or animal subjects. There was only one subject—an inanimate being, Logic Theorist. There was no longer an experiment in which data are generated by either observation or measurement. Experiment took on the meaning of simulation.

In this new kind of experiment, the data were of an unforeseen type—computer printouts of the intermediate results of the program. These new data, in turn, required new methods of hypothesis testing. How did Newell and Simon tell if their program was doing what minds do? There were two methods. For Newell and Simon, simulation was a form of justification itself: A theory that is coded as a working computer program shows that the processes it describes are, at the very least, sufficient to perform the task, or, in the more succinct words of Simon (1992a), "A running program is the moment of truth" (p. 155). Furthermore, a stronger test of the model is made by comparing the output of the computer to the think-aloud protocols of human subjects.

Although all of this was a methodological revolution in the experimental practice of the time, some important parallels exist between the new information-processing approach and the turn-of-the-century German approach to studying mental processes. These parallels concern the analysis of individual subjects (rather than group means), the use of think-aloud procedures, and the status of the subject. In the early German psychology, as well as in American psychology of the time (until about the 1930s), the unit of analysis was the individual person, not the average of a group (Danziger, 1990). The two most prominent kinds of data in early German psychology were reaction times and introspective reports. Introspective reports have been frowned on ever since the inception of American behaviorism, but think-aloud protocols, their grandchildren, are back (as are reaction times). Furthermore, in the tradition of the Leipzig (Wundt) and Würzburg (Külpe) schools, the subject was more prestigious and important than the experimenter. Under the assumption that the thought process is introspectively penetrable, the subject, not the experimenter, was assumed to provide the theoretical description of the thought process. In fact, the main experimental contribution of Külpe, the founder of the Würzburg school, was to serve as a subject, and it was often the subject who published the article. In the true spirit of these schools, Newell and Simon put their subject, the LT, as a coauthor of a paper submitted to the *Journal of Symbolic Logic*. Regrettably, the paper was rejected (as it contained no new results from the point of view of modern logic), and the LT never tried to publish again.

Acceptance

The second dose of information processing administered to psychology (after the 1958 *Psychological Review* article) was the Research Training Institute on the Simulation of Cognitive Processes at the RAND Corporation, organized by Newell and Simon. At the institute, lectures and seminars were conducted; IPL-IV programming was taught; and the LT, the General Problem Solver, and the EPAM model of memory were demonstrated on the RAND computer. In attendance were some scientists who would eventually develop computer-simulation methods of their own—including George Miller, Robert Abelson, Bert Green, and Roger Shepard.

An early but deceptive harbinger of acceptance for the new information-processing theory was the publication, right after the summer institute, of *Plans and the Structure of Behavior* (Miller et al., 1960). Despite the aforementioned 1959 dispute with Newell and Simon over the ownership and validity of the ideas within, this book drew a good deal of attention from all of psychology.

It would seem the table was set for the new information-processing psychology; however, it did not take hold. Simon (1991, p. 232) complained of the psychological community, which took only a "cautious interest" in Newell and Simon's ideas. The "acceptance" part of the tools-to-theories thesis can explain this: Computers were not yet entrenched in the daily routine of psychologists, as we show here.

No Familiar Tools, No Acceptance

We take two institutions as case studies to demonstrate the part of the tools-to-theories hypothesis that concerns acceptance—the Harvard University Center for Cognitive Studies and Carnegie-Mellon University (CMU). The former never came to embrace fully the new information-processing psychology; the latter did but after a considerable delay. Tools-to-theories might explain both phenomena.

George Miller, the cofounder of the Center for Cognitive Studies, was certainly a proponent of the new information-processing psychology. As we said, Miller et al.'s (1960) *Plans and the Structure of Behavior* was so near to Newell et al.'s (1958) ideas that it was at first considered a form of theft, although the version of the book that did see the presses is filled with citations recognizing Newell et al. Given Miller's enthusiasm, one might expect the center, partially under Miller's leadership, to blossom into information-processing research. It never did. Looking at the 1963–1969 annual reports (Harvard University Center for Cognitive Studies, 1963, 1964, 1966, 1968, 1969), we found only a few symposia or papers dealing with computer simulation.

Although the center had a PDP-4C Computer and the reports anticipated the possibility of using it for cognitive simulation, as late as 1969 it never happened. The reports mention that the computer served to run experiments, demonstrate the feasibility of computer research, and draw visitors to the laboratory. However, difficulties involved in using the tool were considerable. The PDP saw 83 hours of use on an average week in 1965–1966, but 56 of these were spent on debugging and maintenance. In the annual reports are several remarks of the type, "It is difficult to program computers. . . . Getting a program to work may take months." The center even turned out a 1966 technical report entitled *Programmanship, or How to Be One-Up on a Computer without Actually Ripping out Its Wires*.

What might have kept the Harvard computer from becoming a metaphor of the mind was that the researchers could not integrate this tool into their everyday laboratory routine. The tool even turned out to be a steady source of frustration. As tools-to-theories suggests, this lack of entrenchment in everyday practice accounted for the lack of acceptance of the new information-processing psychology. Simon (1979) took notice of this:

> Perhaps the most important factors that impeded the diffusion of the new ideas, however, were the unfamiliarity of psychologists with computers and the unavailability on most campuses of machines and associated software (list processing programming languages) that were well adapted to cognitive simulation. The 1958 RAND Summer Workshop, mentioned earlier, and similar workshops held in 1962 and 1963, did a good deal to solve the first problem for the 50 or 60 psychologists who participated

in them; but workshop members often returned to their home campuses to find their local computing facilities ill-adapted to their needs. (p. 365)

At CMU, Newell, Simon, a new information-processing–enthusiastic department head, and a very large National Institute of Mental Health (NIMH) grant were pushing "the new IP [information processing] religion" (H. A. Simon, personal communication, 1994). Even this concerted effort failed to proselytize the majority of researchers within their own department. This again indicates that entrenchment of the new tool in everyday practice was an important precondition for the spread of the metaphor of the mind as a computer.

Acceptance of Theory Follows Familiarity with Tool

At CMU in the late 1950s, the first doctoral theses involving computer simulation of cognitive processes were being written (H. A. Simon, personal communication, 1994). But this was not representative of the national state of affairs. In the mid-1960s, a small number of psychological laboratories were built around computers, including those of CMU, Harvard, Michigan, Indiana, MIT, and Stanford (Aaronson, Grupsmith, & Aaronson, 1976, p. 130). As indicated by the funding history of NIMH grants for cognitive research, the amount of computer-using research tripled over the next decade. In 1967, only 15% of the grants being funded had budget items related to computers (e.g., programmer salaries, hardware, supplies); by 1975, this figure had increased to 46%. The late 1960s saw a turn toward mainframe computers that lasted until the late 1970s, when the microcomputer started its invasion of the laboratory. In the 1978 Behavioral Research Methods & Instrumentation conference, microcomputers were the issue of the day (Castellan, 1981, p. 93). By 1984, the journal *Behavioral Research Methods & Instrumentation* appended the word *Computers* to its title to reflect the broad interest in the new tool. By 1980, the cost of computers had dropped an order of magnitude from what it was in 1970 (Castellan, 1981, 1991). During the last two decades, computers have become the indispensable research tool of the psychologist.

After the tool became entrenched in everyday laboratory routine, a broad acceptance of the view of the mind as a computer followed. In the early 1970s, information-processing psychology finally caught on at CMU. Every CMU-authored article in the proceedings of the 1973 Carnegie Symposium on Cognition mentions some sort of computer simulation. For the rest of the psychological community, which was not as familiar with the tool, the date of broad acceptance was years later. Simon (1979) estimated that, from about 1973 to 1979, the number of active research scientists working in the information-processing vein had "probably doubled or tripled" (p. 390).

This does not mean that the associated methodology became accepted as well. It clashed too strongly with the methodological ritual that was institutionalized during the 1940s and 1950s in experimental psychology. We use the term *ritual* here for the mechanical practice of a curious mishmash between Fisher's and Neyman-Pearson's statistical techniques, which was taught to psychologists as the sine qua non of scientific method (see Chapter 13). Most psychologists assumed, as the textbooks told them, that there is only one way to do good science. But their own heroes—Fechner, Wundt, Pavlov, Köhler, Bartlett, Piaget, Skinner, and Luce, to name a few—had never used this "ritual." Some had used experimental practices that resembled the newly proposed methods used to study the mind as computer.

Pragmatics

Some of our experimental colleagues have objected to our earlier analysis of how statistical tools turned into theories of mind. They have argued that tools are irrelevant in discovery and that our tools-to-theories examples are merely illustrations of psychologists' being quick to realize that the mathematical structure of a tool (e.g., ANOVA) is precisely that of the mind. It is not easy to convince someone who believes (in good Neoplatonic fashion) that today's theory of mind exactly fits the nature of the mind—that such a splendid theory might mirror something other than reality pure and simple. If it were true that tools have no role in discovery and that the new theories just happen to mirror the mathematical structure of the tool, then the pragmatics of the use of a tool—which is independent of the mathematical structure—would find no place in the new theories. In this section, however, we provide evidence that not only the new tool but also its pragmatic uses are projected into the mind. The tools-to-theories heuristic cannot be used to defend a spurious Neoplatonism.

One example is Kelley's (1967) causal attribution theory, which postulates that the mind draws a causal inference in the same way social scientists do, by using Fisher's ANOVA. As described in Chapter 1, the pragmatics, in addition to the mathematics of ANOVA, were projected into the mind. The practical use of a tool is generally undetermined by its mathematical structure. The mathematics of significance testing, as in ANOVA, has been used both for rejecting hypotheses based on data and for rejecting data (e.g., outliers in astronomical observations) based on hypotheses. Scientists have to get rid of both bad hypotheses and bad data. In the psychological laboratories, however, ANOVA was (and is) used almost exclusively for rejecting hypotheses based on data. Dubious data, in contrast, were (and still are) dealt with informally. When Kelley projected ANOVA into the mind, this specific, practical use (i.e., rejecting hypotheses) was projected along with it. In sharp contrast to earlier theoretical accounts, such as Michotte's and Piaget's, causal inference was seen as data driven, as an inductive inference from data to causes. Kelley's new mind used the tool in the same way the researcher uses the tool—to trust the data (the information given) and to mistrust the hypotheses. The inductive view of causal attribution became one of the classic topics of social psychology, even to the point of defining the field.

The same process of projecting pragmatic aspects of the use of a tool into a theory can be shown for the view of the mind as a computer. One example is Levelt's (1989) model of speaking. The basic unit in Levelt's model, which he called the "processing component," corresponds to the computer programmer's concept of a subroutine. We argue that Levelt's model not only borrowed the subroutine as a tool but also borrowed the practical aspects of how subroutines are used and constructed in computer programming.

A subroutine (or "subprocess") is a group of computer instructions (usually serving a specific function) that are separated from the main routine of a computer program. It is common for subroutines to perform often needed functions, such as extracting cube roots or rounding numbers. There is a major pragmatic issue involved in writing subroutines that centers on the "principle of isolation" (Simon & Newell, 1986). The issue is whether subroutines should be black boxes or not. According to the principle of isolation, the internal workings of the subroutine should remain a mystery to the main program, and the outside program should remain a mystery to the subroutine. Black-box subroutines have become known as *program modules*, perfect for the divide-and-conquer strategy programmers often use to tackle large problems. To the computer, however, it makes no difference whether subroutines are isolated or not. Subroutines that are not isolated work just as well as those that are. The only real difference between the two types of subroutine is psychological. Subroutines that violate the principle of isolation are more difficult for the programmer to read, write, debug, maintain, and reuse. For this reason, introductory texts on computer programming stress the principle of isolation as the very essence of good programming style.

The principle of isolation—a pragmatic feature of using subroutines as a programming tool—has a central place in Levelt's model, in which the processing components are "black boxes" that exemplify Fodor's notion of informational encapsulation (Levelt, 1989, p. 15). In this way, Levelt's psychological model embodies a maxim of good computer programming—the principle of isolation. That this practical aspect of the use of the tool shaped a theory of speaking is not an evaluation of the quality of the theory. Our point concerns origins, not validity. However, this pragmatic feature of subroutines has not always served the model well. Kita (1993) and Levinson (1992) have attacked Levelt's model at its Achilles' heel—its insistence on isolated processing components.

To summarize the second part of this chapter, we started with the separation between intelligence and calculation and argued that the realization that computers can do more than arithmetic was an important precondition for the view of the mind as a computer. Newell and Simon seem to have been the first who tried to understand the mind in terms of a computer program, but the acceptance of their information-processing view was delayed until the psychologists became used to computers in their daily laboratory routine. We have argued that, along with the tool, its pragmatic use has been projected into theories of mind. Now that the metaphor is in place, many find it difficult to see how the mind could be anything else: To quote Philip Johnson-Laird (1983): "The computer is the last metaphor; it need never be supplanted" (p. 10).

Social Computers

The tools-to-theories heuristic can reverse the commonly assumed fixed temporal order between discovery and justification—discovery first, justification second. New tools for justification enter the laboratory first, new theories follow. In the case of Babbage's computer, the tool itself was modeled after a new social system, the organization of work in large-scale manufacturing. The model for the machine computer was a social computer.

The argument was that economic changes—the large-scale division of labor in manufacturing and in the "bureaux de calculs"—went along with the breakdown of the Enlightenment conception of the mind, in which calculation was the distinctive essence of intelligence. Once calculation was separated from the rest of intelligence and relegated to the status of a dull and repetitive task, Babbage could envision replacing human computers with mechanical ones. Both human and mechanical computers manufactured numbers as the factories of the day manufactured goods. In the twentieth century, the technology became available to make Babbage's dream a reality. Computers became indispensable scientific tools for everything from number crunching to simulation. Our focus was on the work by Herbert Simon and Allen Newell and their colleagues, who proposed the tool as a theory of mind. Their proposal reunited mere calculation with what was now called "symbol processing," returning to the Enlightenment conception of mind. After personal computers found a place in nearly every psychological laboratory, broad acceptance of the metaphor of the mind as computer followed.[6]

A question remains: Why was the digital computer used as a model of the individual mind rather than of the social organization of many minds? As the social roots of the idea behind Babbage's computer shows, there is nothing inherently individualistic about the business of computation. We can only speculate that it was the traditional focus of psychological research on individuals that suggested the analogy between the computer and the individual mind and that in less individualistic disciplines the computer would have had a better chance of becoming a model of social organization. In fact, anthropologist Ed Hutchins (1995) has proposed using the digital computer as a model of how social groups make decisions, for instance, how a crew on a large ship solves the problem of navigation. Here the computer is used to

6. The reconstruction of the path "from mind to computer and back" also provides an explanation for one widespread type of resistance to the computer metaphor of mind. The post-Enlightenment divorce between intelligence and calculation still holds to this day, and, for those who still associate the computer with mere calculation (as opposed to symbol processing), the mind-as-a-computer is a contradiction in itself.

model the division of labor in the storing, processing, and exchange of information among members of a social group. This notion of distributed intelligence completes the circle traveled by the computer metaphor. Once modeled after the social organization of human work, the computer has now become a model of the social organization of human work.

3

Ideas in Exile

The Struggles of an Upright Man

The sparkling intellectual atmosphere of early twentieth-century Vienna produced Wittgenstein, Popper, Neurath, and Gödel—in addition to a string of other great thinkers. Among them was Karl Bühler, who, when he founded the Vienna Psychological Institute in 1922, was one of the foremost psychologists in the world. Egon Brunswik began to study psychology in Vienna in 1923 and soon became an active participant in Bühler's famous Wednesday evening discussion group; on Thursdays he went to Moritz Schlick's Thursday evening discussion group (Leary, 1987). Schlick was the founder and leading member of the European school of positivist philosophers known as the Vienna Circle. In 1927, Brunswik submitted his doctoral thesis to Bühler and Schlick, the same two advisors to whom Karl Popper submitted his thesis a year later.

The intellectual tension between Wednesday and Thursday evenings was vibrant. The logical positivist doctrine of the Vienna Circle posited that the relation between scientific language and its sense-data referents should and could be unambiguous. Bühler, in contrast, had shown that the relation between perceptual cues and their objects, as well as between words and their objects, was irreducibly ambiguous. Brunswik sided with Bühler. He did try, though, to resolve the tension by adopting the position of Hans Reichenbach, the leader of the Berlin school of logical positivism, who argued that all knowledge is probabilistic.

Influenced by Bühler's biologically motivated concern with the success of organisms in their world, Brunswik's research in the 1920s and 1930s aimed at studying "perceptual achievement" in the presence of ambiguous cues. The three traditional perceptual constancies—size, shape, and color—were the prototype for achievement, that is, how accurate perception is when aspects of the environment change. Brunswik extended the question of how well an organism infers size, shape, and color under varying context variables (such as illumination) to the more general problem of studying the invariance of the perception of one characteristic of an object when the others vary. For instance, he studied how the perceived size of coins changed when their value and the number of coins were varied—coins higher in value appeared to be larger in size and greater in number than those of lesser value (Brunswik, 1934, p. 147). In Brunswik's terms, what we see are *perceptual compromises* that he attributed to the learning of cues from experience (e.g., coins of higher value actually do tend to be larger in size). He manipulated up to four variables simultaneously in factorial designs (he had not yet developed the idea of representative design) and measured how the perception of each variable depended on the values of the others. This Vienna program of "multidimensional psychophysics" measured the context-dependency of judgment (for an introduction see Gigerenzer & Murray, 1987, pp. 61–81). In contrast, its independence from context was assumed in the one-dimensional psychophysics associated with G. T. Fechner and S. S. Stevens, in which one studied a variable in isolation (such as perceived size), held everything else constant, and then compared the perceived with the actual size to obtain the psychophysical function.

In the early 1930s, Brunswik was far ahead of mainstream psychophysics in the study of context dependency. This is not to say that there was no room for theoretical development in his multidimensional psychophysics; for instance, Brunswik treated his two explanatory concepts, perceptual compromises and cue learning, as equivalent, whereas these actually are different and can lead to contradictory predictions about the effect of context (Gigerenzer & Murray, 1987, pp. 70–74). However, his Vienna program had virtually no impact on the future of psychophysics, except for a few scattered studies.

One reason for this lack of influence was that the Vienna Psychological Institute's program was destroyed soon after Brunswik accepted a position at Berkeley in 1937. In early 1938, the Nazis entered Vienna and arrested and dismissed Bühler because of his political views, which were considered dangerous to the "peace and public order of the (Philosophical) Faculty" (Ash, 1987, p. 157). Eventually, he fled to the United States, but no one offered the once celebrated Karl Bühler an adequate position; his brilliant career crumbled in exile. Schlick had died a few years earlier from gunshot wounds inflicted by a deranged student, and the political pressure of fascism caused the Vienna Circle to disband, with many of its members fleeing to the United States. Brunswik had to start practically from scratch at Berkeley.

Brunswik in the Plural

Unlike the Vienna program, Brunswik's Berkeley program—probabilistic functionalism—is well known. It is so well known, in fact, that there is not just one Brunswik, but several. One is the Brunswik absorbed by contemporary psychology: he-was-one-of-us. These good-natured colleagues spell his name "Brunswick," confuse his term *ecological validity* with generalizability from the laboratory to the environment and *representative design* with the representativeness heuristic. In their friendly embrace, Brunswik comes out a forerunner and guardian of today's status quo. No conflict surfaces, all is quiet, nothing must be questioned.

There is a more sophisticated image, in which Brunswik's ideas basically boil down to three correlations and one unorthodoxy. The correlations are functional validities, ecological validities, and cue utilization coefficients, and the heresy is representative design—the frightening idea of sacrificing experimental control and, possibly even worse, of leaving one's laboratory to study people in their real-world environments. Correlations are fine, the unorthodoxy is repugnant. This view gets some work done, but it cuts right through the middle of Brunswik's intellectual heart.

There is a third view of Brunswik: opposition by neglect. This is not an active opposition against an intellectual enemy; Brunswik does not seem to have notable intellectual enemies, unlike many other scholars. The opposition takes the form of silence and a lack of understanding of what the fuss is all about. For instance, in his *Sensation and Perception in the History of Experimental Psychology* (1942), Edwin G. Boring, the dean of the history of psychology and an arch-determinist, covered Brunswik's work in Vienna, which encompassed experimental control in multidimensional designs. But after Brunswik had fleshed out his probabilistic functionalism and representative design, he was not even mentioned in Boring's *A History of Experimental Psychology* (1957) and *History, Psychology, and Science* (1963). As Ken Hammond (1980, p. 9) reported, Boring's verdict was "Brunswik was a brilliant man who wasted his life." Informed neglect can be as toxic to new ideas as an uninformed embrace.

In the following, I describe what I think of when I think of Brunswik. I do not think of correlations; I think of the struggles of an upright man.

Intellectual Integrity

What impresses me deeply is Brunswik's uncompromising intellectual sincerity: the courage to think through the consequences of one's ideas carefully and to speak out in public even when the scientific community does not want to listen and makes one pay a price for these standards. And Brunswik paid dearly. Brunswik's personal struggle was, in my view, about maintaining his *intellectual integrity* in a scientific community in which his ideas fell on hostile ground held by ignorant troops. Great thinkers often learn, to their surprise, that new ideas are less than welcome.

What were these new ideas that inspired so much hostility? Brunswik's probabilistic functionalism can be summarized in the following concepts: achievement, ambiguity of cues, vicarious functioning, and representative design. That is, an organism needs to make inferences about its environment to adjust, survive, and reproduce (achievement); the proximal cues available to it to make these inferences about its environment are uncertain (ambiguity); the organism processes ambiguous cues by substituting or combining them (vicarious functioning); in order to study achievement and vicarious functioning, researchers need to use representative designs. This is Brunswik's linking of biological purpose, environment, cognitive process, and research methodology.

The hostile ground itself was a minefield of dogmas: determinism, the Columbia Bible, and Fisher's experimental design. Determinism was a fading, but still strong, dogma, and the other two were newly emerging dogmas.

Refinancing Determinism

In their struggle to get psychology recognized as a science, many of Brunswik's fellow psychologists in America maintained an old-fashioned ideal no longer characteristic of modern science, from evolutionary biology to quantum physics. This ideal demanded *certain* knowledge and *universal* laws, as Newtonian mechanics had purported to deliver. As an example of this longing for certainty, Edwin Boring declared as late as 1963 that "determinism reigns" (p. 14).

The two debates of Brunswik's program, which were then published in the *Psychological Review* in 1943 and 1955, illustrated the way Brunswik's probabilism collided with the leading experimental psychologists' belief in determinism (see Gigerenzer, 1987b). Probabilism was interpreted as a confession of failure. For instance, Clark Hull (1943) declared in the first debate in Chicago that he and Kurt Lewin believed in uniform laws of behavior that correspond to correlations of 1.00. Because the effort to isolate deterministic laws is laborious and time-consuming, "all of us may as well give it up, as Brunswik seems already to have done" (p. 204).

Twelve years later, in the second debate in Berkeley, David Krech (1955) confronted Brunswik with his personal confession of faith:

> I have always made it a cardinal principle to live beyond my income. And although I have yet to find a one-to-one correlation in psychology . . . I am always ready to make another promissory note and promise that if you bear with us we *will* find uniform laws. . . . And if I can't pay off on my first promissory note I will come seeking refinancing. . . . I have faith that despite our repeated and inglorious failures we will someday come to a theory which is able to give a consistent and complete description of reality. But in the meantime, I repeat, you must bear with us. (p. 230)

Refinancing went on for some time. The fixation on uniform laws of behavior was one of the reasons why many of the commentators did not understand the nature of Brunswik's probabilism—which was located neither in the environment, as Krech and Hilgard interpreted Brunswik, nor in the organism, as Hull seemed to do, but rather in the relationship *between* the organism and the environment.

The dogma of determinism did not survive Brunswik very long, but the next two methodological faiths did. They are still entrenched in the minds of most experimental psychologists—and in their hearts, because these methodologies have been taught as if they were moral principles.

The Columbia Bible

The Henry Holt publishing company advertised in 1938: "THE BIBLE IS OUT." Robert S. Woodworth had finally published his long-awaited *Experimental Psychology*. This textbook, which was known popularly as the "Columbia Bible," narrowed the many existing practices of experimentation (see Danziger, 1990) to one and only one legitimate form: vary an independent variable (or a few), hold all the conditions constant, and observe the effect on the dependent variable. In Brunswik's copy of the Columbia Bible (which Ken Hammond so kindly lent me), on page 2, the passage "all the conditions constant, except for one" is underlined twice and Brunswik's pencil notation "imposs[ible]!" is in the margin. It is not without irony that Brunswik taught courses for years using Woodworth's textbook, as the notes in his copy indicate. An estimated 100,000 North American psychology majors and graduate students learned what experimental research is from the bible and its revised edition (Woodworth & Schlosberg, 1954). The book was translated into many languages and widely used around the world (Evans, 1990). It was enormously successful; many psychologists can no longer envision more than one experimental method in science.

In this book, Woodworth excluded correlation methods and individual differences from the domain of experimental psychology. The bible separated the murky waters of correlation, which obscure the causes of behavior, from the bright sun of experimentation, where cause and effect can be distinguished clearly. The result was a strange institutional partition into "two disciplines of scientific psychology" (Cronbach, 1957), the "Tiny Little Island" of experimental psychology and the "Holy Roman Empire" of correlational psychology.

Brunswik's probabilistic functionalism fit into neither of these disciplines. His intellectual vision was one of coherence between theory and methodology: to start with the purpose or function (achievement in natural environments) and a subject matter (vicarious functioning of perception and judgment) and to choose a matching methodology (representative design).

There is no such intellectual vision behind the creation of the two "scientific disciplines." Each was, and still is, a historically arbitrary collection of purpose, subject matter, and method that have no necessary logical or psychological affinity to each other (Gigerenzer, 1987b). For instance, there is no psychological reason why the study of intelligence is linked with individual differences and correlations, whereas the study of thinking is linked to general laws and experiments. Nor is there a reason why one group should rarely read or cite the other group's work. Like most ordinary humans who bond with their peers, psychologists in one camp looked down on their colleagues in the other camp, declaring their adversaries' methods inferior and their purpose of little scientific interest and public value. The correlation between psychologists' esteem for their colleagues in one camp and their colleagues in the other camp was −.80 (Thorndike, 1954)—alas, a substantial, but not perfect, correlation.

Brunswik found himself and his ideas exiled from his discipline. Ernest Hilgard (1955), an eminent experimental psychologist, put his lack of regard for Brunswik's methods in no uncertain terms: "Correlation is an instrument of the devil" (p. 228). But methods per se are neither good nor bad; the question is whether they match a theory or not. Brunswik's intellectual integrity demanded that he think for himself, deciding what the proper method was, rather than just climbing on the bandwagon. The tragedy is that he found himself in a no-man's-land between the two newly established disciplines.

Fisher's Straitjacket

B. F. Skinner once told me that he had thought of dedicating one of his books to "the statisticians and scientific methodologists with whose help this book would have never been completed." He had second thoughts, and, in fact, dedicated the book to those who actually were helpful, "to the pigeon staff." Skinner had had in mind those statisticians who imposed Sir Ronald Fisher's doctrine that the design of an experiment must match the statistical method, such as analysis of variance.

Fisher's randomized control group experiments were tailor-made to Woodworth's ideal of experimentation, and analysis of variance allowed one to study more than one independent variable. Skinner's resistance arose when researchers started to use Fisher's method compulsively rather than in a thoughtful way, that is, as a tool, which is—like all tools—useful only in specific situations. Editors began to make what they believed was good scientific method a sine qua non for publication: factorial designs, large numbers of participants, and small p values.

Statistical thinking became replaced by a mindless ritual performed in the presence of any set of data (see Chapter 13). Skinner confessed to me that he once tried a factorial design with some two dozen animals. But only once. He lost experimental control because he could not keep so many animals at the same level of deprivation, and the magnitude of error in his data increased. Why increase error just to have a method that measures error?

The Skinnerians escaped the emerging pressure of editors to publish studies with large numbers of animals by founding a new journal in 1958, the *Journal of the Experimental Analysis of Behavior*. Brunswik, however, had no following with which he could found his own journal. Like Skinner, he remarked drolly that "our ignorance of Fisher's work on factorial design and its mathematical evaluation . . . paid off" (1956, p. 102). As almost all great psychologists did, he analyzed individuals rather than comparing group means, and he continued to employ his own nonfactorial representative designs. But he also sometimes felt that he should make concessions, for instance, when he performed "a routine analysis of variance for the factorially orthodox part of our experiment" (1956, p. 106).

In Brunswik's struggle with Fisher's ideas, unlike Skinner's, a classic controversy repeated itself. Karl Pearson, who, with Francis Galton, founded correlation methods, was involved in a terrible intellectual and personal feud with Fisher. This fight between these towering statisticians repeated itself in psychology between the proponents of their respective tools. Just at the time when Brunswik adopted Pearson's correlation methods around 1940, Fisherian methods began to spread. By 1955, when Brunswik died, Fisherian methods had overrun, conquered, and redefined every branch of experimental psychology.

Then the newly institutionalized tools evolved into new theories of mind. When Brunswik's vision of the mind as an intuitive statistician finally became a great success in experimental psychology, the mind's intuitive statistician was not of the Karl Pearson school, as Brunswik had imagined. Rather, the homunculus statistician used the new laboratory tools, such as analysis of variance. For instance, according to Harold Kelley's (1967) causal attribution theory, the mind attributes a cause to an effect in the same way as researchers have come to do—by calculating an intuitive version of analysis of variance (see Chapter 1). Brunswik had never been able to persuade his colleagues from experimental psychology that the mind would use the techniques of the competing discipline of correlational psychology.

The Price of Intellectual Integrity

Woodworth's bible had excommunicated Brunswik from experimental psychology, and the institutionalization of Fisher's methods as the sine qua non of scientific method set Brunswik's ideas outside the realm of what was considered proper scientific method. Brunswik must have soon realized that the edifice he had erected had become, as Ken Hammond (1966) expressed it succinctly, a significant landmark that "was virtually empty; there were visitors, it is true, but no one stayed" (p. v). Although Brunswik, unlike the exiled Bühler, had chosen freely to leave Vienna for the United States, he found his ideas in exile. Unlike in Vienna, at Berkeley he seems not to have had a group of students who worked on his ideas, nor did his working atmosphere support the philosophical and interdisciplinary spirit that continued to enhance his writings. But there was no way back; the Vienna program and the Vienna Circle had been destroyed, and Brunswik himself had moved beyond multidimensional psychophysics. What is one to do if one has lost the old companions and failed to enlist new ones? The obvious easy choice would have been to conform to the new zeitgeist, but the option of surrendering his ideas seems never to have occurred to Brunswik. It is easy to be true to one's ideas if everyone applauds—I admire Brunswik's intellectual integrity because, in his case, only very, very few applauded. Standing upright must have been difficult, lonely, and depressing.

Do the Ideas Matter?

American psychology would hardly remember Brunswik's ideas had not one of his students, Ken Hammond, kept his memory alive to the present day. But is the memory of Egon Brunswik of more than historical interest? Are his ideas still exiled, and if so, does it matter?

Representative Sampling

Brunswik (1956) sadly reported that his success in persuading fellow research-ers to shift to representative sampling of stimuli is "very slow going and hard to maintain" (p. 39). He complained that his colleagues practiced "double stan-dards" by being concerned with the sampling of participants but not of stim-ulus objects. Representative sampling of stimuli is one aspect of the more gen-eral notion of representative design.

It would be an error to introduce representative sampling as a new dogma to replace current methodological dogmas. The point is to choose the appro-priate sampling method for the problem under discussion. For instance, rep-resentative sampling of objects from a class is indispensable if one wants to make general statements about the degree of "achievement," or its flip side, the fallacies of perception and judgment concerning this class of objects. But if the purpose is testing competing models of cognitive strategies and flat max-ima obscure the discriminability of strategies, then using selected stimuli that discriminate between the strategies may be the only choice (see Rieskamp & Hoffrage, 1999).

Is the idea of representative sampling of any relevance for present-day re-search? Imagine Brunswik browsing through recent textbooks on cognitive psy-chology and looking for what we have discovered about achievement in judg-ment—now more fashionably labeled fallacies and cognitive illusions. It would catch his eye that the stimuli used in the demonstrations of fallacies were typically selected rather than representative: the five letters in Tversky and Kahneman's (1973) study from which the availability heuristic was con-cluded; the personality sketches in Kahneman and Tversky's (1973) engineer–lawyer study from which base-rate neglect was concluded; and the general-knowledge questions from which the overconfidence bias was concluded (Lichtenstein, Fischhoff, & Phillips, 1982), among others. Brunswik would have objected that if one wants to measure achievement or demonstrate fal-lacies in a reference class of objects, one needs to take a representative (or random) sample of these objects. If not, one can "demonstrate" almost any level of performance by selecting those objects for which performance is at its worst (or at its best). In fact, when one uses representative (rather than se-lected) samples in these three studies, performance greatly improves: The errors in estimating the frequency of letters largely disappear (Sedlmeier, Hertwig, & Gigerenzer, 1998); the estimated probabilities that a person is an engineer approach Bayes's rule (Gigerenzer et al., 1988); and the over-confidence bias completely disappears (Chapter 7; Juslin, Olsson, & Winman, 1998). These celebrated cognitive illusions, attributed to the participants, are in part due to the selected sampling done by the experimenters.

These examples illustrate that representative sampling of stimuli is still a blind spot in some areas of research. In survey research, it would be a mistake to present the odd views of a few selected citizens as public opinion; that the same applies to stimulus objects is still not commonly acknowledged. Unreflectively selected samples can produce apparently general phenomena that occupy us for years and then finally dissolve into an issue of mere sampling.

Natural Sampling

Imagine Brunswik looking at the studies on Bayesian reasoning, which emerged about 10 years after his death. When he learned that people neglect base rates he might have been surprised because his rats did not (Brunswik, 1939). His rats were not perfect, but they were sensitive to the difference of the base rates of reinforcement in the two sides of a T-maze and to the ratio as well. Sensitized by the frequentist Reichenbach, Brunswik's eye would have caught an essential difference between his study and the base-rate studies of the 1970s and 1980s: His rats learned the base rates from actual experienced frequencies, whereas the humans in almost all studies that reported base-rate neglect could not; they were presented summary information in terms of probabilities or percentages. Rats would not understand probabilities, and humans have only recently in their evolution begun to struggle with this representation of uncertainty. Does representation matter? Christensen-Szalanski and Beach (1982) presented base rates in terms of actual frequencies, sequentially encountered, and reported that base-rate neglect largely disappeared. This process of sampling instances from a population sequentially is known as *natural sampling*. Natural sampling is the everyday equivalent—for rats and humans alike—of the representative sampling done by scientific experimenters. When observed frequencies are based on natural sampling—that is, on raw (rather than normalized) counts of events made in an ecological (rather than experimental) setting—then one can show that Bayesian computations become simpler than with probabilities, and people have more insight into Bayesian problems (Chapter 4).

Structure of Environments

A most important insight I gained from Brunswik's writings is the relevance of the structure of information in environments to the study of judgment. Brunswik tentatively proposed measuring environmental structure by ecological validities and measuring these in turn by correlation coefficients. Brunswik, though, almost as much as Skinner, hesitated to look into the black box, and so he failed to see the important connection between the structure of environments and that of mediation. Adaptive mental strategies can exploit certain structures. For instance, if there is a match between the structure of the environment and that of a strategy, a simple heuristic that processes much less information than multiple regression can nevertheless make as many (or more) accurate inferences about its environment (Martignon & Hoffrage, 1999). Herbert Simon had emphasized the link between cognitive processes and environmental structure in his famous 1956 *Psychological Review* article on bounded rationality. However, in recent years, bounded rationality has been reduced to cognitive limitations, and the structure of environments has been largely forgotten as an indispensable part of understanding bounded rationality, sometimes even by Simon himself (e.g., 1987). The study of the structure of environments is still in its infancy.

Much of psychology after the cognitive revolution is about what is in our heads: Which logic does human reasoning embody? How many primary emotions should we distinguish? It is little concerned with what cognition, emotion, and behavior are for and how they relate to the structure of environments, both physical and social. Brunswik's focus on achievement, in contrast, is functional, focusing on the accuracy of perception and judgment. Accuracy is not the only goal; to be able to act quickly, to come in first, or to establish social relations of trust and cooperation also exemplify achievement in a broader sense.

The structure of environments is essential for understanding cognition and behavior in terms of adaptation, because adaptations are relative to (past) environments. To flesh out the Darwinian aspect of Brunswikian psychology, one needs to distinguish between past and present environments, between ecological validities in past and in present environments, and between social environments composed of conspecifics (where cues are actually signals) and other environments (e.g., physical environments in which humans do not cooperate or bargain with their inhabitants). For instance, smooth skin in female humans may have been a highly valid cue for reproductive capability during most of human evolution, signaling good health (Buss, 1987). In current environments with abundant medical technology, the ecological validity of smooth skin may have decreased to almost nil, but men's proximal mechanisms, cognitive and emotional, may still rely on such cues. A Darwinian psychology is a historical psychology, one that looks into the past to learn about the present (e.g., Cosmides & Tooby, 1992).

Brunswik repeatedly alluded to Darwin, and the notions of function, achievement, and environmental structure all relate to evolution by natural selection. He, however, never developed or carried these ideas any further. Neo-Brunswikians have done little to develop the Darwinian fragment, consistent with the prevailing anxiety about evolution in the American psychology establishment. Given that even Pope John Paul II finally announced in the *Quarterly Review of Biology* (1997) that evolution (of the body, not of the spirit) is a plausible hypothesis, more psychologists might find the courage to think about what we can learn from modern evolutionary theory—even if some still continue to consider such thoughts politically incorrect.

Models of Vicarious Functioning

Schlick's Thursday evening discussion groups seem to have had a lasting effect on Brunswik. The methodological objectivity of the Vienna Circle helped Brunswik to focus his work on the measurement of objective achievement rather than on cognitive processes ("mediation"). He hesitated to speak about the unobservable process of mediation, and even in 1937 still declared that psychology is a science of "what" rather than of "how." The question of how mediation works should be studied only insofar as it throws light on the question of what an organism achieves. Only later did Brunswik (e.g., 1957) grant a place, though only a second place, to the study of cognitive processes.

Given his reluctance to open the black box, I am not sure how Brunswik would look at the process models of vicarious functions that were inspired by his ideas: multiple regression models on the one hand (e.g., Hammond, Hursch, & Todd, 1964) and the theory of probabilistic mental models (PMM theory) and the fast and frugal lens model on the other (Chapter 8). When Brunswik coined the metaphor of the "intuitive statistician," he tentatively suggested that the process of vicarious functioning might be like multiple regression (Doherty & Kurz, 1996). Brunswik's measurement tool turned into a theory of cognitive processes. In the neo-Brunswikian revival, multiple regression became *the* model of vicarious functioning, and, unfortunately, it remains so. Ken Hammond, like Brunswik, has had second thoughts, but by and large, the tool has become part of the message. It structures our thinking about Brunswik.

Brunswik's reluctance to think about processes may explain why his examples for vicarious functioning vacillated back and forth between two different processes, substitution and combination. Some of his examples—such as Hull's habit family hierarchy and the psychoanalytic substitution mechanism in which one cause can manifest itself as various symptoms—referred to substitution without combination, others to the combination of cues. The fast and frugal lens model, based on PMM theory, assumes substitution without combination, emphasizing that judgments need to be made quickly and on the basis of limited knowledge (see Gigerenzer & Kurz, in press). Here Egon Brunswik meets Herbert Simon, creating models of bounded rationality in which simple cognitive heuristics exploit environmental structures.

A Love of History, Philosophy, and Methodology

Just as the human species has a history, so do our theories and methods. Not knowing where they come from can blind one to understanding why one propounds a particular theory or uses a specific method. Nevertheless, looking down at history is symptomatic for much of current psychology. Brunswik had written about the history of his field and had published in philosophical journals; possibly it is just that background that helped him to see that there are differences between methodologies and that one actually needs to make informed choices. Many researchers do not seem to make these choices; rather, they take on the methodological practice of their field and then defend it as if it were religious dogma. If one reads Brunswik, one finds a constant stream of thought about methodology, from preferring matching tasks over numerical response tasks in order to minimize the confounding of perception with judgment to the larger program of representative design. In contrast, the enthusiasm with which some methods have been mechanically applied as general-purpose tools—factor analysis, multidimensional scaling, and analysis of variance, among others—springs from ignorance of history, philosophy, and the methodologies of other scientific disciplines. Methodology is an art, not a science of compulsive hand washing.

This is not to say that every psychologist must be a master of history, but history can protect one against confusing present-day methodological conventions with the sine qua non of scientific research.

The Search for Objectivity in the Twilight of Uncertainty

John Locke (1690/1959) remarked that "God . . . has afforded us only with the twilight of probability; suitable, I presume, to that state of mediocrity and probationership he has been pleased to place us in here. . . ." Bühler's psychology opened the door for Brunswik to the twilight of uncertainty, and the Vienna Circle inspired him to search for objective knowledge behind that door. What Brunswik found there: that we know. What he was looking for is more: not answers, but the right questions. From him, one can learn to rethink that which is taken for granted. I have.

Yet there is another, deeper message in the work of Egon Brunswik: the value of the struggle for intellectual integrity—daring to think ideas through, with all the consequences, and remaining true to them even if they are condemned to exile. Kant's final two words in his lovely essay on the Enlightenment capture the essence of this struggle: *sapere aude*, that is, have the courage to know.

ECOLOGICAL RATIONALITY

The tools-to-theories heuristic generates new ideas about the workings of the mind by looking outside of the mind. So does the program of "ecological rationality." Whereas the first draws on the scientist's laboratory environment, the second draws on people's natural environments, past and present. Ecological rationality refers to the study of how cognitive strategies exploit the representation and structure of information in the environment to make reasonable judgments and decisions. The importance of studying the link between mind and its environment was emphasized by Egon Brunswik, who compared mind and environment to two married people who have to come to terms with each other by mutual adaptation. This couple should not be divorced, as often is done, in research. More recently, Roger Shepard (1990, p. 213) expressed the same insight: "We may look into that window [on the mind] as through a glass darkly, but what we are beginning to discern there looks very much like a reflection of the world." This is well expressed, but how can ecological rationality be used as a tool of research?

For instance, a puzzling phenomenon in human judgment is the apparent neglect of base rates. Even animals do not seem to neglect base rates. Previous attempts to explain base-rate neglect focused on the shoddy software in the human mind that might cause this cognitive illusion—could the culprit be shortcomings in memory, motivation, or computational capabilities? Note that this approach entails looking exclusively inside the head for an explanation. The program of ecological rationality suggests a different question: In what environments, past or present, would neglect of base rates be rational? The answer is, when information is acquired through natural sampling, which yields simple counts (not normalized by base rates; see the three chapters in this section). During most of their history—before the advent of probability theory—humans, like animals, have acquired information about uncertainties and risks through natural sampling of event frequencies rather than in terms of probabilities or percentages. The important point is that under conditions of natural sampling, one can make perfectly rational inferences without paying attention to base rates.

The first two chapters in this section illustrate the practical relevance of this argument for criminal law, medical diagnosis, AIDS counseling, and other professions concerned with uncertainties and risks. Should evidence of wife battering be admissible in the trial of a man accused of murdering his wife? How many 40-year-old women with a positive mammogram in routine screening actually have breast cancer? How likely is it that a man with a positive HIV test actually has the virus? Earlier studies have documented that many experts—and most patients and jurors—do not understand how to answer these questions, possibly because they neglect base rates or are confused by probabilities. I show that the notion of ecological rationality leads to a simple method for helping experts and laypersons alike. One can restore the representation of uncertainty that humans have encountered throughout their evolution by translating probabilities back into natural frequencies—the outcome of natural sampling. This change can turn innumeracy into insight.

The final chapter in this section is theoretical and experimental rather than applied. It defines the concepts of natural sampling, natural frequencies, and reports experimental evidence for the impact of various external representations on statistical thinking. The mental strategies or shortcuts people use, not only their numerical estimates of risks, turn out to be a function of the external representation of numbers we choose.

Ecological rationality can refer to the adaptation of mental processes to the *representation* of information, as in this section. It also can refer to the adaptation of mental processes to the *structure* of information in an environment, as illustrated in the section on bounded rationality and, in more detail, in *Simple Heuristics that Make Us Smart* (Gigerenzer, Todd, & the ABC Research Group, 1999). In both cases, it is important to distinguish between *past* and *present* environments, particularly when we are studying humans, who change their environments rapidly. Studying how past environments differ from present environments reminds us that an ecological perspective has an evolutionary and historical dimension. Here we go beyond Brunswik's metaphor of the married couple, which focuses on the adaptation between the mind and its current spouse while forgetting its previous marriages. The program of ecological rationality is a research heuristic, not a foolproof recipe—just as new laboratory tools do not always lead to good theories for mental processes.

4

Ecological Intelligence

When I left a restaurant in a charming town in Tuscany one night, I looked for my yellow-green rented Renault 4 in the parking lot. There was none. Instead, there was a blue Renault 4 sitting in the lot, the same model but the wrong color. I still feel my fingers hesitating to put my key into the lock of this car, but the lock opened. I drove the car home. When I looked out the window the next morning, there was a yellow-green Renault 4 standing in bright sunlight outside. What had happened? My color-constancy system did not work with the artificial light at the parking lot. Color constancy, an impressive adaptation of the human perceptual system, normally allows us to see the same color under changing illuminations, under the bluish light of day as well as the reddish light of the setting sun. Color constancy, however, fails under certain artificial lights, such as sodium or mercury vapor lamps, which were not present in the environment when mammals evolved (Shepard, 1992).

Human color vision is adapted to the spectral properties of natural sunlight. More generally, our perceptual system has been shaped by the environment in which our ancestors evolved, the environment often referred to as the "environment of evolutionary adaptiveness," or EEA (Tooby & Cosmides, 1992). Similarly, human morphology, physiology, and the nervous and immune systems show exquisite adaptations. The tubular form of the bones maximizes strength and flexibility while minimizing weight; bones are, pound for pound, stronger than solid steel bars, and the best man-made heart valves cannot yet match the way natural valves open and close (Nesse & Williams, 1995). Like color constancy, however, these systems can be fooled and may break down when stable, long-term properties of the environment to which they were adapted change.

In this chapter, I propose that human reasoning processes, like those of color constancy, are designed for information that comes in a format that was present in the EEA. I will focus on a class of inductive reasoning processes technically known as *Bayesian inference*, specifically a simple version

59

thereof in which an organism infers from one or a few indicators which of two events is true.

Bayesian Inference

David Eddy (1982) asked physicians to estimate the probability that a woman has breast cancer given that she has a positive mammogram on the basis of the following information:

> The probability that a patient has breast cancer is 1% (the physician's prior probability).

> If the patient has breast cancer, the probability that the radiologist will correctly diagnose it is 80% (sensitivity or hit rate).

> If the patient has a benign lesion (no breast cancer), the probability that the radiologist will incorrectly diagnose it as cancer is 9.6% (false positive rate).

> QUESTION: What is the probability that a patient with a positive mammogram actually has breast cancer?

Eddy reported that 95 out of 100 physicians estimated the probability of breast cancer after a positive mammogram to be about 75%. The inference from an observation (positive test) to a disease, or more generally, from data D to a hypothesis H, is often referred to as "Bayesian inference," because it can be modeled by Bayes's rule:

$$p(H|D) = \frac{p(H)p(D|H)}{p(H)p(D|H) + p(-H)p(D|-H)}$$

$$= \frac{(.01)(.80)}{(.01)(.80) + (.99)(.096)} = .078$$

(1)

Equation 1 shows how the probability $p(H|D)$ that the woman has breast cancer (H) after a positive mammogram (D) is computed from the prior probability $p(H)$ that the patient has breast cancer, the sensitivity $p(D|H)$, and the false positive rate $p(D|-H)$ of the mammography test. The probability $p(H|D)$ is called the "posterior probability." The symbol $-H$ stands for "the patient does not have breast cancer." Equation 1 is Bayes's rule for binary hypotheses and data. The rule is named after Thomas Bayes (1702 [?]–1761), an English dissenting minister, to whom this solution of the problem of how to make an inference from data to hypothesis (the so-called inverse problem; see Daston, 1988) is attributed.[1] The important point is that Equation 1 results in a probability of 7.8%, not 75% as estimated by the majority of physicians. In other

---

1. As we know from Stephen M. Stigler's *Law of Eponymy*, no scientific discovery is named after its original discoverer, and Bayes's rule seems to be no exception to this law (Stigler, 1983).

words, the probability that the woman has breast cancer is one order of magnitude smaller than estimated.

This result, together with an avalanche of studies reporting that laypeople's reasoning does not follow Bayes's rule either, has (mis-)led many to believe that Homo sapiens would be inept to reason the Bayesian way. Listen to some influential voices: "In his evaluation of evidence, man is apparently not a conservative Bayesian: he is not Bayesian at all" (Kahneman & Tversky, 1972, p. 450). "Tversky and Kahneman argue, correctly, I think, that our minds are not built (for whatever reason) to work by the rules of probability" (Gould, 1992, p. 469).[2] The literature of the last 25 years has reiterated again and again the message that people are bad reasoners, neglect base rates most of the time, neglect false positive rates, and are unable to integrate base rate, hit rate, and false positive rate the Bayesian way (for a review see Koehler, 1996). Probability problems such as the mammography problem have become the stock-in-trade of textbooks, lectures, and party entertainment. It is guaranteed fun to point out how dumb others are. And aren't they? There seem to be many customers eager to buy the message of "inevitable illusions" wired into our brains (Piattelli-Palmarini, 1994).

Ecological Bayesian Inference: An Adaptation for Frequencies

Back to color constancy. If a human visual system enters an environment illuminated by sodium vapor lamps, its color-constancy algorithms will fail. This does not mean, however, that human minds are not built to work by color-constancy algorithms. Similarly, if a human reasoning system enters an environment in which statistical information is formatted differently from that encountered in the environment in which humans evolved, the reasoning algorithms may fail. But this does not imply that human minds are not built to reason the Bayesian way. The issue is not whether nature has equipped our minds with good or with bad statistical software, as the "optimists" versus "pessimists" discussion about human rationality suggests (Jungermann, 1983). The issue I address here is the adaptation of mental algorithms to their environment. By "mental algorithms," I mean induction mechanisms that perform classification, estimation, or other forms of uncertain inferences, such as deciding what color an object is or inferring whether a person has a disease.

For which information formats have mental algorithms been designed? What matters for an algorithm that makes inductive inferences is the format of numerical information. Eddy presented information (about the prevalence of breast cancer, the sensitivity, and the false positive rate of the test) in terms of probabilities and percentages, just as most experimenters did who found hu-

---

2. For a critical discussion of these interpretations, see Cohen (1981), Gigerenzer (1994a, 1996a), Gigerenzer and Murray (1987, chap. 5), and Lopes (1991); for a reply, see Kahneman and Tversky (1996).

mans making irrational judgments. What was the format of the numerical information humans encountered during their evolution? We know too little about these environments, for instance, about the historically normal conditions of childbirth, or how strong a factor religious doctrines were, and most likely, these varied considerably between societies. But concerning the format of numerical information, I believe we can be as certain as we ever can be—probabilities and percentages were not the way organisms encountered information. Probabilities and percentages are quite recent forms of representations of uncertainty. Mathematical probability emerged in the mid-seventeenth century (Hacking, 1975), and the concept of probability itself did not gain prominence over the primitive notion of "expectation" before the mid-eighteenth century (Daston, 1988). Percentages became common notations only during the nineteenth century, after the metric system was introduced during the French Revolution (mainly, though, for interest and taxes rather than for representing uncertainty). Only in the second half of the twentieth century did probabilities and percentages become entrenched in the everyday language of Western countries as representations of uncertainty. To summarize, probabilities and percentages took millennia of literacy and numeracy to evolve as a format to represent degrees of uncertainty. In what format did humans acquire numerical information before that time?

I propose that the original format was *natural frequencies*, acquired by *natural sampling*. Let me explain what this means by a parallel to the mammography problem, using the same numbers. Think about a physician in an illiterate society. Her people have been afflicted by a new, severe disease. She has no books nor statistical surveys; she must rely solely on her experience. Fortunately, she discovered a symptom that signals the disease, although not with certainty. In her lifetime, she has seen 1,000 people, 10 of whom had the disease. Of those 10, eight showed the symptom; of the 990 not afflicted, 95 did. Thus there were 8 + 95 = 103 people who showed the symptom, and only 8 of these had the disease. Now a new patient appears. He has the symptom. What is the probability that he actually has the disease?

The physician in the illiterate society does not need a pocket calculator to estimate the Bayesian posterior probability. All she needs to do is to keep track of the number of symptom and disease cases (8) and the number of symptom and no-disease cases (95). The probability that the new patient actually has the disease can be "seen" easily from these frequencies:

$$p(H|D) = \frac{a}{a+b} = \frac{8}{8+95} \qquad (2)$$

Equation 2 is Bayes's rule for natural frequencies, in which a is the number of cases with symptom and disease and b is the number of cases having the symptom but lacking the disease. The chance that the new patient has the disease is less than 8 out of 100, or 8%. Our physician who learns from experience cannot be fooled as easily into believing that the chances are about 75%, as many of her contemporary colleagues did.

The comparison between Equations 1 and 2 reveals an important theoretical result: Bayesian reasoning is computationally simpler (in terms of the number of operations performed, such as additions and multiplications) when the information is in *natural frequencies* (Equation 2) rather than in *probabilities* (Equation 1) (see Kleiter, 1994). As Equation 2 shows, the base rates of event frequencies (such as 10 in 1,000) need not be kept in memory; they can be ignored as they are implicit in the frequencies *a* and *b*.

Let me be clear how the terms "natural sampling" and "natural frequencies" relate. Natural sampling is the sequential process of updating event frequencies from experience. A foraging organism who, day after day, samples potential resources for food and learns the frequencies with which a cue (e.g., the presence of other species) predicts food performs natural sampling by updating the frequencies *a* and *b* from observation to observation. Natural sampling is different from systematic experimentation, in which the sample sizes (the base rates) of each treatment group are fixed in advance. For instance, in a clinical experiment, one might select 100 patients with cancer and 100 without cancer and then perform tests on these groups. By fixing the base rates, the frequencies obtained in such experimental designs no longer carry information about the base rates. This is not to say that controlled sampling in systematic experiments is useless; it just serves a different purpose. Brunswik's (1955) method of "representative sampling" in a natural environment is an example of applying the idea of natural sampling to experimental design.

Natural frequencies report the final tally of a natural sampling process. There is more than one way to present the final tally. In the case of the physician in the illiterate society, I specified the total number of observations (1,000), the frequency of the disease, and the frequencies *a* and *b* of hits and false positives, respectively: "In her lifetime, she has seen 1,000 people, 10 of whom had the disease. Of those 10, eight showed the symptom; of the 990 not afflicted, 95 did." This is a straightforward translation of the base rates, hit rates, and false positive rates into natural frequencies. Alternatively, one can communicate the frequencies *a* and *b* alone: "In her lifetime, she has seen 8 people with symptom and disease, and 95 people with symptom and no disease." The former natural frequencies use a *standard menu* ("standard" because slicing up the information in terms of base rate, hit rate, and false positive rate is deeply entrenched today), the latter use a *short menu* (see Chapter 6). Both lead to the same result.

Natural frequencies must not to be confused with a representation in terms of relative frequencies (e.g., a base rate of .01, a hit rate of .80, and a false positive rate of .096). Relative frequencies are, like probabilities and percentages, normalized numbers that no longer carry information about the natural base rates. Relative frequencies, probabilities, and percentages are to human reasoning algorithms (that do Bayesian-type inference) as sodium vapor lamps are to human color-constancy algorithms. This analogy has, like every analogy, its limits. For instance, humans can be taught, although with some mental agony, to reason by probabilities, but not, I believe, to maintain color constancy under sodium vapor illumination.

Note that the total number of observations—communicated only when natural frequencies are expressed in the standard menu—need not be the actual total number of observations. It can be any convenient number such as 100 or 1,000. The computational simplicity of natural frequencies holds independently of whether the actual or a convenient number is used. For example, if the actual sample size was 5,167 patients, one can nevertheless represent the information in the same way as above. "For *every* 1,000 patients we expect 10 who have breast cancer, and 8 out of these 10 will test positive."[3]

The hypothesis that mental algorithms were designed for natural frequencies is consistent with (a) a body of studies that report that humans can monitor frequencies fairly accurately (Barsalou & Ross, 1986; Hintzman & Block, 1972; Jonides & Jones, 1992), (b) the thesis that humans process frequencies (almost) automatically, that is, without or with little effort, awareness, and interference with other processes (Hasher & Zacks, 1984), (c) the thesis that probability learning and transfer derive from frequency learning (Estes, 1976), and (d) developmental studies on counting in children and animals (e.g., Gallistel & Gelman, 1992). This is not to say that humans and animals count all possible events equally well, nor could they. A conceptual mechanism must first decide what the units of observation are so that a frequency encoding mechanism can count them. This preceding conceptual process is not dealt with by the hypothesis that mental algorithms are designed for natural frequencies (but see the connection proposed by Brase, Cosmides, & Tooby, 1998).

Thus my argument has two parts: evolutionary (and developmental) primacy of natural frequencies and ease of computation. First, mental algorithms, from color constancy to inductive reasoning, have evolved in an environment with fairly stable characteristics. If there are mental algorithms that perform Bayesian-type inferences from data to hypotheses, these are designed for natural frequencies acquired by natural sampling, and not for probabilities or percentages. Second, when numerical information is represented in natural frequencies, Bayesian computations reduce themselves to a minimum. Both parts of the argument are necessary. For instance, the computational part could be countered by hypothesizing that there might be a single neuron in the human mind that almost instantaneously computes Equation 1 on the basis of probability information. The evolutionary part of the argument makes it unlikely that such a neuron has evolved that computes using an information format that was not present in the environment in which our ancestors evolved.

This argument has testable consequences. First, laypeople—that is, persons with no professional expertise in diagnostic inference—are more likely to reason the Bayesian way when the information is presented in natural frequencies than in a probability format. This effect should occur without any instruction in Bayesian inference. Second, experts such as physicians who make diagnos-

---

3. However, there is a price to be paid if one replaces the actual with a convenient sample size. One can no longer compute second-order probabilities (Kleiter, 1994).

tic inferences on a daily basis should, despite their experience, show the same effect. Third, the "inevitable illusions" (Piattelli-Palmarini, 1994), such as base-rate neglect, should become evitable by using natural frequencies. Finally, natural frequencies should provide a superior vehicle for teaching Bayesian inference. In what follows, I report tests of these predictions and several examples drawn from a broad variety of everyday situations.

This is not to say that probabilities are useless or perverse. In mathematics, they play their role independent of whether or not they suit human reasoning, just as Riemannian and other non-Euclidean geometries play their roles independent of the fact that human spatial reasoning is Euclidean.

Breast Cancer

Eddy (1982) provides only a scant, one-paragraph description of his study of physicians' institutions and refers to a study by Casscells, Schoenberger, and Grayboys (1978) that showed similar results. Both studies used a probability format. Would natural frequencies make any difference to experts such as physicians? Ulrich Hoffrage and I tested 48 physicians in Munich, Germany, on the mammography problem. These physicians had an average professional experience of 14 years. Twenty-four physicians read the information in a probability format as in Eddy's study, the other 24 read the same information in natural frequencies. Physicians were always asked for a single-event probability (as in Eddy's study) when the information was in probabilities; they were always asked for a frequency judgment when the information was in natural frequencies. The two formats of the mammography problem are shown in Table 4.1. Each physician got four diagnostic problems (including the mammography problem), two in a probability format and two in natural frequencies (the details are in Gigerenzer, 1996b; Hoffrage & Gigerenzer, 1996, 1998).

Consider first the thinking of one typical physician, a 59-year-old director of a university clinic, whom I call Dr. Average. He spent 30 minutes on the four problems and another 15 minutes discussing the results with the interviewer. As a high-status physician, he was not used to having his diagnostic intuitions being tested, and he became visibly nervous. He first got the mammography problem in the probability format (Table 4.1) and commented, "I never inform my patients about statistical data. I would tell the patient that mammography is not so exact, and I would, in any case, perform a biopsy." He estimated the probability of breast cancer after a positive mammogram as 80% + 10% = 90%. That is, he added the sensitivity to the false positive rate (this is an unusual strategy). Nervously, he remarked: "Oh, what nonsense. I can't do it. You should test my daughter, she studies medicine." Dr. Average was as helpless with the second problem, Bechterev's disease, in a probability format. Here he estimated the posterior probability by multiplying the base rate by the sensitivity, a common strategy used by laypeople ("joint occurrence," see Tables 6.3 and 6.4 in Chapter 6).

When Dr. Average saw the first problem in a frequency format, his nervousness subsided. "That's so easy," he remarked with relief, and came up with the Bayesian answer, as he did with the second problem in a frequency format. Dr. Average's reasoning turned Bayesian the moment the information was in frequencies, despite his never having heard of, or at least not remembering, Bayes's rule. In the words of a 38-year-old gynecologist faced with the mammography problem in a frequency format: "A first grader could do that. Wow, if someone can't solve this . . . !"

Consider now all the physicians' diagnostic inferences concerning breast cancer. Do natural frequencies foster insight in them?

In the probability format, only 2 out of 24 physicians (8%) came up with the Bayesian answer. The median estimate of the probability of breast cancer after a positive mammogram was 70%, consistent with Eddy's findings. With natural frequencies, however, 11 out of 24 physicians (46%) responded with the Bayesian answer. Across all four diagnostic problems, similar results were obtained—10% Bayesian responses in the probability format and 46% with natural frequencies (Figure 4.1).

Table 4.1 The mammography problem: Probability format and natural frequencies

---

To facilitate early detection of breast cancer, women are encouraged from a particular age on to participate at regular intervals in routine screening, even if they have no obvious symptoms. Imagine you use mammography to conduct such a breast cancer screening in a certain region. For symptom-free women age 40 to 50 who participate in screening using mammography, the following information is available for this region:

Probability format

The probability that one of these women has breast cancer is 1%.

If a woman has breast cancer, the probability is 80% that she will have a positive mammogram.

If a woman does *not* have breast cancer, the probability is 10% that she will still have a positive mammogram.

Imagine a woman (age 40 to 50, no symptoms) who has a positive mammogram in your breast cancer screening. What is the probability that she actually has breast cancer? _____%

Natural frequencies

Ten out of every 1,000 women have breast cancer.

Of these 10 women with breast cancer, 8 will have a positive mammogram.

Of the remaining 990 women *without* breast cancer, 99 will still have a positive mammogram.

Imagine a sample of women (age 40 to 50, no symptoms) who have positive mammograms in your breast cancer screening. How many of these women do actually have breast cancer? _____ out of _____.

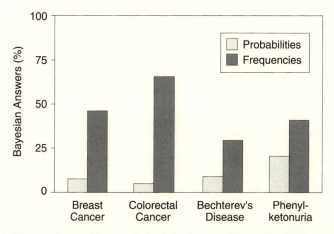

Figure 4.1 How to foster diagnostic insight in physicians. Each of 48 physicians got information about four standard screening tests, two in a probability format and two in natural frequencies. Table 4.1 shows the two forms of information representation for mammography screening. The four diagnostic tasks were to infer the presence of (1) breast cancer from a positive mammogram, (2) colorectal cancer from a positive hemoccult test, (3) Bechterev's disease (ankylosing spondylitis) from a positive HL-antigen-B27 test, and (4) phenylketonuria from a positive Guthrie test. In each diagnostic task, the physicians reasoned more often consistent with Bayes's rule when the numerical information was in natural frequencies. Probabilities tended to cloud their minds.

The lesson of these results is not to blame physicians' or laypeople's minds when they stumble over probabilities. Rather, the lesson is to represent information in textbooks, in curricula, and in physician–patient interactions in natural frequencies that correspond to the way information was encountered in the environment in which human minds evolved.

Colorectal Cancer

The hemoccult test is a widely used and well-known test for colorectal cancer. Windeler and Köbberling (1986) report that just as physicians overestimated the (posterior) probability that a patient has colorectal cancer if the hemoccult test is positive, they also overestimated the base rate of colorectal cancer, the sensitivity (hit rate), and the false positive rate of the test. Windeler and Köbberling asked these physicians about probabilities and percentages. Would natural frequencies improve physicians' estimates of what a positive test tells about the presence of colorectal cancer? The 48 physicians in the study reported previously were given the best available estimates for the base rate, sensitivity, and false positive rate, as published in Windeler and Köbberling

(1986). The following is a shortened version of the full text (structured like the mammography problem in Table 4.1) given to the physicians. In the probability format, the information was:

The probability that a person has colorectal cancer is 0.3%.

If a person has colorectal cancer, the probability that the test is positive is 50%.

If a person does *not* have colorectal cancer, the probability that the test is positive is 3%.

What is the probability that a person who tests positive actually has colorectal cancer?

When one inserts these values in Bayes's rule (Equation 1), the resulting probability is 4.8%. In natural frequencies, the information was:

30 out of every 10,000 people have colorectal cancer.

Of these 30 people with colorectal cancer, 15 will test positive.

Of the remaining 9,970 people *without* colorectal cancer, 300 will still test positive.

Imagine a group of people who test positive. How many of these will actually have colorectal cancer?

When the information was in the probability format, only 1 out of 24 physicians (4%) could find the Bayesian answer, or anything close to it. The median estimate was one order of magnitude higher, namely 47%. When the information was presented in natural frequencies, 16 out of 24 physicians (67%) came up with the Bayesian answer (details are in Gigerenzer, 1996b; Hoffrage & Gigerenzer, 1998).

Wife Battering

Alan Dershowitz, the Harvard law professor who advised the defense in the first O. J. Simpson trial, claimed repeatedly that evidence of abuse and battering should not be admissible in a murder trial. In his best-seller, *Reasonable Doubts: The Criminal Justice System and the O. J. Simpson Case* (1996), Dershowitz says: "The reality is that a majority of women who are killed are killed by men with whom they have a relationship, *regardless of whether their men previously battered them*. Battery, as such, is not a good independent predictor of murder" (p. 105). Dershowitz stated on U.S. television in March 1995 that only about one-tenth of 1% of wife batterers actually murder their wives. In response to Dershowitz, I. J. Good, a distinguished professor emeritus of statistics at the Virginia Polytechnic Institute, published an article in *Nature* to correct for the possible misunderstandings of what that statement implies for the probability that O. J. Simpson actually murdered his wife in 1994 (Good, 1995). Good's argument is that the relevant probability is not the probability that a husband murders his wife if he batters her. Instead, the relevant probability is the probability that a husband has murdered his wife if he battered her *and* if she was actually murdered by someone. More precisely, the relevant probability is not $p(G|Bat)$ but $p(G|Bat$ and $M)$, in which G stands for "the husband is guilty" (that is, did the murder in 1994), *Bat* means that "the husband battered his wife," and M means that "the wife was actually murdered by somebody in 1994."

My point concerns the way Good presents his argument, not the argument itself. Good presented the information in single-event probabilities and odds (rather than in natural frequencies). I will first summarize Good's argument as he made it. I hope I can demonstrate that you the reader—unless you are a trained statistician or exceptionally smart with probabilities—will be confused and have some difficulty following it. Thereafter, I will present the same argument in natural frequencies, and confusion should turn into insight. Let's see.

Good's Argument in Conditional Probabilities

Good bases his calculations of $p(G \mid Bat$ and $M)$ on the odds version of Bayes's rule:

$$\text{posterior odds} = \text{prior odds} \times \text{likelihood ratio}$$

which in the present case is:

$$\frac{p(G|Bat \text{ and } M)}{p(-G|Bat \text{ and } M)} = \frac{p(G|Bat)}{p(-G|Bat)} \times \frac{p(M|G \text{ and } Bat)}{p(M|-G \text{ and } Bat)} \qquad (3)$$

where $-G$ stands for "the husband is not guilty."

The following six equations (Good-1 to Good-6) show Good's method of explaining to the reader how to estimate $p(G|Bat$ and $M)$. Good starts with Dershowitz's figure of one-tenth of 1%, arguing that if the husband commits the murder, the probability is at least 1/10 that he will do it in 1994:[4]

$$p(G|Bat) > (1/10)(1/1,000) = 1/10,000 \qquad \text{(Good-1)}$$

Therefore, the prior odds (O) are:

$$O(G|Bat) > 1/9,999 \approx 1/10,000 \qquad \text{(Good-2)}$$

Furthermore, the probability of a woman being murdered given that her husband has murdered her (whether he is a batterer or not) is unity:

$$p(M|G \text{ and } Bat) = p(M|G) = 1 \qquad \text{(Good-3)}$$

---

4. Good possibly assumed that the average wife batterer is married less than 10 years. Good also made a second calculation assuming a value of $p(G|Bat)$ that is half as large.

Because there are about 25,000 murders per year in the U.S. population of about 250,000,000, Good estimates the probability of a battered woman being murdered, but not by her husband, as:

$$p(M\,|-G \text{ and } Bat) = p(M\,|-G) \approx 1/10,000 \qquad \text{(Good-4)}$$

From Equations Good-3 and Good-4, it follows that the likelihood ratio is about 10,000/1; therefore, the posterior odds can be calculated:

$$O(G\,|\,Bat \text{ and } M) > 10,000/10,000 = 1 \qquad \text{(Good-5)}$$

That is, the probability that a murdered, battered wife was killed by her husband is:

$$p(G\,|\,Bat \text{ and } M) > 1/2 \qquad \text{(Good-6)}$$

Good's point is that "most members of a jury or of the public, not being familiar with elementary probability, would readily confuse this with $P(G\,|\,Bat)$, and would thus be badly misled by Dershowitz's comment" (Good, 1995, p. 541). He adds that he sent a copy of this note to both Dershowitz and the Los Angeles Police Department, reminding us that Bayesian reasoning should be taught at the precollege level.

Good's persuasive argument, I believe, could have been understood more easily by his readers and the Los Angeles Police Department if the information had been presented in natural frequencies rather than in the single-event probabilities and odds in the six equations. As with breast cancer and colorectal cancer, one way to represent information in natural frequencies is to start with a concrete sample of individuals divided into subclasses, in the same way it would be experienced by natural sampling. Here is a frequency version of Good's argument.

Good's Argument in Natural Frequencies

Think of 10,000 battered married women. Within one year, at least one will be murdered by her husband. Of the remaining 9,999 who are not killed by their husbands, one will be murdered by someone else. Thus we expect at least two battered women to be murdered, at least one by her husband and one by someone else. Therefore, the probability $p(G\,|\,Bat \text{ and } M)$ that a murdered, battered woman was killed by her husband is at least ½.

This probability is not to be confounded with the probability that O. J. Simpson is guilty; a jury must take into account much more evidence than battering. But the probability shows that abuse-and-battering is a good predictor of the husband's (or boyfriend's) guilt, disproving Dershowitz's assertion to the contrary.

In natural frequencies, Good's argument is short and transparent. My conjecture is that more ordinary people, including employees of the Los Angeles Police Department and jurors, could understand and communicate the argument if the information were represented in natural frequencies rather than in probabilities or odds.

In legal jargon, evidence of wife battering is probative, not prejudicial. This analysis is consistent with the impressive transcultural evidence about homicide accumulated by Daly and Wilson (1988). The typical function of wife battering seems to be to exert proprietary rights over the sexuality and reproductivity of women, as well as threats against infidelity. Battering can "spill over" into killing, and killing is the tip of a huge iceberg of wife abuse.

AIDS Counseling

Under the headline, "A False HIV Test Caused 18 Months of Hell," the *Chicago Tribune* (3/5/93) published the following letter and response:

Dear Ann Landers: In March 1991, I went to an anonymous testing center for a routine HIV test. In two weeks, the results came back positive.

I was devastated. I was 20 years old and doomed. I became severely depressed and contemplated a variety of ways to commit suicide. After encouragement from family and friends, I decided to fight back.

My doctors in Dallas told me that California had the best care for HIV patients, so I packed everything and headed west. It took three months to find a doctor I trusted. Before this physician would treat me, he insisted on running more tests. Imagine my shock when the new results came back negative. The doctor tested me again, and the results were clearly negative.

I'm grateful to be healthy, but the 18 months I thought I had the virus changed my life forever. I'm begging doctors to be more careful. I also want to tell your readers to be sure and get a second opinion. I will continue to be tested for HIV every six months, but I am no longer terrified.

David in Dallas

Dear Dallas: Yours is truly a nightmare with a happy ending, but don't blame the doctor. It's the lab that needs to shape up. The moral of your story is this: *Get a second opinion. And a third.* Never trust a single test. Ever.

Ann Landers

David does not mention what his Dallas doctors told him about the chances that he actually had the virus after the positive test, but he seems to have inferred that a positive test meant that he had the virus, period. In fact, when we studied AIDS counselors in Germany, we found that many doctors and social workers (erroneously) tell their low-risk clients that a positive HIV test implies that the virus is present (see Chapter 5). These counselors know that a single ELISA (enzyme-linked immunoabsorbent assay) test can produce a false positive, but they erroneously assume that the whole series of ELISA and Western blot tests would wipe out every false positive. How could a doctor have explained the actual risk to David and spared him the nightmare?

I do not have HIV statistics for Dallas, so I will use German figures for illustration. (The specific numbers are not the point here.) In Germany, the prevalence of HIV infections in heterosexual men between the ages of 20 and 30 who belong to no known risk group can be estimated as about 1 in 10,000, or 0.01%. The corresponding base rate for homosexual men is estimated at about 1.5%. The hit rate (sensitivity) of the typical test series (repeated ELISA and Western blot tests) is estimated at about 99.8%. The estimates of the false positive rate vary somewhat; a reasonable estimate seems to be 0.01%. Given these values, and assuming that David was at the time of the routine HIV test a heterosexual man with low-risk behavior, what is the probability that he actually had the virus after testing positive? If his physician had actually given David these probabilities, David nevertheless might not have understood what to conclude.

But the physician could have communicated the information in natural frequencies. She might have said, "Your situation is the following: Think of 10,000 heterosexual men like you. We expect one to be infected with the virus, and he will, with practical certainty, test positive. From the 9,999 men who are not infected, one additional individual will test positive. Thus we get two individuals who test positive, but only one of them actually has the virus. This is your situation. The chances that you actually have the virus after the positive test are about 1 in 2, or 50%." If the physician had explained the risk in this way, David might have understood that there was, as yet, no reason to contemplate suicide or to move to California.

We do not know what risk group David was in. Whatever the statistics are, however, most people of average intelligence can understand the risk of HIV after a positive test when the numbers are represented by a counselor in natural frequencies.

Ann Landers's answer—don't blame the doctor, blame the lab—however, overlooks the fact that despite whatever possible reasons there may be for false positives (such as the presence of cross-reacting antibodies or blood samples being confused in the lab), a doctor should inform the patient that false positives occur, and about how frequently they occur. What information do professional AIDS counselors actually provide? How do they communicate risks? To find this out, a brave student of mine went as a client to 20 public health centers to take 20 HIV tests. The results will be reported in Chapter 5.

Expert Witnesses

Evidentiary problems such as the evaluation of eyewitness testimony constituted one of the first domains of probability theory (Gigerenzer et al., 1989, chap. 1). Statisticians have taken the stand as expert witnesses for almost a century now: In the Dreyfus case in the late nineteenth century in France, or more recently, in *People vs. Collins* in California (Koehler, 1992). The convictions in both cases were ultimately reversed and the statistical arguments discredited. Part of the problem seems to have been that the statistical arguments were couched not in natural frequencies but in probabilities that confused both the prosecution who were making the arguments and the jury and the judges who tried to understand the arguments. I will explain this point with the case of a chimney sweep who was accused of having committed a murder in Wuppertal, Germany (Schrage, n.d.).

The *Rheinischer Merkur* (No. 39, 1974) reported:

On the evening of July 20, 1972, the 40-year-old Wuppertal painter Wilhelm Fink and his 37-year-old wife Ingeborg took a walk in the woods and were attacked by a stranger. The husband was hit by three bullets in the throat and the chest, and fell down. Then the stranger attempted to rape his wife. When she defended herself and, unexpectedly, the shot-down husband got back on his feet to help her, the stranger shot two bullets into the wife's head and fled.

Three days later, 20 kilometers from the scene of the crime, a forest ranger discovered the car of Werner Wiegand, a 25-year-old chimney sweep who used to spend his weekends in the vicinity. The husband, who had survived, at first thought he recognized the chimney sweep in a photo. Later, he grew less certain and began to think that another suspect was the murderer. When the other suspect was found innocent, however, the prosecution came back to the chimney sweep and put him on trial. The chimney sweep had no previous convictions and denied being the murderer. The *Rheinischer Merkur* described the trial:

After the experts had testified and explained their "probability theories," the case seemed to be clear: Wiegand, despite his denial, must have been the murderer. Dr. Christian Rittner, a lecturer at the University of Bonn, evaluated the traces of blood as follows: 17.29% of German citizens share Wiegand's blood group, traces of which have been found underneath the fingernails of the murdered woman; 15.69% of German share [her] blood group that was also found on Wiegand's boots; based on a so-called "cross-combination" the expert subsequently calculated an overall probability of 97.3% that Wiegand "can be considered the murderer." And concerning the textile fiber traces which were found both on Wiegand's clothes and on those of the victim. . . . Dr. Ernst Röhm from the Munich branch of the State Crime Department explained: "The probability that textile microfibers of this kind are transmitted from a human to another human who was not in contact with the victim is at most 0.06%. From this results a 99.94% certainty for Wiegand being the murderer."

Both expert witnesses agreed that, with a high probability, the chimney sweep was the murderer. These expert calculations, however, collapsed when the court discovered that the defendant was in his hometown, 100 kilometers away from the scene of the crime at the time of the crime.

So what was wrong with the expert calculations? One can dispel the confusion in court by representing the uncertainties in natural frequencies. Let us assume that the blood underneath the fingernails of the victim was indeed the blood of the murderer, that the murderer carried traces of the victim's blood (as the expert witnesses assumed), and that there were 10 million men in Germany who could have committed the crime (these and the following figures are from Schrage, n.d., but the specific figures do not matter for my argument). Let us assume further that on one of every 100 of these men a close examination would find microscopic traces of foreign blood, that is, on 100,000 men. Of these, some 15,690 men (15.69%) will carry traces from blood that is of the victim's blood type. Of these 15,690 men, some 2,710 (17.29%) will also have the blood type that was found underneath the victim's fingernails (here, I assume independence between the two pieces of evidence). Thus there are some 2,710 men (including the murderer) who might appear guilty based on the two pieces of blood evidence. The chimney sweep is one of these men. Therefore, given the two pieces of blood evidence, the probability that the chimney sweep is the murderer is about 1 in 2,710, and not 97.3%, as the first expert witness testified.

The same frequency method can be applied to the textile traces. Let us assume that the second expert witness was correct when he said that the probability of the chimney sweep carrying the textile trace, if he were not the murderer, would be at most 0.06%. Let us assume as well that the murderer actually carries that trace. Then some 6,000 of the 10 million would carry this textile trace, and only one of them would be the murderer. Thus the probability that the chimney sweep was the murderer, given the textile fiber evidence, was about 1 in 6,000, and not 99.94%, as the second expert witness testified.

What if one combines both the blood and the textile evidence together, which seems not to have happened at the trial? In this case, one of the 2,710 men who satisfy both pieces of blood type evidence would be the murderer, and he would show the textile traces. Of the remaining innocent men, we expect one or two (0.06%) to also show the textile traces (assuming mutual independence of the three pieces of evidence). Thus there would be two or three men who satisfy all three types of evidence. One of them is the murderer. Therefore, the probability that the chimney sweep was the murderer, given the two pieces of blood sample evidence and the textile evidence, would be between .3 and .5. This probability would not be beyond reasonable doubt.

Teaching Statistical Reasoning

The teaching of statistical reasoning is, like that of reading and writing, part of forming an educated citizenship. Our technological world, with its abundance of statistical information, makes the art of dealing with uncertain information particularly relevant. Reading and writing is taught to every child in modern Western democracies, but statistical thinking is not (Shaughnessy, 1992). The result has been termed "innumeracy" (Paulos, 1988). But can statistical reasoning be taught? Previous studies that attempted to teach Bayesian inference, mostly by corrective feedback, had little or no training effect (e.g., Peterson, DuCharme, & Edwards, 1968; Schaefer, 1976). This result seems to be consistent with the view that the mind does not naturally reason the Bayesian way. However, the argument developed in this chapter suggests a "natural" method of teaching: Instruct people how to represent probability information in natural frequencies.

Peter Sedlmeier and I designed a tutorial program that teaches Bayesian reasoning, based on the assumption that cognitive algorithms have evolved for dealing with natural frequencies (Sedlmeier, 1997; Sedlmeier & Gigerenzer, in press). The goal of this tutorial is to teach participants how to reason the Bayesian way when the information is represented in probabilities, as is usually the case in newspapers, medical textbooks, and other information sources. The computerized tutorial instructs participants in how to represent the probability information in terms of natural frequencies, rather than teaching them how to insert probabilities into Bayes's rule (Equation 1). The tutorial consists of two parts. In the first part, participants are shown how to translate probability information into natural frequencies, visually aided by a frequency tree (or a frequency grid); the method is illustrated by two medical problems, one of them the mammography problem. In the second part, participants solve eight other problems, with step-by-step guidance on what to do as well as step-by-step feedback. If participants have difficulties, the system provides immediate help that ensures that every participant solves all problems correctly. To see how effective this "representation training" is, we compared it with standard "rule training" in which people are taught how to insert probabilities into Bayes's rule. Both training procedures were computerized, and both were supported with the same visual aids (frequency trees). There were three criteria: immediate learning effect after training, transfer to new questions, and stability over time. Stability over time has proven to be the most difficult to obtain, in experimental studies as well as in teaching practice. For instance, many who teach statistical reasoning report that students often successfully perform in the final exam, but a few weeks later they have already forgotten most of what they learned.

In three studies, the immediate effect of the representation training was always larger than that of the rule training, by 10 percentage points or more. Transfer was about the same. The most striking difference was obtained in stability. For instance, in the study with the longest interval—people were called back three months after training—the median performance in the group that had received the representation training was a strong 100%. That is, all problems were solved—even after three months. In contrast, the performance in the group that had received the rule training was 57%, reflecting the well-known steep forgetting curve. Teaching how to translate probabilities into frequencies seems to have a more lasting effect than teaching rules for processing probabilities.

Thus there is evidence that (what I take to be) the natural format of information in the environment in which humans evolved can be used to teach people how to deal with probability information. This may be good news both for instructors who plan to design precollege curricula that teach young people how to infer risks in a technological world and for those unfortunate souls among us charged with teaching undergraduate statistics.

Conclusions

Information needs representation. If a representation is recurrent and stable during human evolution, one can expect that mental algorithms are designed to operate on this representation. In this chapter, I applied this argument to the understanding of human inferences under uncertainty. The thesis is that mental algorithms were designed for natural frequencies, the recurrent format of information until very recently. I have dealt with a specific class of inferences that correspond to a simple form of Bayesian inferences, in which one of several possible states is inferred from one or a few cues. Here, mental computations are simpler when information is encountered in the same form as in the environment in which our ancestors evolved, rather than in the modern form of probabilities or percentages. The evidence from a broad variety of everyday situations and laboratory experiments shows that natural frequencies can make human minds more insightful.

5

AIDS Counseling for Low-Risk Clients

Former Senator Lawton Chiles of Florida reported at an AIDS conference in 1987 that of 22 blood donors in Florida who were notified that they tested HIV-positive with the ELISA test, seven committed suicide. In the same medical text that reported this tragedy, the reader is informed that "even if the results of both AIDS tests, the ELISA and WB (Western blot), are positive, the chances are only 50–50 that the individual is infected" (Stine, 1996, pp. 333, 338). Situations like this can occur when people with low-risk behavior, such as blood donors, test positive. The discrepancy between what clients believe a positive HIV test means and what it actually does mean seems to have cost human lives in addition to the toll the disease itself has taken. One of the goals of AIDS counseling is to explain the actual risk to the client. This chapter deals with pretest HIV counseling of low-risk clients concerning the meaning of a positive HIV test in German public AIDS counseling centers. We address three questions: What information do counselors communicate to the client concerning the chances of an HIV infection given a positive test? Is this information communicated in a way the client can understand? How can the communication and the accuracy of the information be improved?

Counseling Clients with Low-Risk Behavior

We are interested in the counseling received by members of the largest population group: heterosexuals who do not engage in risky behavior, such as IV-drug use. These people take HIV tests for various reasons: voluntarily, because they want to find out whether they are infected before getting married, having children, or for other reasons; or involuntarily, because they are immigrants, applicants for health or life insurance, military personnel, blood donors, or members of other groups that are required by law to take the test. The Swedish

The work on which this chapter is based was coauthored with U. Hoffrage and A. Ebert.

government, for instance, has encouraged voluntary testing to the point that "people who are unlikely to be infected are the ones who take the test, in droves" (Månsson, 1990). Involuntary testing is a legal possibility in several countries, one that insurers exploit to protect themselves against losses. For instance, in 1990, Bill Clinton (then governor of Arkansas) had to take an HIV test to get his life insurance renewed. People with low-risk behavior may be subjected to HIV tests not only involuntarily but also unknowingly. For instance, large companies in Bombay have reportedly subjected their employees to blood tests without telling them that they were being tested for AIDS; when a test was positive, the employee was fired.

Counseling people at low risk requires paying particular attention to false positives, that is, to the possibility that the client has a positive HIV test even though he or she is not infected with the virus. The lower the prevalence of HIV in a group, the larger the proportion of false positives among those who test positive. In other words, if a client with high-risk behavior tests positive, the probability that he actually is infected with HIV is very high, but if someone with low-risk behavior tests positive, this probability may be as low as 50%, as indicated previously. If clients are not informed about this fact, they tend to believe that a positive test means that they are infected with absolute certainty. The case of the young man from Dallas described in the previous chapter is one example. If he had committed suicide, as the blood donors in the Florida case did, we might never have found out that his test was a false positive. Emotional pain and lives can be saved if counselors inform the clients about the possibility of false positives.[1]

We do not know of any study that has investigated what AIDS counselors tell their clients about the meaning of a positive test. We pondered long over the proper methodology, such as sending questionnaires to counselors or asking them to participate in paper-and-pencil tests. However, we decided against questionnaires and similar methods because they are open to the criticism that they tell us little about actual counseling sessions. For instance, these methods have been criticized for not allowing physicians to pose their own questions to get further information, to use their own estimates of the relevant statistical information rather than those provided by the experimenter, and for removing the element of actual concern for the patient, because either the patient is fictional or the case was resolved years ago.

In the end, we decided to take a direct route. One of us went as a client to 20 counseling sites and took a series of counseling sessions and HIV tests. We

1. In their review of suicidal behavior and HIV infection, Catalan and Pugh (1995) conclude that "suicidal ideas, completed suicide and deliberate self-harm are not uncommon in people with HIV-infection" (p. 119). However, as they themselves point out, the evidence is far from conclusive: Many reports are anecdotal or involve few cases, results vary between countries, and methodological problems make matching with comparison groups difficult (e.g., Marzuk & Perry, 1993; Pugh et al., 1993). A recent prospective cohort study that controlled for several factors found a 1.35-fold increase in suicides in HIV-positives relative to HIV-negatives, whereas earlier studies reported a 7- to 36-fold increase in risk for HIV-positives (Dannenberg et al., 1996).

were interested in one important issue that AIDS counselors have to explain to the client: What does a positive test result mean? To answer this question, it is useful to know: (a) the base rate of HIV in heterosexual men with low risk, which is referred to as the *prevalence*, (b) the probability that the test is positive if the client is infected, which is referred to as the *sensitivity* (or hit rate) of the test, and (c) the probability that the test is positive if the client is not infected, which is known as the *false positive rate* (or 1 − *specificity*). From this information, one can estimate what a positive test actually means, that is, the probability of being infected if one tests positive, also known as the *positive predictive value* (PPV). Let us first get the best estimates for these values from the literature.

Prevalence

Germany has a relatively small number of reported AIDS cases. The cumulative number by the end of 1995 was 13,665, as compared with some 30,000 in Italy, 38,000 in France, and more than 500,000 in the USA (World Health Organization, 1996). Thus one can assume that the prevalence of HIV is also comparatively low. The client in our study was 27 years old, a German heterosexual male who did not engage in risky behavior. What is the prevalence of the HIV virus in 20- to 30-year-old heterosexual men in Germany who do not engage in risky behavior? A reasonable estimate is about one in 10,000 or 0.01%.[2] This figure is in the range of the prevalence of HIV in blood donors in the United States (a group with low prevalence within the United States),

2. This is a crude estimate, given that there seem to be no published figures for the prevalence of HIV for 20- to 30-year-old men with low-risk behavior in Germany. This value is based on two approximations. One is to estimate the unknown prevalence by the known prevalence in first-time male blood donors (as opposed to repeat donors, who are a highly selected group). The proportion of HIV-positives in some 130,000 first-time male blood donors (1986–1991, state of Baden-Württemberg) was 1.5 in 10,000 (Maurer et al., 1993). For comparison, the proportion among repeat donors was one order of magnitude smaller, about 1.2 in 100,000 (Maurer et al., 1993). Because false positives occur, the proportion of men actually infected is smaller than 1.5 in 10,000. This estimate is crude in several respects; for instance, it does not differentiate by age group and assumes that men with low-risk behavior are comparable to first-time blood donors.

A second way to estimate the unknown prevalence is by the proportion of HIV-positives who report infection through heterosexual contact. Dietz et al. (1994, p. 1998) found that 3.8% of HIV-positives reported that they were infected by heterosexual contact, as opposed to homosexual/bisexual behavior, injecting drug use, and other risks (for similar figures see Glück et al., 1990; Hoffman-Valentin, 1991; Schering, 1992). In 1994, when our study was begun, the number of HIV-positives in Germany was about 65,000, of which some 29% were in the 20- to 30-year-old age group. If one assumes that the figure of 3.8% also holds for this age group, this results in an estimated 700 HIV-positives in this age group reporting infection through heterosexual contact. Because in 1994 there were an estimated 6 million German men between 20 and 30 who were in no known risk group (a total of 6,718,500 men minus an estimated 11% who belong to one or more of the known risk groups; see Statistisches Bundesamt, 1994), the proportion of HIV-positives who report infection through heterosexual contact can be estimated as 1.2 in 10,000.

which has been estimated at one in 10,000 (Busch, 1994, p. 229) or two in 10,000 (George & Schochetman, 1994, p. 90).

Sensitivity and Specificity

HIV testing typically involves the following sequence. If the first test, ELISA, is negative, the client is notified that he or she is HIV-negative. If positive, at least one more ELISA (preferably from a different manufacturer) is conducted. If the result is again positive, then the more expensive and time-consuming Western blot test is performed. If the Western blot is also positive, then the client is notified of being HIV-positive, and sometimes a second blood sample is also tested. Thus two errors can occur. First, a client who is infected is notified that he is HIV-negative. The probability of this error (false negative) is the complement of the sensitivity of the ELISA test. The estimates for the sensitivity typically range between 98% and 99.8% (Eberle et al., 1988; George & Schochetman, 1994; Schwartz et al., 1990; Spielberg et al., 1989; Tu et al., 1992; Wilber, 1991). Second, a client who is not infected is notified of being HIV-positive. The probability of this second error (false positive) is the complement of the combined specificity of the ELISA and Western blot tests. Although all surveys agree that false positives do occur, the quantitative estimates vary widely.[3] This is in part due to the fact that what constitutes a positive Western blot test has not been standardized (various agencies use different reagents, testing methods, and test-interpretation criteria), that the ELISAs and the Western blot tests are not independent (that is, one cannot simply multiply the individual false positive rates of the tests to calculate the combined false positive rate), and that the higher the prevalence in a group, the lower the specificity seems to be for this group (Wittkowski, 1989). For instance, 20 samples—half with HIV antibodies and half without (the laboratories were not informed which samples were which)—were sent in 1990 to each of 103 laboratories in six World Health Organization (WHO) regions (Snell et al., 1992).

Both ways to estimate the unknown prevalence give consistent numbers; nevertheless, they should only be taken as rough approximations. Because not all of these HIV-positives have the virus (due to false positives), we need to correct these numbers downward. A prevalence of about 1 in 10,000 seems to be a reasonable estimate for the unknown prevalence of the HIV virus in 20- to 30-year-old heterosexual German men with low-risk behavior.

3. Among the reasons for false positives are the presence of cross-reacting antibodies (Stine, 1996); false positive reactions with nonspecifically "sticky" IgM antibodies (Epstein, 1994, p. 56); false positives from samples placed in the wrong wells; and contamination of wells containing negative specimens by positive samples from adjacent wells. In addition, heat-treated, lipemic, and hemolyzed sera may cause false positives; false positive results have been reported to occur in 19% of hemophilia patients and in 13% of alcoholic patients with hepatitis (George & Schochetman, 1994, p. 69). People who have liver disease, have received a blood transfusion or gamma globulin within six weeks of the test, or have received vaccines for influenza and hepatitis B may test false positive as well (Stine, 1996, p. 333).

About 70 different combinations of tests were applied. Of the samples without HIV antibodies, 1.3% were incorrectly classified as positive. A combined specificity of only 98.7%, as in this blind proficiency testing, however, is an unusually low estimate. Most of the estimates in the literature are considerably higher, usually higher than 99.9% (Burke et al., 1988; Eberle et al., 1988; Peichl-Hoffman, 1991; Tu et al., 1992). For instance, the German Red Cross achieved for first-time blood donors a combined specificity of 99.98% (Wittkowski, 1989). From the figures published, a reasonable estimate for the combined specificity (two ELISAs, one Western blot, one blood sample) seems to be about 99.99%. That is, the false positive rate is about one in 10,000. This is an estimate, and more accurate numbers may be available from future research.

Positive Predictive Value

What the client needs to understand is the probability of being infected with HIV if he tests positive. The predictive value of a positive test (*PPV*) can be calculated from the prevalence $p(HIV)$, the sensitivity $p(pos \mid HIV)$, and the false positive rate $p(pos \mid no\ HIV)$:

$$PPV = \frac{p(HIV)p(pos \mid HIV)}{p(HIV)p(pos \mid HIV) + p(no\ HIV)p(pos \mid no\ HIV)} \qquad (1)$$

where $p(no\ HIV)$ equals $1 - p(HIV)$. Equation 1 is known as Bayes's rule. This rule expresses the important fact that the smaller the prevalence, the smaller the probability that a client is infected if the test is positive. What is the predictive value of a positive test (repeated ELISA and Western blot, one blood sample) for a 20- to 30-year-old heterosexual German man who does not engage in risky behavior? Inserting the previous estimates—a prevalence of 0.01%, a sensitivity of 99.8%, and a specificity of 99.99%—into Bayes's rule, the *PPV* results in 0.50, or 50%.

An estimated *PPV* of about 50% for heterosexual men who do not engage in risky behavior is consistent with the report of the Enquete Committee of the German Bundestag, which estimated the *PPV* for low-risk people as "less than 50%" (Deutscher Bundestag, 1990, p. 121).

How to Communicate the Positive Predictive Value

Even if a counselor understands this formula, ordinary people rarely do. Moreover, we know from paper-and-pencil studies in the United States and in Germany that even experienced physicians have great difficulties when asked to infer the *PPV* from probability information. But we also have seen in Chapter 4 that physicians' performance can be substantially improved, by a factor of more than four, if the information is presented in *natural frequencies* rather than in terms of probabilities or percentages.

How would a counselor communicate information in natural frequencies? She might explain to the patient the meaning of a positive test in the following way: "Imagine 10,000 heterosexual men like you being tested. One has the virus, and he will with practical certainty test positive. Of the remaining non-infected men, one will also test positive (the false positive rate of 0.01%). Thus we expect that two men will test positive, and only one of them has HIV. This is the situation you are in if you test positive; the chance of having the virus is one out of two, or 50%."

This simple method can be applied whatever the relevant numbers are assumed to be. If the prevalence is two in 10,000, the *PPV* would be two out of three, or 67%. The numbers can be adjusted; the point is that clients can understand more easily if the counselor communicates in natural frequencies than in probabilities. With a frequency representation the client can "see" how the *PPV* depends on the prevalence. If the prevalence of HIV among German homosexuals is about 1.5%, then the counselor might explain: "Think of 10,000 homosexual men like you. About 150 have the virus, and they all will likely test positive. Of the remaining noninfected men, one will also test positive. Thus we expect that 151 men will test positive, and 150 of them have HIV. This is the situation you are in if you test positive; the chance of having the virus is 150 out of 151, or 99.3%."

In general, the *PPV* is the number of true positives (*TP*) divided by the number of true positives plus false positives (*FP*):

$$PPV = \frac{TP}{TP + FP} \tag{2}$$

The comparison between Equations 1 and 2 shows that natural frequencies make mental computations easier. Physicians and laypeople alike can understand risks better when the information is communicated in natural frequencies rather than in probabilities or percentages.

Public HIV Counseling

Some 300 German public health centers ("Gesundheitsämter") offer free HIV tests and AIDS counseling for the general public. By 1990, these centers had hired 315 counselors, 43% of whom were physicians, 22% social workers, and 7% psychologists. The rest had various professional training (Fischer, 1990). As in other countries, counseling before testing is designed to make sure that the client understands the testing procedure, the risks for HIV infection, and the meaning of either a positive or negative test (Ward, 1994). The report of the Enquete Committee of the German Bundestag (Deutscher Bundestag, 1990, p. 122) directs the counselor explicitly to perform a "quantitative and qualitative assessment of the individual risk" and to "explain the reliability of the test result" before a test is taken. If the client decides to take a test, anonymity is guaranteed in all German states (unlike in the United States, where in 25 states the patient's name is reported; Stine, 1996, p. 346). Counseling requires both social tact and knowledge about the uncertainties involved in testing, and the fact that in 1990 about 37% of clients tested at publicly funded clinics in the United States failed to return for their test results suggests that counseling is not always successful (Doll & Kennedy, 1994).

What information concerning the meaning of a positive test do counselors in German public health centers give a client with low-risk behavior? How is this information communicated (e.g., in probabilities or in natural frequencies)?

Method

Counseling Centers

The "client" visited 20 public AIDS counseling centers in 20 German cities, including large cities such as Berlin, Hamburg, and Munich. Two additional counseling centers were visited in a pilot study that was conducted to design the details of the interview. The 20 counseling centers were distributed over nine German states in former West Germany. Of the 20 counselors, 14 were physicians and 6 were social workers; 12 were female and 8 were male.

The client first contacted the health centers by telephone and made an appointment. He could visit two centers in short sequence, followed by a break of at least two weeks to allow the hematomas from the perforation of the veins in his arms to heal. These breaks were necessary, otherwise signs in the arm might have suggested to the counselor that the client was a drug addict.

Investigating AIDS counselors' performance without their knowledge raises ethical problems. We consulted the Ethics Committee of the German Association of Psychology, which informed us that in the present case the expected utility of the results of the study could justify deceiving the counselors. Public counseling is public behavior; nevertheless, in deference to the Ethics Committee's interpretation of German privacy laws, we decided not to tape the sessions. Moreover, we protect the anonymity of the counselors. We apologize to all of the counselors for having used this covert method but believe that the results of this study justify the approach by revealing what can be improved in future AIDS counseling.

The Interview

The client asked the counselor the following questions (unless the counselor provided the information unprompted):

1. *Sensitivity of the HIV test.* If one is infected with HIV, is it possible to have a negative test result? How reliable does the test identify a virus if the virus is present?
2. *False positives.* If one is not infected with HIV, is it possible to have a positive test result? How reliable is the test with respect to a false positive result?
3. *Prevalence of HIV in heterosexual men.* How frequent is the virus in my risk group, that is, heterosexual men, 20 to 30 years old, with no known risk such as drug use?
4. *Predictive value of a positive test.* What is the probability that men in my risk group actually do have HIV after a positive test?

5. *Window period.* How much time has to pass between infection and test, so that antibodies can be detected?

The pilot study indicated a tendency in counselors to provide vague and noninformative answers, such as, "Don't worry; the test is very reliable; trust me." It also indicated that if the client asked for clarification more than twice, the counselors were likely to become upset and angry, experiencing the client's insistence on clarification as a violation of social norms of communication. Based on these pilot sessions, the interview included the following scheme for clarifying questions: If the counselor's answer was a quantitative estimate (a number or a range) or if the counselor said that he or she could not (or did not want to) give a more precise answer, then the client went on to the next question. If the answer was qualitative (e.g., "fairly certain") or if the counselor misunderstood or avoided answering the question, then the client asked for further clarification and, if necessary, repeated this request for clarification one more time. If, after the third attempt, there was still no success, the client did not push further and went on to the next question. When the client needed to ask for clarification concerning the prevalence of HIV (Question 3), he always repeated his specific risk group; when asking for clarification concerning the *PPV* (Question 4), he always referred to the specific prevalence in his risk group.

As mentioned previously, when the client asked for the prevalence of HIV in his risk group, he specified this group as "heterosexual men, 20 to 30 years old, with no known risk such as drug use." When counselors asked for more information, which happened in only 11 of the sessions, the client explained that he was 27 years old, monogamous, and that neither his current nor his (few) previous sexual partners used drugs or engaged in risky behavior. In two of these 11 cases, the client was given a detailed questionnaire to determine his risk; in one of these cases the counselor did not look at the questionnaire, and the client still had it in his hands when he left the site.

The client was trained in simulated sessions to use a coding system (question number; number of repetitions of a question; the counselor's answer at each repetition; e.g., "1; 2; 99.9%") that allowed him to write down the relevant information in shorthand during the counseling or, if the session was very brief, to rehearse the code in memory and write it down immediately after the counseling session.

After the counseling session, the client took the HIV test, except for three cases (in two he would have had to wait several hours to take the test, and in one case the counselor suggested that the client might first consider it overnight before making the decision of whether or not to take the test).

Results

Four counseling sessions are shown, for illustration, in Table 5.1. The client's questions are abbreviated (e.g., *sensitivity?*), and the information provided by the counselor directly follows the question. The counselors' answers to the client's clarifying questions are preceded by a dash in subsequent lines.

Table 5.1 Four sample counseling sessions

Session 1. The counselor is a female social worker

Sensitivity? False negatives really never occur. Although, if I think about the literature, there were reports about such cases.
—I don't know exactly how many.
—It happened only once or twice.
False positives? No, because the test is repeated; it is absolutely certain.
—If there are antibodies, the test identifies them unambiguously and with absolute certainty.
—No, it is absolutely impossible that there are false positives; by repeating the test it is absolutely certain.
Prevalence? I can't tell you this exactly.
—Between about 1 of 500 to 1 of 1,000.
Positive predictive value? As I have now told you repeatedly, the test is absolutely certain.

Session 2. The counselor is a male physician

Sensitivity? When there are enough antibodies, then the test identifies them in every case. Two tests are performed; the first test is in its fourth generation and is tuned to be very specific and sensitive. Nevertheless, it is tuned in a way that it is more likely to identify positives than negatives.
—99.8% sensitivity and specificity. But we repeat the test, and when it comes out positive, then the result is as solid as cast iron.
False positives? With certainty, they don't occur; if there are false results, then only false negatives, occurring when the antibodies have not formed.
—If you take the test here, including a confirmatory test, it is extremely certain: in any case the specificity is 99.7%. This is as solid as cast iron. We exclude confusions by using two tests.
Prevalence? The classification of individuals into risk groups is by now outdated, therefore one cannot look at it that way.
—I don't remember this. There is a trend of the virus spreading in the general public. Statistics are of no use for the individual case!
Positive predictive value? As I already have said: extremely certain, 99.8%.

Session 3. The counselor is a female physician

Sensitivity? The test is very, very reliable, that is, about 99.98%.
False positives? The test will be repeated. After the first test, one does not speak of positive, but only of reactive. When all tests are performed, then the result is sure.
—It is hard to say how many false positives occur.
—How many precisely? I would have to look up the literature to see if I could find this information there.
Prevalence? That depends on the region.
—Of the circa 67,000 infected people [in Germany], 9% are heterosexual.
—In Munich we have 10,000 infected people, that is, 1% of the population. But these are only numbers, which tell you nothing about whether you have the virus or not.
Positive predictive value? As I already have mentioned, the result is 99.98% sure. If you get a positive result, you can trust it.

—continued

Table 5.1 (continued)

Session 4: The counselor is a female social worker

Sensitivity? Very, very reliable.
>   —No, not absolutely sure, such a thing doesn't exist in medicine, because it may be possible that the virus cannot be identified.
>   —Close to 100%; I don't know exactly.

False positives? They exist but are extremely rare.
>   —In the order of a tenth of a percent. Probably less. However, in your risk group, compared to high-risk groups, false positives are proportionally more frequent [than true positives].
>   —I don't know the exact value.

Prevalence? With the contacts you had, the infection is unlikely.
>   —Generally one can't say. In our own institution, among some 10,000 tests in the last seven years, there were only three or four heterosexuals, non-drug addicts, or similar non-risk-group persons who tested positive.

Positive predictive value? As mentioned, the test is not 100% sure. If the test confuses the [HIV] antibodies with others, then other methods such as repeated tests do not help. And if someone like you does not have a real risk, then I could imagine that even 5% to 10% of those who get a positive result will have gotten a false positive result.

When the client asked a question, he did not use the technical terms shown here (such as sensitivity) but the wording specified in the "interview" section. The answer of the counselor is given after each question. The following lines (beginning with a '—') are the counselor's responses to the client's request for clarification.

Sensitivity and Window Period

Nineteen of 20 counselors gave the client information concerning sensitivity. (The twentieth refused to give any information concerning sensitivity, specificity, and the predictive value before the test result was obtained. When the client picked up the test result, he got no information either.) Most counselors gave the client realistic information concerning the sensitivity (Table 5.2). However, five of the 19 counselors incorrectly informed the client that it would be impossible to get a false negative result, except during the window period.

Table 5.2 Information provided by the counselors

	100% certainty	≥ 99.9%	≥ 99%	≥ 90%	Range
Sensitivity	5 (of 19)	5	6	3	90–100%
Specificity	13 (of 19)	3	3	0	99.7–100%
Prevalence	—	—	—	—	0.0075–6%
PPV	10 (of 18)	5	1	2	90–100%

Note: Not all counselors provided numerical estimates. The verbal assertion "absolutely certain" is treated here as equivalent to 100% certain; verbal assertions such as "almost absolutely certain" and "very, very certain" are classified as ≥ 99%, and assertions such as "very reliable" are classified as ≥ 90%.

Fifteen counselors provided information concerning the window period when asked for the sensitivity. The median estimate for the window period was 12 weeks.

False Positives

Thirteen of 19 counselors informed the client incorrectly that false positives do not occur (e.g., Session 1). Eleven of these explained that the reason is that repeated testing with ELISA and Western blot eliminates all false positives. Five of these 13 counselors told the client that false positives had occurred in the 1980s but no longer today, and two said that false positives would occur only in foreign countries, such as France, but not in Germany. In addition to these 13 counselors, three other counselors first suggested that false positives would not occur, but became less certain when the client repeated his question and admitted the possibility of false positives (e.g., Sessions 2 and 3). Only the three remaining counselors informed the client right away about the existence of false positives. One of them (Session 4) was the only counselor who informed the client about the important fact that the proportion of false positives to true positives is particularly high in heterosexuals such as the client.

Prevalence

The question concerning the prevalence of HIV in heterosexual men with low-risk behavior produced the most uncertainty among the counselors. Sixteen of 20 (all counselors responded) expressed uncertainty or ignorance or argued that the prevalence for heterosexual men with low-risk behavior cannot be determined (e.g., because of unreported cases) or that it would be of no use for the individual case (e.g., Session 2). Several counselors searched for publications in response to the client's question but found only irrelevant statistics, such as the large number of HIV-positives in West Berlin: "The Wall was the best condom for East Berlin," one counselor answered. Twelve counselors provided numerical estimates, with a median of 0.1%. The variability of the estimates was considerable (Table 5.2), including the extreme estimate that in people such as the client an HIV infection is "less probable than winning the lottery three times" (we have not included this value in Table 5.2). Four counselors asserted that information concerning prevalence is of little or no use: "But statistics don't help us in the individual case—and we also have no precise data" (see also Sessions 2 and 3). Two counselors said that they have problems remembering numbers or reasoning with numbers; for instance: "I have difficulties reasoning with statistical information. It's about groups and the transfer is problematic. It reminds me of playing the lottery. The probability of getting all six correct is very small; nevertheless, every week someone wins."

Positive Predictive Value

Recall that under the currently available estimates, only some 50% of heterosexual German men with low-risk behavior actually have HIV if they test positive. The information provided by the counselors was quite different. Half of the counselors (10 of 18; two repeatedly ignored this question) told the client that if he tested positive it was absolutely certain (100%) that he has HIV (Table 5.2 and Session 1). Five told him that the probability is 99.9% or higher (e.g., Session 3). Thus, if the client had tested positive and trusted the information provided by these 15 counselors, he might indeed have contemplated suicide, as many have before (Stine, 1996).

How did the counselors arrive at this inflated estimate of the predictive value? They seemed to have two lines of thought. A total of eight counselors confused the sensitivity with the *PPV* (a confusion also reported by Eddy, 1982, and Elstein, 1988); that is, they gave the same number for the sensitivity and the *PPV* (e.g., Sessions 2 and 3). Three of these eight counselors explained that, except for the window period, the sensitivity is 100% and therefore the *PPV* was also 100%. Another five counselors reasoned by the second strategy. They (erroneously) assumed that false positives would be eliminated through repeated testing and concluded from this (consistently) that the *PPV* is 100%. For both groups, the client's question concerning the *PPV* must have appeared as one they had already answered. In fact, more than half of the counselors (11 of 18) explicitly introduced their answers with a phrase such as, "As I have already said . . ." (e.g., Sessions 1–3). Consistent with this observation, the answers to the question concerning the *PPV* came rather quickly, and the client did not need to ask for clarification as often as before. The average number of questions asked by the client on the *PPV* was only 1.8, compared to 2.4, 2.4, and 2.5 for sensitivity, specificity, and prevalence, respectively.

Table 5.2 lists two counselors who provided estimates of the *PPV* in the correct direction (between 99% and 90%). Only one of these (Session 4), however, arrived at this estimate by reasoning that the proportion of false positives among all positives increases when the prevalence decreases. She was also the only one who explained to the client that there are reasons for false positives that cannot be eliminated by repeated testing, such as that the test reacts to antibodies that it confuses with HIV antibodies. The second counselor first asserted that after a positive test an HIV infection is "completely certain," but when the client asked what "completely certain" meant, the physician had second thoughts and said that the *PPV* is "at least in the upper 90s" and "I can't be more exact."

How Is the Information Communicated?

There was not a single counselor who communicated the information in natural frequencies, the representation physicians and laypeople can understand best. Except for the prevalence of HIV, all numerical information was communicated to the client in terms of percentages. The four sessions in Table 5.1 illustrate this fact. As a consequence, clients will most likely not understand, and several counselors also seemed not to understand the numbers they were communicating. This can be inferred from the fact that several counselors gave the client inconsistent pieces of information but seemed not to notice.

Two examples illustrate this disturbing fact. One physician told the client that the prevalence of HIV in men such as the client is 0.1% or slightly higher, and the sensitivity, specificity, and the *PPV* are each 99.9%. To see that this information is contradictory, we represent it in natural frequencies. Imagine 1,000 men taking an HIV test. One of these men (0.1%) is infected, and he will test positive with practical certainty. Of the remaining uninfected men, one will also test positive (because the specificity is assumed to be 99.9%, which implies a false positive rate of 0.1%). Thus two test positive, and one of them is infected. Therefore, the odds of being infected with HIV are 1 to 1 (50%), and not 999 to 1 (99.9%). (Even if the physician assumed a prevalence of 0.5%, the odds are 5 to 1 rather than 999 to 1.)

Next consider the information the client received in Session 2. Assume for the prevalence (which the counselor did not provide) the median estimate of the other counselors, namely 0.1%. Again imagine 1,000 men. One has the virus, and he will test positive with practical certainty (the counselor's esti- mated sensitivity: 99.8%). Of the remaining uninfected men, three will also test positive (the counselor's estimated specificity: 99.7%). Thus we expect four to test positive, one of whom actually has the virus. Therefore, the prob- ability of being infected if the test is positive is 25% (one in four), not 99.8% as the counselor told the client.

If the counselors had been trained to represent information in natural fre- quencies, these inconsistencies could have been easily detected. But the coun- selors seem to have had no training in how to represent and communicate information concerning risk. A hypothetical session in which an "ideal" coun- selor uses natural frequencies is given here. Because the client did not find such a counselor, the following session is fictional:

Sensitivity? The test will be positive in about 998 of 1,000 persons with an HIV infection. Depending on circumstances, such as the specific tests used, this estimate can vary slightly.

False positives? About 1 in 10,000. False positives can be largely reduced by repeated testing (ELISA and Western blot), but not completely elim- inated. Among the reasons for false positives are . . .

Prevalence? About 1 in 10,000 German heterosexual men with low-risk behavior is HIV infected.

Positive predictive value? Think about 10,000 heterosexual men like you. One is infected, and he will test positive with practical certainty. Of the remaining noninfected men, one will also test positive. Thus we expect that two men will test positive, and only one of them has HIV. This is the situation you are in if you test positive. Your chance of having the virus is about 1 in 2.

Do the brochures available in AIDS centers, a source from which the coun- selors might draw, provide help in understanding what a positive test means when prevalence is low? We studied 78 different brochures from the 20 centers, some of them handed to the client by counselors, ranging from publications of the federal government to reports from the local counseling sites. These brochures contained a flood of useful pieces of information, such as facts concerning the media through which the virus can and cannot be transmitted, but very little about what a positive test means when prevalence is low. In particular, there was no information about the prevalence in men and women with no risky behavior. The most frequently available literature was a series of ten issues edited by the Federal Center for Health Education (Bundeszentrale für gesundheitliche Aufklärung, 1988–1993). In the first issue, the problem of false positives is mentioned, and it is remarked that the repeated test is "reliable." In the second issue, false positives are again briefly mentioned, and the reasonable recommendation is made that people who have no known risk and nevertheless test positive should head for a second test, for instance in a public counseling site. (One might wonder what those counselors who believe that a positive result is absolutely certain will tell such a person.) The third issue promises "in the near future" antibody tests that identify HIV-1 and HIV-2 infections with certainty—in contradiction to the statement of the Enquete Committee of the German Bundestag (Deutscher Bundestag, 1988, p. 79) that there will be no absolute certainty in identifying HIV, as there is none with other viral infections. Nor do the remaining issues provide quantitative estimates of the uncertainties involved with the test. Estimates are only provided for the window period, which is irrelevant for the number of false positives. In no case is an attempt made to explain to the reader the relation between prevalence, sensitivity, false positives, and the positive predictive value in an understandable way. Thus, based on these brochures, neither the counselor nor the client can learn what a positive test means when prevalence is low.

Conclusions

This study shows, for a sample of public AIDS counseling centers in Germany, that counselors were not prepared to explain to a man with low-risk behavior what it would mean if he tested positive for HIV. This is not to say that the counselors were generally ignorant; on the contrary, several counselors gave long and sophisticated lectures concerning immunodiagnostic techniques, the nature of proteins, and the pathways of infection. But when it came to explaining to the client the risk of being infected if he tests positive, there was a lack of information as well as a lack of knowledge of how to communicate risks.

The key problems identified in this study are:

1. All counselors communicated information in terms of probabilities and percentages rather than in a format that helps the clients (and themselves) to understand, such as natural frequencies.

2. Only one of 20 counselors (Session 4) explained the fact that the lower the prevalence, the higher the proportion of false positives among positive tests.

3. A majority of counselors incorrectly assured the client that false positives would never occur. Counselors had a simple, deterministic explanation: False positives would be eliminated through repeated testing (and similarly, false negatives would be eliminated after the window period).

4. Half of the counselors asserted incorrectly that if a low-risk person tests positive, it is absolutely certain (100%) that he is infected with the virus. Counselors arrived at this erroneous judgment by one of two strategies. One group confused the sensitivity of the test with the *PPV*. A second group assumed that there are no false positives because of repeated tests, which implies that a positive test indicates an infection with absolute certainty.

We do not know how representative these results are for AIDS counseling of low-risk client groups in other centers in Germany or in other countries. This study seems to be the first one of this kind, but there is no reason to believe that the sample of counseling centers visited is not representative of Germany (precisely, former West Germany). The lesson of this study is the importance of teaching counselors how to explain to clients in simple terms the risks involved. The counselors need rough estimates of false positives, sensitivity, and the prevalence of HIV in various risk groups. Then they can be taught to communicate this information in an understandable way. Experimental evidence suggests that the most efficient and simple method is to train counselors to represent the relevant information in natural frequencies and to communicate it to the client in the same way.[4] Such training takes little time, and is cost-effective, and participants do not show the usual decay of what they had learned over time (Chapter 4).

The competence to explain in simple language what a positive result means is certainly not all that a counselor needs to be able to do, but it is an important part. Proper information may prevent self-destructive reactions in clients. These reactions are avoidable, an unnecessary toll on top of the one the disease itself takes from humankind.

4. There is also experimental evidence that the error made most often by AIDS counselors in this study, confusing the sensitivity with the *PPV* of the test, is markedly reduced (from 19% to 5% of all diagnostic inferences) when information is represented in terms of frequencies rather than probabilities (Hoffrage & Gigerenzer, 1998).

6

How to Improve Bayesian Reasoning without Instruction

Is the mind, by design, predisposed against performing Bayesian inference? The classical probabilists of the Enlightenment, including Condorcet, Poisson, and Laplace, equated probability theory with the common sense of educated people, who were known then as "hommes éclairés." Laplace (1814/1951) declared that "the theory of probability is at bottom nothing more than good sense reduced to a calculus which evaluates that which good minds know by a sort of instinct, without being able to explain how with precision" (p. 196). The available mathematical tools, in particular the rules of Bayes and Bernoulli, were seen as descriptions of actual human judgment (Daston, 1981, 1988). However, the years of political upheaval during the French Revolution prompted Laplace, unlike earlier writers such as Condorcet, to issue repeated disclaimers that probability theory, because of the interference of passion and desire, could not account for all relevant factors in human judgment. The Enlightenment view—that the laws of probability are the laws of the mind—moderated as it was through the French Revolution, had a profound influence on nineteenth- and twentieth-century science. This view became the starting point for seminal contributions to mathematics, as when George Boole (1854/1958) derived the laws of algebra, logic, and probability from what he believed to be the laws of thought. It also became the basis of vital contributions to psychology, as when Piaget and Inhelder (1951/1975) added an ontogenetic dimension to their Enlightenment view of probabilistic reasoning. And it became the foundation of contemporary notions of rationality in philosophy and economics.

Ward Edwards and his colleagues (Edwards, 1968; Phillips & Edwards, 1966; and earlier Rouanet, 1961) were the first to test experimentally whether human inference follows Bayes's rule. Edwards concluded that inferences, although "conservative," were usually proportional to those calculated from Bayes's rule. In the 1970s and 1980s, proponents of the heuristics-and-biases program, however, arrived at the opposite conclusion: that people systemati-

The work on which this chapter is based was coauthored with U. Hoffrage.

cally neglect base rates in Bayesian inference problems. "The genuineness, the robustness, and the generality of the base-rate fallacy are matters of established fact" (Bar-Hillel, 1980, p. 215). Bayes's rule, like Bernoulli's theorem, was no longer thought to describe the workings of the mind. But passion and desire were no longer blamed as the causes of the disturbances. The new claim was stronger. The discrepancies were taken as tentative evidence that "people do not appear to follow the calculus of chance or the statistical theory of prediction" (Kahneman & Tversky, 1973, p. 237). It was proposed that as a result of "limited information-processing abilities" (Lichtenstein, Fischhoff, & Phillips, 1982, p. 333), people are doomed to compute the probability of an event by crude, nonstatistical rules such as the "representativeness heuristic."

Here is the problem. There are contradictory claims as to whether people naturally reason according to Bayesian inference. The two extremes are represented by the Enlightenment probabilists and by proponents of the heuristics-and-biases program. Their conflict cannot be resolved by finding further examples of good or bad reasoning; text problems generating one or the other can always be designed. Our particular difficulty is that after more than two decades of research, we still know little about the cognitive processes underlying human inference, Bayesian or otherwise. This is not to say that there have been no attempts to specify these processes. For instance, it is understandable that when the "representativeness heuristic" was first proposed in the early 1970s to explain base-rate neglect, it was only loosely defined. Yet at present, representativeness remains a vague and ill-defined notion. For some time it was hoped that factors such as "concreteness," "vividness," "causality," "salience," "specificity," "extremeness," and "relevance" of base-rate information would be adequate to explain why base-rate neglect seemed to come and go (e.g., Ajzen, 1977; Bar-Hillel, 1980; Borgida & Brekke, 1981). However, these factors have led neither to an integrative theory nor even to specific models of underlying processes (Hammond, 1990; Koehler, 1996; Lopes, 1991; Scholz, 1987).

Some have suggested that there is perhaps something to be said for both sides, that the truth lies somewhere in the middle: Maybe the mind does a little of both Bayesian computation and quick-and-dirty inference. This compromise avoids the polarization of views but makes no progress on the theoretical front.

Both views, however, are based on an incomplete analysis: They focus on cognitive processes, Bayesian or otherwise, without making the connection between what we will call a *cognitive algorithm* and an *information format*. We (a) provide a theoretical framework that specifies why frequency formats should improve Bayesian reasoning and (b) present two studies that test whether they do. Our goal is to lead research on Bayesian inference out of the present conceptual cul-de-sac and to shift the focus from human errors to human engineering (see Edwards & von Winterfeldt, 1986): how to help people reason the Bayesian way without even teaching them.

Algorithms Are Designed for Information Formats

Our argument centers on the intimate relationship between a cognitive algorithm and an information format. This point was made in a more general form by the physicist Richard Feynman. In his classic *The Character of Physical Law*, Feynman (1967) placed great emphasis on the importance of deriving different formulations for the same physical law, even if they are mathematically equivalent (e.g., Newton's law, the local field method, and the minimum principle). Different representations of a physical law, Feynman reminded us, can evoke varied mental pictures and thus assist in making new discoveries: "Psychologically they are different because they are completely unequivalent when you are trying to guess new laws" (p. 53). We agree with Feynman. The assertion that mathematically equivalent representations can make a difference to human understanding is the key to our analysis of intuitive Bayesian inference.

We use the general term *information representation* and the specific terms *information format* and *information menu* to refer to *external* representations, recorded on paper or on some other physical medium. Examples are the various formulations of physical laws included in Feynman's book and the Feynman diagrams. External representations need to be distinguished from the *internal* representations stored in human minds, whether the latter are propositional (e.g., Pylyshyn, 1973) or pictorial (e.g., Kosslyn & Pomerantz, 1977). In this article, we do not make specific claims about internal representations, although our results may be of relevance to this issue.

Consider numerical information as an example of external representation. Numbers can be represented in Roman, Arabic, and binary systems, among others. These representations can be mapped one to one onto each other and are in this sense mathematically equivalent. But the form of representation can make a difference for an algorithm that does, say, multiplication. The algorithms of our pocket calculators are tuned to Arabic numbers as input data and would fail badly if one entered binary numbers. Similarly, the arithmetic algorithms acquired by humans are designed for particular representations (Stigler, 1984). Contemplate for a moment long division in Roman numerals.

Our general argument is that mathematically equivalent representations of information entail algorithms that are not necessarily computationally equivalent (although these algorithms are mathematically equivalent in the sense that they produce the same outcomes; see Larkin & Simon, 1987; Marr, 1982). This point has an important corollary for research on inductive reasoning. Suppose we are interested in figuring out what algorithm a system uses. We will not detect the algorithm if the representation of information we provide the system does not match the representation with which the algorithm works. For instance, assume that in an effort to find out whether a system has an algorithm for multiplication, we feed that system Roman numerals. The observation that the system produces mostly garbage does not entail the conclusion that it lacks an algorithm for multiplication.

In the previous two chapters, we applied this argument to statistical thinking—more precisely, to an elementary form of Bayesian inference. These chapters illustrate how one can help experts turn innumeracy into insight. In this chapter, we will explore in more depth the differences between natural frequencies and probabilities and extend this analysis to other representations.

Natural Sampling

Natural sampling is the process of encountering instances in a population sequentially. The outcome of natural sampling is natural frequencies. Figure 6.1a illustrates the natural frequencies observed in a sample of 1,000 women, in which 10 have breast cancer and 990 do not.

There are two ways to arrive at frequencies that are not natural frequencies. The first is through systematic sampling, in which the base rates are fixed

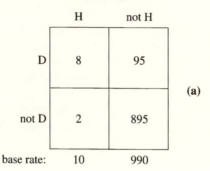

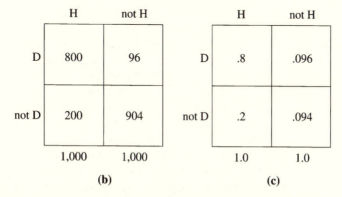

Figure 6.1 (a) Natural frequencies; (b) absolute frequencies that are not natural frequencies (obtained by systematic sampling or by normalizing natural frequencies with respect to base rates); (c) relative frequencies or probabilities. H = hypothesis; D = data.

before any observations are made. Systematic sampling is typically employed in experiments that test the effect of a treatment. Figure 6.1b shows an example in which 1,000 women with and 1,000 women without breast cancer were tested. Note that Figure 6.1b contains absolute frequencies that were not obtained through natural sampling. Unlike natural frequencies, they do not contain information about the base rates of women with and without cancer.

There is a second way to arrive at frequencies that are not natural frequencies. This is by normalizing natural frequencies with respect to the base rates, that is, by setting the base rates to the same value, such as 1,000 (Figure 6.1b) or 1.0 (Figure 6.1c). For instance, consider the 10 women with cancer in Figure 6.1a (left column), of whom 8 test positive. Normalizing this natural frequency results in 800 of 1,000 (Figure 6.1b), or .8 (Figure 6.1c). Normalized natural frequencies, like absolute frequencies obtained through systematic sampling, thus have the base-rate information filtered out of them.

Natural frequencies, such as those in Figure 6.1a, result from the most common form of direct observation (outside systematic experimentation in science). Young children can count events from an early age but do not understand fractions and other kinds of normalized counts until much later in their development (Dehaene, 1997). Examples of natural frequencies in science can be found in medical and epidemiological screening data from which base rates, hit rates, and false positive rates are derived. The qualifier "natural" in the terms natural sampling and natural frequencies emphasizes that they are based on observations made in an ecological (rather than an experimental) setting and on raw (rather than normalized) counts of events.

The important point is that natural frequencies facilitate Bayesian computations. The reason for this is that they carry information about base rates, whereas normalized frequencies and probabilities do not (Kleiter, 1994). If information is presented in normalized values, one has to multiply these by the base rates in order to bring the base rates "back in." Natural frequencies need not be multiplied in this way.

To summarize, natural sampling yields natural frequencies, which carry information about base rates and thereby facilitate Bayesian computations. Systematic sampling and normalization do not lead to natural frequencies. Systematic sampling does not capture information about base rates because they are fixed *before* the observations are made. Normalization entails discarding the base-rate information *after* the observations are made.

How exactly do natural frequencies facilitate Bayesian computations? Consider first the *standard probability format* (Table 6.1) that is one interpretation of Figure 6.1c (another one is in terms of relative frequencies). Here the information is represented in terms of *single-event probabilities*: All information—a base rate of 1%, a hit rate of 80%, and a false alarm rate of 9.6%—is in the form of probabilities attached to a single person, and the task is to estimate a single-event probability. The probabilities are expressed as percentages; alternatively, they can be represented as numbers between zero and one. We refer to this representation (base rate, hit rate, and false alarm rate expressed as single-event probabilities) as the *standard probability format*.

Table 6.1 Information formats and menus for the mammography problem

Format and menu	Description of problem
Standard probability format	The probability of breast cancer is 1% for a woman at age forty who participates in routine screening. If a woman has breast cancer, the probability is 80% that she will get a positive mammogram. If a woman does not have breast cancer, the probability is 9.6% that she will also get a positive mammogram. A woman in this age group had a positive mammogram in a routine screening. What is the probability that she actually has breast cancer? _____%
Standard frequency format	10 out of every 1,000 women at age forty who participate in routine screening have breast cancer. 8 out of every 10 women with breast cancer will get a positive mammogram. 95 out of every 990 women without breast cancer will also get a positive mammogram. Here is a new representative sample of women at age forty who got a positive mammogram in routine screening. How many of these women do you expect to actually have breast cancer? _____ out of _____
Short probability format	The probability that a woman at age forty will get a positive mammogram in routine screening is 10.3%. The probability of breast cancer *and* a positive mammogram is 0.8% for a woman at age forty who participates in routine screening. A woman in this age group had a positive mammogram in a routine screening. What is the probability that she actually has breast cancer? _____%
Short frequency format	103 out of every 1,000 women at age forty get a positive mammogram in routine screening. 8 out of every 1,000 women at age forty who participate in routine screening have breast cancer *and* a positive mammogram. Here is a new representative sample of women at age forty who got a positive mammogram in routine screening. How many of these women do you expect to actually have breast cancer? _____ out of _____

What is the algorithm needed to calculate the Bayesian posterior probability $p(\text{cancer} | \text{positive})$ from the standard probability format? Again, we use the symbols H and $-H$ for the two hypotheses or possible outcomes (breast cancer and no breast cancer) and D for the data obtained (positive mammogram). As shown in Chapter 4, a Bayesian algorithm for computing the posterior probability $p(H|D)$ with the values given in the standard probability format amounts to solving the following equation:

$$p(H|D) = \frac{p(H)p(D|H)}{p(H)p(D|H) + p(-H)p(D|-H)}$$

$$= \frac{(.01)(.80)}{(.01)(.80) + (.99)(.096)}$$

(1)

The result is 0.078. However, physicians, college students, and staff at Harvard Medical School all have equally great difficulties with this and similar medical problems and typically estimate the posterior probability $p(\text{cancer} | \text{positive})$ to be between 70% and 80%, rather than 7.8% (Chapter 4).

The experimenters who have amassed the apparently damning body of evidence that humans fail to meet the norms of Bayesian inference have usually given their research participants information in the standard probability format (or its variant, in which one or more of the three percentages are relative frequencies; see below). Studies on the cab problem (Bar-Hillel, 1980), the lightbulb problem (Lyon & Slovic, 1976), and various disease problems (Casscells et al., 1978; Eddy, 1982; Hammerton, 1973) are examples. Results from these and other studies have generally been taken as evidence that the human mind does not reason with Bayesian algorithms. Yet this conclusion is not warranted, as explained before. One would be unable to detect a Bayesian algorithm within a system by feeding it information in a representation that does not match the representation with which the algorithm works.

In the last few decades, the standard probability format has become a common way to communicate information ranging from medical and statistical textbooks to psychological experiments. But we should keep in mind that it is only one of many mathematically equivalent ways of representing information; it is, moreover, a recently invented notation. Neither the standard probability format nor Equation 1 was used in Bayes's (1763) original essay. As Figure 6.2 shows, with natural frequencies one does not need a pocket calculator to estimate the Bayesian posterior. All one needs is the number of cases that had both the symptom and the disease (here, 8) and the number of symptom cases (here, 8 + 95). A Bayesian algorithm for computing the posterior probability $p(H|D)$ from the frequency format (see Figure 6.2, left side) requires solving the following equation:

$$p(H|D) = \frac{d\&h}{d\&h + d\&-h} = \frac{8}{8 + 95}$$

(2)

where $d\&h$ (data and hypothesis) is the number of cases with symptom and disease, and $d\&-h$ is the number of cases having the symptom but lacking the

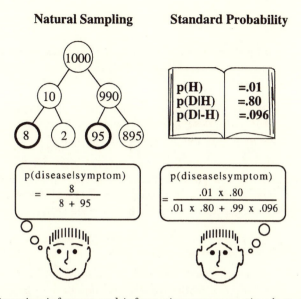

Natural Sampling   **Standard Probability**

Figure 6.2 Bayesian inference and information representation (natural sampling of frequencies and standard probability format).

disease. One does not even need to keep track of the base rate of the disease. A medical student who struggles with single-event probabilities presented in medical textbooks may on the other hand have to rely on a calculator and end up with little understanding of the result (see Figure 6.2, right side).[1] Henceforth, when we use the term *frequency format*, we always refer to natural frequencies as defined by the natural sampling tree in Figure 6.2.

Comparison of Equations 1 and 2 leads to our first theoretical result:

Result 1: Computational demands. Bayesian algorithms are computationally simpler when information is encoded in a frequency format rather than a standard probability format.

By "computationally simpler" we mean that (a) fewer operations (multiplication, addition, or division) need to be performed in Equation 2 than Equation 1, and (b) the operations can be performed on natural numbers (absolute frequencies) rather than fractions (such as percentages).

Equations 1 and 2 are mathematically equivalent formulations of Bayes's rule. Both produce the same result, $p(H|D) = .078$. Equation 1 is a standard version of Bayes's rule in today's textbooks in the social sciences, whereas

---

1. This clinical example illustrates that the standard probability format is a convention rather than a necessity. Clinical studies often collect data that have the structure of frequency trees as in Figure 6.2. Such information can always be represented in frequencies as well as probabilities.

Equation 2 corresponds to Thomas Bayes's (1763) original "Proposition 5" (see Earman, 1992).

Equation 2 implies three further (not independent) theoretical results concerning the estimation of a Bayesian posterior probability $p(H|D)$ in frequency formats (Kleiter, 1994).

> *Result 2: Attentional demands. Only two kinds of information need to be attended to in natural sampling: the absolute frequencies d&h and d&−h (or, alternately d&h and d, where d is the sum of the two frequencies).*

An organism does not need to keep track of the whole tree in Figure 6.2 but only of the two pieces of information contained in the bold circles. These are the hit and false alarm *frequencies* (not to be confused with hit and false alarm *rates*).

> *Result 3: Base rates need not be attended to.*

Neglect of base rates is perfectly rational in natural sampling. For instance, one does not need to pay attention to the base rate of the disease (10 out of 1,000; see Figure 6.2).

> *Result 4: Posterior distributions can be computed.*

Natural frequencies can carry more information than probabilities. Information about the sample size allows inference beyond single-point estimates, such as the computation of posterior distributions, confidence intervals for posterior probabilities, and second-order probabilities (Kleiter, 1994; Sahlin, 1993). In this chapter, however, we focus only on single-point estimation.

For the design of the experiments reported herein, it is important to note that the Bayesian algorithms (Equations 1 and 2) work on the final tally of frequencies (see Figure 6.2), not on the sequential record of updated frequencies. Thus, the same four results still hold even if nothing but the final tally is presented to the participants in an experiment.

Information Format and Menu

We propose to distinguish two aspects of information representation, *information format* and *information menu*. The standard probability format has a *probability format*, whereas a *frequency format* is obtained by natural sampling. However, as the second result (attentional demands) shows, there is another difference. The standard probability format displays three pieces of information, whereas two are sufficient in natural sampling. We use the term *information menu* to refer to the manner in which information is segmented into pieces within any format. The standard probability format displays the three pieces $p(H)$, $p(D|H)$, and $p(D|-H)$ (often called base rate, hit rate, and false alarm rate, respectively). We refer to this as the *standard menu*. Natural

sampling yields a more parsimonious menu with only two pieces of information, *d&h* and *d&−h* (or alternatively, *d&h* and *d*). We call this the *short menu*.

So far we have introduced the probability format with a standard menu and
the frequency format with a short menu. However, information formats and
menus can be completely crossed. For instance, if we replace the probabilities
in the standard probability format with frequencies, we get a standard menu
with a frequency format, or the *standard frequency format*. Table 6.1 uses the
mammography problem to illustrate the four versions that result from crossing
the two menus with the two formats. All four displays are mathematically
equivalent in the sense that they lead to the same Bayesian posterior probability. In general, within the same format information can be divided into various menus; within the same menu, it can be represented in a range of formats.

To transform the standard probability format into the standard frequency
format, we simply replaced 1% with "10 out of 1,000," "80%" with "8 out of
10," and so on (following the tree in Figure 6.2) and phrased the task in terms
of a frequency estimate. All else went unchanged. Note that whether the frequency format actually carries information about the sample size (e.g., that
there were exactly 1,000 women) or not (as in Table 6.1, where it is said "in
every 1,000 women") makes no difference for Results 1 to 3 because these
relate to single-point estimates only (unlike Result 4).

What are the Bayesian algorithms needed to draw inferences from the two
new format–menu combinations? The complete crossing of formats and menus
leads to two important results. A Bayesian algorithm for the *short probability
format*, that is, the probability format with a short menu (as in Table 6.1),
amounts to solving the following equation:

$$p(H \mid D) = \frac{p(D\&H)}{p(D)} \tag{3}$$

This version of Bayes's rule is equivalent to Equation 1. The algorithm for
computing $p(H \mid D)$ from Equation 3, however, is computationally simpler than
the algorithm for computing $p(H \mid D)$ from Equation 1.

What Bayesian computations are needed for the standard frequency format?
Equation 2 specifies the computations for both the standard and short menus
in frequency formats. The same algorithm is sufficient for both menus. In the
standard frequency format of the mammography problem, for instance, the
expected number of actual breast cancer cases among positive tests is computed as 8/(8 + 95). Thus we have the following two important theoretical
results concerning formats (probability vs. frequency) and menus (standard vs.
short):

*Result 5: With a probability format, the Bayesian computations are sim-
pler in the short menu than in the standard menu.*

*Result 6: With a frequency format, the Bayesian computations are the
same for the two menus.*

If the two pieces of information in the short menu are *d*&*h* and *d*, as in Table 6.1, rather than *d*&*h* and *d*&−*h*, then the Bayesian computations are even simpler because the sum in the denominator is already computed.

Relative Frequencies

Several studies of Bayesian inference have used standard probability formats in which one, two, or all three pieces of information were presented as relative frequencies rather than as single-event probabilities—although the task still was to estimate a single-event probability (e.g., Tversky & Kahneman's, 1982b, cab problem). For instance, in the following version of the mammography problem, all information is represented in relative frequencies (in %).

> *Relative frequency version (standard menu)*
> 1% of women at age forty who participate in routine screening have breast cancer. 80% of women with breast cancer will get positive mammograms. 9.6% of women without breast cancer will also get positive mammograms. A woman in this age group had a positive mammogram in a routine screening. What is the probability that she actually has breast cancer?___%

Is the algorithm needed for relative frequencies computationally equivalent to the algorithm for natural frequencies? The relative frequency format does not display the natural frequencies needed for Equation 2. Rather, the numbers are the same as in the probability format, making the Bayesian computation the same as in Equation 1. This yields the following result:

> *Result 7: Algorithms for relative frequency versions are computationally equivalent to those for the standard probability format.*

We tested several implications of Results 1 through 7 (except Result 4) in the studies reported below.

The Format of the Single-Point Estimate

Whether estimates relate to single events or frequencies has been a central issue within probability theory and statistics since the decline of the classical interpretation of probability in the 1830s and 1840s. The question has polarized subjectivists and frequentists, additionally subdividing frequentists into moderate frequentists, such as R. A. Fisher, and strong frequentists, such as J. Neyman. A single-point estimate can be interpreted as a probability or a frequency. For instance, clinical inference can be about the probability that a particular person has cancer or about the frequency of cancer in a new sample of people. Foraging (Simon, 1956; Stephens & Krebs, 1986) provides an excellent example of a single-point estimate reasonably being interpreted as a frequency. The foraging organism is interested in making inferences that lead to satisfying results in the long run. Will it more often find food if it follows Cue *X* or Cue *Y*? Here the single-point estimate can be interpreted as an expected frequency for a new sample. In the experimental research of the past two decades, participants were almost always required to estimate a single-event probability. But this need not be. In the experiments reported herein, we asked people both for single-event probability and frequency estimates.

To summarize, mathematically equivalent information need not be computationally and psychologically equivalent. We have shown that Bayesian algorithms can depend on information format and menu, and we derived several specific results for when algorithms are computationally equivalent and when they are not.

Cognitive Strategies for Bayesian Inference

How might the mind draw inferences that follow Bayes's rule? Surprisingly, this question seems rarely to have been posed. Psychological explanations typically were directed at "irrational" deviations between human inference and the laws of probability; the "rational" seems not to have demanded an explanation in terms of cognitive processes. The cognitive account of probabilistic reasoning by Piaget and Inhelder (1951/1975), as one example, stops at the precise moment the adolescent turns "rational," that is, reaches the level of formal operations.

We propose three classes of cognitive strategies for Bayesian inference: first, the algorithms corresponding to Equations 1 through 3; second, physical analogs of Bayes's rule, as anticipated by Bayes's (1763) billiard table; and third, shortcuts that simplify the Bayesian computations in Equations 1 through 3.

Physical Analogs

We illustrate physical analogs and shortcuts by drawing on actual performance from the studies reported here, in which none of the participants was familiar with Bayes's rule. The German measles problem (in standard probability format and with the numerical information given in Study 2) serves as our example.

> German measles during early pregnancy can cause severe prenatal damage in the child. Therefore, pregnant women are routinely tested for German measles infection. In one such test, a pregnant woman is found to be infected. In order best to advise this woman what to do, the physician first wants to determine the probability of severe prenatal damage in the child if a mother has German measles during early pregnancy. The physician has the following information: The probability of severe prenatal damage in a child is 0.5%. The probability that a mother had German measles during early pregnancy if her child has severe prenatal damage is 40%. The probability that a mother had German measles during early pregnancy if her child does not have severe prenatal damage is 0.01%. What is the probability of severe prenatal damage in the child if the mother has German measles during early pregnancy?____%

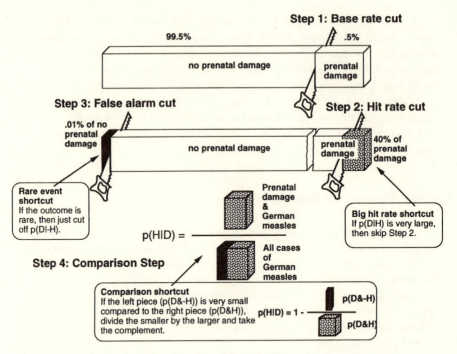

Figure 6.3 A physical analog developed by a brilliant student. The "beam cut" is illustrated for the German measles problem in the standard probability format. H = severe prenatal damage in the child, D = mother had German measles in early pregnancy. The information is $p(H) = 0.5\%$, $p(D|H) = 40\%$, and $p(D|-H) = 0.01\%$. The task is to infer $p(H|D)$.

The "beam analysis" (see Figure 6.3) is a physical analog of Bayes's rule developed by one of our research participants. This student represented the class of all possible outcomes (child has severe prenatal damage and child does not have severe prenatal damage) by a beam. He drew inferences (here, about the probability that the child has severe prenatal damage) by cutting off two pieces from each end of the beam and comparing their size. His algorithm was as follows:

Step 1: Base rate cut. Cut off a piece the size of the base rate from the right end of the beam.

Step 2: Hit rate cut. From the right part of the beam (base rate piece), cut off a proportion $p(D|H)$.

Step 3: False alarm cut. From the left part of the beam, cut off a proportion $p(D|-H)$.

Step 4: Comparison. The ratio of the right piece to both pieces is the posterior probability.

This algorithm amounts to Bayes's rule in the form of Equation 1.

Shortcuts: Probability Format

Shortcuts exploit the structure of environments. Used in the right situation, they are ecologically rational—they can ignore information and reduce computations without substantial loss of accuracy. We have observed in our experiments three elementary shortcuts and several combinations thereof. For instance, by ignoring small "slices," one can simplify the computation without much loss of accuracy, which is easily compensated for by the fact that less computation means a reduced chance of computational errors. We illustrate these shortcuts using the beam analysis (see Figure 6.3). However, these shortcuts are not restricted to physical analogs, and they were used by many of our participants.

Rare-Event Shortcut   Rare events—that is, outcomes with small base rates, such as severe prenatal damage—enable simplification of the Bayesian inference with little reduction in accuracy. If an event is rare, that is, if $p(H)$ is very small, and $p(-H)$ is therefore close to 1.0, then $p(D\,|-H)p(-H)$ can be approximated by $p(D\,|-H)$. That is, instead of cutting the *proportion* $p(D\,|-H)$ off the left part of the beam (Step 3), it is sufficient to cut a piece of *absolute* size $p(D\,|-H)$. The rare-event shortcut (see Figure 6.3) is as follows:

IF the event is rare,
THEN simplify Step 3: Cut a piece of absolute size $p(D\,|-H)$.

This shortcut corresponds to the approximation

$$p(H\,|\,D) \approx p(H)p(D\,|\,H)/[p(H)p(D\,|\,H) + p(D\,|-H)].$$

The shortcut works well for the German measles problem, where the base rate of severe prenatal damage is very small, $p(H) = .005$. The shortcut estimates $p(H\,|\,D)$ as .9524, whereas Bayes's rule gives .9526. It also works with the mammography problem, where it generates an estimate of .077, compared with .078 from Bayes's rule.

Big Hit-Rate Shortcut   Large values of $p(D\,|\,H)$ (such as high sensitivities in medical tests; that is, excellent hit rates) allow one to skip Step 2 with little loss of accuracy. If $p(D\,|\,H)$ is very large, then the $p(H)$ piece is practically the same size as the piece one obtains from cutting all but a tiny sliver from the $p(H)$ piece. The big hit-rate shortcut is then as follows:

IF $p(D\,|\,H)$ is very large,
THEN skip Step 2.

This shortcut corresponds to the approximation

$$p(H\,|\,D) \approx p(H)/[p(H) + p(-H)p(D\,|-H)].$$

The big hit-rate shortcut would not work as well as the rare-event shortcut in the German measles problem because $p(D\,|\,H)$ is only .40. Nevertheless, the shortcut estimate is only a few percentage points removed from that obtained with Bayes's rule (.980 instead of .953). The big hit-rate shortcut works well, to offer one instance, in medical diagnosis tasks where the hit rate of a test is high (e.g., around .99 as in HIV tests).

Comparison Shortcut   If one of the two pieces obtained in Steps 2 and 3 is small relative to the other, then the comparison in Step 4 can be simplified with little loss of accuracy. For example, German measles in early pregnancy and severe prenatal damage in the child occur more frequently than do German measles and no severe damage. More generally, if *D&H* cases are much more frequent than *D&−H* cases (as in the German measles problem), or vice versa (as in the mammography problem), then only two pieces (rather than three) need to be related in Step 4. The comparison shortcuts for these two cases are as follows:

> IF *D&−H* occurs much more often than *D&H*,
> THEN simplify Step 4: Take the ratio of *D&H* (right piece) to *D&−H* (left piece) as the posterior probability.

This shortcut corresponds to the approximation

$$p(H \mid D) \approx p(H)p(D \mid H)/p(-H)p(D \mid -H).$$

Note that the right side of this approximation is equivalent to the posterior odds ratio $p(H \mid D)/p(-H \mid D)$. Thus the comparison shortcut estimates the posterior probability by the posterior odds ratio.

> IF *D&H* occurs much more often than *D&−H*,
> THEN simplify Step 4: Take the ratio of *D&−H* (left piece) to *D&H* (right piece) as the complement of the posterior probability.

This shortcut corresponds to the approximation

$$p(H \mid D) \approx 1 - p(-H)p(D \mid -H)/p(H)p(D \mid H).$$

The comparison shortcut estimates $p(H \mid D)$ as .950 in the German measles problem, whereas Bayes's rule gives .953. The comparison shortcut is simpler when the *D&−H* cases are the more frequent ones, which is typical for medical diagnosis, where the number of false alarms is much larger than the number of hits, as in mammography.

Multiple Shortcuts   Two or three shortcuts can be combined, which results in a large computational simplification. What we call the *quick-and-clean shortcut* combines all three. Its conditions include a rare event, a large hit rate, and many *D&−H* cases compared with *D&H* cases (or vice versa). The quick-and-clean shortcut is as follows:

> IF an event H is rare, p(D | H) high, and D&−H cases much more frequent than D&H cases,
> THEN simply divide the base rate by the false alarm rate.

This shortcut corresponds to the approximation

$$p(H|D) \approx p(H)/p(D|-H).$$

The conditions of the quick-and-clean shortcut seem to be not infrequently satisfied. Consider routine HIV testing: According to present law, the U.S. immigration service makes an HIV test a condition sine qua non for obtaining a green card. Mr. Quick has applied for a green card and wonders what a positive test result (in the first ELISA test) indicates. The information available is a base rate of .002, a hit rate of .99, and a false alarm rate of .02; all three conditions for the quick-and-clean shortcut are thus satisfied. Mr. Quick computes .002/.02 = .10 as an estimate of the posterior probability of actually being infected with the HIV virus if he tests positive. Bayes's rule results in .09. The shortcut is therefore an excellent approximation. Alternately, if $D\&H$ cases are more frequent, then the quick-and-clean shortcut is to divide the false alarm rate by the base rate and to use this as an estimate for $1 - p(H|D)$. In the mammography and German measles problems, where the conditions are only partially satisfied, the quick-and-clean shortcut still leads to surprisingly good approximations. The posterior probability of breast cancer is estimated at .01/.096, which is about .10 (compared with .078), and the posterior probability of severe prenatal damage is estimated as .98 (compared with .953).

Shortcuts: Frequency Format

Does the standard frequency format invite the same shortcuts? Consider the inference about breast cancer from a positive mammogram, as illustrated in Figure 6.2. Would the rare-event shortcut facilitate the Bayesian computations? In the probability format, the rare-event shortcut uses $p(D|-H)$ to approximate $p(-H)p(D|-H)$; in the frequency format, the latter corresponds to the absolute frequency 95 (i.e., $d\&-h$) and no approximation is needed. Thus a rare-event shortcut is of no use and would not simplify the Bayesian computation in frequency formats. The same can be shown for the big hit-rate shortcut for the same reason. The comparison shortcut, however, can be applied in the frequency format:

IF $d\&-h$ occurs much more often than $d\&h$,
THEN compute $d\&h/d\&-h$.

The condition and the rationale are the same as in the probability format.

To summarize, we proposed three classes of cognitive strategies underlying Bayesian inference: (a) algorithms that satisfy Equations 1 through 3; (b) physical analogs that work with operations such as "cutting" instead of multiplying (Figure 6.3); and (c) three shortcuts that can exploit environmental structures.

Predictions

We now derive several predictions from the theoretical results obtained. The predictions specify conditions that do and do not make people reason the

Bayesian way. The predictions should hold independently of whether the cognitive strategies follow Equations 1 through 3, whether they are physical analogs of Bayes's rule, or whether they include shortcuts.

Prediction 1: Frequency formats elicit a substantially higher proportion of Bayesian inferences than probability formats.

This prediction is derived from Result 1, which states that the Bayesian algorithm is computationally simpler in frequency formats.[2]

Prediction 2: Probability formats elicit a larger proportion of Bayesian inferences for the short menu than for the standard menu.

This prediction is deduced from Result 5, which states that with a probability format, the Bayesian computations are simpler in the short menu than in the standard menu.

Prediction 3: Frequency formats elicit the same proportion of Bayesian inferences for the two menus.

This prediction is derived from Result 6, which states that with a frequency format, the Bayesian computations are the same for the two menus.

Prediction 4: Relative frequency formats elicit the same (small) proportion of Bayesian inferences as probability formats.

This prediction is derived from Result 7, which states that the Bayesian algorithms are computationally equivalent in both formats.

Operational Criteria for Identifying Cognitive Strategies

The data we obtained for each of several thousand problem solutions were composed of a participant's (a) probability or frequency estimate and (b) online protocol ("write aloud" protocol) of his or her reasoning. Data type (a) allowed for an outcome analysis, as used exclusively in most earlier studies on Bayesian inference, whereas data type (b) allowed additionally for a process analysis.

Double Check: Outcome and Process

We classified an inferential process as a Bayesian inference only if (a) the estimated probability or frequency was exactly the same as the value calcu-

---

2. At the point when we introduced Result 1, we had dealt solely with the standard probability format and the short frequency format. However, Prediction 1 also holds when we compare formats across both menus. This is the case because (a) the short menu is computationally simpler in the frequency than in the probability format, because the frequency format involves calculations with natural numbers and the probability format with fractions, and (b) with a frequency format, the Bayesian computations are the same for the two menus (Result 6).

lated from applying Bayes's rule to the information given (outcome criterion), and (b) the on-line protocol specified that one of the Bayesian computations defined by Equations 1 through 3 or one (or several) of the shortcuts was used, either by means of calculation or physical representation (process criterion). We applied the same strict criteria to identify non-Bayesian cognitive strategies.

Outcome: Strict Rounding Criterion   By the phrase "exactly the same" in the outcome criterion, we mean the exact probability or frequency, with exceptions made for rounding up or down to the next full percentage point (e.g., in the German measles problem, where rounding the probability of 95.3% down or up to a full percentage point results in 95% or 96%). If, for example, the on-line protocol showed that a participant in the German measles problem had used the rare-event shortcut and the answer was 95% or 96% (by rounding), this inferential process was classified as a Bayesian inference. Estimates below or above were not classified as Bayesian inferences: If, for example, another participant in the same problem used the big hit-rate shortcut (where the condition for this shortcut is not optimally satisfied) and accordingly estimated 98%, this was not classified as a Bayesian inference. Cases of the latter type ended up in the category of "less frequent strategies." This example illustrates the strictness of the joint criteria. The strict rounding criterion was applied to the frequency format in the same way as to the probability format.

When a participant answered with a fraction—such as that resulting from Equation 3—without performing the division, this was treated as if he or she had performed the division. We did not want to evaluate basic arithmetic skills. Similarly, if a participant arrived at a Bayesian equation but made a calculation error in the division, we ignored the calculation error.

Process: "Write Aloud" Protocols   Statistical reasoning often involves pictorial representations as well as computations. Neither are easily expressed verbally, as in "think aloud" methods. Pictorial representations and computations consequently are usually expressed in the form of drawings and by writing down equations and calculations. We designed a "write aloud" technique for tracking the reasoning process without asking the participant to talk aloud either during or after the task.

The "write aloud" method consisted of the following steps. First, participants were instructed to record their reasoning unless merely guessing the answer. We explained that a protocol may contain a variety of elements, such as diagrams, pictures, calculations, or whatever other tools one may use to find a solution. Each problem was on a separate page, which thus allowed ample space for notes, drawings, and calculations. Second, after a participant had completed a problem, he or she was asked to indicate whether the answer was based on a calculation or on a guess. Third, when a "write aloud" protocol was unreadable or the process that generated the probability estimate was unclear, and the participant had indicated that the given result was a calculation, then he or she was interviewed about the particular problem after completing

Table 6.2 Information given and Bayesian solutions for the 15 problems in Study 1

Task: Estimate p(H|D)		Information (standard frequency format)[a]						Bayes[b]
H	D	H		D|H		D|−H		p(H|D)
Breast cancer	Mammogram positive	10	1,000	8	10	95	990	7.77
Prenatal damage in child	German measles in mother	21	10,000	10	21	50	10,000	16.70
Blue cab	Eyewitness says "blue"	15	100	12	15	17	85	41.38
AIDS	HIV test positive	100	1,000,000	100	100	1,000	1,000,000	9.09
Heroin addict	Fresh needle prick	10	100,000	10	10	190	100,000	5.00
Pregnant	Pregnancy test positive	20	1,000	19	20	5	980	79.17
Car accident	Driver drunk	100	10,000	55	100	500	9,900	9.91
Bad posture in child	Heavy books carried daily	50	1,000	20	50	190	950	9.52
Accident on way to school	Child lives in urban area	30	1,000	27	30	388	970	6.51
Committing suicide	Professor	240	1,000,000	36	240	120,000	1,000,000	0.03
Red ball	Marked with star	400	500	300	400	25	100	92.31
Choosing course in economics	Career oriented	300	1,000	210	300	350	700	37.50
Active feminist	Bank teller	5,000	100,000	20	5,000	2,000	95,000	0.99
Pimp	Wearing a Rolex	50	1,000,000	40	50	500	1,000,000	7.41
Admission to school	Particular placement test result	360	1,000	270	360	128	640	67.84

a. The representation of the information is shown only for the standard frequency format (frequency format and standard menu). The other representations (see Table 6.1) can be derived from this. The two numbers for each piece of information are connected by an "out of" relation; for example, the information concerning H in the first problem should be read as "10 out of 1,000."

b. Probabilities are expressed as percentages.

all tasks. This happened only a few times. If a participant could not immediately identify what his or her notes meant, we did not inquire further.

The "write aloud" method avoids two problems associated with retrospective verbal reports: that memory of the cognitive strategies used may have faded by the time of a retrospective report (Ericsson & Simon, 1984) and that participants may have reported how they believe they ought to have thought rather than how they actually thought (Nisbett & Wilson, 1977).

We used the twin criteria of outcome and process to cross-check outcome by process and vice versa. The outcome criterion prevents a shortcut from being classified as a Bayesian inference when the precondition for the shortcut is not optimally satisfied. The process criterion protects against the opposite error, that of inferring from a probability judgment that a person actually used Bayesian reasoning when he or she did not.

We designed two studies to identify the cognitive strategies and test the predictions. Study 1 was designed to test Predictions 1,2, and 3.

Study 1: Information Formats and Menus

Method

Sixty students, 21 men and 39 women from ten disciplines (predominantly psychology) from the University of Salzburg, Austria, were paid for their participation. The median age was 21 years. None of the participants was familiar with Bayes's rule. Participants were studied individually or in small groups of 2 or 3 (in two cases, 5). On the average, students worked 73 min in the first session (range = 25–180 min) and 53 min in the second (range = 30–120 min).

We used two formats, probability and frequency, and two menus, standard and short. The two formats were crossed with the two menus, so four versions were constructed for each problem. There were 15 problems, including the mammography problem (Eddy, 1982; see Table 6.1), the cab problem (Tversky & Kahneman, 1982b), and a short version of Ajzen's (1977) economics problem. The four versions of each problem were constructed in the same way as explained before with the mammography problem (see Table 6.1).[3] In the frequency format, participants were always asked to estimate the frequency of "h out of d"; in the probability format, they were always asked to estimate the probability $p(H|D)$. Table 6.2 shows for each of the 15 problems the information given in the standard frequency format; the information specified in the other three versions can be derived from that.

3. If the Y number in "X out of Y" was large and odd, such as 9,950, we rounded the number to a close, more simple number, such as 10,000. The German measles problem is an example. This made practically no difference for the Bayesian calculation and was meant to prevent participants from being puzzled by odd Y numbers.

Participants were randomly assigned to two groups, with the members of both answering each of the 15 problems in two of the four versions. One group received the standard probability format and the short frequency format; the other, the standard frequency format and the short probability format. Each participant thus worked on 30 tasks. There were two sessions, 1 week apart, with 15 problems each. Formats and menus were distributed equally over the sessions. The two versions of one problem were always given in different sessions. The order of the problems was determined randomly, and two different random orders were used within each group.

Results

Bayesian Reasoning

Predition 1: Frequency formats elicit a substantially higher proportion of Bayesian inferences than probability formats.

Do frequency formats foster Bayesian reasoning? Yes. Frequency formats elicited a substantially higher proportion of Bayesian inferences than probability formats: 46% in the standard menu and 50% in the short menu. Probability formats, in contrast, elicited 16% and 28%, for the standard menu and the short menu, respectively. These proportions of Bayesian inferences were obtained by the strict joint criteria of process and outcome and held fairly stable across 15 different inference problems. Note that 50% Bayesian inferences means 50% of all answers, and not just of those answers where a cognitive strategy could be identified. The percentage of identifiable cognitive strategies across all formats and menus was 84%.

Figure 6.4 shows the proportions of Bayesian inferences for each of the 15 problems. The individual problems mirror the general result. For each problem, the standard probability format elicited the smallest proportion of Bayesian inferences. Across formats and menus, in every problem Bayesian inferences were the most frequent.

The comparison shortcut was used quite aptly in the standard frequency format, that is, only when the precondition of this shortcut was satisfied to a high degree. It was most often used in the suicide problem, in which the ratio between $D\&H$ cases and $D\&-H$ cases was smallest (Table 6.2), that is, in which the precondition was best satisfied. Here, 9 out of 30 participants used the comparison shortcut (and 5 participants used the Bayesian algorithm without a shortcut). In all 20 instances where the shortcut was used, 17 satisfied the strict outcome criterion, and the remaining 3 were accurate to within 4 percentage points.

Because of the strict rounding criterion, the numerical estimates of the participants using Bayesian reasoning can be directly read from Table 6.2. For instance, in the short frequency version of the mammography problem, 43.3% of participants (see Figure 6.4) came up with a frequency estimate of 8 out of 103 (or another value equivalent to 7.8%, or between 7% and 8%).

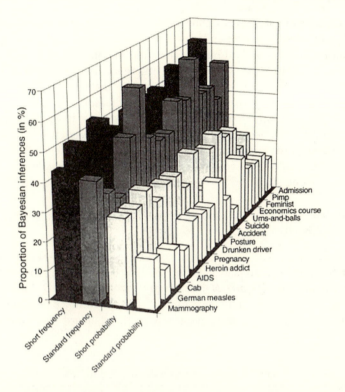

Figure 6.4 Proportion of Bayesian inferences in the 15 problems of Study 1. Standard probability = probability format with standard menu; short frequency = frequency format with short menu; and so on.

The empirical result in Figure 6.4 is consistent with the theoretical result that frequency formats can be handled by Bayesian algorithms that are computationally simpler than those required by probability formats.

Prediction 2: Probability formats elicit a larger proportion of Bayesian inferences for the short menu than for the standard menu.

The percentages of Bayesian inferences in probability formats were 16% and 28% for the standard menu and the short menu, respectively. Prediction 2 holds for each of the 15 problems (Figure 6.4).

Prediction 3: The proportion of Bayesian inferences elicited by the frequency format is independent of the menu.

The effect of the menu largely, but not completely, disappeared in the frequency format. The short menu elicited 3.7 percentage points more Bayesian strategies than the standard menu. The residual superiority of the short menu could have the following cause: Result 2 (attentional demands) states that in natural sampling it is sufficient for an organism to monitor either the frequencies $d\&h$ and d or $d\&h$ and $d\&-h$. We have chosen the former pair for the short menus in our studies and thus reduced the Bayesian computation by one step, that of adding up $d\&h$ and $d\&-h$ to d, which was part of the Bayesian computation in the standard but not the short menu. This additional computational step is consistent with the small difference in the proportions of Bayesian inferences found between the two menus in the frequency formats.

How does the impact of format on Bayesian reasoning compare with that of menu? The effect of the format was about three times larger than that of the menu (29.9 and 21.6 percentage points difference compared with 12.1 and 3.7). Equally striking, the largest percentage of Bayesian inferences in the two probability menus (28%) was considerably smaller than the smallest in the two frequency menus (46%).

Non-Bayesian Reasoning   We found three major non-Bayesian cognitive strategies (see Table 6.3).

Joint Occurrence.   The most frequent non-Bayesian strategy was a computation of the joint occurrence of D and H. Depending on the menu, this involved calculating $p(H)p(D|H)$, or simply "picking" $p(H\&D)$ (or the corresponding values for the frequency format). Joint occurrence does *not* neglect base rates; it neglects the false alarm rate in the standard menu and $p(D)$ in

Table 6.3 Cognitive strategies in Study 1

| | | Information format and menu | | | | | |
| | | Probability | | Frequency | | | |
Cognitive strategy	Formal equivalent	Standard	Short	Standard	Short	Total	% of total
Bayesian	$p(H\|D)$	69	126	204	221	620	34.9
Joint occurrence	$p(H\&D)$	39	97	20	97	253	14.3
Adjusted joint occurrence	$p(H\&D) \pm .05$		64		55	119	6.7
Fisherian	$p(D\|H)$	67		36		103	5.8
Adjusted Fisherian	$p(D\|H) \pm .05$	32		19		51	2.9
Multiply all	$p(D)p(H\&D)$		79		12	91	5.1
Likelihood subtraction	$p(D\|H) - p(D\|-H)$	30		4		34	1.9
Base rate only	$p(H)$	6		13		19	1.1
Less frequent strategies (<1% of total)		71	32	60	29	192	10.8
Not identified		119	52	89	32	292	16.5
Total		433	450	445	446	1,774[a]	100.0

Note: Numbers are absolute frequencies.

a. The sum of total answers is 1,774 rather than 1,800 (60 participants times 30 tasks) because of some participants' refusals to answer and a few missing data.

the short menu. Joint occurrence always underestimates the Bayesian posterior unless $p(D) = 1$. From participants' "write aloud" protocols, we learned about a variant, which we call *adjusted joint occurrence*, in which the participant starts with joint occurrence and adjusts it slightly (5 or fewer percentage points).

Fisherian.   Not all statisticians are Bayesians. Ronald A. Fisher, who invented the analysis of variance and promoted significance testing, certainly was not. In Fisher's (1955) theory of significance testing, an inference from data D to a null hypothesis H_0 is based solely on $p(D|H_0)$, which is known as the "exact level of significance." The exact level of significance ignores base rates and false alarm rates. With some reluctance, we labeled the second most frequent non-Bayesian strategy—picking $p(D|H)$ and ignoring everything else—"Fisherian." Our hesitation lay in the fact that it is one thing to ignore everything else besides $p(D|H)$, as Fisher's significance testing method does, and quite another thing to confuse $p(D|H)$ with $p(H|D)$. For instance, a p value of 1% is often erroneously believed to mean, by both researchers and some statistical textbook authors (see Chapter 13), that the probability of the null hypothesis being true is 1%. Thus the term *Fisherian* refers to this widespread misinterpretation rather than to Fisher's actual ideas (we hope that Sir Ronald would forgive us).

There exist several related accounts of the strategy for inferring $p(H|D)$ solely on the basis of $p(D|H)$ Included in these are the tendency to infer "cue validity" from "category validity" (Medin, Wattenmaker, & Michalski, 1987) and the related thesis that people have spontaneous access to sample spaces that correspond to categories (e.g., cancer) rather than to features associated with categories (Gavanski & Hui, 1992). Unlike the Bayesian algorithms and joint occurrence, the Fisherian strategy is menu specific: It cannot be elicited from the short menu. We observed from participants' "write aloud" protocols the use of a variant, which we call *adjusted Fisherian*, in which the participant started with $p(D|H)$ and then adjusted this value slightly (5 or fewer percentage points) in the direction of some other information.

Likelihood Subtraction.   Jerzy Neyman and Egon S. Pearson challenged Fisher's null-hypothesis testing. They argued that hypothesis testing is a decision between (at least) two hypotheses that is based on a comparison of the probability of the observed data under both, which they construed as the likelihood ratio $p(D|H) / p(D|-H)$. We observed a version of the Neyman–Pearson method, the *likelihood subtraction* strategy, which computes $p(D|H) - p(D|-H)$. As in Neyman–Pearson hypotheses testing, this strategy makes no use of prior probabilities and thus neglects base-rate information. The cognitive strategy is menu specific (it can only be elicited by the standard menu) and occurred predominantly in the probability format. In Robert Nozick's account, likelihood subtraction, also known as ΔR, is considered a measure of evidential support (see Schum, 1994), and McKenzie (1994) has simulated the performance of this and other non-Bayesian strategies.

Others.   There were cases of *multiply all* in the short menu (the logic of which escaped us) and a few cases of *base rate only* in the standard menu (a proportion similar to that reported in Gigerenzer, Hell, & Blank, 1988). We identified a total of 10.8% other strategies; these are not described here because each was used in fewer than 1% of the solutions.

Summary of Study 1

The standard probability format—the information representation used in most earlier studies—elicited 16% Bayesian inferences. When information was presented in a frequency format, this proportion jumped to 46% in the standard menu and 50% in the short menu. The results of Study 1 are consistent with Predictions 1, 2, and 3. Frequency formats, in contrast to probability formats, "invite" Bayesian reasoning, a result that is consistent with the computational simplicity of Bayesian algorithms entailed by frequencies. Two of the three major classes of non-Bayesian strategies our participants used—Fisherian and likelihood subtraction—mimic statistical inferential algorithms used and discussed in the literature.

Study 2: Cognitive Strategies for Probability Formats

In this study we concentrated on probability and relative frequency rather than on frequency formats. Thus, we explored cognitive strategies in the two formats used by almost all previous studies on base-rate neglect. Our goal was to test Prediction 4 and to provide another test of Prediction 2.

We used two formats, probability and relative frequency, and three menus: standard, short, and hybrid. The hybrid menu displayed $p(H)$, $p(D|H)$, and $p(D)$, or the respective relative frequencies. The first two pieces come from the standard menu, the third from the short menu. With the probability format and the hybrid menu, a Bayesian algorithm amounts to solving the following equation:

$$p(H|D) = \frac{p(H)p(D|H)}{p(D)} \qquad (4)$$

The two formats and the three menus were mathematically interchangeable and always entailed the same posterior probability. However, the Bayesian algorithm for the short menu is computationally simpler than that for the standard menu, and the hybrid menu is in between; therefore the proportion of Bayesian inferences should increase from the standard to the hybrid to the short menu (extended Prediction 2). In contrast, the Bayesian algorithms for the probability and relative frequency formats are computationally equivalent; thus there should be no difference between these two formats (Prediction 4).

Method

Fifteen students from the fields of biology, linguistics, English studies, German studies, philosophy, political science, and management at the University of

Konstanz, Germany, served as participants. Eight were men, and 7 were women; the median age was 22 years. They were paid for their participation and studied in one group. None was familiar with Bayes's rule.

We used 24 problems, half from Study 1 and the other half new.[4] For each of the 24 problems, the information was presented in three menus, which resulted in a total of 72 tasks. Each participant performed all 72 tasks. We randomly assigned half of the problems to the probability format and half to the relative frequency format; each participant thus answered half of the problems in each format. All probabilities and relative frequencies were stated in percentages. The questions were always posed in terms of single-event probabilities.

Six 1-hour sessions were scheduled, spaced equally over a 3-week interval. In each session, 12 tasks were performed. Participants received the 72 tasks in different orders, which were determined as follows: (a) Tasks that differed only in menu were never given in the same session, and (b) the three menus were equally frequent in every session. Within these two constraints, the 72 tasks were randomly assigned to six groups of 12 tasks each, with the 12 tasks within each group randomly ordered. These six groups were randomly assigned to the six sessions for each participant. Finally, to control for possible order effects within the three (two) pieces of information (Kroznick, Li, & Lehman, 1990), we determined the order randomly for each participant.

The procedure was the same as in Study 1, except that we had participants do an even larger number of inference problems and that we did not use the "write aloud" instruction. However, participants could (and did) spontaneously "write aloud." After a student had completed all 72 tasks, he or she received a new booklet. This contained copies of a sample of 6 tasks the student had worked on, showing the student's probability estimates, notes, drawings, calculations, and so forth. Attached to each task was a questionnaire in which the student was asked, "Which information did you use for your estimates?" and "How did you derive your estimate from the information? Please describe this process as precisely as you can." Thus, in Study 2, we had only limited "write aloud" protocols and after-the-fact interviews available. A special prize of 25 deutsche marks was offered for the person with the best performance.

Results

We could identify cognitive strategies in 67% of 1,080 probability judgments. Table 6.4 shows the distribution of the cognitive strategies for the two formats as well as for the three menus.

4. Study 2 was performed before Study 1 but is presented here second because it builds on the central Study 1. In a few cases the numerical information in the problems (e.g., German measles problem) was different in the two studies.

Table 6.4 Cognitive strategies in Study 2

Cognitive strategy	Formal equivalent	Information format		Information menu			Total	% of total
		Relative frequency	Probability	Standard	Hybrid	Short		
Joint occurance	$p(H\&D)$	91	88	46	31	102	179	16.6
Bayesian	$p(H\,|\,D)$	60	66	23	40	63	126	11.7
Fisherian	$p(D\,|\,H)$	46	45	41	50		91	8.4
Adjusted Fisherian	$p(D\,|\,H)\pm.05$	20	29	20	29		49	4.5
Multiply all	$p(D)p(H\&D)$	11	27		3	35	38	3.5
False alarm complement	$1 - p(D\,|\,{-}H)$	17	20	37			37	3.4
Likelihood subtraction	$p(D\,|\,H) - p(D\,|\,{-}H)$	19	9	28			28	2.6
Base rate only	$p(H)$	14	10	14	10		24	2.2
Total negatives	$1 - p(D)$	10	7		9	8	17	1.6
Positives times base rate	$p(D)p(H)$	7	7		14		14	1.3
Postives times hit rate	$p(D)p(D\,|\,H)$	4	9		13		13	1.2
Hit rate minus base rate	$p(D\,|\,H) - p(H)$	6	5	3	8		11	1.0
Less frequent strategies (<1% of total)		60	37	37	34	26	97	9.0
Not identified		175	181	111	119	126	356	33.0
Total		540	540	360	360	360	1,080	100.0

Note: Numbers are absolute frequencies.

Bayesian Reasoning

Prediction 4: Relative frequency formats elicit the same (small) proportion of Bayesian inferences as probability formats.

Table 6.4 shows that the number of Bayesian inferences is not larger for the relative frequency format (60) than for the probability format (66). Consistent with Prediction 4, the numbers are about the same. More generally, Bayesian and non-Bayesian inferences were spread about equally between the two formats. Therefore, we do not distinguish probability and relative frequency formats in our further analysis.

Prediction 2 (extended to three menus): The proportion of Bayesian inferences elicited by the probability format is lowest for the standard menu followed in ascending order by the hybrid and short menus.

Study 2 allows for a second test of Prediction 2, now with three menus. Bayesian inferences almost doubled from the standard to the hybrid menu and almost tripled in the short menu (Table 6.4). Thus the prediction holds again. In Study 1, the standard probability menu elicited 16% Bayesian inferences, as opposed to 28% for the short menu. In Study 2, the corresponding percentages of Bayesian inferences in probability formats were generally lower, 6.4% and 17.5%. What remained unchanged, however, was the difference between the two menus, about 12 percentage points, which is consistent with Prediction 2.

Non-Bayesian Reasoning   Study 2 replicated the three major classes of non-Bayesian strategies identified in Study 1: joint occurrence, Fisherian, and likelihood subtraction. There was also a simpler variant of the last, the *false alarm complement* strategy, which computes $1 - p(D|-H)$ and is a shortcut for likelihood subtraction when diagnosticity (the hit rate) is high. The other new strategies—"total negatives," "positives times base rate," "positives times hit rate," and "hit rate minus base rate"—were only or predominantly elicited by the hybrid menu and seemed to us to be trial and error calculations. They seem to have been used in situations in which the participants had no idea of how to reason from the probability or relative frequency format and tried somehow to integrate the information (such as by multiplying everything).

Are Individual Inferences Menu Dependent?   Each participant worked on each problem in three different menus. This allows us to see to what extent the cognitive strategies and probability estimates of each individual were stable across menus. The degree of menu dependence (the sensitivity of strategies and estimates to changes in menu) in probability formats was striking. The number of times the same strategy could be used across the three menus is some number between 0 and 360 (24 problems times 15 participants). The actual number was only 16 and consisted of 10 Bayesian and 6 joint occurrence strategies. Thus in 96% of the 360 triples, the cognitive strategy was never the same across the three menus.

The reasoning of two participants, Rudiger and Oliver, illustrates this dependence of thought on menu. They try to solve the German measles problem, in which the task is to estimate the probability $p(H|D)$ of severe prenatal damage in the child (H) if the mother had German measles during pregnancy (D). In the standard menu, the information (probability expressed in percentages) was $p(H) = 0.5\%$, $p(D|H) = 40\%$, and $p(D|-H) = 0.01\%$; in the hybrid menu, $p(H) = 0.5\%$, $p(D|H) = 40\%$, and $p(D) = 0.21\%$; and in the short menu, $p(D) = 0.21\%$ and $p(D\&H) = 0.2\%$.

> *Rudiger, age 22, management.* In the standard menu, Rudiger focused on $p(D|H)$, explaining that because a child of an infected mother is at such high risk (40%), his estimate would accordingly be high. He adjusted $p(D|H)$ by 5% and estimated the posterior probability of severe prenatal damage as 35% (adjusted Fisherian). In the hybrid menu, he picked the base rate and estimated the same probability as 0.5% with the argument that $p(D|H)$ and $p(D)$ "are without significance" (*base rate only*). In the short menu, he picked $p(H\&D)$ and estimated 0.2% because "this is the information that specifies the probability of severe damage in the child. The percentage of infected mothers, however, is irrelevant" (*joint occurrence*).

> *Oliver, age 22, German literature.* In the standard menu, Oliver stated that the "correlation between not having damage and nevertheless having measles," as he paraphrased $p(D|-H)$, was the only relevant information. He calculated $1 - p(D|-H) = 99.99\%$ and rounded to 100%, which was his estimate (*false alarm complement*). In the hybrid menu, he concluded that the only relevant information was the base rate of severe prenatal damage, and his estimate consequently dropped to 0.5% (*base rate only*). In the short menu, he determined the proportion of severe damage and measles in all cases with German measles, which led him to the Bayesian answer of 95.3%.

The thinking of Rudiger and Oliver illustrates how strongly cognitive strategies can depend on the representation of information, resulting in estimates that may vary as much as from 0.5% to 100% (as in Oliver's case). These cases also reveal how helpless and inconsistent participants were when information was represented in a probability or relative frequency format.

The Effect of Extensive Practice

With 72 inference problems per participant, Study 2 can answer the question of whether mere practice (without feedback or instruction) increased the proportion of Bayesian inferences. There was virtually no increase during the first three sessions, which comprised 36 tasks. Only thereafter did the proportion increase—from .04, .07, and .14 (standard, hybrid, and short menus, respectively) in the first three sessions to .08, .14, and .21 in Sessions 4 through 6. Thus extensive practice seems to be needed to increase the number of Bayesian responses. In Study 1, with "only" 30 problems per participant, the proportion increased slightly from .30 in the first session to .38 in the second. More generally, with respect to all cognitive strategies, we found that when information was presented in a frequency format, our participants became more consistent in their use of strategies with time and practice, whereas there was little if any improvement over time with probability formats.

Summary of Study 2

Our theoretical results were that the computational complexity of Bayesian algorithms varied between the three probability menus but not between the probability and relative frequency formats. Empirical tests showed that the actual proportion of Bayesian inferences followed this pattern; the proportion strongly increased across menus but did not differ between the probability and the relative frequency formats, which is consistent with Predictions 2 and 4.

General Discussion

We return to our initial question: Is the mind, by design, predisposed against performing Bayesian inference? The conclusion of 30 years of heuristics-and-biases research would suggest as much. This previous research, however, has consistently neglected Feynman's (1967) insight that mathematically equivalent information formats need not be psychologically equivalent. An evolutionary point of view suggests that the mind is tuned to frequency formats, which is the information format humans encountered long before the advent of probability theory. We have combined Feynman's insight with the evolutionary argument and explored the computational implications: "Which computations are required for Bayesian inference by a given information format and menu?" Mathematically equivalent representations of information can entail computationally different Bayesian algorithms. We have argued that information representation affects cognitive strategies in the same way. We deduced four novel predictions concerning when information formats and menus make a difference and when they do not. Data from more than 2,800 individual problem solutions are consistent with the predictions. Frequency formats made many participants' inferences strictly conform (in terms of outcome and process) to Bayes's rule without any teaching or instruction. These results were found for a number of inferential problems, including classic demonstrations of non-Bayesian inference such as the cab problem and the mammography problem.

The results of the 15 problems in Study 1 constitute most of the data available today about Bayesian inference with frequency information. We know of only a few studies that have looked at Bayesian inference through frequency formats. Christensen-Szalanski and Beach (1982) sequentially presented symptom and disease information for 100 patients and asked participants to estimate $p(\text{disease} \mid \text{positive})$. Thus, their format was mixed: natural sampling of frequencies with a single-event probability judgment (see also Gavanski & Hui, 1992). The means from the natural sampling condition conformed better to

Bayes's rule than those from the standard probability version; however, only means—and not individual judgments or processes—were analyzed. Cosmides and Tooby (1996) constructed a dozen or so versions of the medical problem presented by Casscells et al. (1978). They converted, piece by piece, probability information into frequencies and showed how this increases, at the same pace, the proportion of Bayesian answers. They reported that when the frequency format was mixed—that is, when the information was represented in frequencies but the single-point estimate was a single-event probability or vice versa—the effect of the frequency format was reduced by roughly half. Their results are consistent with our theoretical framework.

At the beginning of this chapter, we contrasted the belief of the Enlightenment probabilists that the laws of probability theory were the laws of the mind (at least for *hommes éclairés*) with the belief of the proponents of the heuristics-and-biases program that the laws of probability are not the laws of the mind. We side with neither view, nor with those who have settled somewhere in between the two extremes. Both views are based on an incomplete analysis: They focus on cognitive strategies, good or bad, without making the connection between a strategy and the information format it has been designed for. Through exploration of the computational consequences of an evolutionary argument, a novel theoretical framework for understanding intuitive Bayesian inference has emerged.

Why have so many experimental studies used the standard probability format? Part of the reason may be historical accident. There is nothing in Bayes's rule that dictates whether the mathematical probabilities pertain to single events or to frequencies, nor is the choice of format and menus specified by the formal rules of probability. Thomas Bayes himself seemed not to have sided with either single-event probabilities or frequencies. Like his fellow Enlightenment probabilists, he blurred the distinction between warranted degrees of belief and objective frequencies by trying to combine the two (Earman, 1992). Thus the experimental research on Bayesian inference could as well have started with frequency representations, if not for the historical accident that it became tied to Savage's (1954) agenda of bringing singular events back into the domain of probability theory. For instance, if psychological research had been inspired by behavioral ecology, foraging theory, or other ecological approaches to animal behavior in which Bayes's rule figures prominently (e.g., Stephens & Krebs, 1986), then the information format used in human studies might have been frequencies from the very beginning.

We would like to emphasize that our results hold for an elementary form of Bayesian inference, with binary hypotheses and data. Pregnancy tests, mammograms, HIV tests, and the like are everyday examples where this elementary form of inference is of direct relevance. However, there exist other situations in which hypotheses, data, or both are multinomial or continuous and where there is not only one datum, but several. Massaro (1998), for instance, conjectured that when there are two or more pieces of evidence or cues—such as two medical test results—a representation in natural frequencies would no longer help to improve Bayesian reasoning. Krauss, Martignon, and Hoffrage

(1999), in contrast, have shown that natural sampling can be generalized to two cues and observed about the same improvement in Bayesian reasoning with two cues as in the experiments reported here. However, beyond some number of cues, Bayesian calculations, even using natural frequencies, will become extremely complicated or intractable. Here, models of bounded rationality can take over where intuitive Bayesian reasoning leaves off. The following two chapters deal with fast and frugal heuristics that can survive in complex real-world environments by virtue of their simplicity and robustness.

III

BOUNDED RATIONALITY

Trying to change a university is like trying to move a cemetery—this metaphor is easily understood. But why would Herbert A. Simon have proposed a pair of scissors as a metaphor for bounded rationality? To understand the power of human intelligence, one needs to analyze the match between cognitive strategies and the structure of environments. Together they are like a pair of scissors, each blade of little use on its own but effective in concert with the other. The program of "bounded rationality" is the third research strategy explored in this book. Models of bounded rationality address the following question: How do people make decisions in the real world, where time is short, knowledge lacking, and other resources limited?

The program of bounded rationality confronts us with two challenging questions. First, what are the simple heuristics that people use given scarce resources (the cognitive blade)? Second, what structures of information can these heuristics exploit, that is, in what environments do they succeed and fail? The second question concerns the ecological rationality of heuristics (the fit between the cognitive and environmental blades), which emphasizes the interface between bounded and ecological rationality. By analyzing the match between heuristic and environment, we can predict how fast, frugal, and accurate a heuristic will be.

The two chapters in this section focus on the first question, although they also contain the seeds of an answer to the second question, which is explored in depth in two books, *Simple Heuristics That Make Us Smart* (Gigerenzer, Todd, & the ABC Research Group, 1999) and *Bounded Rationality: The Adaptive Toolbox* (Gigerenzer & Selten, 2000). Chapter 7 contains the essence (but not the name) of the "Take The Best" heuristic, which makes decisions on the basis of only one good reason and ignores the rest. The surprisingly good performance of this heuristic, first demonstrated in Chapter 8, initially elicited one or both of two reactions: "It cannot be!" or "We knew it all along!"

I have been asked, How did you discover these fast and frugal heuristics? In fact, most of the credit goes to my students and colleagues in our interdisciplinary research group, the Center for Adaptive Behavior and Cognition. We benefited from a healthy mixture of persistence and luck. The discovery of the recognition heuristic and the less-is-more effect illustrates how insight can emerge from failure to accomplish something else. In an article on probabilistic mental model (PMM) theory (Chapter 7), Ulrich Hoffrage, Heinz Kleinbölting, and I derived a bold prediction about the "hard–easy" effect, in which people are overconfident about their ability to solve hard but not easy questions. The prediction was that the hard–easy effect would disappear when both kinds of questions are representatively sampled.

After the article appeared, we designed an experiment to test the prediction. We needed a hard and an easy set of questions and a domain from which to draw representative samples. At that time, I was teaching at the University of Salzburg, a cheerful architectural blend of postmodern Bauhaus and Austrian Empire-style marble and gold. Common sense dictated that German cities, about which students there knew a lot, would be an easy set, and American cities, about which they knew comparatively little, would be a hard set. How could it be any other way? We drew 100 random pairs of cities from the 75 largest German cities, such as Bielefeld and Heidelberg, and another 100 random pairs of the 75 largest American cities, such as San Diego and San Antonio. The task was to judge which of two cities has the larger population. When we saw the results, we could not believe our eyes. These German-speaking students gave slightly more accurate answers for the American cities (76.0%) than for the German cities (75.6%). How could they have made as many correct judgments in a domain about which they knew little as in one about which they knew a lot?

Salzburg has excellent restaurants. One night our research group had dinner at one of them to mourn the failed experiment—we could not test the prediction because we failed to generate a hard and an easy set of questions. As we tried in vain to make sense of the counterintuitive result, our colleague Anton Kühberger politely remarked: "Why don't you look in your PMM paper? The answer is there." What an embarrassing moment: He was right. Our paper said that having heard of one city and not of the other is a cue that the first city is larger—a fast and frugal strategy that we later named the "recognition heuristic." How could this heuristic explain our puzzling result? Because most of the students in Salzburg had heard of all the largest German cities, they could not use the recognition heuristic in that set. But when it came to American cities, many of which they had never heard, they could use it. By exploiting the wisdom in missing knowledge, the recognition heuristic can lead to highly accurate judgments when lack of recognition is not random but systematically correlated with the criterion (here, population size). Lack of recognition can be highly informative.

So the less-is-more effect was discovered accidentally when it ruined an experiment. After I left the architecturally playful University of Salzburg for the stolidly gothic University of Chicago, I met Daniel Goldstein, with whom

I began to study the recognition heuristic and the less-is-more effect systematically (Goldstein & Gigerenzer, 1999). Meanwhile, others succeeded in testing and confirming our original prediction about the hard–easy effect (Juslin, 1993; Juslin, Winman, & Olsson, 2000; Klayman et al., 1999). This story illustrates how scientific discovery can come by failing to do one thing and yet achieving another.

7

Probabilistic Mental Models

Do people think they know more than they really do? In the last 20 years, cognitive psychologists have amassed a large and apparently damning body of experimental evidence on overconfidence in knowledge, evidence that is in turn part of an even larger and more damning literature on so-called cognitive biases. The cognitive bias research claims that people are naturally prone to making mistakes in reasoning and memory, including the mistake of over-estimating their knowledge. In this chapter, we propose a new theoretical model for confidence in knowledge based on the more charitable assumption that people are good judges of the reliability of their knowledge, provided that the knowledge is representatively sampled from a specified reference class. We claim that this model both predicts new experimental results (that we have tested) and explains a wide range of extant experimental findings on confidence, including some perplexing inconsistencies.

Moreover, it is the first theoretical framework to integrate the two most striking and stable effects that have emerged from confidence studies—the overconfidence effect and the hard–easy effect—and to specify the conditions under which these effects can be made to appear, disappear, and even invert. In most recent studies (including our own, reported herein), participants are asked to choose between two alternatives for each of a series of general-knowledge questions. Here is a typical example: "Which city has more inhabitants? (a) Hyderabad or (b) Islamabad." Participants choose what they believe to be the correct answer and then are directed to specify their degree of confidence (usually on a 50%–100% scale) that their answer is indeed correct. After the participants answer many questions of this sort, the responses are sorted by confidence level, and the relative frequencies of correct answers in each confidence category are calculated. The *overconfidence effect* occurs when the confidence judgments are larger than the relative frequencies of the correct answers; the *hard–easy effect* occurs when the degree of overconfidence increases with the difficulty of the questions, where the difficulty is measured by the percentage of correct answers.

The work on which this chapter is based was coauthored with U. Hoffrage and H. Kleinbölting.

Both effects seem to be stable. Fischhoff (1982) reviewed the attempts to eliminate overconfidence by numerous "debiasing methods," such as giving rewards, clarifying instructions, warning participants in advance about the problem, and using better response modes—all to no avail. He concluded that these manipulations "have so far proven relatively ineffective," and that over-confidence was "moderately robust" (p. 440). Von Winterfeldt and Edwards (1986, p. 539) agreed that "overconfidence is a reliable, reproducible finding." Yet these robust phenomena still await a theory. In particular, we lack a comprehensive theoretical framework that explains both phenomena, as well as the various exceptions reported in the literature, and integrates the several local explanatory attempts already advanced. That is the aim of this chapter. It consists of three parts: (a) an exposition of the proposed theory of probabilistic mental models (PMM theory), including predictions of new experimental findings based on the theory; (b) a report of our experimental tests confirming these predictions; and (c) an explanation of apparent anomalies in previous experimental results by means of PMMs.

PMM Theory

This theory deals with spontaneous confidence—that is, with an immediate reaction, not the product of long reflection. Figure 7.1 shows a flow chart of the processes that generate confidence judgments in two-alternative general-knowledge tasks. There are two strategies. When presented with a two-alternative confidence task, the participant first attempts to construct what we call a *local mental model* (local MM) of the task. This is a solution by memory and elementary logical operations. If this fails, a PMM is constructed that goes beyond the structure of the task in using probabilistic information from a natural environment.

For convenience, we illustrate the theory using a problem from the following experiments: "Which city has more inhabitants? (a) Heidelberg or (b) Bonn." As explained earlier, the participants' task is to choose a or b and to give a numerical judgment of their confidence (that the answer chosen is correct).

Local MM

We assume that the mind first attempts a direct solution that could generate certain knowledge by constructing a local MM. For instance, a participant may recall from memory that Heidelberg has a population between 100,000 and 200,000, whereas Bonn has more than 290,000 inhabitants. This is already sufficient for the answer "Bonn" and a confidence judgment of 100%. In general, a local MM can be successfully constructed if (a) precise figures can be retrieved from memory for both alternatives, (b) intervals that do not overlap can be retrieved, or (c) elementary logical operations, such as the method of exclusion, can compensate for missing knowledge. Figure 7.2 illustrates a suc-

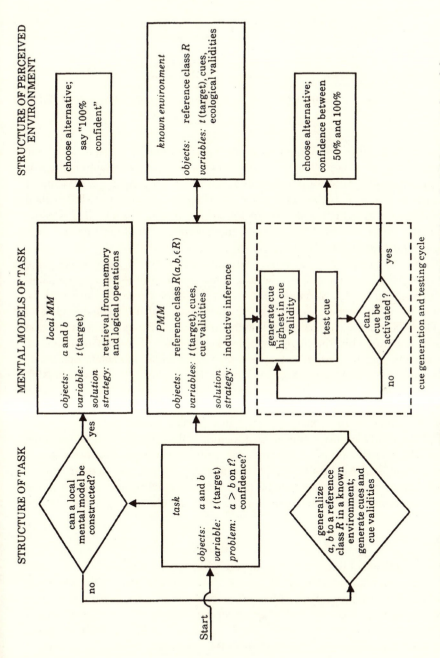

Figure 7.1 Cognitive processes in solving a two-alternative general-knowledge task. MM = mental model; PMM = probabilistic mental model.

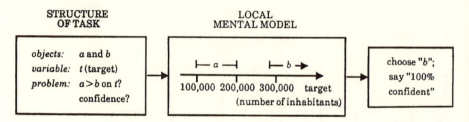

Figure 7.2 Local mental model of a two-alternative general-knowledge task.

cessful local MM for the previous example. Now consider a task in which the target variable is not quantitative (such as the number of inhabitants) but is qualitative: "If you see the nationality letter *P* on a car, is it from Poland or Portugal?" Here, either direct memory about the correct answer or the method of exclusion is sufficient to construct a local MM. The latter is illustrated by a participant reasoning "Since I know that Poland has PL it must be Portugal" (Allwood & Montgomery, 1987, p. 370).

The structure of the task must be examined to define more generally what is referred to as a local MM. The task consists of two objects, *a* and *b* (alternatives), and a target variable *t*. First, a local MM of this task is local; that is, only the two alternatives are taken into account, and no reference class of objects is constructed (see the following discussion). Second, it is direct; that is, it contains only the target variable (e.g., number of inhabitants), and no probability cues are used. Third, no inferences besides elementary operations of deductive logic (such as exclusion) occur. Finally, if the search is successful, the confidence in the knowledge produced is evaluated as certain. In these respects, our concept of a local MM is similar to what Johnson-Laird (1983, pp. 134–142) called a "mental model" in syllogistic inference.

A local MM simply matches the structure of the task; there is no use of the probability structure of an environment and, consequently, no frame for inductive inference as in a PMM. Because memory can fail, the "certain" knowledge produced can sometimes be incorrect. These failures contribute to the amount of overconfidence to be found in 100%-confident judgments.

PMM

Local MMs are of limited success in general-knowledge tasks and in most natural environments, although they seem to be sufficient for solving some syllogisms and other problems of deductive logic (see Johnson-Laird, 1983). If no local MM can be activated, it is assumed that a PMM is constructed next. A PMM solves the task by inductive inference, and it does so by putting the specific task into a larger context. A PMM connects the specific structure of the task with a probability structure of a corresponding natural environment (stored in long-term memory). In our example, a natural environment could be the class of all cities in Germany with a set of variables defined on this

class, such as the number of inhabitants. This task selects the number of inhabitants as the target and the variables that covary with this target as the cues.

A PMM is different from a local MM in several respects. First, it contains
a *reference class* of objects that includes the objects a and b. Second, it uses
a network of variables in addition to the target variable for indirect inference.
Thus it is neither local nor direct. These two features also change the third
and fourth aspects of a local MM. Probabilistic inference is part of the cognitive
process, and uncertainty is part of the outcome.

Reference Class

The term *reference class* refers to the class of objects or events that a PMM
contains. In our example, the reference class "all cities in Germany" may be
generated. To generate a reference class means to generate a set of objects
known from a person's natural environment that contains objects a and b.

The reference class determines which cues can function as probability cues
for the target variable and what their cue validities are. For instance, a valid
cue in the reference class "all cities in Germany" would be the soccer-team
cue; that is, whether a city's soccer team plays in the German soccer Bundesliga, in which the 18 best teams compete. Cities with more inhabitants are
more likely to have a team in the Bundesliga. The soccer-team cue would not
help in the Hyderabad–Islamabad task, which must be solved by a PMM containing a different reference class with different cues and cue validities.

Probability Cues

A PMM for a given task contains a reference class, a target variable, probability
cues, and cue validities. A variable is a probability cue C_i (for a target variable
in a reference class R) if the probability $p(a)$ of a being correct is different from
the conditional probability of a being correct, given that the values of a and b
differ on C_i. If the cue is a binary variable such as the soccer-team cue, this
condition can be stated as follows:

$$p(a) \neq p(a \mid aC_ib; R),$$

where aC_ib signifies the relation of a and b on the cue C_i (e.g., a has a soccer
team in the Bundesliga, but b does not) and $p(a \mid aC_ib; R)$ is the cue validity of
C_i in R.

Thus cue validities are thought of as conditional probabilities, following
Rosch (1978) rather than Brunswik (1955), who defined his "cue utilizations"
as Pearson correlations. Conditional probabilities need not be symmetric as
correlations are. This allows the cue to be a better predictor for the target than
the target is for the cue, or vice versa. Cue validity is a concept in the PMM,
whereas the corresponding concept in the environment is *ecological validity*
(Brunswik, 1955), which is the true relative frequency of any city having more
inhabitants than any other one in R if aC_ib. For example, consider the reference
class *all cities in Germany with more than 100,000 inhabitants*. The ecological

validity of the soccer-team cue here is .91 (calculated for 1988/1989 for what then was West Germany). That is, if one checked all pairs in which one city *a* has a team in the Bundesliga but the other city *b* does not, one would find that in 91% of these cases city *a* has more inhabitants.

Vicarious Functioning

Probability cues are generated, tested, and, if possible, activated. We assume that the order in which cues are generated is not random; in particular, we assume that the order reflects the hierarchy of cue validities. For the reference class *all cities in Germany*, the following cues are examples that can be generated: (a) the soccer-team cue; (b) whether one city is a state capital and the other is not (state capital cue); (c) whether one city is located in the Ruhrgebiet, the industrial center of Germany, and the other in largely rural Bavaria (industrial cue); (d) whether the letter code that identifies a city on a license plate is shorter for one city than for the other (large cities are usually abbreviated by only one letter, smaller cities by two or three; license plate cue); and (e) whether one has heard of one city and not of the other (recognition cue). Consider now the Heidelberg–Bonn problem again. The first probability cue is generated and tested to see whether it can be activated for that problem. Because neither of the two cities has a team in the Bundesliga, the first cue does not work.

In general, with a binary cue and the possibility that the participant has no knowledge, there are nine possibilities (see Figure 7.3). In only two of these can a cue be activated. In all other cases, the cue is useless (although one could further distinguish between the four known–unknown cases and the three remaining cases). If a cue cannot be activated, then a further cue is generated

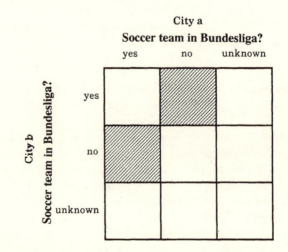

Figure 7.3 Two conditions in which a cue can be activated.

and tested. In the Heidelberg–Bonn task, none of the five cues cited earlier can in fact be activated. Finally, one cue may be generated that can be activated, such as whether one city is the capital of the country and the other is not (capital cue). This cue has a small probability of being activated—a small activation rate in R (because it applies only to pairs that include Bonn)—and it does not have a particularly high cue validity in R because it is well known that Bonn is not exactly London or Paris.

The Heidelberg–Bonn problem illustrates that probability cues may have small activation rates in R, and as a consequence, several cues may have to be generated and tested before one is found that can be activated. The capital cue that can be activated for the Heidelberg–Bonn comparison may fail for the next problem, for instance a Heidelberg–Göttingen comparison. Cues can substitute for one another from problem to problem, a process that Brunswik (1955) called "vicarious functioning."

End of Cue Generation and Testing Cycle

If (a) the number of problems is large or other kinds of time pressure apply and (b) the activation rate of cues is rather small, then one can assume that the cue generation and testing cycle ends after the first cue that can be activated has been found. Both conditions seem to be typical for general-knowledge questions. For instance, even when participants were explicitly instructed to produce all possible reasons for and against each alternative, they generated only about three on the average and four at most (Koriat, Lichtenstein, & Fischhoff, 1980). If no cue can be activated, we assume that choice is made randomly, and "confidence 50%" is chosen.

Choice of Answer and Confidence Judgment

Choice of answer and confidence judgment are determined by the cue validity. Choice follows the rule:

$$\text{choose } a \text{ if } p(a \mid aC_ib; R) > p(b \mid aC_ib; R).$$

If a is chosen, the confidence that a is correct is given by the cue validity:

$$p(a \mid aC_ib; R).$$

Note that the assumption that confidence equals cue validity is not arbitrary; it is both rational and simple in the sense that good calibration is to be expected if cue validities correspond to ecological validities. This holds true even if only one cue is activated.

Thus choice and confidence are inferred from the same activated cue. Both are expressions of the same conditional probability. Therefore, they need not be generated in the temporal sequence choice followed by confidence. The latter is, of course, typical for actual judgments and often enforced by the instructions in confidence studies.

Confidence in the Long Run and Confidence in Single Events

Until now, only confidence in single events—such as the answer "Bonn" is correct—has been discussed. Confidence in one's knowledge can also be expressed with respect to sequences of answers or events, such as "How many of the last 50 questions do you think you answered correctly?" This distinction is parallel to that between probabilities of single events and relative frequencies in the long run—a distinction that is fundamental to all discussions on the meaning of probability (see Gigerenzer et al., 1989). Probabilities of single events (confidences) and relative frequencies are not the same for many schools of probability, and we argue that they are not evaluated by the same cognitive processes either.

Consider judgments of frequency. General-knowledge tasks that involve a judgment of the frequency of correct answers (frequency tasks) can rarely be answered by constructing a local MM. The structure of the task contains one sequence of N questions and answers, and the number of correct answers is the target variable. Only limiting cases, such as small N (i.e., if only a few questions are asked) combined with the belief that all answers were correct, may allow one to solve this task by a local MM. Again, to construct a local MM of the task means that the mental model consists of only the local sequence of total N answers (no reference class), and because one attempts to solve the task by direct access to memory about the target variable, no network of probability cues is constructed.

Similarly, a PMM of a frequency task is different from a PMM of a confidence task. A confidence task about city size in Germany has "cities in Germany" as a reference class; however, a task that involves judgments of frequencies of correct answers in a series of N questions about city size has a different reference class: Its reference class will contain series of similar questions in similar testing situations. Because the target variable also differs (number of correct answers instead of number of inhabitants), the PMM of a fre-

Table 7.1 Probabilistic mental models for confidence task versus frequency task: Differences between target variables, reference classes, and probability cues

PMM	Confidence task	Frequency task
Target variable	Number of inhabitants	Number of correct answers
Reference class	Cities in Germany	Sets of general-knowledge questions in similar testing situations
Probability cues	For example, soccer-team cue or state capital cue	For example, base rates of previous performance or average confidence in N answers

Note: For illustration, questions of the Heidelberg–Bonn type are used. PMM = probabilistic mental model.

quency task will also contain different cues and cue validities. For instance, base rates of performance in earlier general knowledge or similar testing situations could serve as a probability cue for the target variable. Again, our basic assumption is that a PMM connects the structure of the task with a known structure of the participant's environment.

Table 7.1 summarizes the differences between PMMs that are implied by the two different tasks. Note that in our account, both confidences in a single event and judgments of frequency are explained by reference to experienced frequencies. However, these frequencies relate to different target variables and reference classes. We use this assumption to predict systematic differences between these kinds of judgments.

Adaptive PMMs and Representative Sampling

A PMM is an inductive device that uses the "normal" life conditions in known environments as the basis for induction. How well does the structure of probability cues defined on R in a PMM represent the actual structure of probability cues in the environment? This question is also known as that of "proper cognitive adjustment" (Brunswik, 1964, p. 22). If the order of cue validities roughly corresponds to that of the ecological validities, then the PMM is well adapted to a known environment. In Brunswik's view, cue validities are learned by observing the frequencies of co-occurrences in an environment.

A large literature exists that suggests that (a) memory is often (but not always) excellent in storing frequency information from various environments and (b) the registering of event occurrences for frequency judgments is a fairly automatic cognitive process requiring very little attention or conscious effort (e.g., Gigerenzer, 1984; Hasher, Goldstein, & Toppino, 1977; Howell & Burnett, 1978; Sedlmeier, Hertwig, & Gigerenzer, 1998; Zacks, Hasher, & Sanft, 1982). Hasher and Zacks (1979) concluded that frequency of occurrence, spatial location, time, and word meaning are among the few aspects of the environment that are encoded automatically and that encoding of frequency information is "automatic at least in part because of innate factors" (p. 360). In addition, Hintzman, Nozawa, and Irmscher (1982) proposed that frequencies are stored in memory in a nonnumerical analog mode.

Whatever the mechanism of frequency encoding, we use the following assumption for deriving our predictions: If participants had repeated experience with a reference class, a target variable, and cues in their environment, we assume that cue validities correspond well to ecological validities. (This holds true for the average in a group of participants, but individual idiosyncrasies in learning the frequency structure of the environment may occur.) This is a bold assumption made in ignorance of potential deviations between specific cue validities and ecological validities. If such deviations existed and were known, predictions by PMM theory could be improved. The assumption, however, derives support from both the literature on automatic frequency processing and a large body of neo-Brunswikian research on the correspondence between ecological validities and cue utilization (the latter of which corresponds to our cue validities; e.g., Arkes & Hammond, 1986; Armelius, 1979; Brehmer & Joyce, 1988; MacGregor & Slovic, 1986).

Note that this adaptiveness assumption does not preclude that individuals (as well as the average participant) err. Errors can occur even if a PMM is highly adapted to a given environment. For instance, if an environment is changing or is changed in the laboratory by an experimenter, an otherwise well-adapted PMM may be suboptimal in a predictable way.

Brunswik's notion of "representative sampling" is important here. If a person experienced a representative sample of objects from a reference class, one can expect his or her PMM to be better adapted to an environment than if he or she happened to experience a skewed, unrepresentative sample.

Representative sampling is also important in understanding the relation between a PMM and the task. If a PMM is well adapted, but the set of objects used in the task (questions) is not representative of the reference class in the environment, performance in tasks will be systematically suboptimal.

To avoid confusion with terms such as *calibration*, we will use the term *adaptation* only when we are referring to the relation between a PMM and a corresponding environment—not, however, for the relation between a PMM and a task.

Predictions

A concrete example can help motivate our first prediction. Two of our colleagues, K and O, are eminent wine tasters. K likes to make a gift of a bottle of wine from his cellar to Friend O, on the condition that O guesses what country or region the grapes were grown in. Because O knows the relevant cues, O can usually pick a region with some confidence. O also knows that K sometimes selects a quite untypical exemplar from his ample wine cellar to test Friend O's limits. Thus, for each individual wine, O can infer the probability that the grapes ripened in, say, Portugal as opposed to South Africa with considerable confidence from his knowledge about cues. In the long run, however, O nevertheless expects the relative frequency of correct answers to be lower because K occasionally selects unusual items.

Consider tests of general knowledge, which share an important feature with the wine-tasting situation: Questions are selected to be somewhat difficult and sometimes misleading. This practice is common and quite reasonable for testing people's limits, as in the wine-tasting situation. Indeed, there is apparently not a single study on confidence in knowledge in which a reference class has been defined and a representative (or random) sample of general-knowledge questions has been drawn from this population. For instance, consider the reference class "metropolis" and the geographical north-south location as the target variable. A question like "Which city is farther north? (a) New York or (b) Rome" is likely to appear in a general-knowledge test (almost everyone gets it wrong), whereas a comparison between Berlin and Rome is not.

The crucial point is that confidence and frequency judgments refer to different kinds of reference classes. *A set of questions can be representative with respect to one reference class and, at the same time, selected with respect to the other class.* Thus, a set of 50 general-knowledge questions of the city type may be representative for the reference class "sets of general-knowledge questions" but not for the reference class "cities in Germany" (because city pairs have been selected for being difficult or misleading). Asking for a confidence judgment summons up a PMM on the basis of the reference class "cities in Germany"; asking for a frequency judgment summons up a PMM on the basis of the reference class "sets of general-knowledge questions." The first prediction can now be stated.

1. *Typical general-knowledge tasks elicit both overconfidence and accurate frequency judgments.*

By "typical" general-knowledge tasks we refer to a set of questions that is representative for the reference class "sets of general-knowledge questions."

This prediction is derived in the following way: If (a) PMMs for confidence tasks are well adapted to an environment containing a reference class R (e.g., all cities in Germany) and (b) the actual set of questions is not representative for R but selected for difficult pairs of cities, then confidence judgments exhibit overconfidence. Condition A is part of our theory (the simplifying assumption we just made), and Condition B is typical for the general-knowledge questions used in studies on confidence as well as in other testing situations.

If (a) PMMs for frequency-of-correct-answer tasks are well adapted with respect to an environment containing a reference class R' (e.g., the set of all general-knowledge tests experienced earlier), and (b) the actual set of questions is representative for R', then frequency judgments are expected to be accurate. Again, Condition A is part of our theory, and Condition B will be realized in our experiments by using a typical set of general-knowledge questions.

Taken together, the prediction is that the same person will exhibit overconfidence when asked for her confidence that a particular answer is correct and accurate estimates when asked for a judgment of the frequency of correct answers. This prediction is shown by the two points on the left side of Figure 7.4. This prediction cannot be derived from any of the previous accounts of overconfidence.

To introduce the second prediction, we return to the wine-tasting story. Assume that K changes his habit of selecting unusual wines from his wine cellar and instead buys a representative sample of French red wines and lets O guess from what region they come. However, K does not tell O about the new sampling technique. O's average confidence judgments will now be close to the proportion of correct answers. In the long run, O nevertheless expects the proportion of correct answers to be smaller, still assuming the familiar testing situation in which wines were selected, not randomly sampled. Thus O's frequency judgments will show underestimation.

Consider now a set of general-knowledge questions that is a random sample from a defined reference class in the participant's natural environment. We use

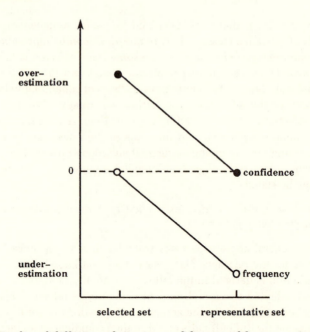

Figure 7.4 Predicted differences between confidence and frequency judgments—
the confidence–frequency effect.

the term *natural environment* to denote a knowledge domain familiar to the
participants in the study. This is a necessary (although not sufficient) condition
to assume that PMMs are, on the average, well adapted. In the experiments
reported herein, we used West German participants and the reference class
"all cities with more than 100,000 inhabitants in West Germany." (The study
was conducted before the unification of Germany.) The second prediction is
about this situation:

> 2. *If the set of general-knowledge tasks is randomly sampled from a nat-*
> *ural environment, we expect overconfidence to be zero, but frequency*
> *judgments to exhibit underestimation.*

Derivation is as before: If PMMs for confidence tasks are well adapted with
respect to R, and the actual set of questions is a representative sample from
R, then overconfidence is expected to disappear. If PMMs for frequency-of-
correct-answers tasks are well adapted with respect to R', and the actual set
of questions is not representative for R', then frequency judgments are expected to be underestimations of true frequencies.

Again, this prediction cannot be derived from earlier accounts. Figure 7.4
shows Predictions 1 and 2. The predicted differences between confidence and
frequency judgments are referred to as the *confidence–frequency effect*.

Testing these predictions also allows for testing the assumption of well-
adapted PMMs for the confidence task. Assume that PMMs are not well

adapted. Then a representative sample of city questions should not generate zero overconfidence but rather over- or underconfidence, depending on whether cue validities overestimate or underestimate ecological validities. Similarly, if PMMs for frequency judgments are not well adapted, frequency judgments should deviate from true frequencies in typical general-knowledge tasks. Independent of the degree of adaptation, however, the confidence–frequency effect should emerge, but the curves in Figure 7.4 would be transposed upward or downward.

We turn now to the standard way in which overconfidence has been demonstrated in previous research, comparing confidence levels with relative frequencies of correct answers at each confidence level. This standard comparison runs into a conceptual problem well known in probability theory and statistics: A discrepancy between subjective probabilities in single events (i.e., the confidence that a particular answer is correct) and relative frequencies in the long run is not a bias in the sense of a violation of probability theory, as is clear from several points of view within probability theory. For instance, for a frequentist such as Richard von Mises (1928/1957), probability theory is about frequencies (in the long run), not about single events. According to this view, the common interpretation of overconfidence as a bias is based on comparing apples with oranges. What if that conceptual problem is avoided and, instead, the relative frequency of correct answers in each confidence category is compared with the estimated relative frequency in each confidence category? PMM theory makes an interesting prediction for this situation, following the same reasoning as for the frequency judgments in Predictions 1 and 2 (which were estimated frequency-of-correct answers in a series of N questions, whereas estimated relative frequencies in each confidence category are the concern here):

3. *Comparing estimated relative frequencies with true relative frequencies of correct answers makes overestimation disappear.*

More precisely, if the set of general-knowledge questions is selected, over- or underestimation is expected to be zero; if the set is randomly sampled, underestimation is expected. Thus PMM theory predicts that the distinction between confidence and relative frequency is psychologically real, in the sense that participants do not believe that a confidence judgment of X% implies a relative frequency of X%, and vice versa. We know of no study on overconfidence that has investigated this issue. Most have assumed instead that there is, psychologically, no difference.

Prediction 4 concerns the hard–easy effect, which says that overconfidence increases when questions get more difficult (e.g., Lichtenstein & Fischhoff, 1977). The effect refers to confidence judgments only, not to frequency judgments. In our account, the hard–easy effect is not simply a function of difficulty. Rather, it is a function of difficulty and a separate dimension, selected versus representative sampling. (Note that the terms *hard* and *easy* refer to the relative difficulty of two samples of items, whereas the terms *selected* and *representative* refer to the relation between one sample and a reference class in the person's environment.) PMM theory specifies conditions under which the hard–easy effect occurs, disappears, and is reversed. A reversed hard–easy effect means that overconfidence decreases when questions are more difficult.

In Figure 7.5, the line descending from H to E represents a hard–easy effect: Overconfidence in the hard set is larger than in the easy set. The important distinction (in addition to hard vs. easy) is whether a set was obtained by representative sampling or was selected. For instance, assume that PMMs are well adapted and that two sets of tasks differing in percentage correct (i.e., in difficulty) are both representative samples from their respective reference classes. In this case, one would expect all points to be on the horizontal zero-overconfidence line in Figure 7.5 and the hard–easy effect to be zero. More generally:

4. *If two sets, hard and easy, are generated by the same sampling process (representative sampling or same deviation from representative), the hard–easy effect is expected to be zero.*

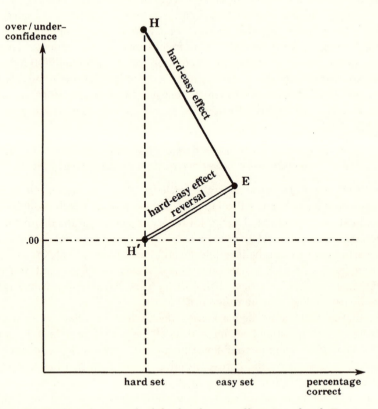

Figure 7.5 Predicted reversal of the hard–easy effect. H = hard; E = easy.

If sampling deviates in both the hard and the easy set equally from representative sampling, points will lie on a horizontal line parallel to the zero-overconfidence line.

Now consider the case that the easy set is selected from a corresponding reference class (e.g., general-knowledge questions), but the hard set is a representative sample from another reference class (denoted as H' in Figure 7.5). One then would predict a reversal of the hard–easy effect, as illustrated in Figure 7.5 by the double line from E to H'.

5. *Given two sets, one a representative sample from a reference class in a natural environment, the other selected from another reference class for being difficult, if the representative set is harder than the selected set, then the hard–easy effect is reversed.*

In the next section, Predictions 1, 2, and 3 are tested in two experiments; in the Explaining Anomalies in the Literature section, Predictions 4 and 5 are checked against results in the literature.

Experiment 1

Method

Two sets of questions were used, which we refer to as the *representative* and the *selected* set. The representative set was determined in the following way. We used as a reference class in a natural environment (an environment known to our participants) the set of all cities in West Germany with more than 100,000 inhabitants. There were 65 cities (Statistisches Bundesamt, 1986). From this reference class, a random sample of 25 cities was drawn, and all pairs of cities in the random sample were used in a complete paired comparison to give 300 pairs. No selection occurred. The target variable was the number of inhabitants, and the 300 questions were of the following kind: "Which city has more inhabitants? (a) Solingen or (b) Heidelberg." We chose city questions for two reasons. First, and most important, this content domain allowed for a precise definition of a reference class in a natural environment and for random sampling from this reference class. The second reason was for comparability. City questions have been used in earlier studies on overconfidence (e.g., Keren, 1988; May, 1987).

In addition to the representative set, a typical set of 50 general-knowledge questions, as in previous studies, was used. Two examples are "Who was born first? (a) Buddha or (b) Aristotle" and "When was the zipper invented? (a) before 1920 or (b) after 1920."

After each answer, the participant gave a confidence judgment (that this particular answer was correct). Two kinds of frequency judgments were used. First, after each block of 50 questions, the participant estimated the number of correct answers among the 50 answers given. Because there were 350 questions, every participant gave seven estimates of the number of correct answers. Second, after the participants answered all questions, they were given an enlarged copy of the confidence scale used throughout the experiment and were asked for the following frequency judgment: "How many of the answers that you classified into a certain confidence category are correct? Please indicate for every category your estimated relative frequency of correct answers."

In Experiment 1, we also introduced two of the standard manipulations in the literature. The first was to inform and warn half of our participants of the overconfidence effect, and the second was to offer half of each group a monetary incentive for good performance. Both are on a list of "debiasing" methods known as being relatively ineffective (Fischhoff, 1982), and both contributed to the view that overconfidence is a robust phenomenon. If PMM theory is correct, the magnitude of effects resulting from the manipulations in this chapter—confidence versus frequency judgment and selected versus representative sampling—should be much larger than those resulting from the two standard "debiasing" manipulations.

Participants   Participants were 80 students (43 men and 37 women) at the University of Konstanz who were paid for participation. Participants were tested in small groups of a maximum of 12 persons.

Design and Procedure   This was a 2 × 2 × 2 design with representative–selected set varied within participants and warning–no warning about overconfidence and monetary incentive–no incentive as independent variables varied between participants. Half of the participants answered the representative set first; the other half, the selected set. Order of questions was determined randomly in both sets.

The confidence scale consisted of seven categories, 50%, 51%–60%, 61%–70%, 71%–80%, 81%–90%, 91%–99%, and 100% confident. The 50%- and 100%-confidence values were introduced as separate categories because previous research showed that participants often tend to use these particular values. Participants were told first to mark the alternative that seemed to be the correct one, and then to indicate with a second cross their confidence that the answer was correct. If they only guessed, they should cross the 50% category; if they were absolutely certain, they should cross the 100% category. We explained that one of the alternatives was always correct. In the warning condition, participants received the following information: "Most earlier studies found a systematic tendency to overestimate one's knowledge; that is, there were many fewer answers correct than one would expect from the confidence ratings given. Please keep this warning in mind." In the incentive condition, participants were promised 20 German marks (or a bottle of French champagne) for the best performance in the group, in addition to the payment that everyone received (7.50 marks).

To summarize, 350 questions were presented, with a confidence judgment after each question, a frequency judgment after each 50 questions, and a judgment of relative frequencies of correct answers in each confidence category at the end.

For comparison with the literature on calibration, we used the following measure:

$$\text{over- or underconfidence} = \frac{1}{n} \sum_{i=1}^{I} n_i(p_i - f_i) = \bar{p} - \bar{f}$$

where n is the total number of answers, n_i is the number of times the confidence judgment p_i was used, and f_i is the relative frequency of correct answers for all answers assigned confidence p_i. I is the number of different confidence categories used ($I = 7$), and $\bar{p}$ and $\bar{f}$ are the overall mean confidence judgment and percentage correct, respectively. A positive difference is called overconfidence. For convenience, we report over- and underconfidence in percentages ($\times$ 100).

Results

Prediction 1   PMM theory predicts that in the selected set (general-knowledge questions), people show overestimation in confidence judgments (overconfidence) and, simultaneously, accurate frequency judgments.

The open-circle curve in Figure 7.6 shows the relation between judgments of confidence and the true relative frequency of correct answers in the selected set—that is, the set of mixed general-knowledge questions. The relative frequency of correct answers (averaged over all participants) was 72.4% in the 100%-confidence category, 66.3% in the 95% category, 58.0% in the 85% category, and so on. The curve is far below the diagonal (calibration curve) and similar to the curves reported by Lichtenstein, Fischhoff, and Phillips (1982, Figure 2). It replicates and demonstrates the well-known overconfidence effect. Percentage correct was 52.9, mean confidence was 66.7, and overconfidence was 13.8.

Participants' frequency judgments, however, are fairly accurate, as Table 7.2 (last row) shows. Each entry is averaged over the 20 participants in each condition. For instance, the figure −1.8 means that, on average, participants in this condition underestimated the true number of correct answers by 1.8. Averaged across the four conditions, we get −1.2, which means that participants missed the true frequency by an average of only about 1 correct answer in the set of 50 questions. Quite accurate frequency judgments coexist with overconfidence. The magnitude of this confidence–frequency effect found is shown in Figure 7.7 (left side). PMM theory predicts this systematic difference between confidence and frequency judgments, within the same person and the same general-knowledge questions.

Prediction 2   PMM theory predicts that in the representative set (city questions) people show zero overconfidence and, at the same time, underestimation in frequency judgments.

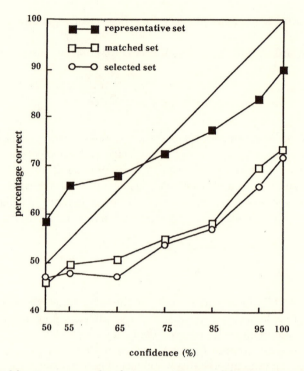

Figure 7.6 Calibration curves for three sets. Overconfidence appears when questions are selected (open circles) but disappears when questions are representative (black squares). The matched set controls for the different content of the two sets. Here, questions are selected from the representative set to match the difficulty of the selected set, and overconfidence is again produced.

Table 7.2 Mean differences between estimated and true frequencies of correct answers

Set	No warning–no incentive	Incentive only	Warning only	Warning and incentive
Representative				
1–50	−9.9	−9.4	−8.8	−8.7
51–100	−9.5	−10.4	−12.0	−11.3
101–150	−9.9	−10.9	−10.9	−9.9
151–200	−6.7	−6.7	−9.4	−5.9
201–250	−9.8	−9.8	−8.0	−5.3
251–300	−9.5	−10.8	−9.4	−9.1
Average	−9.2	−9.7	−9.7	−8.4
Selected	−1.8	−0.6	−2.7	0.3

Note: Negative signs denote underestimation of true number of correct answers.

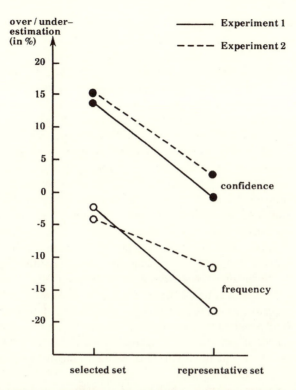

Figure 7.7 Confidence–frequency effect in representative and selected sets. Frequency judgments are long-run frequencies, $N = 50$.

The solid-square curve in Figure 7.6 shows the relation between confidence and percentage correct in the representative set—that is, the city questions. For instance, percentage correct in the 100%-confidence category was 90.8%, instead of 72.4%. Overconfidence disappeared (−0.9%). Percentage correct and mean confidence were 71.7 and 70.8, respectively.

The confidence curve for the representative set is similar to a regression curve for the estimation of relative frequencies by confidence, resulting in underconfidence in the left part of the confidence scale, overconfidence in the right, and zero overconfidence on the average.

Table 7.2 shows the differences between estimated and true frequencies for each block of 50 items and each of the conditions, respectively. Again, each entry is averaged over the 20 participants in each condition. For instance, participants who were given neither information nor incentive underestimated their true number of correct answers by 9.9 (on the average) in the first 50 items of the representative set. Table 7.2 shows that the values of the mean differences were fairly stable over the six subsets, and, most important, they are, without exception, negative (i.e., underestimation).

The following is an illustration at the individual level: Participant 1 estimated 28, 30, 23, 25, 23, and 23, respectively, for the six subsets, compared with 40, 38, 40, 36, 35, and 32 correct solutions, respectively. An analysis of individual judgments confirmed average results. Among the 80 participants, 71 underestimated the number of correct answers, whereas only 8 participants overestimated it (frequency judgments were missing for 1 participant). Incidentally, 7 of these 8 participants were male. In the selected set, for comparison, 44 participants underestimated and 35 participants overestimated the number of correct answers, and 1 participant got it exactly right.

We have attributed the emergence and disappearance of overconfidence to selection versus use of a representative set. One objection to this analysis is that the difference between the open-circle and the solid-square curve in Figure 7.6 is confounded with a difference in the content of both sets. The selected set includes a broad range of general-knowledge questions, whereas the domain of the representative set (cities) is necessarily more restricted. To check for this possible confound, we determined the item difficulties for each of the 50 general-knowledge questions and selected a subset of 50 city questions that had the same item difficulties. If the difference in Figure 7.6 is independent of content but results from the selection process, this "matched" subset of city questions should generate the same calibration curves showing overconfidence as the selected set of general-knowledge questions did. Figure 7.6 shows that this is the case (open-square curve). Both content domains produce the same results if questions are selected.

To summarize, in the representative set, overestimation disappears in confidence judgments, and zero-overconfidence coexists with frequency judgments that show large underestimation. Results confirm Prediction 2. Figure 7.7 (right side) shows the magnitude of the confidence–frequency effect found. No previous theory of confidence can predict the results depicted in Figure 7.7.

Prediction 3   PMM theory predicts that overestimation will disappear if the relative frequencies of correct answers (percentage correct) in each confidence category are compared with the estimated relative frequencies. Because participants estimated percentage correct for all confidence judgments—that is, including both the selected and the representative set—we expect not only that overestimation will disappear (the prediction from the selected set) but also that it will turn into underestimation (the prediction from the representative set).

The solid line in Figure 7.8 shows the results for Experiment 1: Estimated relative frequencies are well calibrated and show underestimation in five out of seven confidence categories. Overestimation of one's knowledge disappears. The only exception is the 100%-confidence category. The latter is the confidence category that contains all solutions by local MMs, and errors in memory or elementary logical operations may account for the difference. Figure 7.8 is a "frequentist" variant of the calibration curve of Figure 7.6. Here, true percentage correct is compared with estimated percentage correct, rather than

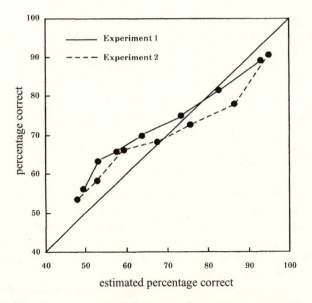

Figure 7.8 Calibration curves for judgments of percentage correct in confidence categories. Values are averaged across both sets of questions.

with confidence. For instance, in the 100%-confidence category, true and estimated percentage correct were 88.8% and 93.0%, respectively.

Averaged across experimental conditions, the ratio between estimated frequency in the long run and confidence value is fairly constant, around .87, for confidence ratings between 65% and 95%. It is highest in the extreme categories (see Table 7.3).

To summarize, participants explicitly distinguished between confidence in single answers and the relative frequency of correct answers associated with

Table 7.3 Estimated and true percentage correct in each confidence category (summarized over the representative and the selected sets)

Confidence category	No. of confidence judgments	% correct		Over-/under-estimation
		Estimated	True	
100	5,166	93.0	88.8	4.2
91–99	1,629	82.7	81.6	1.1
81–90	2,534	73.1	74.6	−1.5
71–80	2,950	64.3	70.1	−5.8
61–70	3,506	57.3	65.6	−8.3
51–60	4,036	53.7	63.3	−9.6
50	8,178	49.8	56.3	−6.5
Σ or M	27,999	64.8	69.1	−4.2

a confidence judgment. This result is implied by PMM theory, according to which different reference classes are cued by confidence and frequency tasks. As stated in Prediction 3, overestimation disappeared. However, the magnitude of underestimation was not, as might be expected, as pronounced as in the frequency judgments dealt with in Predictions 1 and 2. Except for this finding, results conformed well to Prediction 3. Note that no previous theory of confidence in knowledge we are aware of makes this conceptual distinction and that prediction. Our results contradict much of what has been assumed about how the untutored mind understands the relation between confidence and relative frequency of correct answers.

Warning about Overconfidence and Monetary Incentive   Mean confidence judgments were indistinguishable between participants warned of overconfidence and those uninformed. If a monetary incentive was announced, overconfidence was more pronounced with incentive than without incentive in five categories (65%–100%) and less pronounced in the 50% category, with an average increase of 3.6 percentage points.

The monetary incentive effect resulted from the incentive/no-warning group, in which confidence judgments were higher than in all three other groups (but we found the same percentage correct in all groups). One reason for this interaction could be that we did not specify in the instructions a criterion for best performance. If warned of overconfidence, participants could easily infer that the incentive was for minimizing overconfidence. If not warned, at least some participants could also have attempted to maximize percentage correct. None of these attempts, however, was successful, consistent with PMM theory and earlier studies (e.g., Fischhoff, Slovic, & Lichtenstein, 1977). The effort to raise the percentage correct seems to have raised confidence instead, an outcome that cannot be accounted for by PMM theory. The size of this effect, however, was small compared with both the confidence–frequency effect and that of selected versus representative sampling.

To summarize, neither warning of overconfidence nor associated monetary incentive decreased overconfidence or increased percentage correct, replicating earlier findings that knowledge about overconfidence is not sufficient to change confidence. An incentive that participants seem to have interpreted as rewarding those who maximize the percentage correct, however, increased confidence.

Order of Presentation and Sex   Which set (representative vs. selected) was given first had no effect on confidences, neither in Experiment 1 nor in Experiment 2. Arkes, Christensen, Lai, and Blumer (1987) found an effect of the difficulty of one set of items on the confidence judgments for a second set when participants received feedback for their performance in the first set. In our experiment, however, no feedback was given. Thus, participants had no reason to correct their confidence judgments, such as by subtracting a constant value. Sex differences in degree of overconfidence in knowledge have been claimed by both philosophy and folklore. Our study, however, showed no significant differences between the sexes in either overconfidence or calibration, in either Experiment 1 or in Experiment 2. (The men's confidence judgments were on the average 5 percentage points higher than women's, but so was their percentage correct. This replicates Lichtenstein and Fischhoff's, 1981, findings about students at the University of Oregon.)

To summarize, as predicted by PMM theory, we can experimentally make overconfidence (overestimation) appear, disappear, and invert. Experiment 1 made our participants consistently switch back and forth among these responses. The key to this finding is a pair of concepts that have been neglected by the main previous explanations of confidence in one's knowledge—confidence versus frequency judgment and representative versus selected sampling.

Experiment 2

We tried to replicate the results and test several objections. First, to strengthen the case against PMM theory, we instructed the participants both verbally and in written form that confidence is subjective probability, and that among all cases where a subjective probability of X% was chosen, X% of the answers should be correct. Several authors have argued that such a frequentist instruction could enhance external calibration or internal consistency (e.g., Kahneman & Tversky, 1982; May, 1987). According to PMM theory, however, confidence is already inferred from frequency (with or without this instruction)— but from frequencies of co-occurrences between, say, number of inhabitants and several cues, and not from base rates of correct answers in similar testing situations (see Table 7.1). Thus, in our view, the preceding caution will be ineffective because the base rate of correct answers is not a probability cue that is defined on a reference class such as cities in Germany.

Second, consider the confidence–frequency effect. We have shown that this new effect is implied by PMM theory. One objection might be that the difference between confidence and frequency judgments is an artifact of the response function, just as overconfidence has sometimes been thought to be. Consider the following interpretation of overconfidence. If (a) confidence is well calibrated but (b) the response function that transforms confidence into a confidence judgment differs from an identity function, then (c) overconfidence or underconfidence "occurs" on the response scale. Because an identity function has not been proven, Anderson (1986), for instance, denoted the overconfidence effect and the hard–easy effect as "largely meaningless" (p. 91): They might just as well be response function artifacts.

A similar objection could be made against the interpretation of the confidence–frequency effect within PMM theory. Despite the effect's stability across selected and representative sets, it may just reflect a systematic difference between response functions for confidence and frequency judgments. This conjecture can be rephrased as follows: If (a) the difference between "internal" confidence and frequency impression is zero, but (b) the response functions that transform both into judgments differ systematically, then (c) a confidence–

frequency effect occurs on the response scales. We call this the *response-function conjecture*.

How can this conjecture be tested? According to PMM theory, the essential basis on which both confidence and frequency judgments are formed is the probability cues, not response functions. We assumed earlier that frequency judgments are based mainly on base rates of correct answers in a reference class of similar general-knowledge test situations. If we make another cue available, then frequency judgments should change. In particular, if we make the confidence judgments more easily retrievable from memory, these can be used as additional probability cues, and the confidence–frequency effect should decrease. This was done in Experiment 2 by introducing frequency judgments in the short run, that is, frequency judgments for a very small number of questions. Here, confidence judgments can be more easily retrieved from memory than they could in the long run. Thus, if PMM theory is correct, the confidence–frequency effect should decrease in the short run. If the issue were, however, different response functions, then the availability of confidence judgments should not matter because confidence and frequency impression are assumed to be identical in the first place. Thus, if the conjecture is correct, the confidence–frequency effect should be stable.

In Experiment 2, we varied the length N of a series of questions from the long-run condition $N = 50$ in Experiment 1 to the smallest possible short run of $N = 2$.

Third, in Experiment 1 we used a response scale ranging from 50% to 100% for confidence judgments but a full-range response scale for frequency judgments ranging from 0 to 50 correct answers (which corresponds to 0% to 100%). Therefore one could argue that the confidence–frequency effect is an artifact of the different ranges of the two response scales. Assume that (a) there is no difference between internal confidence and frequency, but (b) because confidence judgments are limited to the upper half of the response scale, whereas frequency judgments are not, (c) the confidence–frequency effect results as an artifact of the half-range response scale in confidence judgments. We refer to this as the *response-range conjecture*. It can be backed up by at least two hypotheses.

1. Assume that PMM theory is wrong and participants indeed use base rates of correct answers as a probability cue for confidence in single answers. Then confidence should be considerably lower. If participants anticipate misleading questions, even confidences lower than 50% are reasonable to expect on this conjecture. Confidences below 50%, however, cannot be expressed on a scale with a lower boundary at 50%, whereas they can at the frequency scale. Effects of response range such as those postulated in range–frequency theory (Parducci, 1965) or by Schönemann (1983) may enforce the distorting effect of the half-range format. In this account, both the overconfidence effect and the confidence–frequency effect are generated by a response-scale effect. With respect to overconfidence, this conjecture has been made and has claimed some support (e.g., May, 1986, 1987; Ronis & Yates, 1987). We call this the *base rate hypothesis*.

2. Assume that PMM theory is wrong in postulating that choice and confidence are essentially one process and that the true process is a temporal sequence: choice, followed by search for evidence, followed by confidence judgment. Koriat et al. (1980), for instance, proposed this sequence. Assume further, contrary to Koriat, that the mind is "Popperian," searching for disconfirming rather than for confirming evidence to determine the degree of "corroboration" of an answer. If the participant is successful in retrieving disconfirming evidence from memory but is not allowed to change the original answer, confidence judgments less than 50% will result. Such disconfirmation strategies, however, can hardly be detected using a 50%–100% format, whereas they could in a full-scale format. We call this the *disconfirmation strategy hypothesis.*

To test the response-range conjecture, half of the participants in Experiment 2 were given full-range response scales, whereas the other half received the response scales used in Experiment 1.

Method

Participants   Ninety-seven new participants at the University of Konstanz (not enrolled in psychology) were paid for their participation. There were 59 males and 38 females. As in Experiment 1, participants were tested in small groups of no more than 7.

Design and procedure   This was a 4 × 2 × 2 design, with length of series (50, 10, 5, and 2) and response scale (half range vs. full range) varied between participants and type of knowledge questions (selected vs. representative set) varied within participants.

The procedure and the materials were like that in Experiment 1, except for the following. We used a new random sample of 21 (instead of 25) cities. This change decreased the number of questions in the representative set from 300 to 210. As mentioned earlier, we explicitly instructed the participants to interpret confidences as frequencies of correct answers: "We are interested in how well you can estimate subjective probabilities. This means, among all the answers where you give a subjective probability of X%, there should be X% of the answers correct." This calibration instruction was orally repeated and emphasized to the participants.

The response scale contained the means (50%, 55%, 65%, . . . , 95%, 100%) of the intervals used in Experiment 1 rather than the intervals themselves to avoid the problematic assumption that means would represent intervals. Endpoints were marked *absolutely certain that the alternative chosen is correct* (100%), *both alternatives equally probable* (50%), and, for the full-range scale, *absolutely certain that the alternative chosen is incorrect* (0%). In the full-range scale, one reason for using confidences between 0% and 45% was explained in the following illustration: "If you think after you have made your choice that you would have better chosen the other alternative, do not change your choice, but answer with a probability smaller than 50%."

After each set of $N = 50$ (10, 5, or 2) answers, participants gave a judgment of the number of correct answers. After having completed $50 + 210 = 260$ confidence judgments and 5, 26, 52, or 130 frequency judgments (depending on the participant's group), participants in both response-scale conditions were presented the same enlarged copy of the 50%–100% response scale and asked to estimate the relative frequency of correct answers in each confidence category.

Results

Response-Range Conjecture   We tested the conjecture that the systematic difference in confidence and frequency judgments stated in Predictions 1 and 2 (confidence–frequency effect) and shown in Experiment 1 resulted from the availability of only a limited response scale for confidence judgments (50% to 100%).

Forty-seven participants were given the full-range response scale for confidence judgments. Twenty-two of these never chose confidences below 50%; the others did. The number of confidence judgments below 50% was small. Eleven participants used them only once (in altogether 260 judgments), 5 did twice, and the others 3 to 7 times. There was one outlier, a participant who used them 67 times. In total, participants gave a confidence judgment smaller than 50% for only 1.1% of their answers (excluding the outlier: 0.6%). If the response-range conjecture had been correct, participants would have used confidence judgments below 50% much more frequently.

In the representative set, overconfidence was 3.7% ($SE_M = 1.23$) in the full-range scale condition and 1.8% ($SE_M = 1.15$) in the half-range condition. In the selected set, the corresponding values were 14.4 ($SE_M = 1.54$) and 16.4 ($SE_M = 1.43$). Averaging all questions, we got slightly larger overconfidence in the full-range condition (mean difference = 1.2). The response-range conjecture, however, predicted a strong effect in the opposite direction. Frequency judgments were essentially the same in both conditions. Hence, the confidence–frequency effect can also be demonstrated when both confidence and frequency judgments are made on a full-range response scale.

To summarize, there was (a) little use of confidences below 50% and (b) no decrease of overconfidence in the full-range condition. These results contradict the response-range conjecture.

A study by Ronis and Yates (1987) seems to be the only other study that has compared the full-range and the half-range format in two-alternative choice tasks, but it did not deal with frequency judgments. These authors also reported that only about half their participants used confidence judgments below 50%, although they did so more frequently than our participants. Ronis and Yates concluded that confidences below 50% had only a negligible effect on overconfidence and calibration (pp. 209–211). Thus results in both studies are consistent. The main difference is that Ronis and Yates seem to consider only "failure to follow the instructions" and "misusing the probability scale" (p. 207) as possible explanations for confidence judgments below 50%. In contrast, we argue that there are indeed plausible cognitive mechanisms—the base rate and disconfirmation strategy hypotheses—that imply these kind of judgments, although they would contradict PMM theory.

Both Experiment 2 and the Ronis and Yates (1987) study do not rule out, however, a more fundamental conjecture that is difficult to test. This argument is that internal confidence (not frequency) takes a verbal rather than a numerical form and that it is distorted on any numerical probability rating scale, not just on a 50%–100% response scale. Zimmer (1983, 1986) argued that verbal expressions of uncertainty (such as "highly improbably" and "very likely") are more realistic, more precise, and less prone to overconfidence and other so-called judgmental biases than are numerical judgments of probability. Zimmer's fuzzy-set modeling of verbal expressions, like models of probabilistic reasoning that dispense with the Kolmogoroff axioms (e.g., Cohen, 1989; Kyburg, 1983; Shafer, 1978), remains a largely unexplored source of alternative accounts of confidence.

For the remaining analysis, we do not distinguish between the full-range and the half-range response format. For combining the data, we recoded answers like "alternative *a*, 40% confident" as "alternative *b*, 60% confident," following Ronis and Yates (1987).

Predictions 1 and 2: Confidence–Frequency Effect   The question is whether the confidence–frequency effect can be replicated under the explicit instruction that subjective probabilities should be calibrated to frequencies of correct answers in the long run. Calibration curves in Experiment 2 were similar to those in Figure 7.6 and are not shown here for this reason. Figure 7.7 shows that the confidence–frequency effect replicates. In the selected set, mean confidence was 71.6%, and percentage correct was 56.2. Mean estimated number of correct answers (transformed into percentages) in the series of $N = 50$ was 52.0%. As stated in Prediction 1, overconfidence in single answers coexists with fairly accurate frequency judgments, which once again show slight underestimation.

In the representative set, mean confidence was 78.1% and percentage correct was 75.3%. Mean estimated number of correct answers per 50 answers was 63.5%. As forecasted in Prediction 2, overconfidence largely disappeared (2.8 percentage points), and frequency judgments showed underestimation (−11.8 percentage points).

An individual analysis produced similar results. The confidence–frequency effect (average confidence higher than average frequency judgment) held for 82 (83) participants in the selected (representative) set (out of 97). Answering the selected set, 92 respondents showed overconfidence, and 5 showed underconfidence. In the representative set, however, 60 exhibited overconfidence and 37 exhibited underconfidence.

Prediction 3: Estimated Percentage Correct in Confidence Categories   After the participants answered the 260 general-knowledge questions, they were asked what percentage they thought they had correct in each confidence category. As shown by the dashed line in Figure 7.8, results replicated well. Average estimated percentage correct differed again from confidence and was close to the actual percentage correct.

Despite the instruction not to do so, our participants still distinguished between a specific confidence value and the corresponding percentage of correct responses. Therefore *confidence* and hypothesized percentage correct should not be used as synonyms. As suggested by this experiment, an instruction alone cannot override the cognitive processes at work.

In the 100%-confidence category, for instance, 67 participants gave estimates below 100%. In a postexperimental interview, we pointed out to them that these judgments imply that they assumed they had not followed the calibration instruction. Most explained that in each single case, they were in fact 100% confident. But they also knew that, in the long run, some answers would nonetheless be wrong, and they did not know which ones. Thus they did not know which of the 100% answers they should correct. When asked how they made the confidence judgments, most answered by giving examples of probability cues, such as "I know that this city is located in the Ruhrgebiet (industrial belt), and most cities there are rather large." Interviews provided evidence for several probability cues, but no evidence that base rate expectations, as reported in frequency judgments, were also used in confidence judgments.

Response–Function Conjecture: Frequency Judgments in the Short and Long Runs   We tested the conjecture that the confidence–frequency effect stated in Predictions 1 and 2 and shown in Experiment 1 might be due to different response functions for confidence and frequency judgments, rather than to different cognitive processes, as postulated by PMM theory. If the conjecture were true, the availability of confidence judgments in the short run should not change the confidence–frequency effect (see the previous discussion).

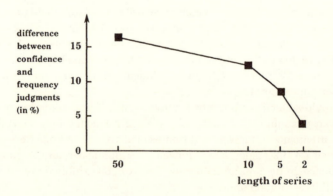

Figure 7.9 Decrease of the confidence–frequency effect in short runs ($N = 50$, 10, 5, and 2). Values are differences between mean confidence and estimated percentage correct in a series of length N. Values are averaged across all questions.

Contrary to the response–function conjecture, the length of series showed an effect on the judgments of frequency of correct answers. Figure 7.9 shows the extent of the disappearance of the confidence–frequency effect in the short run. The curve shows that the effect decreased from $N = 50$ to $N = 2$, averaged across both sets of items. The decrease was around 12 percentage points, an amount similar in the selected set (from 18.9% to 6.9%) and in the representative set (from 15.7% to 3.3%).

The breakdown of the confidence–frequency effect in the short run is inconsistent with the objection that the effect can be reduced to a systematic difference in response functions. This result is, however, consistent with the notion that the shorter the run, the more easily are confidence judgments available from memory, and, thus, the more they can be used as probability cues for the true number of correct answers.

Discussion

Our starting point was the overconfidence effect, reported in the literature as a fairly stable cognitive illusion in evaluating one's general knowledge and attributed to general principles of memory search, such as confirmation bias (Koriat et al., 1980), to general motivational tendencies such as fear of invalidity (Mayseless & Kruglanski, 1987), to insensitivity to task difficulty (see von Winterfeldt & Edwards, 1986, p. 128), and to wishful thinking and other "deficits" in cognition, motivation, and personality. Our view, in contrast, proposes that one evaluates one's knowledge by probabilistic mental models. In our account, the main deficit of most cognitive and motivational explanations is that they neglect the structure of the task and its relation to the structure of a corresponding environment known to the participants. If people want to search for confirming evidence or to believe that their answers are more correct than they are because of some need, wish, or fear, then overestimation of accuracy should express itself independently of whether they judge single answers or frequencies, a selected or representative sample of questions, and hard or easy questions.

Our experiments also do not support the explanation of overconfidence and the hard–easy effect by assuming that participants are insensitive to task difficulty: In frequency tasks we have shown that participants' judgments of their percentage correct in the long run are in fact close to actual percentage correct, although confidences are not. Overconfidence does not imply that participants are not aware of task difficulty. At least two more studies have shown that estimated percentage correct can correspond closely to true percentage correct in general-knowledge tasks. Allwood and Montgomery (1987) asked their participants to estimate how difficult each of 80 questions was for their peers and found that difficulty ratings ($M = 57\%$) were more realistic (percentage correct $= 61\%$) than confidence judgments ($M = 74\%$). May (1987) asked her participants to estimate their percentage of correct answers after they completed an experiment with two-alternative questions. She found that judgments of percentage correct accorded better with the true percentage correct than did confidences.

In our account, overconfidence results from one of two causes, or both: (a) a PMM for a task is not properly adapted to a corresponding environment (e.g., cue validities do not correspond to ecological validities), or (b) the set of objects used is not a representative sample from the corresponding reference class in the environment but is selected for difficulty. If a is the true cause, using a representative sample from a known environment should not eliminate overconfidence. If b is true, it should. In both experiments, overconfidence in knowledge about city populations was eliminated, as implied by b. Thus experimental results are consistent with both PMM theory and the assumption that individual PMMs are on the average well adapted to the city environment we used. Overconfidence resulted from a set of questions that was selected for difficulty. Underconfidence, conversely, would result from questions selected to be easy.

The foregoing comments do *not* mean that overestimation of knowledge is just an artifact of selected questions. If it were, then judgments of frequency of correct answers should show a similar degree of overestimation. What we have called the confidence–frequency effect shows that this is not the case.

Several authors have proposed that judgments in the frequency mode are more accurate, realistic, or internally consistent than probabilities for single events (e.g., Teigen, 1974, p. 62; Tversky & Kahneman, 1983). Our account is different. PMM theory states conditions under which mean judgments of confidence are systematically larger than judgments of relative frequency. PMM theory does not, however, imply that frequency judgments are generally better calibrated. On the contrary, frequency judgments may be miscalibrated for the same reasons as confidence judgments. The set of tasks may not be representative for the reference class from which the inferences are made.

The experimental control of overestimation—how to make overestimation appear, disappear, and invert—gives support to PMM theory. These predictions, however, do not exhaust the inferences that can be derived from PMM theory.

Explaining Anomalies in the Literature

In this section, we explain a series of apparently inconsistent findings and integrate these into PMM theory.

Ronis and Yates (1987)   We have mentioned that the Ronis and Yates study is the only other study that tested a full-range response scale for two-alternative tasks. The second purpose of that study was to compare confidence judgments in situations in which the participant knows that the answers are known to the experimenter (general-knowledge questions) with outcomes of upcoming basketball games, in which answers are not yet known. In all three (response-scale) groups, percentage correct was larger for general-knowledge questions

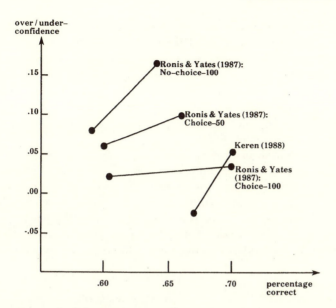

Figure 7.10 Reversal of the hard–easy effect in Ronis and Yates (1987) and Keren (1988).

than for basketball predictions. Given this result, what would current theories predict about overconfidence? The insensitivity hypothesis proposes that people are largely insensitive to percentage correct (see von Winterfeldt & Edwards, 1986, p. 128). This implies that overconfidence will be larger in the more difficult (hard) set: the hard–easy effect. (The confirmation bias and motivational explanations are largely mute on the difficulty issue.) PMM theory, in contrast, predicts that overconfidence will be larger in the easier set (hard–easy effect reversal; see Prediction 5) because general-knowledge questions (the easy set) were selected and basketball predictions were not; only with clairvoyance could one select these predictions for percentage correct.

In fact, Ronis and Yates (1987) reported an apparent anomaly: three hard–easy effect reversals. In all groups, overconfidence was larger for the easy general-knowledge questions than for the hard basketball predictions (Figure 7.10). Prediction 5 accounts for these observed reversals of the hard–easy effect.

Koriat et al. (1980)   Experiment 2 of Koriat et al.'s study provided a direct test of the confirmation bias explanation of overconfidence. The explanation is this: (a) participants first choose an answer based on their knowledge, then (b) they selectively search for confirming memory (or for evidence disconfirming the alternative not chosen), and (c) this confirming evidence generates overconfidence. Between the participants' choice of an answer and their confidence judgment, the authors asked them to give reasons for the alternative chosen.

Three groups of participants were asked to write down one confirming reason, one disconfirming reason, or one of each, respectively. Reasons were given for half of the general-knowledge questions; otherwise, no reasons were given (control condition). If the confirmation bias explanation is correct, then asking for a contradicting reason (or both reasons) should decrease overconfidence and improve calibration. Asking for a confirming reason, however, should make no difference "since those instructions roughly simulate what people normally do" (Koriat et al., 1980, p. 111).

What does PMM theory predict? According to PMM theory, choice and confidence are inferred from the same activated cue. This cue is by definition a confirming reason. Therefore, the confirming-reason and the no-reason (control) tasks engage the same cognitive processes. The difference is only that in the former the supporting reason is written down. Similarly, the disconfirming-reason and both-reason tasks involve the same cognitive processes. Furthermore, PMM theory implies that there is no difference between the two pairs of tasks.

This result is shown in Table 7.4. In the first row we have the no-reason and confirming-reason tasks, which are equivalent. Here, only one cue is activated, which is confirming. There is no disconfirming cue. Now consider the second row, the disconfirming-reason and both-reason tasks, which are again equivalent. Both tasks are solved if one additional cue, which is disconfirming, can be activated. Thus, for PMM theory, the cue generation and testing cycle is started again, and cues are generated according to the hierarchy of cue validities and tested as to whether they can be activated for the problem at hand. The point is that the next cue that can be activated may turn out to be either confirming or disconfirming.

For simplicity, assume that the probability that the next activated cue turns out to be confirming or disconfirming is the same. If it is disconfirming, the cycle is stopped, and two cues in total have been activated, one confirming

Table 7.4 Predictions of PMM theory for the effects of asking for a disconfirming reason

Task	No. of cues activated			CON	DIS	Probability	Predicted change in confidence
					Cues activated		
No; CON	1	CON		1	0	—	—
DIS; both	2	DIS CON		1	1	.5	Decrease
DIS; both	3	DIS CON		2	1	.25	Increase
DIS; both	4	DIS CON		3	1	.125	Increase
DIS; both >4		. . .		>3	1	.125	Increase

Note: CON = confirming reason; DIS = disconfirming reason; No = no reason; both = both reasons.

and one disconfirming. This stopping happens with probability .5, and it decreases both confidence and overconfidence. (Because the second cue activated has a lower cue validity, however, confidence is not decreased below 50%.) If the second cue activated is again confirming, a third has to be activated, and the cue generation and testing cycle is entered again. If the third cue is disconfirming, the cycle stops with two confirming cues and one disconfirming cue activated, as shown in the third row of Table 7.4. This stopping is to be expected with probability .25. Because the second cue has higher cue validity than the third, disconfirming, cue, overall an increase in confidence and overconfidence is to be expected. If the third cue is again confirming, the same procedure is repeated. Here and in all subsequent cases confidence will increase. As shown in Table 7.4, the probabilities of an increase sum up to .5 (.25 + .125 + .125), which is the same as the probability of a decrease.

Thus PMM theory leads to the prediction that, overall, asking for a disconfirming reason will not change confidence or overconfidence. As just shown, the confirmation-bias hypothesis, in contrast, predicts that asking for a disconfirming reason should decrease confidence and overconfidence.

What were the results of the Koriat study? In both crucial conditions, disconfirming reason and both reasons, the authors found only small and nonsignificant decreases of overconfidence (2% and 1%, respectively) and similar small improvements in calibration (.006 each, significant only in the disconfirming-reason task). These largely insignificant differences are consistent with the prediction by PMM theory that asking for a disconfirming reason makes no difference and are inconsistent with the confirmation-bias explanation. Further evidence comes from a replication of the Koriat study by Fischhoff and MacGregor (1982), who reported zero effects of disconfirming reasons.

To summarize, the effects on confidence of giving confirming and disconfirming reasons in the Koriat study can be both explained by and integrated into PMM theory. There is no need to postulate a confirmation bias.

Dawes (1980)   Overconfidence has been attributed to people's tendency to "overestimate the power of our 'intellect' as opposed to that of our coding abilities." Such overestimation "has been reinforced by our realization that we have developed a technology capable of destroying ourselves" (Dawes, 1980, p. 328). Dawes proposed that overconfidence is characteristic for general-knowledge questions but absent in perceptual tasks; he designed a series of experiments to test this proposal. PMM theory, however, gives no special treatment to perceptual tasks. On the contrary, it predicts overconfidence if perceptual tasks are selected for perceptual illusions—that is, for being misleading—whereas zero overconfidence is to be expected if tasks are not selected. Pictures in textbooks on visual illusions are probably the set of items that produces the most extreme overconfidence yet demonstrated. Nevertheless, in a natural environment, perception is generally reliable.

Dawes reported inconsistent results. When perceptual stimuli were systematically constructed from a Square × Circle matrix, as in the area task, and no selection for stimuli that generated perceptual illusions took place, over-confidence was close to zero (perception of areas of squares is quite well adapted in adults; see Gigerenzer & Richter, 1990). This result is predicted by both accounts. The anomaly arises with the second perceptual task used—judging which of two subsequent tones is longer. If the second tone was longer, Dawes reported almost perfect calibration, but if the first tone was longer, par-ticipants exhibited large overconfidence.

PMM theory predicts that in the inconsistent acoustic task, perceptual stim-uli have been selected (albeit unwittingly) for a perceptual illusion. This is in fact the case. From the literature on time perception, we know that of two subsequently presented tones, the tone more recently heard appears to be longer. This perceptual illusion is known as the *negative presentation effect* (e.g., Fraisse, 1964; Sivyer & Finlay, 1982). It implies a smaller percentage of correct answers in the condition in which the tone presented first was longer, because this tone is perceived to be shorter. A decrease in percentage correct in turn increases overconfidence. In Dawes's (1980) experiments, this is exactly the inconsistent condition in which overconfidence occurred. Thus, from the perspective we propose, this inconsistent result can be reconciled.

Keren (1988)   A strict distinction between perceptual judgment and intellec-tual judgment cannot be derived from many views of perception, such as signal-detection theory (Tanner & Swets, 1954). Reflecting on this fact, Keren (1988) proposed a slightly modified hypothesis: The more perception-like a task is, the less overconfident and the better calibrated participants will be. "As a task requires additional higher processing and transformation of the original sensory input, different kinds of possible cognitive distortions may exist (such as inappropriate inferences) that may limit the ability to accurately monitor our higher cognitive processes" (Keren, 1988, p. 99).

Keren (1988, Experiment 1) used general-knowledge questions and two kinds of perceptual tasks, one of them more difficult than the general-knowledge task, the other less difficult. Keren tested the hypothesis that con-fidence judgments in perceptual tasks are better calibrated than in general-knowledge tasks. He could not support it, however. Instead, he found an anomaly: The comparison between the general-knowledge task and the more difficult perceptual task reversed the hard–easy effect (see Figure 7.10). As derived in Prediction 5, this puzzling reversal is implied by PMM theory if the Landolt rings used in the more difficult perceptual task were not selected for perceptual illusions, as seems to be the case (Keren, 1988, p. 100).

Note that the kind of general-knowledge questions used (population of cities or countries, and distances between cities) would easily permit defining a ref-erence class in a known environment and obtaining representative samples. But no representative sample of general-knowledge questions was generated. This lack makes the other predictions from PMM theory coincide with Keren's (1988): overconfidence in general-knowledge, and zero overconfidence in the two perceptual tasks. Results show this outcome, except for the large-gap Lan-dolt rings condition, which generated considerable underconfidence. PMM theory cannot account for the latter, nor can the notion of degree of perception-likeness.

A second perceptual task was letter identification. In Experiment 3, Keren (1988) used two letter-identification tasks, which were identical except that the exposure time of the letters to be recognized was either short or long. Mean percentages correct were 63.5 for short and 77.2 for long exposures. According to earlier explanations, such as participants' insensitivity to task difficulty, a hard–easy effect should result. According to PMM theory, however, the hard–easy effect should be zero, because both tasks were generated by the same sampling process (Prediction 4). In fact, Keren (1988, p. 112) reported that in both tasks, overconfidence was not significantly different from zero. Prediction 4 accounts for this disappearance of the hard–easy effect in a situation in which differences in percentage correct were large.

The Brunswikian Perspective

PMM theory draws heavily on the Brunswikian notions of a natural environment known to an individual, reference classes in this environment, and representative sampling from a reference class. We went beyond the Brunswikian focus on achievement (rather than process) by providing a theoretical framework of the processes that determine choice, confidence, and frequency judgment.

Choice and confidence are a result of a cue-testing and activation cycle, which is analogous to Newell and Simon's (1972) postulate that "problem solving takes place by search in a problem space" (p. 809). Furthermore, the emphasis on the structure of the task in PMM theory is similar to Newell and Simon's proposition that "the structure of the task determines the possible structures of the problem space" (p. 789). Unlike PMM theorists, however, Newell and Simon also assumed in the tasks they studied (cryptarithmetic, logic, and chess) a relatively simple mapping between the external structure of the task and the internal representation in a problem space (see Allport, 1975). Although it is cued by the task structure, we assume that a PMM (the functional equivalent of a problem space) has a large surplus structure (the reference class and the cues), which is taken from a known structure in the problem solver's natural environment. The emphasis on the structure of everyday knowledge or environment (as distinguished from the task environment) has been most forcefully defended by Brunswik. Although Newell and Simon (1972, p. 874) called Brunswik and Tolman "the real forerunners" of their work, they seem not to distinguish clearly between the notions of a probabilistic everyday environment and a task environment. This theory is an attempt to combine both views. Brunswik's focus on achievement (during his behavioristic phase; see Leary, 1987) corresponds more closely to the part of research on probabilistic judgment that focuses on calibration, rather than on the underlying cognitive processes.

The importance of the cognitive representation of the task was studied by the Würzburg school and emphasized in Gestalt theoretical accounts of thinking (e.g., Duncker, 1935/1945), and this issue has regained favor (e.g., Brehmer, 1988; Hammond, Stewart, Brehmer, & Steinmann, 1975). In their review, Einhorn and Hogarth (1981) emphasized that "the cognitive approach has been concerned primarily with *how* tasks are represented. The issue of *why* tasks are represented in particular ways has not yet been addressed" (p. 57). PMM theory addresses this issue. Different tasks, such as confidence and frequency tasks, cue different reference classes and different probability cues from known environments. It is these environments that provide the particular representation, the PMM, of a task.

Many parts of PMM theory need further expansion, development, and testing. Open issues include the following: (a) What reference class is activated? For city comparisons, this question has a relatively clear answer, but in general, more than one reference class can be constructed to solve a problem. (b) Are cues always generated according to their rank in the cue validity hierarchy? Alternative models of cue generation could relax this strong assumption, assuming, for instance, that the first cue generated is the cue activated in the last problem. The latter would, however, decrease the percentage of correct answers. (c) What are the conditions under which we may expect PMMs to be well adapted? There exists a large body of neo-Brunswikian research that, in general, indicates good adaptation but also points out exceptions (e.g., Armelius, 1979; Björkman, 1987; Brehmer & Joyce, 1988; Hammond & Wascoe, 1980). (d) What are the conditions under which cue substitution without cue integration is superior to multiple cue integration? PMM theory assumes a pure cue substitution model—a cue that cannot be activated can be replaced by any other cue—without integration of two or more cues. We focused on the substitution and not the integration aspect of Brunswik's vicarious functioning (see Gigerenzer & Murray, 1987, pp. 66–81), in contrast to the multiple regression metaphor of judgment. Despite its simplicity, the substitution model produces zero overconfidence and a large number of correct answers, if the PMM is well adapted. There may be more reasons for simple substitution models. Armelius and Armelius (1974), for instance, reported that participants were well able to use ecological validities, but not the correlations between cues. If the latter is the case, then multiple cue integration may not work well.

Conclusions

We conjecture that confidence in one's knowledge of the kind studied here—immediate and spontaneous rather than a product of long-term reflection—is largely determined by the structure of the task and the structure of a corresponding, known environment in a person's long-term memory. We provided experimental evidence for this hypothesis by showing how changes in the task (confidence vs. frequency judgment) and in the relationship between task and environment (selected vs. representative sampling) can make the two stable effects reported in the literature—overconfidence and the hard–easy effect—emerge, disappear, and invert at will. We have demonstrated a new phenomenon, the confidence–frequency effect. One cannot speak of a general over-confidence bias anymore, in the sense that it relates to deficient processes of cognition or motivation. In contrast, participants seem to be able to make fine conceptual distinctions—confidence versus frequency—of the same kind as probabilists and statisticians do. Earlier attempts postulating general deficiencies in information processing or motivation cannot account for the experimental results predicted by PMM theory and confirmed in two experiments. PMM theory seems to be the first theory in this field that gives a coherent account of these various effects by focusing on the relation between the structure of the task, the structure of a corresponding environment, and a PMM.

8

Reasoning the Fast and Frugal Way

Organisms make inductive inferences. Darwin (1872/1965) observed that people use facial cues, and such as eyes that waver and lids that hang low, to infer a person's guilt. Male toads, roaming through swamps at night, use the pitch of a rival's croak to infer its size when deciding whether to fight (Krebs & Davies, 1987). Stockbrokers must make fast decisions about which of several stocks to trade or invest when only limited information is available. The list goes on. Inductive inferences are typically based on uncertain cues: The eyes can deceive, and so can a tiny toad with a deep croak in the darkness.

How does an organism make inferences about unknown aspects of the environment? There are three directions in which to look for an answer. From Pierre Laplace to George Boole to Jean Piaget, many scholars have defended the now classical view that the laws of human inference are the laws of probability and statistics (and to a lesser degree logic, which does not deal as easily with uncertainty). Indeed, the Enlightenment probabilists derived the laws of probability from what they believed to be the laws of human reasoning (Daston, 1988). Following this time-honored tradition, much contemporary research in psychology, behavioral ecology, and economics assumes standard statistical tools to be the normative and descriptive models of inference and decision making. Multiple regression, for instance, is both the economist's universal tool (McCloskey, 1985) and a model of inductive inference in multiple-cue learning (Hammond, 1990) and clinical judgment (Brehmer, 1994); Bayes's rule is a model of how animals infer the presence of predators or prey (Stephens & Krebs, 1986) as well as of human reasoning and memory (Anderson, 1990). This Enlightenment view that probability theory and human reasoning are two sides of the same coin crumbled in the early nineteenth century but has remained strong in psychology and economics.

In the past 25 years, this stronghold came under attack by proponents of the heuristics-and-biases program, who concluded that human inference is systematically biased and error prone, suggesting that the laws of inference are

The work on which this chapter is based was coauthored with D. G. Goldstein.

quick-and-dirty heuristics and not the laws of probability (Tversky & Kahneman, 1974). This second perspective appears diametrically opposed to the classical rationality of the Enlightenment, but this appearance is misleading. It has retained the normative kernel of the classical view. For example, a discrepancy between the dictates of classical rationality and actual reasoning is what defines a *reasoning error* in this program. Both views accept the laws of probability and statistics as normative, but they disagree about whether humans can live up to these norms.

Many experiments have been conducted to test the validity of these two views, identifying a host of conditions under which the human mind appears more rational or irrational. But most of this work has dealt with simple situations, such as Bayesian inference with binary hypotheses, one single piece of binary data, and all the necessary information conveniently laid out for the participant (Chapter 6). In many real-world situations, however, there are multiple pieces of information, which are not independent, but redundant. Here, Bayes's rule and other "rational" algorithms quickly become mathematically complex and computationally intractable, at least for ordinary human minds. These situations make neither of the two views look promising. If one were to apply the classical view to such complex real-world environments, this would suggest that the mind is a supercalculator like a Laplacean demon (Wimsatt, 1976)—carrying around the collected works of Kolmogoroff, Fisher, or Neyman—and simply needs a memory jog, like the slave in Plato's *Meno*. On the other hand, the heuristics-and-biases view of human irrationality would lead us to believe that humans are hopelessly lost in the face of real-world complexity, given their supposed inability to reason according to the canon of classical rationality, even in simple laboratory experiments.

There is a third way to look at inference, focusing on the psychological and ecological rather than on logic and probability theory. This view questions classical rationality as a universal norm and thereby questions the very definition of "good" reasoning on which both the Enlightenment and the heuristics-and-biases views were built. Herbert Simon, possibly the best known proponent of this third view, proposed looking for models of *bounded rationality* instead of classical rationality. Simon (1956, 1982) argued that information-processing systems typically need to *satisfice* rather than to optimize. *Satisficing*, a blend of *sufficing* and *satisfying*, is a word of Scottish origin, which Simon uses to characterize strategies that successfully deal with conditions of limited time, knowledge, or computational capacities. His concept of satisficing postulates, for instance, that an organism would choose the first object (a mate, perhaps) that satisfies its aspiration level—instead of the intractable sequence of taking the time to survey all possible alternatives, estimating probabilities and utilities for the possible outcomes associated with each alternative, calculating expected utilities, and choosing the alternative that scores highest.

Let us stress that Simon's notion of bounded rationality has two sides, one cognitive and one ecological. As early as in *Administrative Behavior* (1945), he emphasized the cognitive limitations of real minds as opposed to the omniscient Laplacean demons of classical rationality. As early as in his *Psychological Review* article titled "Rational Choice and the Structure of the Environment" (1956), Simon emphasized that minds are adapted to real-world environments. The two go in tandem: "Human rational behavior is shaped by a scissors whose two blades are the structure of task environments and the computational capabilities of the actor" (Simon, 1990, p. 7). For the most part, however, theories of human inference have focused exclusively on the cognitive side, equating the notion of bounded rationality with the statement that humans are limited information processors, period. In a Procrustean-bed fashion, *bounded rationality* became almost synonymous with *heuristics and biases*, thus paradoxically underpinning classical rationality as the normative standard for both biases and bounded rationality (for a discussion of this confusion see Lopes, 1992). Simon's insight that the minds of living systems should be understood relative to the environment in which they evolved, rather than to the tenets of classical rationality, has had little impact so far in research on human inference. Simple psychological strategies that were observed in human inference, reasoning, or decision making were often discredited without a fair trial, because they looked so stupid by the norms of classical rationality. For instance, when Keeney and Raiffa (1993) discussed the lexicographic ordering strategy they had observed in practice—a procedure related to the models of bounded rationality we propose in this chapter—they concluded that this procedure "is naively simple" and "will rarely pass a test of 'reasonableness' " (p. 78). They did not report such a test. We do.

Initially, the concept of bounded rationality was only vaguely defined, often as that which is not classical economics, and one could "fit a lot of things into it by foresight and hindsight," as Simon (1992b, p. 18) himself put it. We wish to do more than oppose the Laplacean demon view. We strive to come up with something positive that could replace this unrealistic view of mind. What are these simple, intelligent heuristics capable of making near-optimal inferences? How fast and how accurate are they? In this chapter, we propose a class of heuristics that exhibit bounded rationality in both of Simon's senses. These "fast and frugal heuristics" operate with simple psychological principles that satisfy the constraints of limited time, knowledge, and computational might, rather than those of classical rationality. At the same time, they are designed to be fast and frugal without a significant loss of inferential accuracy, because they can exploit the structure of environments.

The chapter is organized as follows. We begin by describing the task the cognitive heuristics are designed to address, the Take The Best heuristic, and the real-world environment on which its performance will be tested. Next, we report on a competition in which the heuristic competes with "rational" strategies in making inferences about a real-world environment. The "rational" strategies start with an advantage: They use more time, information, and computational might to make inferences. Finally, we study variants of the heuristic that make faster inferences and get by with even less knowledge.

The Task

We deal with inferential tasks in which a choice must be made between two alternatives on a quantitative dimension. Consider the following example:

Which city has a larger population? (a) Hamburg (b) Cologne.

Two-alternative-choice tasks occur in various contexts in which inferences need to be made with limited time and knowledge, such as in decision making and risk assessment during driving (e.g., exit the highway now or stay on); treatment-allocation decisions (e.g., who to treat first in the emergency room: the 80-year-old heart attack victim or the 16-year-old car accident victim); and financial decisions (e.g., whether to buy or sell in the trading pit). Inference concerning population demographics, such as city populations of the past, present, and future (e.g., Brown & Siegler, 1993), is of importance to people working in urban planning, industrial development, and marketing. Population demographics, which is better understood than, say, the stock market, will serve us later as a "drosophila" environment that allows us to analyze the behavior of heuristics.

We study two-alternative-choice tasks in situations in which a person has to make an inference based solely on knowledge retrieved from memory. We refer to this as *inference from memory*, as opposed to *inference from givens*. Inference from memory involves search in declarative knowledge and has been investigated in studies of, inter alia, confidence in general knowledge (e.g., Juslin, 1994; Sniezek & Buckley, 1993); the effect of repetition on belief (e.g., Hertwig, Gigerenzer, & Hoffrage, 1997); hindsight bias (e.g., Fischhoff, 1977); quantitative estimates of area and population of nations (Brown & Siegler, 1993); and autobiographic memory of time (Huttenlocher, Hedges, & Prohaska, 1988). Studies of inference from givens, on the other hand, involve making inferences from information presented by an experimenter (e.g., Hammond, Hursch, & Todd, 1964). In the tradition of Ebbinghaus's nonsense syllables, attempts are often made here to prevent individual knowledge from having an impact on the results by using problems about hypothetical referents instead of actual ones. For instance, in celebrated judgment and decision-making tasks, such as the "cab" problem and the "Linda" problem, all the relevant information is provided by the experimenter, and individual knowledge about cabs and hit-and-run accidents, or feminist bank tellers, is considered of no relevance (Gigerenzer & Murray, 1987). As a consequence, limited knowledge or individual differences in knowledge play a small role in inference from givens. In contrast, the heuristics proposed in this chapter perform inference from memory, they use limited knowledge as input, and as we will show, they can actually profit from a lack of knowledge.

Assume that a person does not know or cannot deduce the answer to the Hamburg–Cologne question but needs to make an inductive inference from related real-world knowledge. How is this inference derived? How can we predict choice (Hamburg or Cologne) from a person's state of knowledge?

Theory

The cognitive heuristics we propose are realizations of a framework for modeling inferences from memory, the theory of *probabilistic mental models* (Chapter 7). The theory of probabilistic mental models assumes that inferences about unknown states of the world are based on probability cues. The theory relates three visions: (a) Inductive inference needs to be studied with respect to natural environments, as emphasized by Brunswik and Simon; (b) inductive inference is carried out by satisficing algorithms, as emphasized by Simon; and (c) inductive inferences are based on frequencies of events in a reference class, as proposed by Reichenbach and other frequentist statisticians. The theory of probabilistic mental models accounts for choice and confidence, but only choice is addressed in this chapter.

The major thrust of the theory is that it replaces the canon of classical rationality with simple, plausible psychological mechanisms of inference— mechanisms that a mind can actually carry out under limited time and knowledge and that could have possibly arisen through evolution. Most traditional models of inference, from linear multiple regression models to Bayesian models to neural networks, try to find some optimal integration of all information available: Every bit of information is taken into account, weighted, and combined in a computationally expensive way. The family of heuristics based on PMM theory does not implement this classical ideal. Search in memory for relevant information is reduced to a minimum, and there is no integration (but rather a substitution) of pieces of information. These boundedly rational heuristics dispense with the fiction of the omniscient Laplacean demon, who has all the time and knowledge to search for all relevant information, to compute the weights and covariances, and then to integrate all this information into an inference.

Limited Knowledge

A PMM is an inductive device that uses limited knowledge to make fast inferences. Different from mental models of syllogisms and deductive inference (Johnson-Laird, 1983), which focus on the logical task of truth preservation and where knowledge is irrelevant (except for the meanings of connectives and other logical terms), PMMs perform intelligent guesses about unknown features of the world, based on uncertain indicators. To make an inference about which of two objects, a or b, has a higher value, knowledge about a reference class R is searched, with $a, b \in R$. In our example, knowledge about the reference class "cities in Germany" could be searched. The knowledge consists of probability cues C_i ($i = 1, \ldots, n$) and the cue values a_i and b_i of the objects for the ith cue. For instance, when making inferences about populations of German cities, the fact that a city has a professional soccer team in the major league (*Bundesliga*) may come to a person's mind as a potential cue. That is, when considering pairs of German cities, if one city has a soccer team

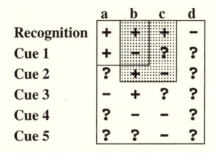

	a	b	c	d
Recognition	+	+	+	–
Cue 1	+	–	?	?
Cue 2	?	+	–	?
Cue 3	–	+	?	?
Cue 4	?	–	–	?
Cue 5	?	?	–	?

Figure 8.1 Illustration of bounded search through limited knowledge. Objects *a, b,* and *c* are recognized; object *d* is not. Cue values are positive (+) or negative (–); missing knowledge is shown by question marks. Cues are ordered according to their validities. To infer whether $a > b$, the Take The Best heuristic looks up only the cue values in the shaded space; to infer whether $b > c$, search is bounded to the dotted space. The other cue values are not looked up.

in the major league and the other does not, then the city with the team is likely, but not certain, to have the larger population.

Limited knowledge means that the matrix of objects by cues has missing entries (i.e., objects, cues, or cue values may be unknown). Figure 8.1 models the limited knowledge of a person. She has heard of three German cities, *a, b,* and *c,* but not of *d* (represented by three positive and one negative recognition values). She knows some facts (cue values) about these cities with respect to five binary cues. For a binary cue, there are two cue values, positive (e.g., the city has a soccer team) or negative (it does not). *Positive* refers to a cue value that signals a higher value on the target variable (e.g., having a soccer team is correlated with a large population). Unknown cue values are shown by a question mark. Because she has never heard of *d,* all cue values for object *d* are, by definition, unknown.

People rarely know all the information on which an inference could be based, that is, knowledge is limited. We model limited knowledge in two respects: A person can have (a) incomplete knowledge of the objects in the reference class (e.g., she recognizes only some of the cities), (b) limited knowledge of the cue values (facts about cities), or (c) both. For instance, a person who does not know all of the cities with soccer teams may know some cities with positive cue values (e.g., Munich and Hamburg certainly have teams), many with negative cue values (e.g., Heidelberg and Potsdam certainly do not have teams), and several cities for which cue values will not be known.

The Take The Best Heuristic

The first fast and frugal heuristic presented is called *Take The Best*, because its policy is "take the best, ignore the rest." It is the basic heuristic in the

PMM framework. Variants that work faster or with less knowledge are described later. We explain the steps of Take The Best for binary cues (the heuristic can be easily generalized to many valued cues), using Figure 8.1 for illustration.

Take The Best assumes a rank order of cues according to their subjective validities (as in Figure 8.1). We call the highest ranking cue (that discriminates between the two alternatives) the best cue. The heuristic is shown in the form of a flow diagram in Figure 8.2.

Step 0: Recognition Heuristic   The recognition heuristic is invoked when the mere recognition of an object is a predictor of the target variable (e.g., population). The recognition heuristic states the following: If only one of the two objects is recognized, then choose the recognized object. If neither of the two objects is recognized, then choose randomly between them. If both of the objects are recognized, then proceed to Step 1.

Example: If a person in the knowledge state shown in Figure 8.1 is asked to infer which of city a and city d has more inhabitants, the inference will be city a, because the person has never heard of city d before.

Step 1. Search Rule   Choose the cue with the highest validity that has not yet been tried for this choice task. Look up the cue values of the two objects.

Step 2. Stopping Rule   If one object has a positive cue value and the other does not (i.e., either a negative or an unknown value; see Figure 8.3), then stop

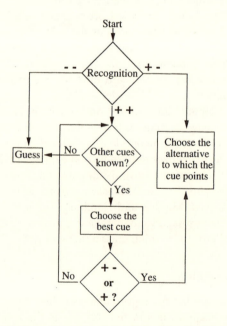

Figure 8.2 Flow diagram of the Take The Best heuristic.

search and go on to Step 3. Otherwise go back to Step 1 and search for another cue. If no further cue is found, then guess.

Step 3. Decision Rule (one-reason decision making)   Predict that the object with the positive cue value has the higher value on the criterion.

Examples: Suppose the task is judging which of city *a* or *b* is larger (Figure 8.1). Both cities are recognized (Step 0), and search for the best cue results in a positive and a negative cue value for Cue 1 (Step 1). The cue discriminates, and search is terminated (Step 2). The person makes the inference that city *a* is larger (Step 3).

Suppose now the task is judging which city *b* or *c* is larger. Both cities are recognized (Step 0), and search for the cue values results in a negative cue value on object *b* for Cue 1, but the corresponding cue value for object *c* is unknown (Step 1). The cue does not discriminate, so search is continued (Step 2). Search for the next cue results in positive and negative cue values for Cue 2 (Step 1). This cue discriminates and search is terminated (Step 2). The person makes the inference that city *b* is larger (Step 3).

The features of this heuristic are (a) search extends through only a portion of the total knowledge in memory (as shown by the shaded and dotted parts of Figure 8.1) and is stopped immediately when the first discriminating cue is found, (b) the algorithm does not attempt to integrate information but uses one-reason decision making instead, and (c) the total amount of information processed is contingent on each task (pair of objects) and varies in a predictable way among individuals with different knowledge. This fast and computationally simple heuristic is a model of bounded rationality rather than of classical rationality. There is a close parallel with Simon's concept of "satisficing": Take The Best stops search after the first discriminating cue is found, just as Simon's satisficing algorithm stops search after the first option that meets an aspiration level.

The heuristic is hardly a standard statistical tool for inductive inference: It does not use all available information, it is non-compensatory and nonlinear,

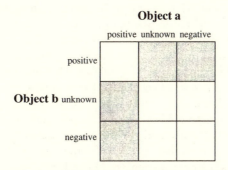

Figure 8.3 Stopping rule. A cue discriminates between two alternatives if one has a positive cue value and the other does not. The four discriminating cases are shaded. If a cue discriminates, search is stopped.

and variants of it can violate transitivity. Thus it differs from standard linear tools for inference such as multiple regression, as well as from nonlinear neural networks that are compensatory in nature. Take The Best is noncompensatory because only the best discriminating cue determines the inference or decision; no combination of other cue values can override this decision. In this way, the heuristic does not conform to the classical economic view of human behavior (e.g., Becker, 1976), where, on the assumption that all aspects can be reduced to one dimension (e.g., money), there always exists a trade-off between commodities or pieces of information. That is the heuristic violates the Archimedian axiom, which implies that for any multidimensional object a $(a_1, a_2, \ldots, a_n)$ preferred to b $(b_1, b_2, \ldots, b_n)$, where a_1 dominates b_1, this preference can be reversed by taking multiples of any one or a combination of $b_2, b_3, \ldots, b_n$. As we discuss, variants of this heuristic also violate transitivity, one of the cornerstones of classical rationality (McClennen, 1990).

Empirical Evidence

Despite their flagrant violation of traditional standards of rationality, Take The Best and PMM theory have been successful in integrating various extant phenomena in inference from memory and predicting novel phenomena. These include conditions under which overconfidence occurs, disappears, and inverts to underestimation (Gigerenzer, 1993b; Juslin, 1993, 1994; Juslin, Winman, & Persson, 1995; but see Griffin & Tversky, 1992), and those in which the hard–easy effect occurs, disappears, and inverts—predictions that have been experimentally confirmed by Hoffrage (1994) and by Juslin (1993).

Fast and frugal heuristics allow for predictions of individual choices, including individual differences based on each person's knowledge. Bröder (in press) reported that when search for information is costly, about 65% of the participants' choices were consistent with Take The Best, compared to fewer than 10% with a linear strategy. (For similar results, see Rieskamp & Hoffrage, 1999.) Hoffrage and Hertwig (1999) showed that a memory updating model with Take The Best could correctly predict some 75% of all individual occurrences of hindsight bias. Goldstein and Gigerenzer (1999) showed that the recognition heuristic predicted individual participants' choices in about 90% to 100% of all cases, even when participants were taught information that suggested doing otherwise (negative cue values for the recognized objects). Among the evidence for the empirical validity of Take The Best are the tests of a bold prediction, the less-is-more effect, which postulates conditions under which people with little knowledge make better inferences than those who know more. This surprising prediction has been experimentally confirmed. For instance, U.S. students make slightly more correct inferences about German city populations (about which they know little) than about U.S. cities, and vice versa for German students (Gigerenzer, 1993b; Goldstein & Gigerenzer, 1999; Hoffrage, 1994). The recognition heuristic has been successfully applied to stock investment (Borges et al., 1999); on rumor-based stock market trading, see DiFonzo (1994). Other species also practice one-reason decision making closely resembling Take The Best, such as when female guppies choose between males on the basis of an order of cues (Dugatkin, 1996). For general reviews, see Gigerenzer et al. (1999) and McClelland and Bolger (1994).

The reader familiar with the original heuristic presented in Gigerenzer et al. (1991, see Chapter 7) will have noticed that we simplified the stopping rule.[1] In the present version, search is already terminated if one object has a positive cue value and the other does not, whereas in the earlier version, search was terminated only when one object had a positive value and the other a negative one (cf. Figure 7.3 in Chapter 7 with Figure 8.3 in this chapter). This change follows empirical evidence that participants tend to use this faster, simpler stopping rule (Hoffrage, 1994).

This chapter does not attempt to provide further empirical evidence. For the moment, we assume that the model is descriptively valid and investigate how accurate this fast and frugal heuristic is in drawing inferences about unknown aspects of a real-world environment. Can a heuristic based on simple psychological principles that violate the norms of classical rationality make a fair number of accurate inferences?

The Environment

We tested the performance of Take The Best on how accurately it made inferences about a real-world environment. The environment was the set of all cities in Germany with more than 100,000 inhabitants (83 cities after German reunification), with population as the target variable. The model of the environment consisted of 9 binary ecological cues and the actual 9×83 cue values. The full model of the environment is shown in Gigerenzer and Goldstein (1996a).

Each cue has an associated validity that is indicative of its predictive power. The *ecological validity* of a cue is the relative frequency with which the cue correctly predicts the target, defined with respect to the reference class (e.g., all German cities with more than 100,000 inhabitants). For instance, if one checks all pairs in which one city has a soccer team but the other city does not, one finds that in 87% of these cases, the city with the team also has the higher population. This value is the ecological validity of the soccer team cue. The validity v_i of the ith cue is

$$v_i = p[t(a) > t(b) \mid a_i \text{ is positive and } b_i \text{ is negative}],$$

where $t(a)$ and $t(b)$ are the values of objects a and b on the target variable t and p is a probability measured as a relative frequency in R.

The ecological validity of the nine cues ranged over the whole spectrum: from .51 (only slightly better than chance) to 1.0 (certainty), as shown in Table

---

1. Also, we now use the term *stopping rule* instead of *activation rule*.

Table 8.1 Cues, ecological validities, and discrimination rates

Cue	Ecological validity	Discrimination rate
National capital (Is the city the national capital?)	1.00	.02
Exposition site (Was the city once an exposition site?)	.91	.25
Soccer team (Does the city have a team in the major league?)	.87	.30
Intercity train (Is the city on the Intercity line?)	.78	.38
State capital (Is the city a state capital?)	.77	.30
License plate (Is the abbreviation only one letter long?)	.75	.34
University (Is the city home to a university?)	.71	.51
Industrial belt (Is the city in the industrial belt?)	.56	.30
East Germany (Was the city formerly in East Germany?)	.51	.27

8.1. A cue with a high ecological validity, however, is often not useful if its discrimination rate is small.

Table 8.1 also shows the *discrimination rates* for each cue. The discrimination rate of a cue is the relative frequency with which the cue discriminates between any two objects from the reference class. The discrimination rate is a function of the distribution of the cue values and the number N of objects in the reference class. Let the relative frequencies of the positive and negative cue values be x and y, respectively. Then the discrimination rate d_i of the ith cue is

$$d_i = \frac{2x_iy_i}{1 - \dfrac{1}{N}}$$

as an elementary calculation shows. Thus, if N is very large, the discrimination rate is approximately $2x_iy_i$.[2] The larger the ecological validity of a cue, the better the inference. The larger the discrimination rate, the more often a cue can be used to make an inference. In the present environment, ecological validities and discrimination rates are negatively correlated. The redundancy of

2. For instance, if $N = 2$ and one cue value is positive and the other negative ($x_i = y_i = .5$), $d_i = 1.0$. If N increases, with x_i and y_i held constant, then d_i decreases and converges to $2x_iy_i$.

cues in the environment, as measured by pairwise correlations between cues, ranges between −.25 and .54, with an average absolute value of .19.[3]

The Competition

The question of how well a fast and frugal heuristic performs in a real-world environment has rarely been posed in research on inductive inference. The present simulations seem to be the first to test how well one-reason decision making does compared with standard integration strategies, which require more knowledge, time, and computational power. This question is important for Simon's postulated link between the cognitive and the ecological: If the simple psychological principles in fast and frugal heuristics are tuned to ecological structures, these heuristics should not fail outright. We propose a competition between various inferential strategies. The contest will go to the strategy that scores the highest proportion of correct inferences (accuracy) using the smallest number of cues (frugality).

Simulating Limited Knowledge

We simulated people with varying degrees of knowledge about cities in Germany. Limited knowledge can take two forms. One is limited recognition of objects in the reference class. The other is limited knowledge about the cue values of recognized objects. To model limited recognition knowledge, we simulated people who recognized between 0 and 83 German cities. To model limited knowledge of cue values, we simulated 6 basic classes of people, who knew 0%, 10%, 20%, 50%, 75%, or 100% of the cue values associated with the objects they recognized. Combining the two sources of limited knowledge resulted in 6 × 84 types of people, each having different degrees and kinds of limited knowledge. Within each type of people, we created 500 simulated in-

---

3. There are various other measures of redundancy besides pairwise correlation. The important point is that whatever measure of redundancy one uses, the resultant value does not have the same meaning for all strategies. For instance, all that counts for Take The Best is what proportion of correct inferences the second cue adds to the first in the cases where the first cue does not discriminate, how much the third cue adds to the first two in the cases where they do not discriminate, and so on. If a cue discriminates, search is terminated, and the degree of redundancy in the cues that were not included in the search is irrelevant. Integration strategies, in contrast, integrate all information and, thus, always work with the total redundancy in the environment (or knowledge base). For instance, when deciding among objects a, b, c, and d in Figure 8.1, the cue values of Cues 3, 4, and 5 do not matter from the point of view of Take The Best (because search is terminated before reaching Cue 3). However, the values of Cues 3, 4, and 5 affect the redundancy of the ecological system, from the point of view of all integration algorithms. The lesson is that the degree of redundancy in an environment depends on the kind of strategy that operates on the environment. One needs to be cautious in interpreting measures of redundancy without reference to a strategy.

dividuals, who differed randomly from one another in the particular objects and cue values they knew. All objects and cue values known were determined randomly within the appropriate constraints, that is, a certain number of objects known, a certain total percentage of cue values known, and the validity of the recognition heuristic (as explained in the following paragraph).

The simulation needed to be realistic in the sense that the simulated people could invoke the recognition heuristic. Therefore, the sets of cities the simulated people knew had to be carefully chosen so that the recognized cities were larger than the unrecognized ones a certain percentage of the time. We performed a survey to get an empirical estimate of the actual covariation between recognition of cities and city populations. Let us define the *recognition validity* α to be the probability, in a reference class, that one object has a greater value on the target variable than another, in the cases where one object is recognized and the other is not:

$$\alpha = p[t(a) > t(b) | a_r \text{ is positive and } b_r \text{ is negative}],$$

where $t(a)$ and $t(b)$ are the values of objects a and b on the target variable t, a_r and b_r are the recognition values of a and b, and p is a probability measured as a relative frequency in R.

In a pilot study of 26 undergraduates at the University of Chicago, we found that the cities they recognized (within the 83 largest in Germany) were larger than the cities they did not recognize in about 80% of all possible comparisons. We incorporated this value into our simulations by choosing sets of cities (for each knowledge state, i.e., for each number of cities recognized) where the known cities were larger than the unknown cities in about 80% of all cases. Thus the cities known by the simulated individuals had the same relationship between recognition and population as did those of the human individuals. Let us first look at the performance of Take The Best.

Testing the Take The Best Heuristic

We tested how well individuals using Take The Best did at answering real-world questions such as, Which city has more inhabitants: (a) Heidelberg or (b) Bonn? Each of the 500 simulated individuals in each of the 6 × 84 types was tested on the exhaustive set of 3,403 city pairs, resulting in a total of 500 × 6 × 84 × 3,403 tests, that is, about 858 million.

The curves in Figure 8.4 show the average proportion of correct inferences for each proportion of objects and cue values known. The x axis represents the number of cities recognized, and the y axis shows the proportion of correct inferences that Take The Best drew. Each of the 6 × 84 points that make up the six curves is an average proportion of correct inferences taken from 500 simulated individuals, who each made 3,403 inferences.

When the proportion of cities recognized was zero, the proportion of correct inferences was at chance level (.5). When up to half of all cities were recognized, performance increased at all levels of knowledge about cue values. The maximum percentage of correct inferences was around 77%. The striking re-

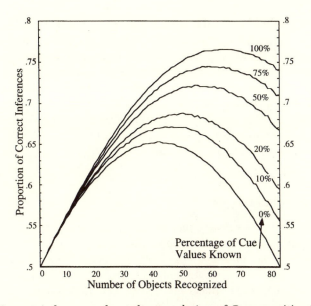

Figure 8.4 Correct inferences about the population of German cities (two-alternative-choice tasks) by Take The Best. Inferences are based on actual information about the 83 largest cities and nine cues for population (see text). Limited knowledge of the simulated individuals is varied across two dimensions: (a) the number of cities recognized (x axis) and (b) the percentage of cue values known (the six curves).

sult was that this maximum was not achieved when individuals knew all cue values of all cities, but rather when they knew less. This result shows the ability of the heuristic to exploit limited knowledge, that is, to do best when not everything is known. Thus, Take The Best produces the *less-is-more* effect. At any level of limited knowledge of cue values, learning more German cities will eventually cause a decrease in the proportion correct. Take, for instance, the curve where 75% of the cue values were known and the point where the simulated participants recognized about 60 German cities. If these individuals learned about the remaining German cities, their proportion correct would decrease. The rationale behind the less-is-more effect is the recognition heuristic, and it can be understood best from the curve that reflects 0% of total cue values known. Here, all decisions are made on the basis of the recognition heuristic, or by guessing. On this curve, the recognition heuristic comes into play most when half of the cities are known, so it takes on an inverted-U shape. When half the cities are known, the recognition heuristic can be activated most often, that is, for roughly 50% of the questions. Because we set the recognition validity in advance, 80% of these inferences will be correct. In the remaining half of the questions, when recognition cannot be used (either both cities are recognized or both cities are unrecognized), then the organism is forced to guess and only 50% of the guesses will be correct. Using the 80% effective recognition validity half of the time and guessing the other half of the time, the organism scores 65% correct, which is the peak of the bottom curve. The mode of this curve moves to the right with increasing knowledge about cue values. Note that even when a person knows everything, all cue values of all cities, there are states of limited knowledge in which the person would make more accurate inferences. We are not going to discuss the conditions of this counterintuitive effect and the supporting experimental evidence here (see Goldstein & Gigerenzer, 1999). Our focus is on how much better integration strategies can do in making inferences.

Integration Strategies

We asked several colleagues in the fields of statistics and economics to devise decision strategies that would do better than Take The Best. The five integration strategies we simulated and pitted against Take The Best in a competition were among those suggested by our colleagues. These competitors include "proper" and "improper" linear models (Dawes, 1979; Lovie & Lovie, 1986). These strategies, in contrast to Take The Best, embody two classical principles of rational inference: (a) complete search—they use all available information (cue values)—and (b) complete integration—they combine all these pieces of information into a single value. In short, we refer in this chapter to strategies that satisfy these principles as "rational" (in quotation marks) strategies.

Contestant 1: Tallying   Let us start with a simple integration strategy: tallying of positive evidence (Goldstein, 1994). In this strategy, the number of positive cue values for each object is tallied across all cues ($i = 1, \ldots, n$), and the object with the largest number of positive cue values is chosen. Integration strategies are not based (at least explicitly) on the recognition heuristic. For this reason, and to make the integration strategies as strong as possible, we allow all the integration strategies to make use of recognition information (the positive and negative recognition values; see Figure 8.1). Integration strategies treat recognition as a cue, like the nine ecological cues in Table 8.1. That is, in the competition, the number of cues (n) is thus equal to 10 (because recognition is included). The decision criterion for tallying is the following:

$$\text{If } \sum_{i=1}^{n} a_i > \sum_{i=1}^{n} b_i, \text{ then choose city } a.$$

$$\text{If } \sum_{i=1}^{n} a_i < \sum_{i=1}^{n} b_i, \text{ then choose city } b.$$

$$\text{If } \sum_{i=1}^{n} a_i = \sum_{i=1}^{n} b_i, \text{ then guess.}$$

The assignments of a_i and b_i are the following:

$$a_i, b_i = \begin{vmatrix} 1 \text{ if the } i\text{th cue value is positive} \\ 0 \text{ if the } i\text{th cue value is negative} \\ 0 \text{ if the } i\text{th cue value is unknown.} \end{vmatrix}$$

Let us compare cities a and b from Figure 8.1. By tallying the positive cue values, a would score 2 points and b would score 3. Thus, tallying would choose b to be the larger, in opposition to Take The Best, which would infer that a is larger. Variants of tallying, such as the frequency-of-good-features heuristic, have been discussed in the decision literature (Alba & Marmorstein, 1987; Payne, Bettman, & Johnson, 1993).

Contestant 2: Weighted Tallying   Tallying treats all cues alike, independent of cue validity. Weighted tallying of positive evidence is identical with tallying, except that it weights each cue according to its ecological validity, v_i. The ecological validities of the cues appear in Table 8.1. We set the validity of the recognition cue to .8, which is the empirical average determined by the pilot study. The decision rule is as follows:

$$\text{If } \sum_{i=1}^{n} a_i v_i > \sum_{i=1}^{n} b_i v_i, \text{ then choose city } a.$$

$$\text{If } \sum_{i=1}^{n} a_i v_i < \sum_{i=1}^{n} b_i v_i, \text{ then choose city } b.$$

$$\text{If } \sum_{i=1}^{n} a_i v_i = \sum_{i=1}^{n} b_i v_i, \text{ then guess.}$$

Note that weighted tallying needs more information than either tallying or Take The Best, namely, quantitative information about ecological validities. In the simulation, we provided the real ecological validities to give this strategy a good chance.

Calling again on the comparison of objects a and b from Figure 8.1, let us assume that the validities would be .8 for recognition and .9, .8, .7, .6, .51 for Cues 1 through 5. Weighted tallying would thus assign 1.7 points to a and 2.3 points to b. Thus weighted tallying would also choose b to be the larger.

Both tallying strategies treat negative information and missing information identically. That is, they consider only positive evidence. The following strategies distinguish between negative and missing information and integrate both positive and negative information.

Contestant 3: Unit-Weight Linear Model   The unit-weight linear model is a special case of the equal-weight linear model (Huber, 1989) and has been advocated as a good approximation of weighted linear models (Dawes, 1979; Einhorn & Hogarth, 1975). The decision criterion for unit-weight integration is the same as for tallying; only the assignment of a_i and b_i differs:

$$a_i, b_i = \begin{vmatrix} 1 \text{ if the } i\text{th cue value is positive} \\ -1 \text{ if the } i\text{th cue value is negative} \\ 0 \text{ if the } i\text{th cue value is unknown.} \end{vmatrix}$$

Comparing objects a and b from Figure 8.1 would involve assigning 1.0 points to a and 1.0 points to b and, thus, choosing randomly. This simple linear model corresponds to Model 2 in Einhorn and Hogarth (1975, p. 177) with the weight parameter set equal to 1.

Contestant 4: Weighted Linear Model   This model is like the unit-weight linear model except that the values of a_i and b_i are multiplied by their respective ecological validities. The decision criterion is the same as with weighted tallying. The weighted linear model (or some variant of it) is often viewed as an optimal rule for preferential choice, under the idealization of independent dimensions or cues (e.g., Keeney & Raiffa, 1993; Payne et al., 1993). Comparing objects a and b from Figure 8.1 would involve assigning 1.0 points to a and 0.8 points to b and, thus, choosing a to be the larger.

Contestant 5: Multiple Regression   The weighted linear model reflects the different validities of the cues but not the dependencies between cues. Multiple regression creates weights that reflect the covariances between predictors or cues and is commonly seen as an "optimal" linear way to integrate various pieces of information into an estimate (e.g., Brunswik, 1955; Hammond, 1966). Neural networks using the delta rule determine their "optimal" weights by the same principles as multiple regression does (Stone, 1986). The delta rule carries out the equivalent of a multiple linear regression from the input patterns to the targets.

The weights for the multiple regression could simply be calculated from the full information about the nine ecological cues. To make multiple regression an even stronger competitor, we also provided information about which cities the simulated individuals recognized. Thus the multiple regression used nine ecological cues and the recognition cue to generate its weights. Because the weights for the recognition cue depend on which cities are recognized, we calculated 6 × 500 × 84 sets of weights: one for each simulated individual. Unlike any of the other strategies, regression had access to the actual city populations (even for those cities not recognized by the hypothetical person) in the calculation of the weights.[4] During the quiz, each simulated person used the set of weights provided to it by multiple regression to estimate the populations of the cities in the comparison.

There was a missing-values problem in computing these 6 × 84 × 500 sets of regression coefficients, because most simulated individuals did not know certain cue values, for instance, the cue values of the cities they did not recognize. We strengthened the performance of multiple regression by substituting

---

4. We cannot claim that these integration strategies are the best ones, nor can we know a priori which small variations will succeed in our bumpy real-world environment. An example: After we had completed the simulations, we learned that regressing on the ranks of the cities does slightly better than regressing on the city populations. The key issue is what are the structures of environments in which particular strategies and variants thrive.

unknown cue values with the average of the cue values the person knew for the given cue.[5] This was done both in creating the weights and in using these weights to estimate populations. Unlike cross-validation procedures in which weights are estimated from one half of the data and inferences based on these weights are made for the other half, the regression strategy had access to all the information (except, of course, the unknown cue values)—more information than was given to any of the competitors. In the competition, multiple regression and, to a lesser degree, the weighted linear model approximate the ideal of the Laplacean demon.

Results

Frugality   Take The Best is designed to enable quick decision making. Compared with the integration strategies, how frugal is it, measured by the amount of information searched in memory? For instance, in Figure 8.1, Take The Best would look up four cue values (including the recognition cue values) to infer that *a* is larger than *b*. None of the integration strategies use limited search; thus they always look up all cue values.

Figure 8.5 shows the number of cue values retrieved from memory by Take The Best for various levels of limited knowledge. Take The Best reduces search in memory considerably. Depending on the knowledge state, this heuristic needed to search for between 2 (the number of recognition values) and 20 (the maximum possible cue values: Each city has nine cue values and one recognition value). For instance, when a person recognized half of the cities and knew 50% of their cue values, then, on average, only about 4 cue values (that is, one fifth of all possible) were searched for. The average across all simulated participants was 5.9, which was less than a third of all available cue values.

Accuracy   Given that it searches only for a limited amount of information, how accurate is Take The Best, compared with the integration strategies? We ran the competition for all states of limited knowledge shown in Figure 8.4. We first report the results of the competition in the case where each strategy achieved its best performance: when 100% of the cue values were known. Figure 8.6 shows the results of the simulations, carried out in the same way as those in Figure 8.4.

To our surprise, Take The Best drew as many correct inferences as any of the other strategies, and more than some. The curves for Take The Best, multiple regression, weighted tallying, and tallying are so similar that there are only slight differences among them. Weighted tallying performed about as well as tallying, and the unit-weight linear model performed about as well as the weighted linear model—demonstrating that the previous finding that weights

---

5. If no single cue value was known for a given cue, the missing values were substituted by .5. This value was chosen because it is the midpoint of 0 and 1, which are the values used to stand for negative and positive cue values, respectively.

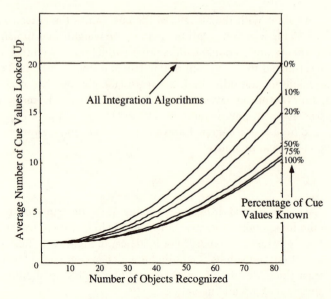

Figure 8.5 Frugality: Number of cue values looked up by Take The Best and by the competing integration strategies (see text), depending on the number of objects recognized (0–83) and the percentage of cue values known.

may be chosen in a fairly arbitrary manner, as long as they have the correct sign (Dawes, 1979), is generalizable to tallying. The two integration strategies that make use of both positive and negative information, unit-weight and weighted linear models, made considerably fewer correct inferences. By looking at the lower-left and upper-right corners of Figure 8.6, one can see that all competitors do equally well with a complete lack of knowledge or with complete knowledge. They differ when knowledge is limited. Note that some strategies can make more correct inferences when they do not have complete knowledge: a demonstration of the less-is-more effect mentioned earlier.

What was the result of the competition across all levels of limited knowledge? Table 8.2 shows the result for each level of limited knowledge of cue values, averaged across all levels of recognition knowledge. (Table 8.2 reports also the performance of two variants of Take The Best, which we discuss later: the Minimalist and Take The Last.) The values in the 100% column of Table 8.2 are the values in Figure 8.6 averaged across all levels of recognition. Take The Best made as many correct inferences as one of the competitors (weighted tallying) and more than the others. Because it was also the most frugal, we judged the competition goes to Take The Best as the highest performing, overall.

To our knowledge, this is the first time that it has been demonstrated that a fast and frugal heuristic, that is, Take The Best, can draw as many correct inferences about a real-world environment as integration strategies, across all

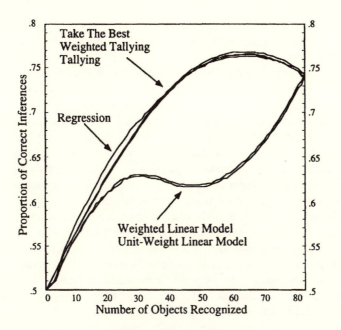

Figure 8.6 Results of the competition. The curve for Take The Best is identical with the 100% curve in Figure 8.4. The results for proportion correct have been smoothed by a running median smoother, to lessen visual noise between the lines.

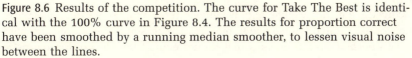

Strategy	10	20	50	75	100	Average
Take the Best	62.1	63.5	66.3	67.8	69.1	65.8
Weighted tallying	62.1	63.5	66.3	67.9	69.3	65.8
Regression	62.5	63.5	65.7	67.4	69.4	65.7
Tallying	62.0	63.3	65.9	67.6	69.1	65.6
Weighted linear model	62.3	62.7	62.3	61.9	62.5	62.3
Unit-weight linear model	62.1	62.2	62.1	62.0	62.2	62.1
Minimalist	61.9	63.1	65.0	66.1	67.4	64.7
Take The Last	61.9	63.0	64.6	65.8	67.5	64.5

Note: Values are rounded; averages are computed from the unrounded values. Bottom two heuristics are variants of Take The Best.

states of limited knowledge. The dictates of classical rationality would have led one to expect the integration strategies to do substantially better than the fast and frugal heuristic.

Two results of the simulation can be derived analytically. First and most obvious is that if knowledge about objects is zero, then all strategies perform at a chance level. Second, and less obvious, is that if all objects and cue values are known, then tallying produces as many correct inferences as the unit-weight linear model. This is because, under complete knowledge, the score under the tallying strategy is an increasing linear function of the score arrived at in the unit-weight linear model.[6] The equivalence between tallying and unit-weight linear models under complete knowledge is an important result. It is known that unit-weight linear models can sometimes perform about as well as proper linear models (i.e., models with weights that are chosen in an optimal way, such as in multiple regression; see Dawes, 1979). The equivalence implies that under complete knowledge, merely counting pieces of positive evidence can work as well as proper linear models. This result clarifies one condition under which searching only for positive evidence, a strategy that has sometimes been labeled *confirmation bias* or *positive test strategy*, can be a reasonable and efficient inferential strategy (Klayman & Ha, 1987; Tweney & Walker, 1990).

Why do the unit-weight and weighted linear models perform markedly worse under limited knowledge of objects? The reason is the simple and bold recognition heuristic. Strategies that do not exploit the recognition heuristic in environments where recognition is strongly correlated with the target variable pay the price of a considerable number of wrong inferences. The unit-weight and weighted linear models use recognition information and integrate it with all other information but do not follow the recognition heuristic, that is, they sometimes choose unrecognized cities over recognized ones. Why is this? In the environment, there are more negative cue values than positive ones, and most cities have more negative cue values than positive ones. From this it follows that when a recognized object is compared with an unrecognized object, the (weighted) sum of cue values of the recognized object will often be smaller than that of the unrecognized object (which is -1 for the unit-weight model and $-.8$ for the weighted linear model). Here the unit-weight and weighted linear models often make the inference that the unrecognized object is the larger one, due to the overwhelming negative evidence for the recognized object. Such inferences contradict the recognition heuristic. Tallying, in contrast, has the recognition heuristic built in implicitly. Because tallying ignores negative information, the tally for an unrecognized object is always 0 and,

---

6. The proof for this is as follows. The tallying score t for a given object is the number n^+ of positive cue values, as defined above. The score u for the unit-weight linear model is $n^+ - n^-$, where n^- is the number of negative cue values. Under complete knowledge, $n = n^+ + n^-$, where n is the number of cues. Thus, $t = n^+$, and $u = n^+ - n^-$. Because $n^- = n - n^+$, by substitution into the formula for u, we find that $u = n^+ - (n - n^+) = 2t - n$.

thus, is always smaller than the tally for a recognized object, which is at least 1 (for tallying, or .8 for weighted tallying, due to the positive value on the recognition cue). Thus tallying always arrives at the inference that a recognized object is larger than an unrecognized one.

Note that this explanation of the different performances puts the full weight in a psychological principle (the recognition heuristic) explicit in Take The Best, as opposed to the statistical issue of how to find optimal weights in a linear function. To test this explanation, we reran the simulations for the unit-weight and weighted linear models under the same conditions but replaced the recognition cue with the recognition heuristic. The simulation showed that the recognition heuristic accounts for all the difference.

Can Heuristics Get by with Even Less Time and Knowledge?

Take The Best produced a surprisingly high proportion of correct inferences, compared with more computationally expensive integration strategies. Making correct inferences despite limited knowledge is an important adaptive feature of a heuristic, but being right is not the only thing that counts. In many situations, time is limited, and acting fast can be as important as being correct. For instance, if you are driving on an unfamiliar highway and you have to decide in an instant what to do when the road forks, your problem is not necessarily making the best choice, but simply making a quick choice. Pressure to be quick is also character-istic for certain types of verbal interactions, such as press conferences, in which a fast answer indicates competence, or commercial interactions, such as having telephone service installed, where the customer has to decide in a few minutes which of a dozen calling features to purchase. These situations entail the dual constraints of limited knowledge and limited time. Take The Best is already faster and more frugal than the integration strategies, because it performs only a limited search and does not compute weighted sums of cue values. Can it be made even faster? It can, if search is guided by the recency of cues in memory rather than by cue validity.

The Take The Last Heuristic

Take The Last first tries the cue that discriminated the last time. If this cue does not discriminate, the heuristic then tries the cue that discriminated the time before last, and so on. The algorithm differs from Take The Best in Step 1, which is now reformulated as Step 1'.

Step 1'. Search Rule   If there is a record of which cues stopped search in pre-vious problems, choose the cue that stopped search in the most recent problem and that has not yet been tried. Look up the cue values of the two objects. Otherwise try a random cue and build up such a record.

Thus, in Step 2, the algorithm goes back to Step 1'. Variants of this search principle have been studied as the "Einstellung effect" in the water jar experiments (Luchins & Luchins, 1994), in which the solution strategy of the most recently solved problem is tried first on the subsequent problem. This effect has also been noted in physicians' generation of diagnoses for clinical cases (Weber, Böckenholt, Hilton, & Wallace, 1993).

This heuristic does not need a rank order of cues according to their validities; all that needs to be estimated is the direction in which a cue points. The rank order of cue validities is replaced by a memory of which cues were last used. Note that such a record can be built up independently of any knowledge about the structure of an environment and neither needs, nor uses, any feedback about whether inferences are right or wrong.

The Minimalist Heuristic

Can reasonably accurate inferences be achieved with even less knowledge? What we call the *Minimalist* heuristic needs neither information about the rank ordering of cue validities nor the discrimination history of the cues. In its ignorance, the heuristic picks cues in a random order. The algorithm differs from Take The Best in Step 1, which is now reformulated as Step 1":

Step 1". Search Rule   Draw a cue randomly (without replacement) and look up the cue values of the two objects.

The Minimalist does not necessarily speed up search, but it tries to get by with even less knowledge than any other strategy.

Results

Frugality   How frugal are the heuristics? The simulations showed that for each of the two variant heuristics, the relationship between amount of knowledge and the number of cue values looked up had the same form as for Take The Best (Figure 8.5). That is, unlike the integration strategies, the curves are concave and the number of cues searched for is maximal when knowledge of cue values is lowest. The average number of cue values looked up was lowest for Take The Last (5.3) followed by the Minimalist (5.6) and Take The Best (5.9). As knowledge becomes more and more limited (on both dimensions: recognition and cue values known), the difference in frugality becomes smaller and smaller. The reason why the Minimalist looks up fewer cue values than Take The Best is that cue validities and cue discrimination rates are negatively correlated (Table 8.1); therefore, randomly chosen cues tend to have larger discrimination rates than cues chosen by cue validity.

Accuracy   What is the price to be paid for speeding up search or reducing the knowledge of cue orderings and discrimination histories to nothing? We tested the performance of the two heuristics in the same environment as all other strategies. Figure 8.7 shows the proportion of correct inferences that the Minimalist achieved. For comparison, the performance of Take The Best with 100% of cue values known is indicated by a dotted line. Note that the Mini-

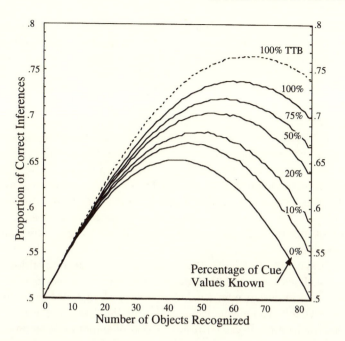

Figure 8.7 Performance of Minimalist. For comparison, the performance of Take The Best (TTB) is shown as a dotted line, for the case in which 100% of cue values are known.

malist performed surprisingly well. The maximum difference appeared when knowledge was complete and all cities were recognized. In these circumstances, the Minimalist did about 4 percentage points worse than Take The Best. On average, the proportion of correct inferences was only 1.1 percentage points less than the best strategies in the competition (Table 8.2).

The performance of Take The Last is similar to Figure 8.7, and the average number of correct inferences is shown in Table 8.2. Take The Last was more frugal but scored slightly lower than the Minimalist. Take The Last has an interesting ability, which fooled us in an earlier series of tests, in which we used a systematic (as opposed to a random) method for presenting the test pairs, starting with the largest city and pairing it with all others, and so on. An integration strategy such as multiple regression cannot "find out" that it is being tested in this systematic way, and its inferences are accordingly independent of the sequence of presentation. However, Take The Last found out and won this first round of the competition, outperforming the other competitors by some 10 percentage points. How did it exploit systematic testing? Recall that it tries, first, the cue that discriminated the last time. If this cue does not discriminate, it proceeds with the cue that discriminated the time before, and so on. In doing so, when testing is systematic in the way described, it tends to find, for each city that is being paired with all smaller ones, the group of cues for which the larger city has a positive value. Trying these cues first increases the chances of finding a discriminating cue that points in the right direction (toward the larger city). We learned our lesson and reran the whole competition with randomly ordered pairs of cities.

Discussion

The competition showed a surprising result: The Take The Best heuristic drew as many correct inferences about unknown features of a real-world environment as any of the integration strategies, and more than some of them. Two further simplifications of the heuristic—Take The Last (replacing knowledge about the rank orders of cue validities with a memory of the discrimination history of cues) and Minimalist (dispensing with both)—showed a comparatively small loss in correct inferences, and only when knowledge about cue values was high.

To the best of our knowledge, this is the first inference competition between fast and frugal heuristics and "rational" strategies in a real-world environment. The result is of importance for encouraging research that focuses on the power of simple psychological mechanisms, that is, on the design and testing of models of bounded rationality. The result is also of importance as an existence proof that cognitive strategies capable of successful performance in a real-world environment do not need to satisfy the classical norms of rational inference. The classical norms may be sufficient but are not necessary for good inference in real environments.

Bounded Rationality

In this section, we discuss the fundamental psychological mechanism postulated by the PMM family of heuristics: one-reason decision making. We discuss how this mechanism exploits the structure of environments in making fast inferences that differ from those arising from standard models of rational reasoning.

One-Reason Decision Making   What we call *one-reason decision making* is a specific form of bounded rationality. The inference, or decision, is based on a single, good reason. There is no compensation between cues. One-reason decision making is probably the most challenging feature of the PMM family of heuristics. As we mentioned before, it is a design feature that is not present in those models that depict human inference as an optimal integration of all information available (implying that all information has been looked up in the first place), including linear multiple regression and nonlinear neural networks. One-reason decision making means that each choice is based exclusively on one reason (i.e., cue), but this reason may be different from decision to decision. This allows for highly context-sensitive modeling of choice. One-reason decision making is not compensatory. Compensation is, after all, the cornerstone of classical rationality, assuming that all commodities can be compared and everything has its price. Compensation assumes commensurability. However, human minds do not trade everything; some things are supposed to be without a price (Elster, 1979). For instance, if a person must choose between two actions that might help him or her get out of deep financial trouble, and one involves killing someone, then no amount of money or other benefits might compensate for the prospect of bloody hands. He or she takes the action that does not involve killing a person, whatever other differences exist between the two options. More generally, hierarchies of ethical and moral values are often noncompensatory: True friendship, military honors, and doctorates are supposed to be without a price.

Noncompensatory strategies—such as lexicographic, conjunctive, and disjunctive rules—have been discussed in the literature, and some empirical evidence has been reported (e.g., Einhorn, 1970; Fishburn, 1988). The closest relative to the PMM family of heuristics is the lexicographic rule. Most evidence for lexicographic processes seems to come from studies on decision under risk (for a recent summary, see Lopes, 1995). However, despite empirical evidence, noncompensatory lexicographic strategies have often been dismissed at face value because they violate the tenets of classical rationality (Keeney & Raiffa, 1993; Lovie & Lovie, 1986). The PMM family is both more general and more specific than the lexicographic rule. It is more general because only Take The Best uses a lexicographic procedure in which cues are ordered according to their validity, whereas the variant heuristics do not. It is more specific, because several other psychological principles are integrated with the lexicographic rule in Take The Best, such as the recognition heuristic and the rules for confidence judgment (which are not dealt with in this chapter; see Chapter 7).

Serious models that comprise noncompensatory inferences are hard to find. One of the few examples is in Breiman, Friedman, Olshen, and Stone (1993), who reported a simple, noncompensatory algorithm with only 3 binary, ordered cues, which classified heart attack patients into high- and low-risk groups and was more accurate than standard statistical classification methods that used up to 19 variables. The practical relevance of this noncompensatory classification algorithm is obvious: In the emergency room, the physician can quickly obtain the measures on one, two, or three variables and does not need to perform any computations because there is no integration. This group of statisticians constructed decision trees that approach the task of classification (and estimation) much as Take The Best handles two-alternative choice. Relevance theory (Sperber, Cara, & Girotto, 1995) postulates that people generate consequences from rules according to accessibility and stop this process when expectations of relevance are met. Although relevance theory has not been as formalized, we see its stopping rule as parallel to that of Take The Best. Finally, optimality theory (Legendre, Raymond, & Smolensky, 1993; Prince & Smolensky, 1991) proposes that hierarchical noncompensation explains how the grammar of a language determines which structural description of an input best satisfies well-formedness constraints. Optimality theory (which is actually a satisficing theory) applies the same inferential principles as PMM theory to phonology and morphology.

Recognition Heuristic   The recognition heuristic is a version of ignorance-based decision making that exploits a lack of knowledge. The very fact that one does not know is used to make accurate inferences. The recognition heuristic is an intuitively plausible principle that seems not to have been used until now in models of bounded rationality. However, it has long been used to good advantage by humans and other animals. For instance, advertisement techniques as used by Benetton put all their effort into making sure that every customer recognizes the brand name, with no effort made to inform about the product itself. The idea behind this is that recognition is a strong force in customers' choices. One of our dear (and well-read) colleagues, after seeing a draft of this chapter, explained to us how he makes inferences about which books are worth acquiring. If he finds a book about a great topic but does not recognize the name of the author, he makes the inference that it is probably not worth buying. If, after an inspection of the references, he does not recognize most of the names, he concludes the book is not even worth reading. The recognition heuristic is also known as one of the rules that guide food preferences in animals. For instance, rats choose the food that they recognize having eaten before (or having smelled on the breath of fellow rats) and avoid novel foods (Gallistel, Brown, Carey, Gelman, & Keil, 1991).

The empirical validity of the recognition heuristic for inferences about unknown city populations, as used in the present simulations, can be directly tested in several ways. First, participants are presented pairs of cities, among them critical pairs in which one city is recognized and the other unrecognized, and their task is to infer which one has more inhabitants. The recognition heuristic predicts the recognized city. In our empirical tests, participants followed the recognition heuristic in roughly 90% to 100% of all cases (Goldstein & Gigerenzer, 1999). Second, participants are taught a cue, its ecological validity, and the cue values for some of the objects (such as whether a city has a soccer team or not). Subsequently, they are tested on critical pairs of cities, one recognized and one unrecognized, where the recognized city has a negative cue value (which indicates lower population). The second test is a harder test for the recognition heuristic than the first one and can be made even harder by using more cues with negative cue values for the recognized object, and by other means. Tests of the second kind have been performed, and participants still followed the recognition heuristic more than 90% of the time, providing evidence for its empirical validity (Goldstein & Gigerenzer, 1999).

The recognition heuristic is a useful strategy in domains where recognition is a predictor of a target variable, such as whether a food contains a toxic substance. In cases where recognition does not predict the target, the PMM algorithms can still perform the inference, but without the recognition heuristic (i.e., Step 0 is canceled).

Limited Search   Both one-reason decision making and the recognition heuristic realize limited search by defining stopping rules. Integration strategies, in contrast, do not provide any model of stopping rules and implicitly assume exhaustive search (although they may provide rules for tossing out some of the variables in a lengthy regression equation). Stopping rules are crucial for modeling inference under limited time, as in Simon's examples of satisficing, where search among alternatives terminates when a certain aspiration level is met.

Nonlinearity   Linearity is a mathematically convenient tool that has dominated the theory of rational choice since its inception in the mid-seventeenth century. The assumption is that the various components of an alternative add up independently to its overall estimate or utility. In contrast, nonlinear inference does not operate by computing linear sums of (weighted) cue values. Nonlinear inference has many varieties, including simple principles such as in the conjunctive and disjunctive algorithms (Einhorn, 1970) and highly complex ones such as in nonlinear multiple regression and neural networks. Take The Best and its variants belong to the family of simple nonlinear models. One advantage of simple nonlinear models is *transparency*; every step in the heuristic can be followed through, unlike fully connected neural networks with numerous hidden units and other free parameters.

Our competition revealed that the unit-weight and weighted versions of the linear models lead to about equal performance, consistent with the finding that the choice of weights, provided the sign is correct, often does not matter much (Dawes, 1979). In real-world domains, such as in the prediction of sudden infant death from a linear combination of eight variables (Carpenter, Gardner, McWeeny, & Emery, 1977), the weights can be varied across a broad range without decreasing predictive accuracy: a phenomenon known as the "flat maximum effect" (Lovie & Lovie, 1986; von Winterfeldt & Edwards, 1982). The competition in addition showed that the flat maximum effect extends to tallying, with unit-weight and weighted tallying performing about equally well. The performance of Take The Best showed that the flat maximum can extend beyond linear models: Inferences based solely on the best cue can be as accurate as any weighted or unit-weight linear combination of all cues.

Most research in psychology and economics has preferred linear models for description, prediction, and prescription (Edwards, 1954, 1962; Lopes, 1994; von Winterfeldt & Edwards, 1982). Historically, linear models such as analysis of variance and multiple regression originated as tools for data analysis in psychological laboratories and were subsequently projected by means of the "tools-to-theories heuristic" into theories of mind (Chapter 1). From the sufficiently good fit of linear models in many judgment studies, it has been interpreted that humans in fact might combine cues in a linear fashion. However, whether this can be taken to mean that humans actually use linear models is controversial (Hammond & Summers, 1965; Hammond & Wascoe, 1980). For instance, within a certain range, data generated from the (nonlinear) law of falling bodies can be fitted well by a linear regression. For the data in this study, a multiple linear regression resulted in $R^2 = .87$, which means that a linear combination of the cues can predict the target variable quite well. But the simpler, nonlinear Take The Best could match this performance. Thus good fit of a linear model does not rule out simpler models of inference.

Shepard (1967) reviewed the empirical evidence for the claim that humans integrate information by linear models. He distinguished between the perceptual transformation of raw sensory inputs into conceptual objects and properties and the subsequent inference based on conceptual knowledge. He concluded that the perceptual analysis integrates the responses of the vast number of receptive elements into concepts and properties by complex nonlinear rules but once this is done, "there is little evidence that they can in turn be juggled and recombined with anything like this facility" (Shepard, 1967, p. 263). Although our minds can take account of a host of different factors, and although we can remember and report doing so, "it is seldom more than one or two that we consider at any one time" (Shepard, 1967, p. 267). In Shepard's view, there is little evidence for integration, linear or otherwise, in what we term *inferences from memory*—even without constraints of limited time and knowledge. A further kind of evidence does not support linear integration as a model of memory-based inference. People often have great difficulties in handling correlations between cues (e.g., Armelius & Armelius, 1974), whereas integration models such as multiple regression need to handle intercorrelations. To summarize, for memory-based inference, there seems to be little empirical evidence for the view of the mind as a Laplacean demon equipped with the computational powers to perform multiple regressions. But this need not be taken as bad news. The beauty of the nonlinear heuristics is that they can match the demon's performance with less searching, less knowledge, and less computational might.

Intransitivity   Transitivity is a cornerstone of classical rationality. It is one of the few tenets that the Anglo-American school of Ramsey and Savage shares with the competing Franco-European school of Allais (Fishburn, 1991). If we prefer a to b and b to c, then we should also prefer a to c. The linear strategies in our competition always produce transitive inferences (except for ties, where the algorithm randomly guessed), and city populations are, in fact, transitive. The PMM family includes heuristics that do not violate transitivity (such as Take The Best), and others that do (e.g., Minimalist). The Minimalist randomly selects a cue on which to base the inference, therefore intransitivities can result. Table 8.2 shows that in spite of these intransitivities, overall performance of the heuristic is only about 1 percentage point lower than that of the best transitive strategy and a few percentage points better than some transitive strategies.

An organism that used Take The Best with a stricter stopping rule (actually, the original version found in Gigerenzer et al., 1991; see Chapter 7) could also be forced into making intransitive inferences. The stricter stopping rule is that search is only terminated when one positive and one negative cue value (but not one positive and one unknown cue value) are encountered. Figure 8.8

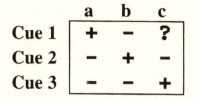

Figure 8.8 Limited knowledge and a stricter stopping rule can produce intransitive inferences.

illustrates a state of knowledge in which this stricter stopping rule gives the result that a dominates b, b dominates c, and c dominates a.[7]

Biological systems, for instance, can exhibit systematic intransitivities based on incommensurability between two systems on one dimension (Gilpin, 1975; Lewontin, 1968). Imagine three species: a, b, and c. Species a inhabits both water and land; species b inhabits both water and air. Therefore, the two only compete in water, where species a defeats species b. Species c inhabits land and air, so it only competes with b in the air, where it is defeated by b. Finally, when a and c meet, it is only on land, and here, c is in its element and defeats a. A linear model that estimates some value for the combative strength of each species independently of the species with which it is competing would fail to capture this nontransitive cycle.

Inferences without Estimation   Einhorn and Hogarth (1975) noted that in the unit-weight model "there is essentially no estimation involved in its use" (p. 177), except for the sign of the unit weight. A similar result holds for the heuristics reported here. Take The Best does not need to estimate regression weights; it only needs to estimate a rank ordering of cue validities. Take The Last and the Minimalist involve essentially no estimation (except for the sign of the cues). The fact that there is no estimation problem has an important consequence: An organism can use as many cues as it has experienced, without being concerned about whether the size of the sample experienced is sufficiently large to generate reliable estimates of weights.

7. Note that missing knowledge is necessary for intransitivities to occur. If all cue values are known, no intransitive inferences can possibly result. Take The Best with the stricter stopping rule allows precise predictions about the occurrence of intransitivities over the course of knowledge acquisition. For instance, imagine a person whose knowledge is described by Figure 8.8, except that she does not know the value of Cue 2 for object c. This person would make no intransitive judgments comparing objects a, b, and c. If she were to learn that object c had a negative cue value for Cue 2, she would produce an intransitive judgment. If she learned one piece more, namely, the value of Cue 1 for object c, then she would no longer produce an intransitive judgment. The prediction is that transitive judgments should turn into intransitive ones and back during learning. Thus intransitivities do not simply depend on the amount of limited knowledge but also on what knowledge is missing.

Cue Redundancy and Performance   Einhorn and Hogarth (1975) suggested that unit-weight models can be expected to perform approximately as well as proper linear models when (a) R^2 from the regression model is in the moderate or low range (around .5 or smaller) and (b) predictors (cues) are correlated. Are these two criteria necessary, sufficient, or both to explain the performance of Take The Best? Take The Best and its variants certainly can exploit cue redundancy: If cues are highly correlated, one cue can do the job.

We have already seen that in the present environment, $R^2 = .87$, which is in the high rather than the moderate or low range. As mentioned earlier, the pairwise correlations between the nine ecological cues ranged between −.25 and .54, with an absolute average value of .19. Thus, despite a high R^2 and only moderate-to-small correlation between cues, the heuristics performed quite successfully. Their excellent performance in the competition can be explained only partially by cue redundancy, because the cues were only moderately correlated. High cue redundancy, thus, does seem sufficient but is not necessary for the successful performance of the heuristics.

A New Perspective on the Lens Model   Ecological theorists such as Brunswik (1955) emphasized that the cognitive system is designed to find many pathways to the world, substituting missing cues with whatever cues happen to be available. Brunswik labeled this ability *vicarious functioning*, in which he saw the most fundamental principle of a science of perception and cognition. His proposal to model this adaptive process by linear multiple regression has inspired a long tradition of neo-Brunswikian research (Brehmer, 1994; Hammond, 1990), although the empirical evidence for mental multiple regression is still controversial (e.g., Brehmer & Brehmer, 1988). However, vicarious functioning need not be equated with linear regression. The PMM family of heuristics provides an alternative, nonadditive model of vicarious functioning, in which cue substitution operates without integration. This offers a new perspective on Brunswik's lens model. In a fast and frugal lens model, the first discriminating cue that passes through inhibits any other rays passing through and determines judgment (Gigerenzer & Kurz, in press). Noncompensatory vicarious functioning is consistent with some of Brunswik's original examples, such as the substitution of behaviors in Hull's habit–family hierarchy, and the alternative manifestation of symptoms according to the psychoanalytic writings of Frenkel-Brunswik (see Gigerenzer & Murray, 1987, chap. 3).

It has been reported sometimes that teachers, physicians, and other professionals claim that they use seven or so criteria to make judgments (e.g., when grading papers or making a differential diagnosis) but that experimental tests showed that they in fact often used only one criterion (Shepard, 1967). At first glance, this seems to indicate that those professionals make outrageous claims. But it need not be. If experts' vicarious functioning works according to the PMM heuristics, then they are correct in saying that they use many predictors, but the decision is made by only one at any time.

What Counts as Good Reasoning?   Much of the research on reasoning in the last decades has assumed that sound reasoning can be reduced to principles of internal consistency, such as additivity of probabilities, conformity to truth-table logic, and transitivity. For instance, research on the Wason selection task, the "Linda" problem, and the "cab" problem has evaluated reasoning almost exclusively by some measure of internal consistency (Gigerenzer, 1995, 1996a). Cognitive strategies, however, need to meet more important constraints than internal consistency: (a) They need to be psychologically plausible, (b) they need to be fast, and (c) they need to make accurate inferences in real-world environments. In real time and real environments, the possibility that a heuristic (e.g., the Minimalist) can make intransitive inferences does not mean that it will make them all the time or that this feature will significantly hurt its accuracy. What we have not addressed in this chapter are constraints on human reasoning that emerge from the fact that *Homo sapiens* is a social animal. For instance, some choices (e.g., who to treat first in an emergency room) need to be justified (Tetlock, 1992). Going with the single best reason, the strategy of Take The Best, has an immediate appeal for justification and can be more convincing and certainly easier to communicate than some complicated weighting of cues.

Future Research   Among the questions that need to be addressed in future research are the following. First, how can we generalize the present heuristics from two-alternative-choice tasks to other inferential tasks, such as classification and estimation? The reported success of the classification and regression tree models (Breiman et al., 1993), which use a form of one-reason decision making, is an encouraging sign that what we have shown here for two-alt0ernative-choice tasks might be generalizable. In fact, Berretty, Todd, and Martignon (1999) recently proposed fast and frugal heuristics for classification, as have Hertwig, Hoffrage, and Martignon (1999) for estimation. Second, what is the structure of real-world environments that allows simple heuristics to perform so well? We need to develop a conceptual language that can capture important aspects of the structure of environments that simple cognitive heuristics can exploit. For instance, Martignon and Hoffrage (1999) have identified two structures that Take The Best can take advantage of: noncompensatory information and scarce information. For more on these new results, see Gigerenzer, Todd, and the ABC Research Group (1999).

Can Reasoning Be Rational and Psychological?

At the beginning of this chapter, we pointed out the common opposition between the rational and the psychological, which emerged in the nineteenth century after the breakdown of the classical interpretation of probability. Since then, rational inference is commonly reduced to logic and probability theory, and psychological explanations are called on when things go wrong. This division of labor is, in a nutshell, the basis on which much of the current research on reasoning and decision making under uncertainty is built.

We believe that after 40 years of toying with the notion of bounded rationality, it is time to overcome the opposition between the rational and the psychological and to reunite the two. The PMM family of heuristics provides precise computational models that attempt to do so. They differ from the Enlightenment's unified view of the rational and psychological, in that they focus on simple psychological mechanisms that operate under constraints of limited time and knowledge and are supported by empirical evidence. The single most important result in this chapter is that simple psychological mechanisms can yield about as many (or more) correct inferences more quickly and with less information than integration strategies that embody classical properties of rational inference. The demonstration that a fast and frugal heuristic won the competition defeats the widespread view that only "rational" strategies can be accurate. Models of inference do not have to forsake accuracy for simplicity. The mind can have it both ways.

IV

SOCIAL RATIONALITY

The study of human thinking is deeply suspicious of introducing anything genuinely social into the world of "pure" rationality. As in much of cognitive science, most researchers have fallen in love with syllogisms, first-order logic, probability theory, and other systems that abstract and distract from the semantics and pragmatics of thinking, not to mention social motives.

In 1987, I spent the fall at the Department of Psychology at Harvard. One day, I asked my colleagues whether they knew of a theory of thinking that starts with a social motive rather than a logical structure. Sheldon White answered by handing me a copy of a 1985 dissertation he had supervised. The 280-page work, entitled "Deduction or Darwinian algorithms?" and written by Leda Cosmides, dealt with the Wason selection task—a classical stock-in-trade of research on reasoning. It set forth the first theory applied to the selection task that began with an adaptive problem, cheating detection in social exchange, rather than with material conditionals, truth tables, and the like. I read the dissertation in one long sitting and designed a critical test of the theory using perspective change. The result is reported in Chapter 10.

Social rationality is a specific form of ecological rationality, one in which the environment consists of other humans (or, more generally, conspecifics). The program of social rationality explains human judgment and decision making in terms of the structure of *social* environments. Chapter 9 illustrates how behaviors that look irrational from an individualistic point of view can turn out to be well adapted to a specific social environment. Social environments foster different strategies than physical environments, such as imitation instead of deliberation, and demand attention to information that is unique to social interaction, such as cues that could reveal that one is being cheated or bluffed.

In this section, I argue for the domain specificity of mental strategies and the heuristic value of evolutionary theory in guessing what the relevant domains are. Domain-specific processes allow organisms to solve adaptive problems quickly with specialized tools, such as specific emotions. There are several ways in which the mind might implement such a division of labor. For instance, some have proposed mental modules for intuitive physics, mathematics, and biology—a view that turns academic subjects into domains. An evolutionary perspective suggests that a different division of labor has evolved, one directed at solving important adaptive problems, such as attachment development, mate search, parenting, social exchange, coalition formation, and maintaining and upsetting dominance hierarchies. The module dedicated to solving each of these problems needs to integrate motivation, perception, thinking, emotion, and behavior into a functional unit. This is not to say that domain-specific modules are encapsulated and dissociated; they are probably as coordinated as the violins, violas, cellos, oboes, and French horns in an orchestra, or the liver, kidneys, lungs, and heart in a human body.

The idea of modules specialized for certain adaptive problems conflicts with the compartmentalization of psychology. Today's areas of specialization are defined in terms of faculties, such as memory, thinking, decision making, intelligence, motivation, and emotion. These faculties have become institutionalized in modern university curricula and grant agencies. They determine the professional self-perception of our colleagues, what they read and what they ignore, their departmental alliances, and the hiring of professors. If you ask a psychologist at a conference what she is doing, you will probably get an answer such as "I am a cognitive psychologist," "I do emotions," "I am a judgment and decision-making person," or "My field is motivation." Evolutionary thinking is an antidote to this faculty view of the mind. Adaptive problems and their modern equivalents, such as foraging and dieting and social exchange and markets, demand the orchestration of these faculties, not their segregation.

In my opinion, the partitioning of psychological research into faculties is one of the greatest barriers to progress. Research on modularity forces us to reconsider the borders that have gone unquestioned for many decades. Rethinking rationality means rethinking the organization of the fields that study it. Most interesting problems do not respect today's disciplinary boundaries. Nor should we.

9

Rationality
Why Social Context Matters

I want to argue against an old and beautiful dream. It was Leibniz's dream, but not his alone. Leibniz (1677/1951) hoped to reduce rational reasoning to a universal calculus, which he termed the Universal Characteristic. The plan was simple: to establish characteristic numbers for all ideas, which would reduce every question to calculation. Such a rational calculus would put an end to scholarly bickering; if a dispute arose, the contending parties could settle it quickly and peacefully by sitting down and calculating. For some time, the Enlightenment probabilists believed that the mathematical theory of probability had made this dream a reality. Probability theory rather than logic became the flip side of the newly coined rationality of the Enlightenment, which acknowledged that humankind lives in the twilight of probability rather than the noontime sun of certainty, as John Locke expressed it. Leibniz guessed optimistically of the Universal Characteristic that "a few selected persons might be able to do the whole thing in five years" (Leibniz, 1677/1951, p. 22). By around 1840, however, mathematicians had given up as thankless and even antimathematical the task of reducing rationality to a calculus (Daston, 1988). Psychologists and economists have not.

Contemporary theories embody Leibniz's dream in various forms. Piaget and Inhelder's (1951/1975) theory of cognitive development holds that, by roughly age 12, human beings begin to reason according to the laws of probability theory; Piaget and Inhelder thus echo the Enlightenment conviction that human rationality and probability theory are two sides of the same coin. Neoclassical economic theories center on the assumption that Jacob Bernoulli's expected utility maximization principle or its modern variants, such as subjective expected utility, define rationality in all contexts. Similarly, neo-Bayesians tend to claim that the formal machinery of Bayesian statistics defines rational inferences in all contexts. In cognitive psychology, formal axioms and rules—consistency, transitivity, and Bayes's rule, for example, as well as entire statistical techniques—figure prominently in recent theories of mind and warrant the rationality of cognition (Chapter 1).

All these theories have been criticized as *descriptively* incomplete or inadequate, most often by showing that principles from logic or probability theory (such as consistency) are systematically violated in certain contexts. Piaget himself wondered why adults outside of Geneva seemed not to reach the level of formal operations. But even critics have generally retained the beautifully simple principles drawn from logic and probability theory as normative, albeit not descriptively valid—that is, as definitions of how we *should* reason. In this chapter, I will address the question of whether these principles are indeed normative: sufficient for defining rational behavior.

My discussion will challenge one central assumption in the modern variants of Leibniz's dream: that formal axioms and rules of choice can define rational behavior without referring to factors external to choice behavior. To the contrary, I will argue that these principles are incomplete as behavioral norms in the sense that their normative validity depends on the *social* context of the behavior, such as social objectives, values, and motivations.

The point I wish to defend is that formal axioms and rules cannot be *imposed* as universal yardsticks of rationality independent of social objectives, norms, and values; they can, however, be *entailed* by certain social objectives, norms, and values. Thus I am not arguing against axioms and rules, only against their a priori imposition as context-independent yardsticks of rationality.

Leibniz's dream was of a formal calculus of reasonableness that could be applied to everything. Modern variants tend to go one step further and assume that the calculus of rationality has already been found and can be imposed in all contexts. I will focus only on the *social* context in this chapter, arguing that the idea of imposing a context-independent, general-purpose rationality is a limited and confused one. The several examples that follow seek to demonstrate that only by referring to something external to the rules or axioms, such as social objectives, values, and norms, can we decide whether an axiom or choice rule entails rational behavior.

Consistency: Property Alpha

Internal consistency of choice figures prominently as a basic requirement for human rationality in decision theory, behavioral economics, game theory, and cognitive theories. It is often seen as *the* requirement of rational choice. One basic condition of the internal consistency of choice is known as "Property Alpha," also called the "Chernoff condition" or "independence of irrelevant alternatives" (Sen, 1993). The symbols S and T denote two (nonempty) sets of alternatives, and x (S) denotes that alternative x is chosen from the set S:

Property Alpha:
$$x(S) \text{ and } x \; \varepsilon \; T \subseteq S \Rightarrow x(T).$$

Property Alpha demands that if x is chosen from S, and x belongs to a subset T of S, then x must be chosen from T as well. The following two choices would be inconsistent in the sense that they violate Property Alpha:

1. x is chosen given the options $\{x, y\}$.
2. y is chosen given the options $\{x, y, z\}$.

Property Alpha is violated here because x is chosen when the two alternatives $\{x, y\}$ are offered, but y is chosen when z is added to the menu. (Choosing x is interpreted here as a rejection of y, not as a choice that results from mere indifference.) It may indeed appear odd and irrational that someone who chooses x and rejects y when offered the choice set $\{x, y\}$ would choose y and reject x when offered the set $\{x, y, z\}$.

Property Alpha formulates consistency exclusively in terms of the internal consistency of choice behavior with respect to sets of alternatives. No reference is made to anything external to choice—for instance, intentional states such as people's social objectives, values, and motivations. This exclusion of every-thing psychological beyond behavior is in line with Samuelson's (1938) pro-gram of freeing theories of behavior from any traces of utility and from the priority of the notion of "preference." As Little (1949) commented on the un-derlying methodological program, Samuelson's "revealed preference" formu-lation "is scientifically more respectable [since] if an individual's behavior is consistent, then it must be possible to explain the behavior without reference to anything other than behavior" (p. 90). Sen (1993) has launched a forceful attack on internal consistency, as defined by Property Alpha and similar prin-ciples, and what follows is based on his ideas and examples.

The last apple. At a dinner party, a fruit basket is passed around. When it reaches Mr. Polite, one apple is left in the basket. Dining alone, Mr. Polite would face no dilemma; he would take it. In company, however, he must choose between the apple (y) or nothing (x). He decides to be-have decently and go without (x). If the basket had contained another apple (z), he could reasonably have chosen y over x without violating standards of good behavior. Choosing x over y from the choice set $\{x, y\}$ and choosing y over x from the choice set $\{x, y, z\}$ violates Property Alpha, even though there is nothing irrational about Mr. Polite's behavior given his scruples in social interaction. If he had not held to such values of politeness, then Property Alpha might have been entailed. But it can-not be imposed independent of his values.

Waiting for dinner. Consider a second example. Mr. Pleasant is invited to his colleague's home on Sunday at 9:00 P.M. On arriving, he takes a seat in the living room, and his host offers him crackers and nuts (y). Mr. Pleasant decides to take nothing (x), because he is hungry for a sub-stantial meal and does not want to fill up before dinner. After a while, the colleague's wife comes in with tea and cake (z). The menu has thereby been extended to $\{x, y, z\}$, but there is a larger implication: The new option z also has destroyed an illusion about what the invitation included. Now Mr. Pleasant chooses the crackers and nuts (y) over noth-ing (x). Again, this preference reversal violates Property Alpha. Given the guest's expectations of what the invitation entailed, however, there is nothing irrational about his behavior.

Tea at night. Here is a final example similar to the last. Mr. Sociable has met a young artist at a party. When the party is over, she invites him to come back to her place for tea. He chooses to have tea with her (x) over returning home (y). The young lady then offers him a third choice—to share some cocaine at her apartment (z). This extension of the choice set may quite reasonably affect Mr. Sociable's ranking of x and y. Depending on his objectives and values, he may consequently choose to go home (y).

All three examples seek to illustrate the same point: Property Alpha will or will not be entailed depending on the social objectives, values, and expectations of the individual making the choice. To impose Property Alpha as a general yardstick of rational behavior independent of social objectives or other factors external to choice behavior seems fundamentally flawed.

The conclusion is not that consistency is an invalid principle; rather, consistency, as defined by Property Alpha or similar principles, is indeterminate. The preceding examples illustrate different kinds of indeterminateness. With respect to the last apple, social values define what the alternatives in the choice set are and, thereby, *what* consistency is about. If there are many apples in the basket, the choice is between "apple" and "nothing." If a single apple remains and one does not share the values of Mr. Polite, the alternatives are the same; for Mr. Polite, however, they become "last apple" and "nothing." In the dinner and tea examples, one learns something new about the old alternatives when a new choice is introduced. The fresh option provides new information—that is, it reduces uncertainty about the old alternatives.

To summarize the argument: Consistency, as defined by Property Alpha, cannot be imposed on human behavior independent of something external to choice behavior, such as social objectives and expectations. Social concerns and moral views (e.g., politeness), as well as inferences from the menu offered (learning from one option as to what others may involve), determine whether internal consistency is or is not entailed.

Maximizing: Choice under Uncertainty

The birth year of the mathematical theory of probability is usually dated at 1654, when the French mathematicians Blaise Pascal and Pierre Fermat exchanged letters about gambling problems. One of these problems, the *double-six problem*, was posed by the Chevalier de Méré, a notorious gambler. From his rich experience, de Méré knew it was advantageous to bet on the occurrence of at least one six in a series of four dice tosses. Therefore, he reasoned, it must be as advantageous to bet on the occurrence of at least one double-six in 24 tosses of a pair of dice. Fortune, however, disappointed him. Was he unlucky but right, or unlucky because he was wrong?

The mathematical theory of probability that emerged from the exchange between Pascal and Fermat showed how to compute the expectation of an event. Because the probability of *not* getting a six with a fair die is 5/6, the probability of *not* getting a six in four throws is $(5/6)^4$, which is .482. Thus, de Méré was right that it is advantageous to bet on the occurrence of at least one six in four tosses, which is .518. In the same way, the answer to his puzzle can be calculated. The probability of *not* getting a double six in one toss of a pair of dice is 35/36, therefore the probability of *not* getting at least one double six in 24 tosses is $(35/36)^{24}$, which is .509. Thus de Méré was unlucky because his reasoning was wrong.

In general terms, maximizing expected utility means maximizing the product between probabilities and utilities. In the simple case of a choice between two options, x and y (e.g., *no six* and *at least one six*), with probabilities $p(x)$ and $p(y)$, and utilities $U(x)$ and $U(y)$, one can maximize the gain according to the rule:

Maximizing expected utility:
Choose x if $p(x)U(x) > p(y)U(y)$.

For de Méré, the utilities were equal, because he and his gambling partner bet the same amount of money on x and y, respectively. All this seems to be straightforward once the mathematical theory is in place.

Now consider the following situation, which seems to be, formally, essentially equivalent. The choice set is again $\{x, y\}$. Choosing x will lead to a reinforcement with a probability $p(x) = .80$, whereas choosing y will only lead to the same reinforcement with a probability $p(y) = .20$. That is, the utilities of the outcomes (reinforcements) are the same, but their probabilities differ. It is easy to see that when the choice is repeated n times, the expected number of reinforcements will be maximized if an organism always chooses x:

Maximizing with equal utilities:
Always choose x if $p(x) > p(y)$.

Consider a hungry rat in a T-maze where reinforcement is obtained at the left end in 80% of cases and at the right end in 20% of cases. The rat will maximize reinforcement if it always turns left. Imagine students who watch the rat running and predict on which side the reinforcement will appear in each trial. They will also maximize their number of correct predictions by always saying "left." But neither rats nor students seem to maximize. Under a variety of experimental conditions, organisms choose both alternatives with relative frequencies that roughly match the probabilities (Gallistel, 1990):

Probability matching:
Choose x with probability $p(x)$;
choose y with probability $p(y)$.

In the preceding example, the expected rate of reinforcements is 80% for maximizing, but only 68% for probability matching (this value is calculated by $.80^2 + .20^2 = .68$). The conditions of the seemingly irrational behavior of probability matching are discussed in the literature (e.g., Brunswik, 1939; Estes, 1976; Gallistel, 1990).

Violations of maximizing by probability matching pose a problem for a context-independent account of rational behavior in animals and humans. What looks irrational for an individual, however, can be optimal for a group.

Again, the maximizing principle does not capture the distinction between the individual in social isolation and in social interaction. Under natural conditions of foraging, there will not be just one rat but many who compete to exploit food resources. If all choose to forage in the spot where previous experience suggests food is to be found in greatest abundance, then each may get only a small share. The one mutant organism that sometimes chooses the spot with less food would be better off. Natural selection will favor those exceptional individuals who sometimes choose the less attractive alternative. Thus maximizing is not always an evolutionarily stable strategy in situations of competition among individuals. Given certain assumptions, probability matching may in fact be an evolutionarily stable strategy, one that does not tend to create conditions that select against it (Fretwell, 1972; Gallistel, 1990).

To summarize the argument: The maximization rule cannot be imposed on behavior independent of social context. Whether an organism performs in isolation or in the context of other organisms can determine, among other things, whether maximization is entailed as an optimal choice rule.

Betting against the Probabilities

Mr. Smart would like to invest the $10,000 in his savings account in the hope of increasing his capital. After some consideration, he opts to risk the amount in a gamble with two possible outcomes, x and y. The outcomes are determined by a fair roulette wheel with 10 equal sections, 6 of them white (x) and 4 black (y). Thus the probability $p(x)$ of obtaining white is .6, and the probability $p(y)$ of obtaining black is .4. The rules of the game are that he has to bet *all* his money ($10,000) either on black or on white. If Mr. Smart guesses the outcome correctly, his money will be doubled; otherwise, he will lose three-quarters of his investment. Could it ever be advantageous for Mr. Smart to bet on black?

If Mr. Smart bets on white, his expectation is $20,000 with a probability of .6, and $2,500 with a probability of .4. The expected value $E(x)$ is (.6 × $20,000) + (.4 × $2,500) = $13,000. But if he bets on black, the expected value $E(y)$ is only (.4 × $20,000) + (.6 × $2,500) = $9,500. Betting on white would give him an expectation larger than the sum he invests. Betting on black, on the other hand, would result in an expectation lower than the sum he invests. A maximization of the expected value implies betting on white:

Maximizing expected value:
Choose x if $E(x) > E(y)$,

where $E(x) = \Sigma\, p(x)V(x)$. The principle of maximizing the expected value (or subjective variants such as expected utility) is one of the cornerstones of classical definitions of rationality. Mr. Smart would be a fool to bet on black, wouldn't he?

Let me apply the same argument again. The principle of maximizing the expected value does not distinguish between the individual in social isolation and in social interaction. If many individuals face the same choice, could it be to the benefit of the whole group that some sacrifice themselves and bet on black? Let us first look at an example from biology.

Cooper (1989; Cooper & Kaplan, 1982) discussed conditions under which it is essential for the survival of the group that some individuals bet against the probabilities and do *not*, at the individual level, maximize their expected value. Consider a hypothetical population of organisms whose evolutionary fitness (measured simply by the finite rate of increase in their population) depends highly on protective coloration. Each winter predators pass through the region, decimating those within the population that can be spotted against the background terrain. If the black soil of the organisms' habitat happens to be covered with snow at the time, the best protective coloration is white; otherwise, it is black. The probability of snow when predators pass through is .6, and protectively colored individuals can expect to survive the winter in numbers sufficient to leave an average of two surviving offspring each, whereas the conspicuous ones can expect an average of only 0.25 offspring each. This example assumes a simple evolutionary model with asexual breeding (each offspring is genetically identical to its parent), seasonal breeding (offspring are produced only in spring), and semelparous breeding (each individual produces offspring only once in a lifetime at the age of exactly one year).

Adaptive Coin-Flipping

Suppose two genotypes, W and WB, are in competition within a large population. Individuals of genotype W always have white winter coloration; that is, W is a genotype with a uniquely determined phenotypic expression. Genotype WB, in contrast, gives rise to both white and black individuals, with a ratio of 5 to 3. Thus, 3 out of 8 individuals with genotype WB are "betting" on the low probability of no snow. Each of these individuals' expectation to survive and reproduce is smaller than that of all other individuals in both W and WB.

How will these two genotypes fare after 1,000 generations (1,000 years)? We can expect that there was snow cover in about 600 winters, exposed black soil in about 400 winters. Then the number of individuals with genotype W will be doubled 600 times and reduced to one-fourth 400 times. If n is the original population size, the population size after 1,000 years is

$$n2^{600}(1/4)^{400} \approx 6n \times 10^{-61}.$$

That is, genotype W will have been wiped out with practical certainty after 1,000 years. How does genotype WB do? In the 600 snowy winters, $5/8$ of the population will double in number and three-eighths will be reduced to 25%, with corresponding proportions for the 400 winters without snow. The number of individuals after 1,000 years is then

$$n\left(\frac{5}{8} \times 2 + \frac{3}{8} \times \frac{1}{4}\right)^{600} \left(\frac{5}{8} \times \frac{1}{4} + \frac{3}{8} \times 2\right)^{400} \approx 8n \times 10^{59}.$$

Thus genotype *WB* is likely to win the evolutionary race easily.[1] (The large estimated number is certainly an overestimation, however, because it does not take account of such other constraints as food resources.) The reason why *WB* has so much better a chance of survival than *W* is that a considerable proportion of the *WB* individuals do not maximize their individual expectations but "bet" on small probabilities.

This violation of individual maximization has been termed "adaptive coin-flipping" (Cooper & Kaplan, 1982), meaning that individuals are genetically programmed to "flip coins" to adopt phenotypic traits. Thus the phenotype is ultimately determined by the nature of the coin-flipping process, rather than uniquely specified by the genotype.[2]

Back to Mr. Smart. Assume he won and wants to try again. So do his numerous brothers, sisters, and cousins, who all are willing to commit their entire investment capital to this gamble. The game is offered every week, and the rules are as before: Each person's choice is every week to bet *all* his or her investment capital either on black or on white (no hedging of bets). If everyone wanted solely to maximize his or her individual good, his or her money would be better invested in white than in black, because the chances to double one's assets are 60% for white compared with only 40% for black. Investing in black would appear irrational. But we know from our previous calculations that someone who invests all his or her money every week in white will, with a high probability, lose every dollar of assets in the long run.

If Mr. Smart and his extended family, however, acted as one community rather than as independent individuals—that is, create one investment capital fund in which they share equally—they can quickly increase their capital with a high probability. Every week they would need to instruct three-eighths of their members to invest in black, the rest in white. This social sharing is essentially the same situation as the "adaptive coin-flipping" example. Thus Mr. Smart's betting on black needs to be judged against his motivation: If he is

---

1. I have reported the numbers only for the most likely event (i.e., 600 snowy winters out of 1,000 winters). If one looks at all possible events, one finds that those in which *W* would result in a larger population size than *WB* are extremely rare (Cooper, 1989). Nevertheless, the expected value is larger for *W* than for *WB*, due to the fact that in those very few cases in which *W* results in a larger population size, this number is astronomically large. The reader who is familiar with the St. Petersburg paradox will see a parallel (Wolfgang Hell has drawn my attention to this fact). The parallel is best illustrated in Lopes's (1981) simulations of businesses selling the St. Petersburg gamble. Although these businesses sold the gamble far below its expected value, most nonetheless survived with great profits.

2. Adaptive coin-flipping is a special case of a general phenomenon: In variable environments (in which the time scale of variation is greater than the generation time of the organism, as in the example given), natural selection does not maximize expected individual fitness but geometric mean fitness (Gillespie, 1977).

cooperating with others for their common interest, then betting on the wrong side of a known probability is part of an optimal strategy. If he is not cooperating but, rather, investing for his own immediate benefit, then betting on black is the fastest way to ruin.

This example, like the preceding ones, attempts to illustrate that a rule such as maximizing the expected value cannot be imposed on behavior without consideration of the social context. Is this context a single individual wagering all his or her assets at once or a population that risks their collective assets or offspring at regular intervals? It makes all the difference, because individual maximization can lead to the extinction of the genotype.

Conclusions

These examples show that general principles such as consistency and maximizing are insufficient for capturing rationality. I have argued that there is no way of determining whether a behavioral pattern is consistent or maximizes without first referring to something external to choice behavior (Sen, 1993). The external factor investigated in this chapter is the *social context* of choice behavior, including objectives, motivations, and values. I am not arguing against consistency, maximization, or any given rule per se but against the a priori imposition of a rule or axiom as a requirement for rationality, independent of the social context of judgment and decision and, likewise, of whether the individual operates in isolation or within a social context (see Chapter 12; Elster, 1990).

One way to defend general principles against this argument would be to say that maximization poses no restrictions on what individuals maximize, be it their own good (utilities) or the fitness of their genotype. Switching from individual goals to genotypic fitness can save the concept of maximization. Such a defense would imply, however, that maximization cannot be imposed independent of the motivations and goals built into living systems, which is precisely the point I have asserted. By the same token, to claim that consistency poses no restrictions on whatever consistency is about would destroy the very idea of behavioral consistency, because Property Alpha would as a result be open to any external interpretation and would no longer impose any constraint on choice.

More generally, the formal principles of logic, probability theory, rational choice theory, and other context-independent principles of rationality are often rescued and defended by post hoc justifications. Post hoc reasoning typically uses the social objectives, values, and motivations of organisms to make room for exceptions or to reinterpret the alternatives in axioms or rules until they are compatible with the observed result. Contemporary neoclassical economics, for instance, provides little theoretical basis for specifying the content and shape of the utility function; it thus affords many degrees of freedom for fitting any phenomenon to the theory (Simon, 1986). In Elster's (1990) formulation, a theory of rationality can fail through indeterminacy (rather than through inadequacy) to the extent that it fails to yield unique predictions.

The challenge is to go beyond general-purpose principles of rationality that allow context to slip in through the back door. What would a theory of reasoning that lets social context in through the front door look like? In the next chapter, I present and discuss one example of such a "front door" theory. Inspired by evolutionary theory, it uses the theory of reciprocal altruism to define social objectives and motivations underlying human reasoning.

10

Domain-Specific Reasoning

Social Contracts and Cheating Detection

What counts as human rationality? Reasoning processes that embody content-independent formal theories, such as propositional logic, or reasoning processes that are well designed for solving specific adaptive problems? What would a theoretical framework look like that starts with an adaptive problem rather than with logical structure? In this chapter, I first introduce the challenge of domain specificity and then apply a domain-specific theory for a specific adaptive problem, social exchange, to a reasoning task that has puzzled researchers for several decades.

Are Mental Processes Domain Specific?

The psychological flip side of Leibniz's dream of a universal calculus of reasonableness is the assumption that there is one—or at most a few—universal mechanisms that govern all of reasoning, learning, memory, inference, imitation, imagery, and so on. I will call these assumed mechanisms *general-purpose* mechanisms because they have no features specialized for processing particular kinds of content. For instance, when Piaget started to work on mental imagery and memory, he did not expect and search for processes different from logical thinking. Rather, he attempted to demonstrate that at each stage in development, imagery and memory express the same logical structure as the one he had found in his earlier studies on children's thinking (Gruber & Vonèche, 1977). Similarly, B. F. Skinner's laws of operant behavior were designed to be general purpose: to hold true for all stimuli and responses (the assumption of the *equipotentiality* of stimuli).

John Garcia's anomalous findings (e.g., Garcia & Koelling, 1966) challenged not only the notion of the equipotentiality of stimuli but also the law of contiguity, which postulates the necessity of immediate reinforcement, independent of the nature of the stimulus and response. For instance, when the taste of flavored water is repeatedly paired with an electric shock immediately after tasting, rats have great difficulty learning to avoid the flavored water. Yet in just one trial the rat can learn to avoid the flavored water when it is followed by experimentally induced nausea, even when the nausea occurs 2 hours later:

> From the evolutionary view, the rat is a biased learning machine designed by natural selection to form certain CS–US [conditioned stimulus–unconditioned stimulus] associations rapidly but not others. From a traditional learning viewpoint, the rat was an unbiased learner able to make any association in accordance with the general principles of contiguity, effect, and similarity. (Garcia y Robertson & Garcia, 1985, p. 25)

Garcia's evolutionary challenge, however, was not welcomed by mainstream neobehaviorists. In 1965, after 10 years of research, he openly pointed out the clash between the data and the ideal of general-purpose mechanisms—and his manuscripts suddenly began to be rejected by the editors of the APA (American Psychological Association) journals. This pattern continued for the next 13 years until, in 1979, Garcia was awarded the APA's Distinguished Scientific Contribution Award (Lubek & Apfelbaum, 1987). By then, stimulus equipotentiality was driven out of behaviorism but had found new fertile ground in cognitive psychology.

The view that psychological mechanisms such as those described in the laws of operant behavior are designed for specific classes of stimuli rather than being general purpose is known as *domain specificity* (e.g., Hirschfeld & Gelman, 1994a), *biological preparedness* (Seligman & Hager, 1972), or, in biology, *special-design* theories (Williams, 1966).

Mainstream cognitive psychology, however, still tries to avoid domain specificity. The senses, language, and emotions have occasionally been accepted as domain-specific adaptations (Fodor, 1983). But the "central" cognitive processes that define the rationality of *Homo sapiens*—reasoning, inference, judgment, and decision making—have not. Even such vigorous advocates of domain specificity as Fodor (1983) have held so-called central processes to be general purpose. Research on probabilistic, inductive, and deductive reasoning tends to define good reasoning exclusively in terms of formal axioms and rules similar to those discussed in Chapter 9. Mental logic, Johnson-Laird's mental models, and Piaget's formal operations all are examples of the hope that reasoning can be understood without reference to its content.

A glance at textbooks on cognitive psychology reveals how we have bottle-fed our students on the idea that whenever thinking is the object of our investigation, content does not matter. Typically, a chapter on "deductive reasoning" teaches propositional logic and violations thereof by human reasoning, whereas a chapter on "probabilistic reasoning" teaches the laws of probability theory and violations thereof by human reasoning. Similarly, "fallacies" of reasoning are defined against formal structure—the base-rate fallacy, the conjunction fallacy, and so on. Content is merely illustrative and cosmetic, as it is in textbooks of logic. Whether a problem concerns white and black swans, blue and green taxicabs, or artists and beekeepers does not seem to matter. Content has not yet assumed a life of its own. For the most part, it is seen only as a disturbing factor that sometimes facilitates and sometimes hinders formal, rational reasoning.

Is there an alternative? In what follows, I shall describe a domain-specific theory of cognition that relates reasoning to the evolutionary theory of reciprocal altruism (Cosmides & Tooby, 1992). This theory turns the traditional approach upside down. It does not start out with a general-purpose principle from logic or probability theory or a variant thereof; it takes social objectives as fundamental, which in turn makes content fundamental, because social objectives have specific contents. Traditional formal principles of rationality are not imposed; they can be entailed or not, depending on the social objectives.

Cheating Detection in Social Contracts

One feature that sets humans and some other primates apart from almost all animal species is the existence of cooperation among genetically unrelated individuals within the same species, known as *reciprocal altruism* or *cooperation*. The thesis that such cooperation has been practiced by our ancestors since ancient times, possibly for at least several million years, is supported by evidence from several sources. First, our nearest relatives in the hominid line, chimpanzees, also engage in certain forms of sophisticated cooperation (de Waal & Luttrell, 1988), and in more distant relatives, such as macaques and baboons, cooperation can still be found (e.g., Packer, 1977). Second, cooperation is both universal and highly elaborated across human cultures, from hunter–gatherers to technologically advanced societies. Finally, paleoanthropological evidence also suggests that cooperation is extremely ancient (e.g., Tooby & DeVore, 1987).

Why altruism? Kin-related helping behavior, such as that by the sterile worker castes in insects, which so troubled Darwin, has been accounted for by generalizing "Darwinian fitness" to "inclusive fitness"—that is, to the number of surviving offspring an individual has *plus* the individual's effect on the number of offspring produced by its relatives (Hamilton, 1964). But why reciprocal altruism, which involves cooperation among two or more nonrelated individuals? The now-classic answer draws on the economic concept of trade and its analogy to game theory (Axelrod, 1984; Williams, 1966). If the reproductive benefit of being helped is greater than the cost of helping, then individuals who engage in reciprocal helping can outreproduce those who do not, causing the helping design to spread. A vampire bat, for instance, will die if it fails to find food for two consecutive nights, and there is high variance in food-gathering success. Food sharing allows the bats to reduce this variance, and the best predictor of whether a bat, having foraged successfully, will share its food with a hungry nonrelative is whether the nonrelative has shared food with the bat in the past (Wilkinson, 1990).

But "always cooperate" would not be an evolutionarily stable strategy. This can be seen using the analogy of the prisoner's dilemma. If a group of individuals always cooperates, then individuals who always defect—that is, who take the benefit but do not reciprocate—can invade and outreproduce the cooperators. Where the opportunity for defecting (or cheating) exists, indiscriminate cooperation would eventually be selected out. "Always defect" would not be an evolutionarily stable strategy, either. A group of individuals who always defect can be invaded by individuals who cooperate in a selective (rather than indiscriminate) way. A simple heuristic for selective cooperation is "Cooperate on the first move; for subsequent moves, do whatever your partner did on the preceding move" (a strategy known as Tit For Tat). There are several rules in addition to Tit For Tat that lead to cooperation with other "selective cooperators" and exclude or retaliate against cheaters (Axelrod, 1984).

The important point is that selective cooperation would not work without a cognitive heuristic for detecting cheaters—or, more precisely, a heuristic for directing an organism's attention to information that could reveal that it (or its group) is being cheated (Cosmides & Tooby, 1992). Neither indiscriminate cooperation nor indiscriminate cheating demands such a heuristic. In vampire bats, who exchange only one thing—regurgitated blood—such a heuristic can be restricted to a sole commodity. Cheating, or more generally noncooperation, would mean, "That other bat took my blood when it had nothing, but it did not share blood with me when I had nothing." In humans, who exchange many goods (including such abstract forms as money), a cheating-detection heuristic needs to work on a more general level of representation—in terms, for example, of "benefits" and "costs."

To summarize, cooperation between two or more individuals for their mutual benefit is a solution to a class of important adaptive problems, such as the sharing of scarce food when foraging success is highly variable. Rather than being indiscriminate, cooperation needs to be selective, requiring a cognitive heuristic that directs attention to information that can reveal cheating. This evolutionary account of cooperation, albeit still general, can be applied to a specific puzzle in the psychology of reasoning.

The Selection Task

In 1966, Peter Wason invented the "selection task" to study reasoning about conditionals. This was to become one of the most extensively researched subjects in cognitive psychology during the following decades. The selection task involves four cards and a conditional statement in the form "If P then Q." One example is, "If there is a 'D' on one side of the card, then there is a '3' on the other side." The four cards are placed on a table so that the participant can read only the information on the side facing upward. For instance, the four cards may read "D," "E," "3," and "4." The participant's task is to indicate which of the four cards need(s) to be turned over to find out whether the statement has been violated. Table 10.1 shows two examples of selection tasks, each with a different content: a numbers-and-letters rule and a transportation rule.

Because the dominant approach has been to impose propositional logic as a general-purpose standard of rational reasoning in the selection task (inde-

Table 10.1 Two selection tasks

Numbers-and-letters rule
  If there is a "D" on one side of the card, then there is a "3" on the other side.

  Each of the following cards has a letter on one side and a number on the other. Indicate only the card(s) you definitely need to turn over to see if the rule has been violated.

D	E	3	4

Transportation rule
  If a person goes in to Boston, then he takes the subway.

  The cards below have information about four Cambridge residents. Each card represents one person. One side of the card tells where the person went and the other side tells how the person got there. Indicate only the card(s) you definitely need to turn over to see if the rule has been violated.

SUBWAY	ARLINGTON	CAB	BOSTON

---

pendent, of course, of the content of the conditional statements), it is crucial to recall that, according to propositional logic, a conditional "If P then Q" can be violated only by "P & not-Q." That is, the logical falsity of a material conditional is defined within propositional logic in the following way:

Logical falsity:
  "If P then Q" is logically false if and only if "P & not-Q."

Thus the "P" and "not-Q" cards, and no others, must be selected, because only these can reveal "P & not-Q" instances. In the numbers-and-letters rule, these cards correspond to the "D" and "4" cards and, in the transportation problem, to the "Boston" and "cab" cards.

Wason's results showed, however, that human inferences did not generally follow propositional logic. An avalanche of studies has since confirmed this, reporting that, with numbers-and-letters rules, only about 10% of the participants select both the "P" and "not-Q" cards, whereas most select the "P" card and the "Q" card or only the "P" card. It was soon found that the selections were highly dependent on the content of the conditional statement. This was labeled the "content effect." For instance, about 30% to 40% of participants typically choose the "P" and "not-Q" cards in the transportation problem (Cosmides, 1989). These results seem to be inconsistent with Piaget's claim that adults should have reached the stage of formal operations (Legrenzi & Murino, 1974; Wason, 1968; Wason & Johnson-Laird, 1970).

Within a decade it was clear that these results—a low overall proportion of "P & not-Q" answers and the content effect—contradicted the model of human reasoning provided by propositional logic. One might expect that propositional logic was then abandoned; but it was abandoned only as a *descriptive* model of reasoning. Propositional logic was, however, retained as the *normative*, content-independent yardstick of good reasoning, and actual human reasoning was blamed as irrational. The experimental manipulations were evaluated, as is still the case today, in terms of whether or not they "facilitated logical reasoning." Much effort was directed at explaining participants' apparent irrationality, including their "incorrigible conviction that they are right when they are, in fact, wrong" (Wason, 1981, p. 356). It was proposed that the mind runs with deficient mental software—for example, confirmation bias, matching bias, and availability heuristic—rather than by propositional logic. Yet these proposals were as general purpose as propositional logic; they could be applied to any content. It seems fair to say that these vague proposals have not led to an understanding of what participants do in the selection task.

Only since the mid-1980s have a few dissidents dared to design theories that start with the *content* of the conditional statement rather than with propositional logic (Cheng & Holyoak, 1985; Cosmides, 1989; Cummins, 1998; Light, Girotto, & Legrenzi, 1990; Over & Manktelow, 1993). I will concentrate here exclusively on Cosmides's proposal, which takes the evolutionary theory of cooperation as its starting point (for a different evolutionary account, see Klix, 1993).

Cosmides's (1989) central point is that selective cooperation demands the ability to detect cheaters. This ability presupposes several others, including that of distinguishing different individuals, recognizing when a reciprocation (social contract) is offered, and computing costs and benefits, all of which I ignore here (Cosmides & Tooby, 1992). Being cheated in a social contract of the type

If you take the benefit, then you have to pay the cost

means that the other party has exhibited the following behavior:

Benefit taken and cost not paid.

The evolutionary perspective suggests that humans, who belong to one of the few species practicing reciprocal altruism since time immemorial, have evolved a cognitive system for directing attention to information that could reveal cheaters. That is, once a cognitive system has classified a situation as one of cooperation, attention will be directed to information that could reveal "benefit taken and cost not paid." Note that cheating detection in social contracts is a domain-specific mechanism; it would not apply if a conditional statement is coded as a threat, such as "If you touch me, then I'll kill you." But how does this help us to understand the content effect in the selection task?

The thesis is that the cheating-detection mechanism required by the theory of reciprocal altruism guides reasoning in the selection task:

If the conditional statement is coded as a social contract, and the subject is cued in to the perspective of one party in the contract, then attention is directed to information that can reveal being cheated.

In other words, a participant should select those cards that correspond to "benefit taken" and "cost not paid," whatever the cards' logical status is. This application of the theory of reciprocal altruism to an unresolved issue in human reasoning is, of course, a bold thesis.

Cheating Detection in the Selection Task

The numbers-and-letters rule and the transportation rule are not social contracts. There are not two partners who have engaged in a contract; the rules are descriptive ones rather than obligations, permissions, or other contracts with mutual costs and benefits. Therefore, social contract theory is mute on these problems. Cosmides (1989), however, showed that if a rule expressed a social contract, then the percentage of "benefit taken" and the "costs not paid" selections was very high. But this result can also be consistent with competing accounts that do not invoke reciprocal altruism, so we need to look more closely at tests that differentiate between competing accounts. Below is a sample of tests with that aim.

What Guides Reasoning: Availability or Cheater Detection?

The major account of the content effect in the 1970s and 1980s was variously called "familiarity" and "availability" (Manktelow & Evans, 1979; Pollard, 1982), without ever being precisely defined. The underlying idea is that the more familiar a statement is, the more often a participant may have experienced associations between the two propositions in a conditional statement, including those that are violations ("benefit taken" and "cost not paid") of the conditional statement. In this view, familiarity makes violations more "available" in memory, and selections may simply reflect availability. According to this conjecture, therefore, familiarity and not social contracts accounts for selecting the "benefit taken" and "cost not paid" cards. If familiarity were indeed the guiding cognitive principle, then *unfamiliar* social contracts should not elicit the same results. However, Cosmides (1989), Gigerenzer and Hug (1992), and Platt and Griggs (1993) showed that social contracts with unfamiliar propositions elicit the same high number of "benefit taken" and "cost not paid" selections, in contradiction to the availability account.

Social Contracts without Cheater Detection

Are People Simply Good at Reasoning about Social Contracts?

The game-theoretic models for the evolution of cooperation require, as argued earlier, some mechanism for detecting cheaters in order to exclude them from

Table 10.2 A social contract

Overnight rule
  If someone stays overnight in the cabin, then that person must bring along a bundle of wood from the valley.

The cards below have information about four hikers. Each card represents one person. One side of the card tells whether the person stayed overnight in the cabin, and the other side tells whether he or she carried a bundle of wood. Indicate only the card(s) you definitely need to turn over to see if the rule has been violated.

| STAYS OVERNIGHT IN THE CABIN | CARRIED WOOD | DOES NOT STAY OVERNIGHT | CARRIED NO WOOD |

the benefits of cooperation. The second conjecture, however, rejects any role of cheating detection in the selection task, claiming that people are, for some reason, better at reasoning about social contracts than about numbers-and-letters problems. Social contracts may be more "interesting" or "motivating," or people may have some "mental model" for social contracts that affords "clear" thinking. Although this alternative is nebulous, it needs to be taken into account; in her tests, Cosmides (1989) never distinguished between social contracts and cheating detection.

But one can experimentally disentangle social contracts from cheating detection. Klaus Hug and I also used social contracts but varied whether the search for violations constituted looking for cheaters or not (Gigerenzer & Hug, 1992). For instance, consider the following social contract: "If someone stays overnight in the cabin, then that person must bring along a bundle of wood from the valley" (Table 10.2). This was presented in one of two context stories.

The "cheating" version explained that a cabin high in the Swiss Alps serves as an overnight shelter for hikers. Because it is cold and firewood is not otherwise available at this altitude, the Swiss Alpine Club has made the rule that each hiker who stays overnight in the cabin must bring along a bundle of firewood from the valley. The participants were cued to the perspective of a guard who checks whether any of four hikers has violated the rule. The four hikers were represented by four cards (Table 10.2).

In the "no-cheating" version, the participants were cued to the perspective of a member of the German Alpine Association, visiting the same cabin in the Swiss Alps to find out how it is managed by the local Alpine Club. He observes people carrying firewood into the cabin, and a friend accompanying him suggests that the Swiss may have the same overnight rule as the Germans, namely, "If someone stays overnight in the cabin, then that person must bring along a bundle of wood from the valley." That this is also the Swiss Alpine Club's rule is not the only possible explanation; alternatively, only its members (who do not stay overnight in the cabin), and not the hikers, might bring firewood. The participants were now in the position of an observer who checks information to find out whether the social contract suggested by his friend actually holds.

This observer does not represent a party in a social contract. The participants instruction was the same as in the cheating version.

Thus, in the cheating scenario, the observation "benefit taken and cost not paid" means that the party represented by the guard is being cheated; in the no-cheating scenario, the same observation suggests only that the Swiss Alpine Club never made the supposed rule in the first place.

Assume as true the conjecture that what matters is only that the rule is a social contract, making the game-theoretic model (which requires a cheating mechanism) irrelevant. Because in both versions the rule is always the same social contract, such a conjecture implies that there should be no difference in the selections observed. In the overnight problem, however, 89% of the participants selected "benefit taken" and "cost not paid" when cheating was at stake, compared with 53% in the no-cheating version (Figure 10.1). Similarly, the averages across all four test problems used were 83% and 45%, respectively, consistent with the game-theoretic account of cooperation (Gigerenzer & Hug, 1992).

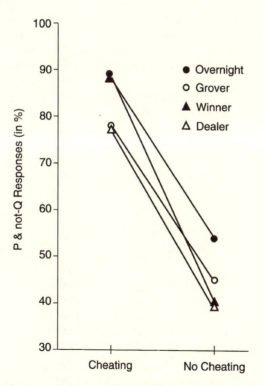

Figure 10.1 The absence of the possibility of being cheated reduces the "benefit taken and cost not paid" selections (which coincide with the P & not-Q selections), even when all rules are social contracts. From Gigerenzer and Hug (1992).

The "availability theory," in contrast, predicts no difference between the cheating and the no-cheating versions because the rules are identical and the context stories are similar in content and length. Pragmatic reasoning schema theory (Cheng & Holyoak, 1985) also predicts no difference, because the rules are in both versions permission or obligation rules, and cheating detection motivations and perspectives do not enter this theory.

These results support the assumption of a cheater-detection mechanism that guides information selection, as postulated by social contract theory. The study also shows that the concepts of a social contract rule and a cheater-detection mechanism can be experimentally separated.

Perspective Change

Do Social Contracts Simply Facilitate Logical Reasoning?

In most of Cosmides's tests, the predicted "benefit taken" and "cost not paid" selections corresponded to the truth conditions of conditionals in propositional logic. Thus a third conjecture would be that social contracts may somehow facilitate logical reasoning, which we tested by deducing predictions from the cheating-detection hypothesis that contradicted propositional logic (Gigerenzer & Hug, 1992). The key to these tests is that cheating detection is pragmatic and perspectival, whereas propositional logic is aperspectival. For instance, in the day-off problem in Table 10.3, one group of participants was cued to the perspective of an employee, in which case cheating detection and propositional logic indeed predict the same cards. For a second group of participants, we switched the perspective from employee to employer but held everything else constant (the conditional statement, the four cards, and the instruction shown in Table 10.3). For the employer, being cheated means "did not work on the weekend and did get a day off"; that is, in this perspective participants should select the "did not work on the weekend" and the "did

Table 10.3 A social contract with perspective change

Day-off rule
If an employee works on the weekend, then that person gets a day off during the week.

The cards below have information about four employees. Each card represents one person. One side of the card tells whether the person worked on the weekend, and the other side tells whether the person got a day off during the week. Indicate only the card(s) you definitely need to turn over to see if the rule has been been violated.

WORKED ON THE WEEKEND	DID GET A DAY OFF	DID NOT WORK ON THE WEEKEND	DID NOT GET A DAY OFF

get a day off" cards, which correspond to the "not-P" and "Q" cards. (Note that "not-P & Q" selections have rarely been observed in selection tasks.) Thus perspective change can play cheating detection against general-purpose logic. The two competing predictions are: If the cognitive system attempts to detect instances of "benefit taken and cost not paid" in the other party's behavior, then a perspective switch implies switching card selections; if the cognitive system reasons according to propositional logic, however, pragmatic perspectives are irrelevant and there should be no switch in card selections.

The results showed that when the perspective was changed, the cards selected also changed in the predicted direction (Figure 10.2). The effects were strong and robust across the three rules tested (Gigerenzer & Hug, 1992). For instance, in the employee perspective of the day-off problem, 75% of the participants had selected "worked on the weekend" and "did not get a day off," but only 2% had selected the other pair of cards. In the employer perspective, this 2% (who had selected "did not work on the weekend" and "did get a day off") rose to more than 60%. The result is consistent with the thesis that attention is directed toward information that could reveal oneself (or one's group) as being cheated in a social contract but is inconsistent with the claim that reasoning is directed by propositional logic independent of content.

Thus social contracts do not simply facilitate logical reasoning. I believe that the program of reducing context merely to an instrument for "facilitating" logical reasoning is misguided. My point is the same as for Property Alpha (Chapter 9). Reasoning consistent with propositional logic is entailed by some perspectives (e.g., the employee's), but is not entailed by other perspectives (e.g., the employer's).

Two additional conjectures can be dealt with briefly. First, several authors have argued that the cheating-detection thesis can be invalidated because "logical facilitation" (large proportions of "P & not-Q" selections) has also been found in some conditional statements that were not social contracts (e.g., Cheng & Holyoak, 1989; Politzer & Nguyen-Xuan, 1992). This conjecture misconstrues the thesis in two respects. The thesis is not about "logical facilitation"; the conjunction "benefit taken and cost not paid" is not the same as the logical conjunction "P & not-Q," as we have seen. Furthermore, a domain-specific theory makes, by definition, no prediction about performance outside its own domain; it can only be refuted within that domain.

The second conjecture also tries to reduce the findings to propositional logic, pointing out that a conditional that states a social contract is generally understood as a biconditional "if and only if." In this case all four cards can reveal logical violations and need to be turned over. However, it is not true that four-card selections are frequent when cheating detection is at stake. We found in about half of the social contract problems (12 problems, each answered by 93 students) that *not a single participant* had selected all four cards; for the remaining problems, the number was very small. Only when cheating detection was excluded (the no-cheating versions) did four-card selections increase to a proportion of about 10% (Gigerenzer & Hug, 1992). There is, then,

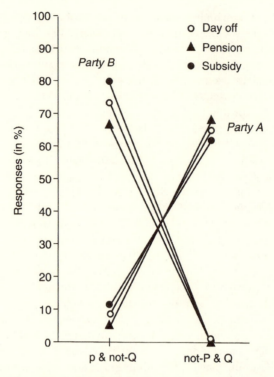

Figure 10.2 Social contracts in which both parties have the option to cheat allow us to test whether reasoning about social contracts follows aperspectival propositional logic (that is, the hypothesis that the conditional rule is interpreted as a material conditional) or the pragmatic and domain-specific goal of cheating detection. Results show that in both perspectives (Party A and Party B; e.g., employer and employee), participants search for information that could reveal that their party is being cheated, whether this information corresponds to P & not-Q (as the material conditional would suggest) or to not-P & Q. This result also does not support the hypothesis that participants interpret the rule as a biconditional, which implies that they would have to check all four cards. Four-card selections were rare. From Gigerenzer and Hug (1992).

no evidence that participants follow propositional logic even if we assume that they interpret the implication as a biconditional. In other words, people were not looking for cheaters per se but only for evidence of being cheated themselves. Our participants were not reasoning with a Kantian moral but with a Machiavellian intelligence.

Logical reductionism cannot explain how the mind infers that a particular conditional should be understood as a material implication, a biconditional, or something else. This inference is accomplished, I believe, by coding the specific content of the conditional statement as an instance of a larger domain, such as social contract, threat, and warning (Fillenbaum, 1977).

Conclusions

The evolutionary theory of cooperation illustrates how to begin constructing a theory of cognition situated in social interaction. The idea is to start with a specific design that a cognitive system requires for social interaction, rather than with a general-purpose, formal system—in other words, to start with the functional and see what logic it entails, rather than to impose some logic a priori. The virtues of this approach are as evident as its unresolved questions. Among these questions are: How can we precisely describe the "Darwinian algorithms" that determine when a social contract is in place? How does the mind infer that the conditional statement "If you touch me, then I'll kill you" does not imply a social contract but a threat? What are the cues coding this specific statement into the domain of "threats" rather than "social contracts"? Once a statement is categorized into a particular domain, what distribution of attention is implicated by that domain? In a threat, for example, attention needs to be directed to information that can reveal being bluffed or double-crossed rather than cheated (Fillenbaum, 1977). The challenge is to design theoretical proposals for reasoning and inference processes in other domains of human interaction beyond cooperation in social contracts.

To approach reasoning as situated in social interaction is to assume that the cognitive system (a) generalizes a specific situation as an instance of a larger domain and (b) reasons about the specific situation by applying a domain-specific cognitive module. This raises two questions about the nature of the domains and the design of the modules.

What Are the Domains and at What Level of Abstraction Are They Located?

Imagine a vertical dimension of abstraction, in which the specific problem corresponds to the lowest level of abstraction, and some formal representation of the problem, stripped of any content and context, to the highest. Two diametrically opposed views correspond to the ends of this continuum of abstraction. First, it may be argued that the cognitive system operates at the lowest level of abstraction, guided by familiarity and availability of instances in memory (e.g., Griggs & Cox, 1982). Second, it may be argued that the cognitive system generalizes the specific problem to the highest level of abstraction (e.g., propositional logic), performs some logical operations on this formal representation, and translates the result back into application to the specific problem. Variants of the latter view include Piaget's theory of formal operations and mental logics.

The primary challenge of domain specificity is to find a level of abstraction between the two extremes, where some content is stripped but an adequate amount retained. For instance, the level of social contracts and cheating detection could turn out to be too abstract, because cheating may assume different forms (e.g., in contracts in which both or only one side can be cheated; Gigerenzer & Hug, 1992), requiring different procedures of cheating detection. In contrast, the notions of social contracts and cheating detection may not be abstract enough, needing to be stripped of some content and placed at the more general level of social regulations, such as obligations, permissions, and other kinds of deontic reasoning (Cheng & Holyoak, 1985, 1989; Over & Manktelow, 1993). This focus on level of abstraction parallels Rosch's (1978) concern with "basic level objects."

What Is the Design of a Domain-Specific Cognitive Module?

A cognitive module organizes the processes—such as inference, emotion, and the distribution of attention—that have been evolved and learned to handle a domain. To classify a specific situation as an instance of a given domain, a cognitive module must be connected to an inferential mechanism. For instance, David Premack and others assume that humans and primates first classify an encounter as an instance of either social interaction (in the broadest sense) or interaction with the nonliving world. There is evidence that the cues used for this inference involve motion patterns, analyzed by cognitive systems to classify objects in the world as "self-propelled" or not; this analysis is reminiscent of Fritz Heider's and Albert Michotte's work (Premack, 1990; Sperber, 1994; Thinès, Costall, & Butterworth, 1991). Cognitive modules dealing with something external that has been coded as "self-propelled" attend to information such as whether it is friend or enemy, prey or predator. For a module that deals with inanimate things, no attention needs to be directed to information of this kind. Domain-specific modules can thus distribute attention in a more focused way than a domain-general mechanism. The challenge now before us is to come up with rich and testable models about the design of cognitive modules.

Toward a Social Rationality

Researchers in several disciplines are converging on a domain-specific program of studying reasoning and inference situated in social interaction. Primatologists have joined philosophers and psychologists in studying "social intelligence" (Kummer et al., 1997) and "Machiavellian intelligence" (Byrne & Whiten, 1988). Linguists and philosophers have begun to reinterpret the conclusions of experimental research, in particular the so-called fallacies and biases, by arguing that the interaction between participant and experimenter is constrained by conversational rather than formal axioms (e.g., Adler, 1991; Grice, 1975; Sperber & Wilson, 1986). Social psychologists have tested some of these proposals experimentally, concluding among other things that pervasive reasoning "biases" may not reflect universal shortcomings of the human mind but instead the application of Gricean conversational principles that conflict with what formal logic seems to dictate (e.g., Hertwig & Gigerenzer, 1999; Hilton, 1995; Schwarz et al., 1991). Similarly, Tetlock's (1992) concept of "accountability" models the social side of decision making by emphasizing that people do not simply choose the better alternative, but in certain social interactions, choose the alternative they can better justify. Developmental psychologists have departed from Piaget's general-purpose processes and investigate the domain-specific processes and their change during development (Hirschfeld & Gelman, 1994a). The convergence of these approaches promises a new vision of reasoning and rationality situated in social context.

I can only hope that this chapter will inspire some readers to rethink the imposition of formal axioms or rules as "rational," independent of context. The challenging alternative is to put the psychological and the social first—and then to examine what formal principles these entail. We need less Aristotle and more Darwin in order to understand the messy business of how to be rational in the uncertain world of interacting human beings. And we may have to abandon a dream. Leibniz's vision of a sovereign calculus, the Universal Characteristic, was a beautiful one. If only it had proved true.

11

The Modularity of Social Intelligence

In a "protected threat," a baboon induces a dominant member of its group to attack a third one. The baboon appeases the dominant member, whom it uses as a tool to threaten the target, and maneuvers to prevent the target from doing the same (Kummer, 1988). This "social tool use" is mastered by baboons at puberty, whereas chimpanzees are adult before they learn to use a stone as a tool for cracking hard nuts (Boesch & Boesch, 1984). Primates appear to manipulate social objects with more ease and sophistication than physical tools.

Observations such as these have suggested that primate intelligence is designed primarily for the social rather than the physical and have led to the *Machiavellian intelligence* hypothesis (Whiten & Byrne, 1988) or *social intelligence* hypothesis (Kummer et al., 1997). The social intelligence hypothesis assumes that social intelligence preceded (evolutionary headstart), influences, and qualitatively differs from nonsocial intelligence. The term *Machiavellian intelligence* emphasizes the besting of rivals for personal gain over cooperation, whereas the term *social intelligence* (which is the more general term) is neutral on the balance between exploitation and cooperation.

The social intelligence hypothesis is both stimulating and vague. It is stimulating because it reminds us that whenever psychologists study intelligence and learning in humans or animals, it is almost invariably about inanimate objects: symbols, sticks, and bananas. It is vague because the nature of the intelligence it invokes is largely unclear, and as a consequence, the mechanisms of social intelligence have not yet been specified. The modular version of the social intelligence hypothesis I propose assumes that social intelligences come in the plural, as do nonsocial intelligences. The notion of modularity is nothing new, but, as the introduction to a recent book on this topic illustrates, it means many things to many people (Hirschfeld & Gelman, 1994b). There exist several important approaches to modularity (e.g., Baron-Cohen, 1995; Leslie, 1994; Millikan, 1984; Pinker, 1994). It will soon become clear which ones inspired my own ideas. I will now describe the modular organization of social intelligence. Reader be warned: from here on is speculation.

The thesis that social intelligence is modular is motivated by two reasons: the shortsightedness of natural selection and the combinatorial explosion of intelligent systems. Natural selection works without a big plan but results in specific adaptations accumulated over generations. Thus it seems unlikely that natural selection designed a general-purpose intelligence that embodies, say, the Piagetian formal operations or a Bayesian inference machine. Even if this had happened, such a general-purpose intelligence runs into the problem of combinatorial explosion, as evidenced by the frame problem in artificial intelligence: Unless the infinite possibilities to combine elements and relations in a general-purpose system are drastically reduced by semantic constraints, an organism would be paralyzed and unable to react in time. For instance, unless attention is constrained to specific types of interactors and interactions, and semantic structure is a priori built in that tells the organism what to learn, what to look for, and what to ignore, an intelligent organism would be unable to perform even the most elementary tasks: to detect predators, prey, and mates and be fast enough to survive and reproduce.

I propose the following assumptions about the nature of modular social intelligence:

A Module for Social Intelligence Is a Faculty, Not a General Factor

Intelligence is often assumed to be of one kind, one general ability that helps an organism cope with all situations—such as Francis Galton's "natural ability," Spearman's general intelligence factor *g*, and the numberless definitions that start with "intelligence is the general ability to . . ." The thesis that intelligence is a unified general ability has been created only recently, in the mid-19th century, by Francis Galton, Herbert Spencer, and Hippolyte Taine, among others (Daston, 1992). The idea of one general intelligence was motivated by Darwin's theory of evolution (Galton was Darwin's cousin) and seemed to provide the missing continuum between animals and humans, as well as between human races, and last but not least, between men and women.

Such a unified general ability was alien to the earlier *faculty* psychology, which dated back to Aristotle. Faculty psychology posited a collection of faculties and talents in the mind, such as imagination, memory, and judgment. These faculties organized an intricate division of mental labor, and no single one nor their sum coincided with our concept of intelligence (Daston, 1992). Faculty psychology was revived, in the language of factor analysis, in the late 1930s when L. L. Thurstone claimed about seven primary mental abilities. In the second half of the 20th century, the mind has become again a crowded place. Evidence has been announced for dozens of factors of intelligence, and Guilford and Hoepfner (1971) even claimed the confirmation of some 98 factors of cognitive ability (see Carroll, 1982). Cognitive psychologists who use experiments rather than IQ tests also divide up cognition in terms of faculties (but you will not catch one using that term): deductive reasoning, inductive reasoning, problem solving, memory, attention, judgment and decision making, and so forth.

A modular organization of intelligence assumes, similar to the earlier faculty psychology before Galton, several intelligences that have special designs, and not one general-purpose intelligence. The general thesis is that social intelligence is an "adaptive toolbox" with several special tools rather than one single general-purpose hammer (Gigerenzer & Todd, 1999).

A Module for Social Intelligence Is Domain Specific, Not Domain General

Intelligence modules, however, are not like Thurstone's primary mental abilities and faculties such as reasoning. I distinguish between two types of faculties: *domain specific* and *domain general*. Faculties such as deductive reasoning, memory, and numerical ability (as well as such factors as "fluid" and "crystallized" intelligence) are assumed to treat any content identically, that is, to operate in a domain-general way. The laws of memory, for instance, in this view, are not about *what* is memorized; they are formulated without reference to content. Fodor (1983) called these domain-general faculties "horizontal" as opposed to "vertical" domain-specific faculties. The modularity of social intelligence, I propose, is vertical.

The doctrine of domain-general mechanisms flourished in Skinner's behaviorism, before it was generally rejected following experimental work by John Garcia and others (see Chapter 10). Learning through imitation (rather than reinforcement) is also reported to be domain specific. Rhesus monkeys, for instance, reared in the laboratory show no fear toward venomous snakes. However, one will show fear if it sees another monkey exhibiting a fear reaction toward snakes. Yet the monkey does not become afraid of just any stimulus: If it sees another monkey emit a fear reaction toward a flower, it does not acquire a fear of flowers (Cosmides & Tooby, 1994b; Mineka & Cook, 1988). Learning by imitation of others, like learning by association, is simultaneously *enabled* and *constrained* by specific "expectations" of what to avoid, what to fear, or more generally, what causal connections to establish. Without domain-specific mechanisms, an organism would not "know" what to look for, nor which of the infinite possible causal connections to check. Such an organism would be paralyzed by data analysis like the quantophrenic researcher who measures everything one can think of, computes correlation matrices of dinosaurian dimensions, and blindly searches for significant correlations. Despite the available evidence to the contrary, Skinner's ideal of domain generality has survived the cognitive revolution and is flourishing in present-day conceptions of the mind.

Domain generality is possibly the most influential and suspect idea in 20th-century psychology. Psychologists love to organize their field by horizontal faculties such as attention, memory, perception, problem solving, and judgment and decision making. Terms such as these organize the chapter structure of textbooks, the specialties of scientific journals, the divisional structure in grant agencies, and the self-identity of numerous colleagues. Psychologists tend to identify with horizontal faculties, not with domains.

I propose, in contrast, that modules for social intelligence are domain specific. How should we think about these modules? Fodor (1983), a vehement proponent of modularity, has argued that modularity is restricted to input systems (the senses) and language, whereas central processes such as reasoning are domain general. I term this the "weak modularity thesis." In his view, modules are specifically designed mechanisms for voice recognition in conspecifics, for face recognition in conspecifics, and color perception, among others. I disagree with Fodor's opposition between modular sensory processes (and language) and general-purpose central processes. Social intelligence involves both perceptual processes and mechanisms for reasoning and inductive inference. For instance, assume there is a module for social contracts, that is, a module that enables cooperation between unrelated conspecifics for their mutual benefit. Such a module would need to incorporate both "central" processes, such as cost–benefit computations and search algorithms for information that could reveal that one is being cheated, and sensory processes such as face recognition. Without both "peripheral" and "central" mechanisms, neither social contracts nor cheating detection would be possible.

What I call the "strong modularity thesis" postulates that modules include central processes as well as sensory mechanisms (and language). The function of modules is not tied to "peripheral" as opposed to "central" processes. Rather, their function is to solve specific problems of adaptive significance and to do this quickly. A problem of adaptive significance can be described as an evolutionarily recurrent problem whose solution promoted reproduction (Cosmides & Tooby, 1994a, b; Miller & Todd, 1995, 1998). Candidates include coalition forming and cooperation, foraging, predator avoidance, navigation, mate selection, and rearing children. To solve such problems, modules need to combine "peripheral" and "central" processes. Thus the domains (more precisely, the "proper" domains; see next section) of modules are important adaptive problems and not just perceptual (plus language) tasks.

A Module for Social Intelligence Has a Proper and an Actual Domain

Assume there is a social intelligence module designed for handling social contracts in a hunter–gatherer society. The *proper* domain of the module may have been the exchange of food for the mutual benefit of both parties involved in the contract (because food sharing is not too common among animals, an alternative hypothesis would be that the proper domain concerned social services such as alliance formation; see Harcourt & de Waal, 1992). Generations later, currency has been developed, and the module's representation of possible benefits and costs exchanged in a social contract needs to be expanded to tokens that can be exchanged for benefits. Soon economic systems will be invented in which the exchange of hard currency is no longer the norm, and benefits and costs become more and more abstract. The *actual* domain of the module has shifted from the exchange of grain and meat to buying futures and options. The mechanisms of the module, however, perform largely the same task: a routine that leads individuals to enter into social contracts (sharing) when resources (such as meat) are highly variable and scarce; a representation of what the benefits and costs are for oneself and for one's kin; perceptual algorithms and a memory that allows identification of the partner by face, voice, or name recognition; and a search heuristic that looks for information that could reveal that one is being cheated.

Thus the *proper* domain of a module is that for which the module actually evolved; the *actual* domain is one to which the module is transferred or extended, following changes in the environment (Sperber, 1994). By being transferred to new domains, the mechanisms of the modules themselves may change; adaptations (modules) can become exaptations for new adaptations (Gould & Vrba, 1982). The distinction between proper and actual domain is a matter of degree rather than of kind, and the actual domain is most likely larger than the proper domain. Modules for social intelligence in humans seem to differ from those in primates in that they have larger actual domains and in that the actual domains may have less overlap with the proper domain.

The actual domains of modules for human social intelligence can extend beyond the human. Anthropomorphism is social intelligence reaching out beyond *Homo sapiens*. Anthropomorphism has counted as a scientific sin since the 17th century, and earlier as a theological sin; nevertheless human intelligence cannot resist projecting human social categories, intentions, and morals onto nonhumans (Mitchell et al., 1997). Darwin himself practiced empathic anthropomorphism (but not anthropocentrism) in particular with respect to dogs; animal rights activists often invoke the same sentiment. Anthropomorphism of a less empathic nature extends to phylogenetically distant species: "Rape" in scorpion flies and "ant slavery" are examples. In opposition to all this, behaviorism values purifying scientific language, and a story told about the Columbia University philosopher Sidney Morgenbesser illustrates this. After B. F. Skinner gave a talk at Columbia, Sidney stood up and said: "Professor Skinner, I always tried to understand what the essence of behaviorism is. Now I think I know. Behaviorism is the denial of anthropomorphism for humans."

Social intelligence can reach beyond animals and still create powerful metaphors. Dawkins's (1976) "selfish gene" lives in a world of savage competition, exploitation, and deceit. Physicists, chemists, and astronomers certainly censor similar anthropomorphic descriptions in press, but in scientists' informal and private conversations, intentions are frequently attributed to particles and matter (Atran, 1990).

A Module Is Activated by a Triggering Algorithm

Assume there is a simple social organism with two modules for social intelligence: One deals with social contracts, the other with threats. Thus this organism knows only two ways to deal with conspecifics: to engage with them in the exchange of certain goods to their mutual benefit and to threaten individuals to get one's way (and react when others do so). As simple as the social intelligence of this organism is, the organism needs to decide when to activate the social contract module and when the threat module. All modules cannot be activated at the same time because the very advantage of modularity is to focus attention and to prevent combinatorial explosion. For instance, the social contract module focuses attention on information that can reveal that the organism is being cheated, whereas this information is of no relevance for a threat module. A threat module needs to attend to information that can reveal, for instance, whether the other side is bluffing or whether high-status individuals are present who could be used for "protected threat" (Kummer, 1988).

How is one of the two modules activated? I assume that there is a triggering algorithm that attends to a small set of cues whose presence signals either threat or social contract. These signals can include facial expressions, gestures, body movements, and verbal statements. Assume that the organisms do have language. A simple algorithm can quickly recognize whether a verbal statement of the type "if you do X, then I do Y" is a threat or a social contract. If Y is a negative consequence for me, and follows X in time, then I am being threatened. If Y is a benefit for me and the temporal sequence can be either way, then I am being offered a social contract. I call such simple heuristics "triggering algorithms" because their function is to activate a module that can focus attention, emotion, and behavioral responses so that fast reaction is possible.

Triggering algorithms can err, that is, not activate the appropriate module, such as mistaking a serious threat for pretend play. The likelihood of triggering the wrong module may increase when there are more than two modules, but redundancy in cues, such as verbal cues, facial cues, and gestures, may reduce errors.

Modules Are Hierarchically Organized

When a mind has not just two but a large number of modules, a single triggering algorithm may be too slow to discriminate between all possibilities simultaneously. In such a socially more intelligent mind, modules can be hierarchically connected by triggering algorithms, as in a sequential decision tree. Hierarchical organization corresponds to the idea that species started out with a few modules, to which more specialized modules were added later in phylogeny, and to Wimsatt's (1986) notion of generative entrenchment.

Assume I march through a forest at night. Visibility is poor, a storm is coming up, and I suddenly see the contours of a large dark object that seems to move slowly. A triggering algorithm needs to decide quickly whether the object is "self-propelled" (animal or human) or not (plant or physical object; Premack & Premack, 1994). According to the Premacks, this decision is based on the object's motion pattern. Recall the demonstrations by Fritz Heider in which the motion patterns of two points in two-dimensional space make us "see" the points as animate or inanimate, chasing, hunting, hurting, or supporting one another (e.g., Heider & Simmel, 1944). These are beautiful demonstrations, but they include no descriptions of the algorithms that make us see all these social behaviors. How could the first triggering algorithm work? A simple algorithm would analyze only external movements (such as the direction and accelera-tion of the object) and not internal movements (the relative movement of the body parts). For instance, if a motion pattern centers on my own position, such as an object that circles around me or speeds up toward me, the algorithm infers a self-propelled object. Moreover, it infers a self-propelled object that takes some interest in me. Motion patterns that center around the object's own center of gravity, in contrast, indicate that the object is a plant (e.g., a tree). Now, if the motion pattern indicates that the object is self-propelled, the trig-gering algorithm may activate a module for unrecognized self-propelled ob-jects. This module will immediately set the organism into a state of physio-logical and emotional arousal, initiate behavioral routines such as stopping and preparing to run away, and activate a second, more specialized triggering algorithm whose task is to decide whether the self-propelled object is animal or human. Assume that this second triggering algorithm infers from shape and motion information that the object is human. A module for social encounters with unknown humans is subsequently activated, which initiates a search for individual recognition in memory and may initiate an appeal for voice contact in order to find out whether the other is friend or enemy, is going to threaten or help me, and so on. This is pure speculation, but one might work out the mechanisms of a hierarchical organization along these lines.

Modules that are hierarchically organized can act quickly, as only a few branches of the combinatorial tree need to be traveled. For instance, if the first triggering algorithm had indicated that the unknown object was not self-propelled, then all subsequent information concerning whether it is human or animal, friend or enemy, or predator or prey could have been ignored.

An Intelligence Module Works with Fast and Frugal Heuristics

There are two views about the machinery of intelligent behavior. The classical view is that the laws of probability theory or logic define intelligent processes: Intelligent agents have rules such as Bayes's rule, the law of large numbers, transitive inference, and consistency built in. This was the view of the Enlight-enment mathematicians, to which Jean Piaget added an ontogenetic dimension, and it still is a dominant view in economics, cognitive psychology, artificial intelligence, and optimal foraging theory. For instance, Bayes's rule has been proposed as a normative or descriptive model of how animals infer the presence of predators and prey (Stephens & Krebs, 1986), as well as how humans reason, categorize, and memorize (Anderson, 1990). The problem with this view is that in any sufficiently rich environment, Bayesian computations become mathematically so complex that one needs to assume that minds are "Laplacean demons" that have unlimited computational power, time, and knowledge. To find a way out of this problem, researchers often make unrealistic assumptions about the structure of natural environments, namely assumptions that reduce the Bayesian computations. Anderson (1990), for instance, found himself forced to make the assumption that environmental features would be generally independent, in order to save the fiction of the Bayesian homunculus in the mind (Gigerenzer, 1991c). Despite their psychological implausibility, Laplacean demons are bustling in contemporary theories of the mind: as models of choice, categorization, estimation, and inference, among others. The rationale seems to be this: Cognition is rational, Bayes's rule defines rationality, ergo cognition works with Bayes's rule. The same rationale seems to hold for other statistical tools that turned into theories of mind, such as multiple regression, Neyman-Pearson decision techniques, and analysis of variance (Chapter 1).

The second view, the one I propose here, is that modules of social intelligence, including the triggering algorithms, work with fast and frugal strategies instead of the costly "optimal" algorithms. There are several reasons that favor simple and specifically designed heuristics rather than expensive and general ones. First, there is, in fact, no single method of inference—statistical or logical—that works best in all real-world contexts. Second, as mentioned before, in real-world situations, "optimal" computations can quickly become so complex that one is forced to make highly simplifying assumptions about the environment. Third, algorithms for social intelligence need to work under constraints of limited time and knowledge—for instance, one may not have the time to search for further information. Fourth, the means and ends of social intelligence are broader than consistency (coherence) and accuracy—the accepted norms of logic and statistics. Social intelligence can involve being inconsistent (e.g., adaptive unpredictability may be optimal in competitive situations: the opponent will be unable to predict one's behavior), taking high risks in trying to come out first (that is, options with low probabilities rather than those that maximize expected value), responding quickly rather than accurately (e.g., to make too long a pause in a conversation in order to think of the best answer can be embarrassing and seen as impolite), and making decisions that one can justify or defend afterward (Todd, 2000a, b).

The key argument against fast and frugal heuristics is that their simplicity raises the suspicion that they are really bad. But this need not be the case: Simple principles can be quick-and-clean rather than quick-and-dirty. Consider a simple heuristic for choice called "Take The Best" (Gigerenzer & Goldstein, 1996). Take The Best infers which of two alternatives scores higher on some criterion, such as which of two food items is more dangerous or which of two cities has a higher population. Take The Best bases decisions on one single reason, namely on the first good reason on which two alternatives differ. The first good reason can be simply that the individual does not recognize (has never heard of) one of the two alternatives. This "recognition heuristic" seems to operate in domains in which recognition is correlated with the variable that needs to be inferred. For instance, rats who can choose between food that they recognize and food that is new to them do not accept the new food unless they have smelled it on the breath of a fellow rat (Gallistel et al., 1991). The surprising result is that simple heuristics such as Take The Best can make as accurate inferences about real-world environments as costly statistical algorithms of the Laplacean demon type (Martignon & Laskey, 1999).

If short-sighted evolution has equipped us with adaptive heuristics rather than with the collected works of logic and probability theory, this result indicates that we need to rethink human rationality. The challenges are to understand what these heuristics are and to describe the structure of the environments in which they can perform well and in which they cannot. My proposal is that both the triggering algorithms and the mechanisms of the module can be modeled as fast and frugal heuristics (Gigerenzer et al., 1999).

Modules Combine Cognitive, Emotional, and Motivational Tools to Guide Inference and Behavior

In each module, various cognitive, emotional, behavioral, and motivational processes are wired together. A social contract module, for instance, includes perceptual machinery to recognize different individuals; a long-term memory that stores the history of past exchanges with other individuals in order to know when to cooperate, when to defect, and when to punish for defection; knowledge about what constitutes a benefit and what a cost for oneself; and emotional reactions such as anger that signal to others that one will go ruthlessly after cheaters (Cosmides & Tooby, 1992; Gigerenzer, 1995). Intelligent modules can use cognitive, emotional, or motivational processes vicariously as means to achieve a goal. For instance, emotional reactions (such as disgust in matters of food) can substitute for learning from experience when events are too rare or too deadly for individual learning.

The very challenge of a modular concept of social intelligence is that it crosses the established boundaries of horizontal faculties. Thereby, the notion of modularity questions the institutionalized subdisciplines of psychology. It opens up a conception of intelligence that integrates cognition with, rather than setting it apart from, other adaptive functions such as motivations and emotions.

Summary

In 1976, Nick Humphrey wrote a stimulating essay on the social function of intellect that provided "the single most important seed" (Byrne & Whiten,

1988, p. 1) for *Machiavellian intelligence*. Humphrey's paper contains thought-provoking ideas about social intelligence but also the seed of a sterile research methodology. In the postscript we are told that his "central thesis" demands "that there should be a positive correlation across species between 'social complexity' and 'individual intelligence' " (Humphrey, 1976/1988, p. 26). A laboratory test of social skill, Humphrey proposes, is urgently needed, which "ought, if I am right, to double as a test of 'high-level intelligence' " (p. 26). This proposal, as innocent as it looks, steers toward repeating a grave error that has swamped research on (nonsocial) intelligence. The error is to start with no theory but with seductive everyday concepts such as social skill and creative intelligence, then go on to design tests to measure these vague concepts, and to pray to heaven that these tests miraculously transform loose thinking into precise mechanisms of intelligence.[1] Despite prayers that were backed up by statistics, some 90 years of factor analyzing and correlating IQ tests has not noticeably increased our understanding of the mechanisms of human intelligence. I fear that Humphrey's proposal to look for correlations between some tests for social complexity, social skill, and individual intelligence will be doomed to the same failure.

The alternative is to start boldly and theoretically. The challenge is to design the possible mechanisms of social intelligence and to test these by means of experiment, observation, and simulation. The mechanisms of a modular social intelligence that I have outlined, as speculative as they are, can serve as a start. We will have to take up some hard questions. What are the domains (proper and actual) for a given species? What is the mechanism of a module? What is the algorithm that triggers a module? If we join forces, we can do it.

---

1. The notion of test intelligence, left undefined in its content, has had many faces, including the moral and the social (Daston, 1992). For instance, the creators of the first intelligence tests, Binet and Simon (1914), asked questions about social skills, such as "Why should one judge a person by his acts rather than by his words?" In the first edition of the Stanford–Binet Test, Louis Terman (1916) expressed the intimate link between lack of intelligence and morally inappropriate behavior in no uncertain terms: "Every feeble-minded woman is a prostitute." In the 1937 revision of the text (with M. A. Merrill), this sentence was deleted. Piece by piece, IQ tests became pure and puritan.

V

COGNITIVE ILLUSIONS AND STATISTICAL RITUALS

The "discovery" of cognitive illusions was not the first assault on human rationality. Sigmund Freud's attack is probably the best known: According to him, the unconscious wishes and desires of the human id are a steady source of intrapsychical conflict that manifests itself in all kinds of irrational fears, beliefs, and behavior. But the cognitive-illusion assault is stronger than the psychoanalytic one. It does not need to invoke a conflict between rational judgment and unconscious wishes and desires to explain humans' apparent irrationality: Judgment is itself fundamentally deficient. *Homo sapiens* appears to be a misnomer. During the last few decades, cognitive illusions have become fodder for classroom demonstrations and textbooks. Isn't it fun to show how dumb everyone else is, and after all, aren't they?

In the spring of 1990, I gave a talk in the Department of Psychology at Stanford University entitled "Beyond heuristics and biases: How to make cognitive illusions disappear." The first chapter in this section is an updated version of this talk. It became the fountainhead of an ongoing, heated debate over the nature of human rationality and the litany of sins people seem to commit routinely against reason (e.g., Gigerenzer, 1996a; Kahneman & Tversky, 1996), the so-called "rationality wars" (Samuels, Stich, & Bishop, in press). Cognitive illusions have been linked to perceptual illusions, suggesting that they are "inevitable illusions" (Piattelli-Palmarini, 1994). The political implications of this view are not hard to see. Given the message that ordinary citizens are unable to estimate uncertainties and risks, one might conclude that a government would be well advised to keep these nitwits out of important decisions regarding new technologies and environmental risks. In Chapter 12, I criticize the narrow norms that make humans look irrational and show how to make inevitable illusions "evitable."

Research on cognitive illusions is but one example of the more general phenomenon of replacing statistical thinking with narrow, simplistic norms. The statistical practices institutionalized in many social and medical sciences are another case in point; they have little to do with statistical thinking and instead promote statistical rituals. Textbooks teach our students the equivalent of compulsive hand washing, the result being confusion and anxiety.

I once asked a well-known author who was busy preparing the latest edition of his best-selling statistical text for psychologists why he promoted the usual incoherent mishmash of Fisherian and Neyman-Pearsonian prescriptions for testing hypotheses (see Chapter 13). He did not try to deny the problem, but he told me whom to blame for it. First, there was his publisher, who had insisted that he supply a statistical cookbook and take out anything that hinted at the existence of alternative tools for statistical inference, which he did. Next, there were his fellow researchers, who did not aim to truly understand statistics but to get their papers published. Finally, he passed the blame on to the editors who demanded a statistical ritual and to his university administration, which determined salary increases by counting the number of papers published. When I asked him in what statistical methods he himself believed, he said that deep in his heart he was a Bayesian. I was shocked. What a Faustian pact—an author successfully sells a method in which he does not believe, which students and researchers then naively mistake for the moral guidelines of doing science.

This is not to say that the many textbook authors who borrowed from him are as aware of the confusion behind the ritual of null hypothesis testing as he was. In my experience, many authors are innocent because ignorant, which is one way to maintain one's intellectual integrity. I wrote Chapter 13 as an antidote to mindless statistics for both students and future textbook writers.

The larger social and intellectual background for this chapter can be found in *The empire of chance: How probability changed science and everyday life* (Gigerenzer et al., 1989). This book was written by an interdisciplinary group of scholars who studied the probabilistic revolution in the sciences at the Center for Interdisciplinary Research in Bielefeld, a place where nothing could distract us from work. Geoffrey Loftus reviewed the book in *Contemporary Psychology* in 1991. When he became the editor of *Memory & Cognition* in 1993, in his editorial statement he asked researchers to stop submitting manuscripts with legions of p-values, t-values, and F-values and instead present sound descriptive statistics, such as figures with error bars around means. I admire him for having the courage to stand up against mindless null hypothesis testing. A few years later, I asked Geoffrey how his crusade was going. To Geoffrey's surprise, the resistance was coming from the researchers. Most of them insisted on going through with the ritual. As this case illustrates, editors alone cannot be blamed for psychologists' continued reliance on misguided statistical procedures. I might add that I have never had a problem publishing experimental papers without null hypothesis tests.

The story of null hypothesis testing in psychology is reminiscent of Hans Christian Andersen's tale of the emperor's new clothes. In a sense, the procedure has no clothes: Its outcome, the p-value, does not inform the reader about the size of the effect, the probability that the null hypothesis is true, the probability that the alternative hypothesis is true, or the probability that the result is replicable. Nevertheless, studies in the United States, Great Britain, and Germany indicate that some 80% to 90% of academic psychologists "see" one or more of these attractive garments on the p-value.

I have been asked what we should do instead of null hypothesis testing. The answer is: not a new ritual. Chapter 6 illustrated one alternative. First, the data is tested against multiple hypotheses—alternative models of cognitive strategies—rather than against one null hypothesis. Second, multiple hypotheses are tested against the judgments of each individual participant rather than against the average across individuals, thus enabling detection of multiple strategies. Third, hypotheses are tested against both outcome and process data rather than outcome data only.

The most important thing is to define candidate hypotheses before starting the business of hypothesis testing. Null hypothesis testing encourages theoretical laziness. To use it, one does not need to specify one's research hypothesis or a substantive alternative except "chance." This scant requirement allows surrogates for theories to grow like weeds (Chapter 14). We need statistical thinking, not statistical rituals.

12

How to Make Cognitive Illusions Disappear

Social psychology was transformed by the "cognitive revolution." Cognitive imperialism has been both praised and lamented. But a second revolution has transformed most of the sciences so fundamentally that it is now hard to see that it could have been different before. It has made concepts such as probability, chance, and uncertainty indispensable for understanding nature, society, and the mind. This sweeping conceptual change has been called the "probabilistic revolution" (Krüger, Daston, & Heidelberger, 1987; Krüger, Gigerenzer, & Morgan, 1987). The probabilistic revolution differs from the cognitive revolution in its genuine novelty and its interdisciplinary scope. Statistical mechanics, Mendelian genetics, Brownian motion, radioactive decay, random drift, randomized experimental design, statistical inference—these are some of the fruits of that transformation. Social psychology was no exception. It currently bears the marks of both the cognitive revolution and the probabilistic revolution.

Probabilistic and statistical concepts were piggybacked onto cognitive concepts. Some of the most popular theories and research programs owed their genesis to an analogy between social cognition and "intuitive statistics." In 1967, for instance, Harold Kelley proposed that the layperson attributes a cause to an effect in the same way as a statistician of the Fisherian school would, by (unconsciously) calculating an analysis of variance (ANOVA). Research on the ANOVA mind soon became mainstream social psychology (Kelley & Michaela, 1980). It is well documented in the history of science that statistics *transformed* almost everything it touched. So has causal attribution (Chapter 1). Just as statistical calculations are those of an *individual* statistician, attribution and social cognition were investigated as the calculations of individual minds, confirming the individualism in social psychology (Newcombe & Rutter, 1982).

More recently, Bayesian statistics, rather than Fisherian statistics, has been used as a yardstick to evaluate social cognition, and as measured by this new yardstick, many people's judgments seemed to be flawed by fallacies and errors in statistical reasoning. "Hot" motivational terms were replaced by the "cold" cognitive language of intuitive statistics. Self-serving perceptions and attributions, ethnocentric beliefs, and many types of human conflict were analyzed as passionless information-processing errors, due to basic shortcomings in intuitive statistical reasoning (e.g., Borgida & Brekke, 1981; Nisbett & Ross, 1980; Sherman, Judd, & Park, 1989). Social cognitive psychologists started to study (what they believed to be) errors in probabilistic reasoning, such as the base-rate fallacy, the conjunction fallacy, and overconfidence bias, and adopted the explanatory language of Kahneman and Tversky's "heuristics," such as representativeness and availability. Some, such as Strack (1988), even pointed to Kahneman and Tversky's heuristics as primary evidence of the end of the "crisis" of social psychology and of new, rising confidence and decisive progress in the field.

Heuristics and Biases

The "heuristics and biases" program of Kahneman, Tversky, and others has generated two main results concerning judgment under uncertainty: (1) a list of so-called biases, fallacies, or errors in probabilistic reasoning, such as the base-rate fallacy and the conjunction fallacy, and (2) explanations of these biases in terms of cognitive heuristics such as representativeness. Table 12.1 gives a taste of the conclusions drawn from this program.

Kahneman and Tversky (1982) see the study of systematic errors in probabilistic reasoning, also called "cognitive illusions," as similar to that of visual illusions. "The presence of an error of judgment is demonstrated by comparing people's responses either with an established fact (e.g., that the two lines are equal in length) or with an accepted rule of arithmetic, logic, or statistics" (p. 493). Their distinction between "correct" and "erroneous" judgments under uncertainty has been echoed by many social psychologists: "We follow conventional practice by using the term 'normative' to describe the use of a rule when there is a consensus among formal scientists that the rule is appropriate for the particular problem" (Nisbett & Ross, 1980, p. 13).

Social psychology is not the only area in which the "heuristics and biases" program has made strong inroads. Experimental demonstrations of "fallacious" judgments have entered law (e.g., Saks & Kidd, 1980), economics (e.g., Frey, 1990), management science (e.g., Bazerman, 1990), medical diagnosis (e.g., Casscells, Schoenberger, & Grayboys, 1978), behavioral auditing (see Shanteau, 1989), philosophy (e.g., Stich, 1990), and many other fields. There is no doubt that understanding judgment under uncertainty is essential in all these fields. It is the achievement of the "heuristics and biases" program to have finally established this insight as a central topic of psychology. Earlier pioneers who studied intuitive statistics (Hofstätter, 1939; Peirce & Jastrow, 1884; Wendt, 1966) had little impact. Even Ward Edwards and his colleagues (e.g., Edwards, 1968), who started the research from which Kahneman and Tversky's "heuris-

Table 12.1 A sample of conclusions from the *heuristics-and-biases* program

In making predictions and judgments under uncertainty, people do not appear to follow the calculus of chance or the statistical theory of prediction. Instead, they rely on a limited number of heuristics which sometimes yield reasonable judgments and sometimes lead to severe and systematic errors.

Daniel Kahneman & Amos Tversky, 1973, p. 237

It appears that people lack the correct programs for many important judgmental tasks. . . . We have not had the opportunity to evolve an intellect capable of dealing conceptually with uncertainty.

Paul Slovic, Baruch Fischhoff, & Sarah Lichtenstein, 1976, p. 174

The genuineness, the robustness, and the generality of the base-rate fallacy are matters of established fact.

Maya Bar-Hillel, 1980, p. 215

The biases of framing and overconfidence just presented suggest that individuals are generally affected by systematic deviations from rationality.

Max Bazerman & M. A. Neale, 1986, p. 317

[Overconfidence bias] has proved so robust that it is hard to acquire much insight into the psychological processes underlying it.

Baruch Fischhoff, 1988, p. 172

. . . mental illusions should be considered the rule rather than the exception.

Richard H. Thaler, 1991, p. 4

[We are] a species that is uniformly probability-blind, from the humble janitor to the Surgeon General. . . . We should not wait until A. Tversky and D. Kahneman receive a Nobel prize for economics. Our self-liberation from cognitive illusions ought to start even sooner.

Massimo Piattelli-Palmarini, 1991, p. 35

tics and biases" program emerged, had no comparable influence on cognitive and social psychology.

Despite its influence, I will argue that the "heuristics and biases" program is merely an important transitional stage, which must be transformed if long-term progress is to be made. I will review some serious shortcomings of that research program and show how they can be overcome.

In this chapter I do three things. First, I discuss the validity of the normative yardstick that is used to define people's judgments as systematic errors in probabilistic reasoning. I will argue that most so-called errors or cognitive illusions are, contrary to the assertions in the literature, in fact *not* violations of probability theory. In their normative claims, Tversky and Kahneman, and social psychologists following in their footsteps, have neglected conceptual distinctions that are fundamental to probability and statistics. Second, I show that if we pay attention to these conceptual distinctions, we can make apparently stable "cognitive illusions" disappear, reappear, or even invert. Third, the interesting fact that intuitive reasoning is highly sensitive to conceptual distinctions made by statisticians (but ignored by many psychologists) leads to a revised understanding of judgment under uncertainty.

Why Biases Are Not Biases

In the "heuristics and biases" program, a bias or error in probabilistic reasoning is defined as a systematic discrepancy between a person's judgment and a norm. What is that norm? It is often referred to as "the normative theory of prediction" (Kahneman & Tversky, 1973, p. 243), as the "normative principles of statistical prediction" (Ajzen, 1977, p. 304), or simply as an "accepted rule" of statistics. Many have understood this rhetoric to imply that there exists precisely one "correct" answer to the cab problem, engineer–lawyer problem, Linda problem, and other problems posed to participants—an answer sanctioned by the authority of the eminent mathematicians, probabilists, and statisticians of this century. The claim that all these problems have *one* correct answer is crucial. If they did *not* have one and only one answer, it would make little sense first to identify "errors" and "cognitive illusions" and then to use these cognitive illusions to understand the principles of inductive reasoning, in the way that visual illusions are used to understand the principles of normal perception. This two-step program, identifying errors and explaining them, in analogy to perceptual research, is the basic idea behind the heuristics-and-biases program (Kahneman & Tversky, 1982, p. 493).

But what does the "heuristics and biases" investigation of judgment under uncertainty have to do with probability and statistics? The short answer to this question is: all too little. The probabilistic rules against which cognitive and social psychologists have measured the proficiency of their participants are in fact a highly (and, I shall argue, often misleadingly) selected sample of those routinely used, consulted, and discussed by working probabilists and statisticians. When claiming "errors" and "fallacies," cognitive and social psychologists have largely ignored conceptual and technical distinctions *fundamental* to probability and statistics.

What in the heuristics-and-biases literature is called the "normative theory of probability" or the like is in fact a very narrow kind of neo-Bayesian view that is shared by some theoretical economists and cognitive psychologists and to a lesser degree by practitioners in business, law, and artificial intelligence. It is *not* shared by proponents of the frequentist view of probability that dominates today's statistics departments, nor by proponents of many other views; it is not even shared by all Bayesians, as I shall show shortly. By this narrow standard of "correct" probabilistic reasoning, the most distinguished probabilists and statisticians of our century—figures of the stature of Richard von Mises and Jerzy Neyman—would be guilty of "biases" in probabilistic reasoning.[1] Let me illustrate this point with some of the best-known demonstrations of "fallacies."

1. Despite the widespread rhetoric of a single "normative theory of prediction," it should be kept in mind that the problem of inductive reasoning still has no universal solution (the "scandal of philosophy") but many competing ones. The controversies

Overconfidence Bias

Confidence in general knowledge is typically studied with questions of the following kind:

Which city has more inhabitants?

(a) Hyderabad, (b) Islamabad

How confident are you that your answer is correct?

50% / 60% / 70% / 80% / 90% / 100%

The participant chooses what he or she believes is the correct answer and then rates his or her confidence that the answer is correct. After many participants answer many questions, the experimenter counts how many answers in each of the confidence categories were actually correct. The typical finding is that in all the cases in which participants said, "I am 100% confident that my answer is correct," the relative frequency of correct answers was only about 80%; in all the cases in which they said, "I am 90% confident that my answer is correct," the relative frequency of correct answers was only about 75%, and so on (for an overview, see Lichtenstein, Fischhoff, & Phillips, 1982). This systematic discrepancy between confidence and relative frequency is termed "overconfidence."

Little has been achieved in explaining this "bias." A common proposal is to explain "biases" by other, deeper mental flaws. For instance, Koriat, Lichtenstein, and Fischhoff (1980) proposed that the overconfidence bias is caused by a "confirmation bias." Their explanation was this: After one alternative is chosen, the mind searches for further information that *confirms* the answer

---

between the Fisherians, the Neyman-Pearsonians, and the Bayesians are evidence of this unresolved rivalry. For the reader who is not familiar with the fundamental issues, two basic themes may help introduce the debate (for more, see Hacking, 1965). The first issue relevant for our topic is whether probability is *additive* (that is, satisfies the Kolmogorov axioms, e.g., that the probabilities of all possible events sum up to 1) or not. The above-mentioned points of view (including that of the heuristics-and-biases program) subscribe to additivity, whereas L. J. Cohen's (e.g., 1982) Baconian probabilities are nonadditive (for more on nonadditive theories, see Shafer, 1976). In my opinion, Cohen correctly criticizes the normative claims in the heuristics-and-biases program insofar as not all uses of "probability" that refer to single events must be additive—but this does not imply that Baconian probability is the only alternative, nor that one should assume, as Cohen did, that all minds reason rationally (or at least are competent to do so) in all situations. I do not deal with this issue in this chapter (but see Gigerenzer, 1991d). The second fundamental issue is whether probability theory is about *relative frequencies in the long run* or (also) about *single events*. For instance, the question "What is the relative frequency of women over 60 who have breast cancer?" refers to frequencies, whereas "What is the probability that Ms. Young has breast cancer?" refers to a single event. Bayesians usually assume that (additive) probability theory is about single events, whereas frequentists hold that statements about single cases have nothing to do with probability theory (they may be dealt with by cognitive psychology, but not by probability theory).

given, but not for information that could falsify it. This selective information search artificially increases confidence. The key idea in this explanation is that the mind is not a Popperian. Despite the popularity of the confirmation bias explanation in social psychology, there is little or no support for this hypothesis in the case of confidence judgments (see Chapter 7).

As with many "cognitive illusions," overconfidence bias seems to be a robust fact waiting for a theory. This "fact" was quickly generalized to account for human disasters of many kinds, such as deadly accidents in industry (Spettell & Liebert, 1986), confidence in clinical diagnosis (Arkes, 1981), and shortcomings in management and negotiation (Bazerman, 1990) and in the legal process (Saks & Kidd, 1980), among others.

The Normative Issue   Is overconfidence bias really a "bias" in the sense of a violation of probability theory? Let me rephrase the question: Has probability theory been violated if one's *degree of belief (confidence) in a single event* (i.e., that a particular answer is correct) is different from the *relative frequency* of correct answers one generates in the long run? The answer is "no." It is in fact *not* a violation according to several interpretations of probability.

Let us look first at the now dominant school of probability: the frequentists (the frequentist interpretation of probability has been dominant since about 1840; see Daston, 1988; Porter, 1986). Most readers of this chapter will have been trained in the frequentist tradition and, for instance, will have been taught that the probabilities of Type I and Type II errors are long-run frequencies of errors in repeated experiments, not probabilities of single outcomes or hypotheses. For a frequentist like the mathematician Richard von Mises, the term "probability," when it refers to a *single event*, "has no meaning at all for us" (1928/1957, p. 11). For predictions of single events, as studied in present-day overconfidence research, he put the issue in crystal-clear terms: "Our probability theory has nothing to do with questions such as: 'Is there a probability of Germany being at some time in the future involved in a war with Liberia?' " (p. 9). In this view, probability theory is about frequencies, not about single events. To compare the two means comparing apples with oranges.

Even the major opponents of the frequentists—subjectivists such as Bruno de Finetti—would not generally think of a discrepancy between confidence and relative frequency as a "bias," albeit for different reasons. For a subjectivist, probability *is* about single events, but rationality is identified with the internal consistency of subjective probabilities. As de Finetti emphasized, "however an individual evaluates the probability of a particular event, no experience can prove him right, or wrong; nor, in general, could any conceivable criterion give any objective sense to the distinction one would like to draw, here, between right and wrong" (1931/1989, p. 174).

Other theories and interpretations of probability are also at odds with the claim that overconfidence is a bias, that is, a violation of probability theory. But I will stop here and summarize the normative issue. A discrepancy between confidence in single events and relative frequencies in the long run is not an error or a violation of probability theory from many experts' points of view. It only looks like it from a narrow interpretation of probability that blurs the distinction between single events and frequencies fundamental to probability theory. (The choice of the word "overconfidence" for the discrepancy put the "fallacy" message into the term itself.)

How to Make the Cognitive Illusion Disappear   If there are any robust cognitive biases at all, overconfidence in one's knowledge would seem to be a good candidate. "Overconfidence is a reliable, reproducible finding" (von Winterfeldt & Edwards, 1986, p. 539). "Can anything be done? Not much" (Edwards & von Winterfeldt, 1986, p. 656). "Debiasing" methods, such as warning the participants of the overconfidence phenomenon before the experiment and offering them money to avoid it, have had little or no effect (Fischhoff, 1982).

Setting the normative issue straight has important consequences for understanding confidence judgments. Let us go back to the metaphor of the mind as an intuitive statistician. I now take the term "statistician" to refer to a statistician of the dominant school in this (and in the last) century, not one adopting the narrow perspective some psychologists and economists have suggested. Assume that the mind is a frequentist. Like a frequentist, the mind should be able to *distinguish* between single-event confidences and frequencies in the long run.

This view has testable consequences. Ask people for their estimated frequencies of correct answers and compare them with true frequencies of correct answers, instead of comparing the latter frequencies with confidences. We are now comparing apples with apples. Ulrich Hoffrage, Heinz Kleinbölting, and I carried out such experiments. Participants answered several hundred questions of the Islamabad–Hyderabad type (see above), and, in addition, estimated their frequencies of correct answers.

Table 12.2 (top row) shows the usual "overconfidence bias" when single-event confidences are compared with actual relative frequencies of correct answers. In both experiments, the difference was around 13 to 15 percentage points, which is a large discrepancy. After each set of 50 general knowledge

Table 12.2 How to make the *overconfidence bias* disappear

Difference between	Experiment 1 (n = 80)	Experiment 2 (n = 97)
Mean confidence and relative frequency of correct answers ("overconfidence bias")	+13.8	+15.4
Estimated frequency and frequency of correct answers	−2.4	−4.2

Note: To make values for frequency and confidence judgments comparable, all frequencies were transformed to relative frequencies. Values shown are differences multiplied by a factor of 100. Positive values denote "overconfidence" (Gigerenzer, Hoffrage, & Kleinbölting, 1991).

questions, we asked the same participants, "How many of these 50 questions do you think you got right?" Comparing their estimated frequencies with actual frequencies of correct answers made "overconfidence" *disappear*. Table 12.2 (second row) shows that estimated frequencies were practically identical with actual frequencies, with even a small tendency toward underestimation. The "cognitive illusion" was gone. Similar results were obtained when participants estimated the relative frequencies of correct answers in each confidence category. In all cases in which participants said they were "100% (90%, 80%, . . .) confident," they estimated that, in the long run, they had a *lower* percentage of answers correct, and their estimates were close to the true relative frequencies of correct answers (May, 1987, reported similar results). Eliminating the experimenter's normative confusion between single events and frequencies made the participants' "overconfidence bias" disappear.

The general point is (i) a discrepancy between probabilities of single events (confidences) and long-run frequencies need not be framed as an "error" and called "overconfidence bias," and (ii) judgments need not be "explained" by a flawed mental program at a deeper level, such as "confirmation bias." Rather, people seem to be able intuitively to make conceptual distinctions similar to those that professional statisticians make. How they do it can be accounted for by the theory of "probabilistic mental models" (PMM), which explains both confidence and frequency judgments in terms of frequentist probability cues (Chapter 7). PMM theory is a frequentist theory of judgment and uncertainty; it can predict overconfidence, good calibration, and *under*estimation within the same participant.

Conjunction Fallacy

The original demonstration of the "conjunction fallacy" was with problems of the following kind (Tversky & Kahneman, 1983, p. 299):

> Linda is 31 years old, single, outspoken and very bright. She majored in philosophy. As a student, she was deeply concerned with issues of discrimination and social justice, and also participated in antinuclear demonstrations.

Participants were asked which of two alternatives was more probable:

> Linda is a bank teller (T)
> Linda is a bank teller and is active in the feminist movement (T&F)

Eighty-five percent of the participants chose T&F in the Linda problem (see Table 12.3). Tversky and Kahneman, however, argued that the "correct" answer is T, because the probability of a conjunction of two events, such as T&F, can never be greater than that of one of its constituents. They explained this "fallacy" as induced by the representativeness heuristic. They assumed that judgments were based on the match (similarity, representativeness) between the description of Linda and the two alternatives T and T&F. That is, since

Table 12.3 Linda problem: How to make the conjunction fallacy disappear

Linda problem	Single-event probability	Frequency
Tversky & Kahneman (1983)		
Which is more probable?	85	–
Probability ratings	82	–
Probability ratings T*	57	–
Betting	56	–
Fiedler (1988)		
Exp. 1	91	22
Exp. 2	83	17
Hertwig & Gigerenzer (1999)		
Studies 1 and 3	83	0
Studies 2 and 4	88	13

Note: Numbers are violations (in %) of the conjunction rule. The various versions of the Linda problem are (i) which is more probable (see text), (ii) probability ratings on a 9-point scale, (iii) probability ratings using the alternative "Linda is a bank teller whether or not she is active in the feminist movement" (T*) instead of "Linda is a bank teller" (T), (iv) hypothetical betting, that is, participants were asked "If you could win $10 by betting on an event, which of the following would you choose to bet on?" Fiedler asked participants to rank order T, T&F, and other alternatives with respect to their probability. In his first frequency version the population size was always 100, in the second it varied. Hertwig and Gigerenzer asked participants to rank order T, T&F, and F with respect to their probability, or estimate their frequency. Tversky and Kahneman (1983, p. 309) had reported a facilitating effect of frequency judgments for a different problem.

Linda was described as if she were a feminist and T&F contains the term "feminist," people believe that T&F is more probable.

This alleged demonstration of human irrationality in the Linda problem has been widely publicized in psychology, philosophy, economics, and beyond. Stephen J. Gould (1992, p. 469) put the message clearly:

> I am particularly fond of [the Linda] example, because I know that the [conjunction] is least probable, yet a little homunculus in my head continues to jump up and down, shouting at me, "but she can't just be a bank teller; read the description." . . . Why do we consistently make this simple logical error? Tversky and Kahneman argue, correctly I think, that our minds are not built (for whatever reason) to work by the rules of probability.

I suggest that Gould should have had more trust in the rationality of his homunculus.

The Normative Issue   Is the "conjunction fallacy" a violation of probability theory, as has been claimed in the literature? Has a person who chooses T&F as the more probable alternative violated probability theory? Again, the answer is "no." Choosing T&F is *not* a violation of probability theory, and for the same reason given previously. For a frequentist, this problem has nothing to do with probability theory. Participants were asked for the probability of a *single event* (that Linda is a bank teller), not for frequencies. For instance, the statistician Barnard (1979) commented thus on subjective probabilities for single events: "If we accept it as important that a person's subjective probability assessments should be made coherent, our reading should concentrate on the works of Freud and perhaps Jung rather than Fisher and Neyman" (p. 171).

Note that problems that are claimed to demonstrate the "conjunction fallacy" are structurally different from "confidence" problems. In the former, subjective probabilities (that Linda is a bank teller or a bank teller and a feminist) are compared with one another; in the latter, they are compared with frequencies.

To summarize the normative issue, what is called the "conjunction fallacy" looks like a violation of *some* subjective theories of probability, including Bayesian theory. It is not, however, a violation of a major view of probability, the frequentist conception.

How to Make the Cognitive Illusion Disappear   What if the mind were a frequentist? If the untutored mind is as sensitive to the distinction between single cases and frequencies as a statistician of the frequentist school is, then we should expect dramatically different judgments if we pose the above problem in a frequentist mode, such as the following:

> There are 100 persons who fit the description above (i.e., Linda's).
> How many of them are:
> (a) bank tellers
> (b) bank tellers and active in the feminist movement.

Participants are now asked for frequency judgments rather than for single-event probabilities. If the mind solves the Linda problem by using a representativeness heuristic, changes in information representation should not matter because they do not change the degree of similarity. The description of Linda is still more representative of (or similar to) the conjunction "teller and feminist" than of "teller." Participants therefore should still exhibit the conjunction fallacy. Table 12.3, however, shows that with frequency judgments, the "conjunction fallacy" largely disappears. The effect is dramatic, from some 80% to 90% conjunction violations in probability judgments to 10% to 20% in frequency judgments, with one study even reporting 0%.

What accounts for this striking effect of frequency judgments? Hertwig and Gigerenzer (1999) analyzed how participants understood the phrase "which is more probable?", for instance, by asking them to paraphrase the problem to another person who is not a native speaker of the language in which the problem was presented. The results indicate that most participants did not understand "probability" in the sense of mathematical probability but as one of the many other legitimate meanings that are listed in, for example, the Oxford English Dictionary (e.g., meaning credibility, typicality, or that there is evidence). The term frequency, unlike probability, narrows down the spectrum of possible interpretations to meanings that follow mathematical probability.

The results in Table 12.3 are consistent with the earlier work by Inhelder and Piaget (1969), who showed children a box containing wooden beads, most of them brown, but a few white. They asked the children, "Are there more wooden beads or more brown beads in this box?" By the age of eight, a majority of children responded that there were more wooden beads, indicating that they understand conjunctions (class inclusions). Note that Inhelder and Piaget asked children for frequency judgments, not probability judgments.

Base-Rate Fallacy

Among all cognitive illusions, the "base-rate fallacy" has probably received the most attention. The neglect of base rates seems in direct contradiction to the widespread belief that judgments are unduly affected by stereotypes (Landman & Manis, 1983), and for this and other reasons it has generated a great deal of interesting research on the limiting conditions for the "base-rate fallacy" in attribution and judgment (e.g., Ajzen, 1977; Borgida & Brekke, 1981). For instance, in their review, Borgida and Brekke argue for the pervasiveness of the "base-rate fallacy" in everyday reasoning about social behavior, ask the question "*Why* are people susceptible to the base-rate fallacy?" (1981, p. 65), and present a list of conditions under which the "fallacy" is somewhat reduced, such as "vividness," "salience," and "causality" of base-rate information.

My analysis is different. Again I first address the normative claims that people's judgments are "fallacies" using two examples that reveal two different aspects of the narrow understanding of good probabilistic reasoning in much of this research.

The first is from Casscells, Schoenberger, and Grayboys (1978, p. 999) and presented by Tversky and Kahneman (1982b, p. 154) to demonstrate the generality of the phenomenon:

> If a test to detect a disease whose prevalence is 1/1000 has a false positive rate of 5%, what is the chance that a person found to have a positive result actually has the disease, assuming you know nothing about the person's symptoms or signs?

Sixty students and staff at Harvard Medical School answered this medical diagnosis problem. Almost half of them judged the probability that the person actually had the disease to be 0.95 (modal answer), the average answer was 0.56, and only 18% of participants responded 0.02. The latter was considered to be the correct answer. Note the enormous variability in judgments. Little has been achieved in explaining *how* people make these judgments and *why* the judgments are so strikingly variable.

The Normative Issue   But do statistics and probability give one and only one "correct" answer to that problem? The answer is again "no." And for the same reason, as the reader will already have guessed. As in the case of confidence and conjunction judgments, participants were asked for the probability of a *single event*, that is, that "a person found to have a positive result actually has the disease." If the mind is an intuitive statistician of the frequentist school, such a question has no necessary connection to probability theory. Furthermore, even for a Bayesian, the medical diagnosis problem has several possible answers. One piece of information necessary for a Bayesian calculation is missing: the test's long-run frequency of correctly diagnosing persons who have the disease (admittedly a minor problem if we can assume a high "true positive rate"). A more serious difficulty is that the problem does not specify whether or not the person was *randomly* drawn from the population to which the base rate refers. Clinicians, however, know that patients are usually not randomly selected—except in screening and large survey studies—but rather "select" themselves by exhibiting symptoms of the disease. In the absence of random sampling, it is unclear what to do with the base rates specified. The modal response, 0.95, would follow from applying the Bayesian principle of indifference (i.e., same prior probabilities for each hypothesis), whereas the answer 0.02 would follow from using the specified base rates and assuming random sampling. In fact, the range of actual answers corresponds quite well to the range of possible solutions.

How to Make the Cognitive Illusion Disappear   The literature overflows with assertions of the generality and robustness of the "base-rate fallacy," such as: "the base-rate effect appears to be a fairly robust phenomenon that often results from automatic or unintentional cognitive processes" (Landman & Manis, 1983, p. 87); and "many (possibly most) subjects generally ignore base rates completely" (Pollard & Evans, 1983, p. 124; see also Table 12.1). Not only are the *normative* claims often simplistic and, therefore, misleading, but so too are the *robustness* assertions.

What happens if we do something similar as for the "overconfidence bias" and the "conjunction fallacy," that is, rephrase the medical diagnosis problem in a frequency format? Cosmides and Tooby (1996) did so. They compared the original problem (above) with a frequency format, in which the same information was given:

> One out of 1000 Americans has disease X. A test has been developed to detect when a person has disease X. Every time the test is given to a person who has the disease, the test comes out positive. But sometimes the test also comes out positive when it is given to a person who is completely healthy. Specifically, out of every 1000 people who are perfectly healthy, 50 of them test positive for the disease.

> Imagine that we have assembled a random sample of 1000 Americans. They were selected by a lottery. Those who conducted the lottery had no information about the health status of any of these people. How many people who test positive for the disease will actually have the disease? _____ out of _____.

In this frequentist version of the medical diagnosis problem, both the information and the question are phrased in terms of frequencies. (In addition, the two pieces of information missing in the original version [see above] are supplied. In numerous other versions of the medical diagnosis problem, Cosmides and Tooby showed that the striking effect [see Table 12.4] on participants' reasoning is mainly due to the transition from a single-event problem to a frequency format, and only to a lesser degree to the missing information.) Participants were Stanford University undergraduates.

If the question was rephrased in natural frequencies, as shown above, then the Bayesian answer of 0.02—that is, the answer "one out of 50 (or 51)"—was given by 76% of the participants. The "base-rate fallacy" disappeared. By comparison, the original single-event version elicited only 12% Bayesian answers in Cosmides and Tooby's study. Chapter 6 provides an explanation for this effect.

Cosmides and Tooby identified one condition in which almost every participant found the Bayesian answer of 0.02. Participants received the frequentist version of the medical diagnosis problem (except that it reported a random sample of "100 Americans" instead of "1000 Americans"), and in addition a page with 100 squares (10 × 10). Each of these squares represented one American. Before the frequentist question "How many people who test positive . . ." was put, participants were asked to (i) circle the number of people who will have the disease and (ii) to fill in squares to represent people who will test positive. After that, 23 out of 25 participants came up with the Bayesian answer (see frequency format, pictorial, in Table 12.4).

All three examples point in the same direction: The mind acts as if it were a frequentist; it distinguishes between single events and frequencies in the long run—just as probabilists and statisticians do. Despite the fact that researchers in the "heuristics and biases" program routinely ignore this distinction fundamental to probability theory when they claim to have identified "errors," it

Table 12.4 How to make the "base-rate fallacy" disappear: The medical diagnosis problem

Medical diagnosis problem	N	Bayesian answers (%)
Original single-event version (Casscells, Schoenberger, & Grayboys, 1978)	60	18
Single-event version, replication (Cosmides & Tooby, 1996)	25	12
Frequency format (Cosmides & Tooby, 1996)	50	76
Frequency format, pictorial (Cosmides & Tooby, 1996)	25	92

would be foolish to label these judgments "fallacies." These results not only point to a truly new understanding of judgment under uncertainty, but they also seem to be relevant for teaching statistical reasoning.

Selected versus Random Sampling: More on the Base-Rate Fallacy

Another conceptual distinction routinely used by probabilists and statisticians is that between random sampling and selected sampling. Again, little attention has been given to that distinction when intuitive statistical reasoning is investigated. The original medical diagnosis problem is silent about whether the patient was randomly selected from the population. That this crucial information is missing is not atypical. For instance, in the "Tom W." problem (Kahneman & Tversky, 1973), *no* information is given about how the personality sketch of Tom W. was selected, whether randomly or not. The same holds for the personality sketches of Gary W. and Barbara T. in Ajzen's (1977) base-rate studies.

But the issue is not necessarily resolved simply by asserting random sampling verbally in the problem. Consider the following famous demonstration of base-rate neglect in which random sampling is actually mentioned. A group of students had to solve the engineer–lawyer problem (Kahneman & Tversky, 1973, pp. 241–242):

> A panel of psychologists have interviewed and administered personality tests to 30 engineers and 70 lawyers, all successful in their respective fields. On the basis of this information, thumbnail descriptions of the 30 engineers and 70 lawyers have been written. You will find on your forms five descriptions, chosen at random from the 100 available descriptions. For each description, please indicate your probability that the person described is an engineer, on a scale from 0 to 100.

Two of these thumbnail descriptions were:

> Jack is a 45-year-old man. He is married and has four children. He is generally conservative, careful, and ambitious. He shows no interest in political and social issues and spends most of his free time on his many hobbies which include home carpentry, sailing, and mathematical puzzles. The probability that Jack is one of the 30 engineers in the sample of 100 is _____%.

> Dick is a 30-year-old man. He is married with no children. A man of high ability and high motivation, he promises to be quite successful in his field. He is well liked by his colleagues.

A second group of students received the same instructions and the same descriptions, but were told that the base rates were 70 engineers and 30 lawyers (as opposed to 30 engineers and 70 lawyers). Kahneman and Tversky found that the mean response in both groups of students was for the most part the same, and concluded that base rates were largely ignored. Their explanation was that participants use a representativeness heuristic, that is, they judge the probability by the similarity (representativeness) between a description and their stereotype of an engineer. Kahneman and Tversky believed that their participants were violating "one of the basic principles of statistical prediction," the integration of prior probability with specific evidence by Bayes's rule. The result was given much weight: "The failure to appreciate the relevance of prior probability in the presence of specific evidence is perhaps one of the most significant departures of intuition from the normative theory of prediction" (p. 243).[2]

The Normative Issue   The phrase "*the* normative theory of prediction," or probability, is standard rhetoric in the "heuristics and biases" program. But what is this normative theory? Certainly it is not frequentist—to name, for example, only the most popular theory of probability. So let us infer what the authors mean by "the normative theory" from what they want their participants to do. This seems to be simply to apply a formula—Bayes's rule—to the engineer–lawyer problem. But there is more to *good* probabilistic reasoning than applying formulas mechanically. There are assumptions to be checked (see Mueser, Cowan, & Mueser, 1999). Is the structure of the problem the same as the structure of the statistical model underlying the formula?

One important structural assumption is random sampling. If the descriptions of Jack, Dick, and the others were not randomly sampled but selected, the base rates of engineers and lawyers specified were indeed irrelevant. In fact, the descriptions were made up and *not* randomly sampled from a population with the base rates specified—although the participants were told the contrary. Whether the single word "random" in the instruction is enough to commit participants to this crucial structural assumption is a problem in itself—particularly because we cannot assume that people are familiar with situations in which profession guessing is about randomly drawn people. For instance, both in the United States and in Germany there is a popular TV program in which a panel of experts guesses the profession of a candidate, who answers only "yes" or "no" to their questions. Here, the experts would perform badly if they started out with the known base rates of professions, say in the United States, and revised them according to Bayes's rule. The candidates were selected, not randomly drawn.

2. The terms "prior probabilities" and "base rates" are frequently used interchangeably in the psychological literature. But these concepts are not identical. It is the prior probabilities that are fed into Bayes's rule, and these priors may be informed by base rates. Base rates are just one piece of information among several that a person can consider relevant for making up her prior probabilities. Equating prior probabilities with *one* particular kind of base-rate information would be a narrow understanding of Bayesian reasoning. Such reasoning might be defensible in those situations in which one knows very little, but not in real-life situations in which one can base judgments on rich knowledge.

Random Sampling Increases Use of Base Rates   One way to understand participants' judgments is to assume that the engineer–lawyer problem activates earlier knowledge associated with profession guessing, which can be used as an inferential framework—a "mental model"—to solve the problem.[3] But, as I have argued, we cannot expect random sampling to be part of this mental model. If my analysis is correct, then base-rate use can be increased if we take care to commit the participants to the crucial property of random sampling—that is, break apart their mental models and insert the new structural assumption. In contrast, if the true explanation is that participants rely on the representativeness heuristic, then the participants should continue to neglect base rates.

There is a simple method of making people aware of random sampling in the engineer–lawyer problem, which we used in a replication of the original study (Gigerenzer, Hell, & Blank, 1988). The participants themselves drew each description (blindly) out of an urn, unfolded the description, and gave their probability judgments. There was no need to tell them about random sampling because they did it themselves. This condition increased the use of base rates. Participants' judgments were closer to Bayesian predictions than to base-rate neglect. When we used, for comparison, the original study's version of the crucial assumption—as a one-word assertion—neglect of base rates appeared again (although less intensely than in Kahneman and Tversky's study).

Worthless Specific Evidence and the Base-Rate Fallacy   The description of "Dick" (see above) is a particularly interesting case. It was constructed to be totally uninformative for distinguishing engineers from lawyers. Kahneman and Tversky (1973) reported that the median probabilities were the same (0.50) in both base-rate groups. That people neglect base rates even when only "worthless specific evidence" is given has been taken by the authors to demonstrate the "strength" (p. 242) of the representativeness heuristic. This striking result led to many a speculation:

> The fact that the base rate is ignored even when the individuating information is useless (for example, the target is 'ambitious' or 'well liked') suggests that the preference for specific-level evidence is so great that the base rate or high-level default information is not even retrieved once the subject tries to make a prediction on the basis of the specific information. (Holland et al., 1986, p. 218)

Such statements need to be corrected. First, if the crucial structural assumption of random sampling is made clear, base rates are no longer ignored in participants' judgments about the "uninformative" description of Dick, just as for "informative" descriptions such as Jack's. Second, and equally striking,

---

3. I use the term "mental model" in a sense that goes beyond Johnson-Laird's (1983). As in the theory of probabilistic mental models (Chapter 7), a mental model is an inferential framework that generalizes the specific task to a reference class (and probability cues defined on it) that a person *knows* from his or her environment.

I show that even with Kahneman and Tversky's original "verbal assertion method," that is, a one-word assertion of random sampling, there is in fact *no* support for the claim that judgments about an uninformative description are guided by a general representativeness heuristic—contrary to assertions in the literature.

Table 12.5 lists all studies of the uninformative description "Dick" that I am aware of—all replications of Kahneman and Tversky's (1973) verbal assertion method. The two base-rate groups were always 30% and 70% engineers. According to Kahneman and Tversky's argument, the difference between the two base-rate groups should approach the difference between the two base rates, that is, 40% (or somewhat less, if the description of Dick was not perceived as totally uninformative by the participants). The last column shows their result mentioned above, a zero difference, which we (Gigerenzer, Hell, & Blank, 1988) could closely replicate. Table 12.5 also shows, however, that several studies found substantial mean differences up to 37%, which comes very close to the actual difference between base-rate groups.

Seen together, the studies seem to be as inconsistent as it is possible to be: Every result between zero difference (base-rate neglect) and the actual base-rate difference has been obtained. This clearly contradicts the rhetoric of robustness and generality of the base-rate fallacy, such as: "Regardless of what kind of information is presented, subjects pay virtually no attention to the base rate in guessing the profession of the target" (Holland et al., 1986, p. 217). And it contradicts the explanation of the so-called fallacy: the proposed general representativeness heuristic.

Table 12.5 How to make the "base-rate fallacy" disappear: The uninformative description "Dick" in the engineer–lawyer problem

Study	No. of descriptions	"Dick" encountered first (relative frequency)	Mean difference between base rate groups[a]
Gigerenzer, Hell, & Blank (1988)[b]	6	1/6	1.2
Kahneman & Tversky (1973)[c]	5	1/5	0.0
Wells & Harvey (1978)	2	1/2	18.0
Ginosssar & Trope (1987)[d]	1	1	24.0
Ginossar & Trope (1980)[c]	1	1	31.0
Gigerenzer, Hell, & Blank (1988)[e]	1	1	37.0

a. Entries are $\{p_{70}(E \mid D) - p_{30}(E \mid D)\} \times 100$, where $p_{70}(E \mid D)$ is the mean probability judgment that "Dick" is an engineer, given the description and the 70% base rate.

b. Order of descriptions systematically varied.

c. Medians (no means reported).

d. Three descriptions were used, but "Dick" was always encountered first.

e. Separate analysis for all participants who encountered "Dick" first.

How to explain these apparently inconsistent results? Table 12.5 gives us a clue. There is a striking correlation between the *number* of descriptions each participant read and judged and the mean difference between base-rate groups. The key variable seems to be the relative frequency with which participants encountered "Dick" first, which is a direct function of the number of descriptions. In all studies in which only Dick was used (i.e., the number of descriptions was 1), or in which a separate analysis was performed for all participants who encountered Dick first, there *is* a strong base-rate effect. If Dick and one informative description (Jack) were used, as in Wells and Harvey (1978), then the base-rate effect is in between, because of averaging across participants who encountered Dick either before or after the informative description. Thus Table 12.5 supports the following conclusions. (1) Contrary to claims in the literature, participants did make use of the base rates if only uninformative information ("Dick") was presented. (2) The neglect of base rates occurred only in a specific condition, that is, when the participants had encountered one or more *informative* descriptions before they judged "Dick"—in other words, when "Dick" occurred in the second, third, fourth, or later position. (3) The more descriptions a participant encountered, the less often "Dick" was in the first position, and—because of averaging across positions (such as in Kahneman and Tversky's study)—the smaller the difference was between base-rate groups.

This result should *not* occur if the intuitive statistician operates with a representativeness heuristic. Again, an explanatory framework using mental models based on knowledge about a particular domain (here, profession guessing) seems to be superior. If an informative description is encountered first, a mental model is activated that contains probability cues for professions, such as hobbies and political attitudes. Once the mental model is activated, the mind uses it as an inferential framework for similar-looking problems, that is, when "Dick" is encountered as the second or subsequent problem. Carrying over mental models to similar problems is analogous to perceptual judgment. We watch the first few steps and then proceed on the hypothesis that the rest are like the first (Gregory, 1974). This practice can sometimes make us stumble, but this kind of uncertain and "risky" inference is what makes our perceptual apparatus superior to any computer available today.

If the uninformative description is encountered first, however, then such a mental model is not activated, because its probability cues would not discriminate, and participants fall back on the only information available, the base rates (which are, as I argued above, not part of the mental model of profession guessing).

To summarize: (1) There is little justification for calling participants' judgments in the engineer–lawyer problem an "error" in probabilistic reasoning, because (aside from the frequentist argument) participants were not committed to random sampling. (2) If one lets the participants do the random drawing, base-rate neglect disappears. (3) That participants are sensitive to the distinction between random and selected (nonrandom) drawings shows again that the framework of so-called "heuristics and biases" is much too narrow for understanding judgments under uncertainty (for similar results see Ginossar & Trope, 1987; Grether, 1980; Hansen & Donoghue, 1977; Wells & Harvey, 1977; but see Nisbett & Borgida, 1975).

Note that the critical variable here is the content of a problem. There seems to be a class of contents for which participants know from their environment that base rates are relevant (as do birds; see Caraco, Martindale, & Whittam, 1980) or that random sampling is common (though they need not represent these concepts explicitly), whereas in other contents this is not the case. Profession guessing seems to belong to the latter category. In contrast, predictions of sports results, such as those of soccer games, seem to belong to the former. For instance, we found that participants revised information about the previous performance of soccer teams (base rates) in light of new information (half-time results) in a way that is indistinguishable from Bayesian statistics (Gigerenzer, Hell, & Blank, 1988). Here verbal assertion of random drawing was sufficient—there was no need for strong measures to break apart mental models.

Heuristics

The concept of a "heuristic" has various meanings and a long history—from Descartes's 21 heuristic rules for the direction of the mind to Duncker's heuristic methods that guide the stepwise reformulation of a problem until it is solved (Groner, Groner, & Bischof, 1983). The cognitive revolution has reintroduced the concept of a heuristic into psychology, in particular in the work of Herbert Simon (1957). Because of limited information-processing abilities, Simon argued, humans have to construct simplified models of the world. Heuristics are a product of these: They are shortcuts that can produce efficient decisions. Simon understood heuristics such as satisficing (i.e., selecting the first option available that meets an aspiration level) as adaptive strategies in a complex environment, in which alternatives for action are not given but must be sought out.

In the 1970s, Kahneman and Tversky borrowed the term "heuristic" from artificial intelligence to explain "errors" in probabilistic reasoning: "People rely on a limited number of heuristic principles which reduce the complex tasks of assessing probabilities and predicting values to simpler judgmental operations. In general, these heuristics are quite useful, but sometimes they lead to severe and systematic errors" (Tversky & Kahneman, 1974, p. 1124). Although they repeatedly asserted that these heuristics are useful, almost all of their work focused on how they lead to "errors." The three heuristics proposed in the early 1970s—representativeness, availability, and anchoring and adjustment—were a first, promising step to connect the rather atheoretical Bayesian research of the 1960s with cognitive theory. But in the 30 years of "heuristics and biases" research since then, a lack of theoretical progress is possibly the most striking result. The absence of a general theory or even of specific models of underlying cognitive processes has been repeatedly criticized (e.g., Jungermann, 1983; Wallsten, 1983), but to no avail. Why is this? I believe that particular features of the use of the term "heuristic" have led to the present conceptual dead end, and more research in a cul-de-sac will not help. In my opinion, these features are the following.

The Function of Heuristics

In artificial intelligence research one hopes that heuristics can make computers smart; in the "heuristics and biases" program one hopes that heuristics can tell why humans are not smart. The fundamental problem with the latter is that most "errors" in probabilistic reasoning that one wants to explain by heuristics are in fact not errors, as I have argued above. Thus heuristics are meant to explain what does not exist. Rather than explaining a *deviation* between human judgment and allegedly "correct" probabilistic reasoning, future research has to get rid of simplistic norms that evaluate human judgment instead of explaining it.

Simon, and earlier Egon Brunswik, has emphasized that cognitive functions are adaptations to a given environment and that we have to study the structure of environments in order to infer the constraints they impose on reasoning. Heuristics such as representativeness have little to say about how the mind adapts to the structure of a given environment.

Redescription as a Substitute for Theorizing

Several of the explanations using heuristics are hardly more than redescriptions of the phenomena reported. Take, for instance, the explanation of base-rate neglect in the engineer–lawyer problem (and similar base-rate problems) by the representativeness heuristic. Representativeness here means the perceived similarity between a personality description and the participants' stereotype of an engineer. In the vocabulary of Bayes's rule, this similarity is a likelihood: that is, the probability of a description given that the person is an engineer. Now we can see that Bayes's rule, in particular its concepts of base rates (prior probabilities) and likelihoods, provides the vocabulary for both the phenomenon and its purported explanation. The phenomenon is neglect of base rates and use of likelihoods. The "explanation" is that participants use representativeness (likelihoods) and do not use base rates. What is called a representativeness heuristic here is nothing more than a redescription of the phenomenon (Gigerenzer & Murray, 1987, pp. 153–155).

Heuristics Are Largely Undefined Concepts

Representativeness means similarity. Although there are numerous specific models of similarity (including Tversky, 1977), the relationship between the representativeness heuristic and these models has never been worked out. Fiedler (1983), for instance, has analyzed the theoretical weakness of explaining estimated frequencies of events by the availability heuristic. All three heuristics, representativeness, availability, and anchoring and adjustment, are largely undefined concepts and can post hoc be used to explain almost everything. After all, what is similar to what (representativeness), what comes into your mind (availability), and what comes first (anchoring) have long been known to be important principles of the mind.

More Undefined Concepts, Less Theory

Instead of giving up the program of explaining *deviations* of human judgment from simplistic norms by means of redescription and largely undefined heuristics, the last 25 years have witnessed the effort to keep that program going and to add further undefined concepts such as "causal base rates" and "vividness" to account for contradictory results (for an analysis of the "causal base rate" concept, see Gigerenzer & Murray, 1987, pp. 157–162). Heuristics such as representativeness are by now riddled with exceptions, but all this tinkering has not given us much purchase in understanding judgment under uncertainty.

Beyond Heuristics and Biases

I have argued that what have been widely accepted to be the "normative principles of statistical prediction" (e.g., Ajzen, 1977, p. 304), against which human judgment has been evaluated as "fallacious," are a caricature of the present state of probability theory and statistics. I have shown that several so-called fallacies are in fact not violations of probability theory. Conceptual distinctions routinely used by probabilists and statisticians were just as routinely ignored in the normative claims of "fallacies." Most strikingly, in the experimental research reviewed, "fallacies" and "cognitive illusions" tend to disappear if we pay attention to these fundamental distinctions. I am certainly not the first to criticize the notion of "robust fallacies." The only novelty in my research is that the variables that bring "cognitive illusions" under experimental control are those important from the viewpoint of probability and statistics (as opposed to, say, whether participants were given more or less "vivid" or "causally relevant" information).

Together, these results point to several ways to develop an understanding of judgment under uncertainty that goes beyond the narrow notion of a "bias" and the largely undefined notion of a "heuristic."

Use Different Statistical Models as Competing Explanatory Models

The existence of different statistical models of inference is a rich resource for developing theories about intuitive inference. This resource has been rarely touched, possibly because of the misleading normative view that statistics speaks with one voice.

For instance, despite the quantity of empirical data that has been gathered on the cab problem, the lack of a theory of the cognitive processes involved in solving it is possibly the most striking result. Tversky and Kahneman claimed that the cab problem has one "correct answer" (1980, p. 62). They attempted to explain the extent to which people's judgments deviated from that "norm" by largely undefined terms such as "causal base rates." But statistics gives several interesting answers to the cab problem, rather than just one "correct" answer (e.g., Birnbaum, 1983; Gigerenzer, 1998c; Levi, 1983). If progress is to be made and people's cognitive processes are to be understood, one should no longer try to explain the *difference* between people's judgments and Tversky and Kahneman's "normative" Bayesian calculations. People's *judgments* have to be explained. Statistical theories can provide highly interesting models of these judgments. The only theoretically rich account of the cognitive processes involved in solving the cab problem (or similar "eyewitness testimony" problems) was in fact derived from a frequentist framework: Birnbaum (1983) combined Neyman–Pearson theory with psychological models of judgments such as range–frequency theory.

Future research should use competing statistical theories as competing explanatory models, rather than pretending that statistics speaks with one voice (see also Cohen, 1982; Wallendael & Hastie, 1990).

Explore the Metaphor of the Mind as a Frequentist

I reported earlier the striking effect of participants' judging frequencies rather than probabilities for single events. These results suggest that the mind distinguishes between frequencies and other meanings of probability, just as a statistician of the frequentist school does. Because "cognitive illusions" tend to disappear in frequency judgments, it is tempting to think of the intuitive statistics of the mind as frequentist statistics.

Processing of frequencies seems to be fairly automatic, like encoding of time and space (e.g., Hasher & Zacks, 1979)—whereas probabilities are in evolutionary terms recent tools of the mind that seem to be processed less automatically. The theory of probabilistic mental models (Chapter 7) seems to be the first frequentist theory of confidence judgments that integrates Brunswik's frequency-learning view with the notion of mental models. The general theoretical point is that both single-case and frequency judgments are explained by learned frequencies (the probability cues), albeit by frequencies that relate to different reference classes and different networks of cues—in short, to different mental models.

Intuitive Statisticians Need to Check the Structure
of the Environment

Good judgment under uncertainty is more than mechanically applying a formula, such as Bayes's rule, to a real-world problem. The intuitive statistician, like his professional counterpart, must first check the structure of the environment (or of a problem) in order to decide whether to apply a statistical algorithm at all, and if so, which (see Gigerenzer & Murray, 1987, pp. 162–174). There is no good (applied) probabilistic reasoning that ignores the structure of the environment and mechanically uses only *one* (usually mathematically convenient) algorithm. I illustrate this point with a thought experiment by Nisbett and Ross (1980, p. 15), which I have shortened and slightly changed here (in respects unimportant to my argument).

(i) You wish to buy a new car. Today you must choose between two alternatives: to purchase either a Volvo or a Saab. You use only one criterion for that choice, the car's life expectancy. You have information from *Consumer Reports* that in a sample of several hundred cars the Volvo has the better record. Just yesterday a neighbor told you that his new Volvo broke down. Which car do you buy?

Nisbett and Ross comment that after the neighbor's information "the number of Volvo-owners has increased from several hundred to several hundred and one" and that the Volvo's record "perhaps should be changed by an iota" (p. 15). The moral of their thought experiment is that good probabilistic reasoning is applying an algorithm (here, updating of base rates) to the world. There is some truth to this message of resisting the temptation of the vivid and personal, but that is only half the story. Good intuitive statistics is more than calm calculation; first and foremost, the structure of the environment has to be examined. I will now vary the content of Nisbett and Ross's thought experiment to make the point intuitively immediate. Here is the same problem, but with a different content (Gigerenzer, 1990):

(ii) You live in a jungle. Today you must choose between two alternatives: to let your child swim in the river, or to let it climb trees instead. You use only one criterion for that choice, your child's life expectancy. You have information that in the last 100 years there was only one accident in the river, in which a child was eaten by a crocodile, whereas a dozen children have been killed by falling from trees. Just yesterday your neighbor told you that her child was eaten by a crocodile. Where do you send your child?

If good probabilistic reasoning means applying the same algorithm again and again, the neighbor's testimony should make no difference. The base rates would be updated by the testimony from one to two cases in 100 years, and by this reasoning one would send the child into the river. The mind of a parent, however, might use the new information to *reject* the updating algorithm instead of *inserting* the new information into the algorithm. A parent may suspect that the small river world has changed—crocodiles may now inhabit the river.

Why do we have different intuitions for the Volvo and the crocodile problems? In the Volvo problem, the prospective buyer may assume that the Volvo world is stable and that the important event (good or bad Volvo) can be considered as an independent random drawing from the same reference class. In the crocodile problem, the parents may assume that the river world has changed and that the important event (being eaten or not) can no longer be considered as an independent random drawing from the same reference class. Updating "old" base rates may be fatal for the child.

The question of whether some part of the world is stable enough to use statistics has been posed by probabilists and statisticians since the inception of probability theory in the mid-seventeenth century—and the answers have varied and will vary, as is well documented by the history of insurance (Daston, 1987). Like the underwriter, the layperson has to check structural assumptions before entering into calculations. For instance, the following structural assumptions are all relevant for the successful application of Bayes's rule: independence of successive drawings, random sampling, an exhaustive and mutually exclusive set of hypotheses, and independence between prior probabilities and likelihoods.

How can the intuitive statistician judge whether these assumptions hold? One possibility is that the mind generalizes the specific content to a broader mental model that uses implicit domain-dependent knowledge about these structural assumptions. If so, then the *content* of problems is of central importance for understanding judgment—it embodies implicit knowledge about the structure of an environment.

The Surplus Structure of the Environment

Analyzing the environment (problem) using structural properties of a given statistical model is one way to understand its structure. But natural environments often have *surplus* structure, that is, a structure that goes beyond prior probabilities and likelihoods (the Bayesian structure) or entailment and contradiction (the structure of binary propositional logic). Surplus structure includes space and time (Björkman, 1984), cheating options, perspective, and social contracts (Cosmides, 1989), among others. Surplus structure is the reason that the notion of "structural isomorphs" has only limited value.

The idea of studying inductive reasoning using structural isomorphs (i.e., use a particular statistical model or formal principle and construct problems that all have the same formal structure but different contents) is implicit in much research on reasoning; it postulates that if two problems have different contents, but the same *formal* structure (say, Bayesian probability-revision structure), then judgments should be the *same*. But the structure of natural environments is usually richer than what Bayes's rule has to offer, and two structural isomorphs may differ on relevant surplus structure. If we understand reasoning as an adaptation to the environment, then it should be sensitive to surplus structure.

One way to deal with this is to devise theories that combine statistical theory and psychological principles—just as the most distinguished statisticians of this century, R. A. Fisher, J. Neyman, and E. S. Pearson, emphasized that good statistical reasoning always consists of mathematics *and* personal judgment. Birnbaum (1983) gave several examples of how the Neyman–Pearson theory can be combined with psychological principles to give a theoretically rich account of intuitive inference. Developing such integrated models is a challenging task for future research on judgments under uncertainty.

The Social Context of Judgment and Decision

Judgment under uncertainty occurs in a social environment in which there are other "players" who make a person's response more or less rational. Here is an anecdote to illustrate this point.

> A small town in Wales has a village idiot. He once was offered the choice between a pound and a shilling, and he took the shilling. People came from everywhere to witness this phenomenon. They repeatedly offered him a choice between a pound and a shilling. He always took the shilling.

Seen as a single choice (and by all monotone utility functions), this choice would seem irrational. Seen in its social context, in which a surprising choice increases the probability of getting to choose again, this behavior looks different.

The following are several aspects of the social context of judgment and decision that have been explored recently. First, human judgment seems to be domain specific rather than guided by some general mental logic. In particular, reasoning about social contracts seems to have its own laws. The striking changes of judgment depending on people's perspective and cheating options in a social contract were shown by Cosmides (1989) and Gigerenzer and Hug (1992). Second, the role of conversational principles in social interactions, such as that participants assume the experimenter's contribution will be cooperative (Adler, 1984; Grice, 1975), has sometimes been acknowledged by, but never been integrated into, the judgment under uncertainty literature. Third, humans share knowledge and decisions, and sharing imposes constraints on information processing and judgment as postulated by shareability theory (Freyd, 1983). Fourth, research on group decision making and judgments negotiated by two or more people is still largely disconnected from "individualistic" social cognition research (see Scholz, 1983).

Conclusion

A key metaphor for understanding inductive reasoning is probability theory. Since its origins in the mid-seventeenth century and throughout the Enlightenment, probability theory was viewed as a mathematical codification of rationality. In Pierre Laplace's famous phrase: probability theory is "only good sense reduced to calculus" (1814/1951, p. 196). When there was a striking discrepancy between the judgment of reasonable people and what probability theory dictated—as with the famous St. Petersburg paradox—then the mathematicians went back to the blackboard and changed the equations (Daston, 1980).

Those good old days have gone, although the eighteenth-century link between probability and rationality is back in vogue in cognitive and social psychology. If, in studies on social cognition, researchers find a discrepancy between human judgment and what probability theory seems to dictate, the blame is now put on the human mind, not on the statistical model.

I have used classical demonstrations of overconfidence bias, conjunction fallacy, and base-rate neglect to show that what have been called "errors" in probabilistic reasoning are in fact *not* violations of probability theory. They only look so from a narrow understanding of good probabilistic reasoning that ignores conceptual distinctions fundamental to probability and statistics. These so-called cognitive illusions largely disappear when one pays attention to these conceptual distinctions. The intuitive statistician seems to be highly sensitive to them—a result unexpected from the view that "mental illusions should be considered the rule rather than the exception" (see Table 12.1).

Why do cognitive illusions largely disappear? The examples in this chapter have illustrated three reasons:

1. *Polysemy: not all probabilities are mathematical probabilities.* Asking a frequency as opposed to a probability question can reduce the multiple meanings (polysemy) of the English terms "probable" and "likely." Frequency questions clarify that the question is actually about mathematical probability and not about one of the other legitimate meanings (see the Oxford English Dictionary), which are often suggested by the cover story of a problem. Reducing polysemy seems to be the major reason the conjunction fallacy in the Linda problem largely disappears (Hertwig & Gigerenzer, 1999).

2. *A mathematical probability refers to a reference class, which may differ depending on the task.* Asking a frequency (as opposed to a probability) question can systematicaly cue different reference classes (and therefore, different probabilistic mental models). Changing reference classes seems to be the reason overconfidence bias appears in probability judgments and disappears in frequency judgments (Chapter 7).

3. *Natural frequencies facilitate Bayesian reasoning.* When information is represented in natural frequencies rather than in conditional probabilities (or relative frequencies), Bayesian computations become simpler. Using natural frequencies is a powerful tool to reduce people's mental confusion and foster Bayesian reasoning (Chaper 6).

This is not to say that frequencies always improve judgment. For instance, the theory of probabilistic mental models specifies conditions under which frequency judgments systematically underestimate actual frequencies, and Chapter 6 explains why natural frequencies but not other kinds of frequencies facilitate Bayesian reasoning. The question is not whether or not, or how often, "cognitive illusions" disappear, but *why*. We need precise models of heuristics that make surprising (and falsifiable) predictions, not vague terms that, post hoc, explain everything and nothing. Future progress will be in understanding, not debunking, human thinking.

13

The Superego, the Ego, and the Id
in Statistical Reasoning

Piaget worked out his logical theory of cognitive development, Köhler the Gestalt laws of perception, Pavlov the principles of classical conditioning, Skinner those of operant conditioning, and Bartlett his theory of remembering and schemata—all without rejecting null hypotheses. But by the time I took my first course in psychology at the University of Munich in 1969, null hypothesis tests were presented as *the* indispensable tool, as the sine qua non of scientific research. Post–World War II German psychology mimicked a revolution of research practice that had occurred between 1940 and 1955 in American psychology.

What I learned in my courses and textbooks about the logic of scientific inference was not without a touch of moralizing, a scientific version of the Ten Commandments: Thou shalt not draw inferences from a nonsignificant result. Thou shalt always specify the level of significance before the experiment; those who specify it afterward (by rounding up obtained *p* values) are cheating. Thou shalt always design thy experiments so that thou canst perform significance testing.

The Inference Revolution

What happened between the time of Piaget, Köhler, Pavlov, Skinner, and Bartlett and the time I was trained? In Kendall's (1942) words, statisticians "have already overrun every branch of science with a rapidity of conquest rivalled only by Attila, Mohammed, and the Colorado beetle" (p. 69).

What has been termed the *probabilistic revolution in science* (Gigerenzer et al., 1989) reveals how profoundly our understanding of nature changed when concepts such as chance and probability were introduced as fundamental theoretical concepts. The work of Mendel in genetics, that of Maxwell and Boltzmann on statistical mechanics, and the quantum mechanics of Schrödinger and Heisenberg that built indeterminism into its very model of nature are key examples of that revolution in thought.

Psychology did not resist the probabilistic revolution, and psychologists in turn actively contributed to the growth of statistics. But psychology is nonetheless a peculiar case. In psychology and in other social sciences, probability and statistics were typically not used to revise the understanding of our *subject matter* from a deterministic to some probabilistic view (as in physics, genetics, or evolutionary biology) but rather to mechanize the *experimenters'* inferences—in particular, their inferences from data to hypothesis. Of course, there have been several attempts to revise our theories as well—for example, to transform Piaget's logical determinism into a more Darwinian view, in which variability and irregularity are seen as the motor of evolution rather than as an annoyance (Gruber, 1977; Gruber & Vonèche, 1977) or to transform Skinner's theory into a probabilistic learning theory (Estes, 1959). But the real, enduring transformation came with statistical inference, which became institutionalized and used in a dogmatic and mechanized way. This use of statistical theory contrasts sharply with physics, in which statistics and probability are indispensable in theories about nature, whereas mechanized statistical inference such as null hypothesis testing is almost unknown.

So what happened with psychology? David Murray and I described the striking change in research practice and named it the *inference revolution* in psychology (Gigerenzer & Murray, 1987). It happened between approximately 1940 and 1955 in the United States and led to the institutionalization of one brand of inferential statistics as *the* method of scientific inference in university curricula, textbooks, and the editorial policies of major journals.

The ground for the inference revolution was prepared by a dramatic shift in experimental practice. During the 1920s, 1930s, and 1940s, the established tradition of experimenting with *single* participants—from Wundt to Pavlov—was replaced in the United States by the *treatment group experiment*, in which group means are compared. For instance, between 1915 and 1950, the percentage of empirical studies reporting only group data in the *American Journal of Psychology* rose from 25% to 80%, and the reporting of only individual data decreased from 70% to 17% (Danziger, 1990). Danziger argued that this shift was in part due to the pressure felt by American academic psychologists to legitimize their work through showing its practical utility. The Wundtian type of experiment was useless to educational administrators, the largest market for psychological products. The treatment group experiment, however, appeared to fit their needs exactly, for example, by allowing them to compare mean performance in two classrooms that were using different instruction methods. After this change in experimental practice, null hypothesis testing of group means appeared to be tailor-made to the new unit of research, the group aggregate. Consistent with Danziger's argument, the institutionalization of both the treatment group and null hypothesis testing spread from the applied fields to the laboratories (Lovie, 1979). The contrast with Germany is informative. German academic psychologists of the early 20th century had to legitimize their work before a different tribunal, the values of a well-entrenched intellectual elite (Danziger, 1990). In contrast to the United States, the German educational system, driven by tradition rather than by experimentation, pro-

vided only a limited market for psychologists. No comparable shift in experimental practice happened in German psychology. It was only after World War
II that a new generation of German psychologists began to assimilate the methodological imperatives imported from their colleagues in the United States.

The figures are telling. Before 1940, null hypothesis testing using analysis
of variance or *t* tests was practically nonexistent: Rucci and Tweney (1980)
found only 17 articles in all from 1934 through 1940. By 1955, more than 80%
of the empirical articles in four leading journals used null hypothesis testing
(Sterling, 1959). Today, the figure is close to 100%. By the early 1950s, half of
the psychology departments in leading U.S. universities had made inferential
statistics a graduate program requirement (Rucci & Tweney, 1980). Editors and
experimenters began to measure the quality of research by the level of significance obtained. For instance, in 1962, the editor of the *Journal of Experimental Psychology*, A. W. Melton (1962, pp. 553–554), stated his criteria for accepting articles. In brief, if the null hypothesis was rejected at the .05 level but
not at the .01 level, there was a "strong reluctance" to publish the results,
whereas findings significant at the .01 level deserved a place in the journal.
The *Publication Manual of the American Psychological Association* (APA,
1974) prescribed how to report the results of significance tests (but did not
mention other statistical methods) and used, as Melton did, the label *negative*
results synonymously with "not having rejected the null" and the label *positive* results with "having rejected the null."

It is likely that Piaget's, Köhler's, Bartlett's, Pavlov's, and Skinner's experimental work would have been rejected for publication under such editorial
policies—these men did not set up null hypotheses and try to refute them.
Some of them were actively hostile toward institutionalized statistics. For his
part, Skinner (1972) disliked the intimate link Fisher had established between
statistics and the design of experiments: "What the statistician means by the
design of experiments is design which yields the kind of data to which his
techniques are applicable" (p. 122). And, "They have taught statistics in lieu
of scientific method" (p. 319). Skinner continued to investigate one or a few
pigeons under well-controlled conditions, rather than run 20 or more pigeons
under inevitably less well-controlled conditions to obtain a precise estimate
for the error variance. In fact, the Skinnerians were forced to found a new
journal, the *Journal of the Experimental Analysis of Behavior*, in order to publish their kind of experiments (Skinner, 1984, p. 138). Their focus was on experimental control, that is, on minimizing error beforehand, rather than on
large samples, that is, on measuring error after the fact.

This is not an isolated case, nor one peculiar to behaviorists. The *Journal of
Mathematical Psychology* is another. One of the reasons for launching this new
journal was again to escape the editors' pressure to perform institutionalized
null hypothesis testing.[1] One of its founders, Luce (1988), called the institution-

---

1. R. Duncan Luce, personal communication, April 4, 1990. See also Luce's (1989)
autobiography, p. 270 and pp. 281–282.

alized practice a "wrongheaded view about what constituted scientific progress" and "mindless hypothesis testing in lieu of doing good research: measuring effects, constructing substantive theories of some depth, and developing probability models and statistical procedures suited to these theories" (p. 582).

Who is to blame for the present state of mindless hypothesis testing? Fisher was blamed by Skinner, as well as by Meehl: "Sir Ronald has befuddled us, mesmerized us, and led us down the primrose path. I believe that the almost universal reliance on merely refuting the null hypothesis ... is ... one of the worst things [that] ever happened in the history of psychology" (Meehl, 1978, p. 817).

I share the sentiments expressed by Luce and Meehl. But to blame Fisher, as Meehl and Skinner did, gives us at best a spurious understanding of the inference revolution. Fisher declared that a significance test of a null hypothesis is only a "weak" argument. That is, it is applicable only in those cases in which we have very little knowledge or none at all. For Fisher, significance testing was the most primitive type of argument in a hierarchy of possible statistical analyses (see Gigerenzer et al., 1989, chap. 3). In this chapter I argue the following points:

1. What has become institutionalized as *inferential statistics* in psychology is not Fisherian statistics. It is an incoherent mishmash of some of Fisher's ideas on the one hand and some of the ideas of Neyman and E. S. Pearson on the other. I refer to this blend as the "hybrid logic" of statistical inference. Fisher, Neyman, and Pearson would all have rejected it, although for different reasons.

2. The institutionalized hybrid carries the message that *statistics is statistics is statistics*, that is, that statistics is a single integrated structure that speaks with a single authoritative voice. This entails the claim that the problem of inductive inference in fact *has* an algorithmic answer (i.e., the hybrid logic) that works for all contents and contexts. Both claims are wrong, and it is time to go beyond this institutionalized illusion. We must write new textbooks and change editorial practices. Students and researchers should be exposed to different approaches (not one) to inductive inference and be trained to use these in a constructive (not mechanical) way. A free market of several good ideas is better than a state monopoly for a single confused idea.

The "Parents" and Their Conflicts

To understand the structure of the hybrid logic that has been taught in psychology for some 50 years, I briefly sketch those ideas of Fisher on the one hand and Neyman and Pearson on the other that are relevant to understanding the hybrid structure of the logic of inference.

Fisher's first book, *Statistical Methods for Research Workers*, published in 1925, was successful in introducing biologists and agronomists to the new techniques. However, it had the agricultural odor of issues like the weight of pigs and the effect of manure, and, such alien topics aside, it was technically far too difficult to be understood by most psychologists.

Fisher's second statistical book, *The Design of Experiments*, first published in 1935, was most influential on psychology. At the very beginning of this book, Fisher rejected the theory of inverse probability (Bayesian theory) and congratulated the Reverend Bayes for having been so critical of his own theory as to withhold it from publication (Bayes's treatise was published posthumously in 1763). Bayes's rule is attractive for researchers because it allows one to calculate the probability $p(H|D)$ of a hypothesis H given some data D, also known as *inverse probability*. A frequentist theory, such as Fisher's null hypothesis testing or Neyman–Pearson theory, however, does not. It deals with the probabilities $p(D|H)$ of some data D given a hypothesis H, such as the level of significance.

Fisher was not satisfied with an approach to inductive inference based on Bayes's rule. The use of Bayes's rule presupposes that a prior probability distribution over the set of possible hypotheses is available. For a frequentist, such as Fisher, this prior distribution must theoretically be verifiable by actual frequencies, that is, by sampling from its reference set. These cases are rare. But if we are ignorant and have no a priori distributional information, then every researcher can express that ignorance in different numbers leading, for Fisher, to an unacceptable subjectivism. As we shall see, however, Fisher wanted to both reject the Bayesian cake and eat it, too.

Fisher proposed several alternative tools for inductive inference. In *The Design of Experiments* (1935), he started with *null hypothesis testing*, also known as *significance testing*, and he gave that tool the most space in his book. It eventually became the backbone of institutionalized statistics in psychology. In a test of significance, one confronts a null hypothesis with observations, to find out whether the observations deviate far enough from the null hypothesis to conclude that the null is implausible. The specific techniques of null hypothesis testing, such as the t test (devised by Gosset, using the pseudonym "Student," in 1908) or the F test (F for Fisher, e.g., in analysis of variance) are so widely used that they may be the lowest common denominator of what psychologists today do and know.

The topic of this chapter is the *logic* of inference rather than specific techniques. Just as with Bayes's rule, the problems we encounter do not concern the formula—the rule is a simple consequence of the definition of conditional probability. The problems arise with its application to inductive inference in science. To what aspect of inductive inference does a particular algorithm, or technique, refer? What do the calculations mean? These are questions that pertain to what I call the *logic* of inference.

Concerning my account of Fisher's logic of significance testing, one thing must be said in advance: Fisher's writings and polemics had a remarkably elusive quality, and people have read his work quite differently. During Fisher's long and acrimonious controversy with Neyman and Pearson, which lasted from the 1930s to his death in 1962, he changed, and sometimes even reversed, parts of his logic of inference. Thus the following brief account of Fisher's logic of inference represents one possible reading (for a more detailed analysis, see Gigerenzer et al., 1989, chap. 3).

How Do We Determine the Level of Significance?

In *The Design*, Fisher suggested that we think of the level of significance as a *convention:* "It is usual and convenient for experimenters to take 5 per cent as a standard level of significance, in the sense that they are prepared to ignore all results which fail to reach this standard" (1935, p. 13). Fisher's assertion that 5% (in some cases, 1%) is a *convention* that is adopted by all experimenters and in all experiments and that nonsignificant results are to be ignored became part of the institutionalized hybrid logic.

But Fisher had second thoughts, which he stated most clearly in the mid-1950s. These did not become part of the hybrid logic. One of the reasons for that revision was his controversy with Neyman and Pearson and Neyman's (e.g., 1950) insistence that one has to specify the level of significance (which is denoted as α in Neyman–Pearson theory) *before* the experiment, in order to be able to interpret it as a long-run frequency of error. Neyman and Pearson took the frequentist position more seriously than Fisher. They argued that the meaning of a level of significance such as 5% is the following: If the null hypothesis is correct and if the experiment is repeated many times, then the experimenter will wrongly reject the null in 5% of the cases. To reject the null if it is correct is called an *error of the first kind* (Type I error) in Neyman–Pearson theory, and its probability is called *alpha* (α). In his last book, *Statistical Methods and Scientific Inference* (1956), Fisher ridiculed this definition as "absurdly academic, for in fact no scientific worker has a fixed level of significance at which from year to year, and in all circumstances, he rejects hypotheses; he rather gives his mind to each particular case in the light of his evidence and his ideas" (p. 42). Fisher rejected the Neyman–Pearson logic of repeated experiments (repeated random sampling from the same population) and thereby rejected his earlier proposal to have a conventional standard level of significance, such as .05 or .01. What researchers should do, according to Fisher's second thoughts, is to publish the *exact level of significance*, say, $p = .03$ (not $p < .05$), and communicate this result to their fellow research workers. This means that the level of significance is determined *after* the experiment, not, as Neyman and Pearson proposed, *before* the experiment.

Thus the phrase "level of significance" has three meanings: (a) the *standard level of significance*, a conventional standard for all researchers (early Fisher), (b) the *exact level of significance*, a communication to research fellows, determined after the experiment (late Fisher), and (c) the *alpha level, the relative frequency of Type I errors in the long run*, to be decided on using cost–benefit considerations *before* the experiment (Neyman & Pearson). The basic difference is this: For Fisher, the exact level of significance is a property of the data (i.e., a relation between a body of data and a theory); for Neyman and Pearson, alpha is a property of the test, not of the data. Level of significance and alpha are not the same thing.

Neyman and Pearson thought their straightforward long-run frequentist interpretation of the significance test—and the associated concepts of power and of stating two statistical hypotheses (rather than only one, the null)—would be an improvement on Fisher's theory and make it more consistent. Fisher disagreed. Whereas Neyman and Pearson thought of mathematical and conceptual consistency, Fisher thought of ideological differences. He accused Neyman, Pearson, and their followers of confusing technology with knowledge: Their focus on Type I and Type II errors, on cost–benefit considerations that determine the balance between the two, and on repeated sampling from the same population has little to do with scientific practice, but it is characteristic for quality control and acceptance procedures in manufacturing. Fisher (1955, p. 70) compared the Neyman–Pearsonians to the Soviets, their five-year plans, and their ideal that "pure science can and should be geared to technological performance." He also compared them to Americans, who confuse the process of attaining knowledge with speeding up production or saving money. (Incidentally, Neyman was born in Russia and went to Berkeley, California, after Fisher made it difficult for him to stay on at University College in London).

What Does a Significant Result Mean?

The basic differences are these: Fisher attached an epistemic interpretation to a significant result, which referred to a particular experiment. Neyman rejected this view as inconsistent and attached a behavioral meaning to a significant result that did not refer to a particular experiment but to repeated experiments. (Pearson found himself somewhere in between.)

In *The Design*, Fisher talked about how to "disprove" a null hypothesis (e.g., 1935, pp. 16–17). Whatever phraseology he used, he always held that a significant result affects our confidence or degree of belief that the null hypothesis is false. This is what I refer to as an *epistemic interpretation:* Significance tells us about the truth or falsehood of a particular hypothesis in a particular experiment. Here we see very clearly Fisher's quasi-Bayesian view that the exact level of significance somehow measures the confidence we should have that the null hypothesis is false. But from a more consistent frequentist viewpoint, as expressed by Neyman, a level of significance does not tell us anything about the truth of a particular hypothesis; it states the relative frequency of Type I errors in the long run.

Neyman (1957, 1977) called his frequentist interpretation *behavioristic:* To accept or reject a hypothesis is a decision to take a particular action. Imagine a typical application of Neyman–Pearson theory: quality control. Imagine you have chosen the probability of Type I errors (false alarms) to be .10 and that of Type II errors (misses) to be .01, because misses are much more costly to your firm than false alarms. Every day you take a random sample from the firm's production. Even if the production is normal, you will expect a significant result (false alarm) on 10% of all days. Therefore, if a significant result occurs, you will act as if the null hypothesis were false, that is, stop production and check for a malfunction; but you will not necessarily believe that it is false—because you expect a lot of false alarms in the long run.

Fisher rejected Neyman's arguments for "inductive behavior" as "childish" (1955, p. 75), stemming from "mathematicians without personal contact with the Natural Sciences" (p. 69). And he maintained his epistemic view: "From a test of significance ... we have a genuine measure of the confidence with which any particular opinion may be held, in view of our particular data" (p. 74). For all his anti-Bayesian talk, Fisher adopted a very similar-sounding line of argument (Johnstone, 1987).

Does "Significant" Imply That There Is a Causal Effect?

Of course not. It is useful to distinguish between the *statistical* null hypothesis and the *substantive* null hypothesis.[2] Only the latter refers to the absence of a particular cause. What is rejected in significance testing is the statistical hypothesis, not the existence or absence of a cause. But in Fisher's writings we can read both "yes" and "no" as answers to the aforementioned question. Sometimes Fisher formulated the null hypothesis as "the treatment has no effect, period," whereas in other places he formulated it as a statistical null hypothesis (see Gigerenzer et al., 1989, pp. 95–97). In the famous Tea-Tasting Experiment (Fisher, 1935), for instance, he stated clearly that we cannot conclude from a significant result (disproving the null) that the opposite hypothesis (which is not formulated as an exact statistical hypothesis in null hypothesis testing) is proven. (This experiment was designed to test a lady's claim that she could tell whether the milk or the tea infusion was first added to a cup.) That is, we cannot infer the existence of a causal process from a significant result—here, that the lady can discriminate between whether the milk or the tea infusion was first added to the cup. For instance, there exist other causal mechanisms (someone told the lady in which cups the tea infusion had been poured first) that are consistent with rejecting the null hypothesis.

What Does a Nonsignificant Result Mean?

In *The Design*, Fisher (1935) proposed asymmetry: A null hypothesis can be disproved, but "never proved or established" (p. 16), so "experimenters ... are prepared to ignore all [nonsignificant] results" (p. 13). This has been understood by many textbook writers as saying that no conclusions can be drawn from a nonsignificant result. And several textbook authors laid down the commandment that I was taught: "Thou shalt not draw inferences from a nonsignificant result." This made nonsignificance appear a negative, worthless, and disappointing result. In Neyman–Pearson theory, in contrast, there is symmetry, and a conclusion is drawn from nonsignificance: Act as if the null hypothesis were true. The reason is that Neyman and Pearson start with a disjunction of two symmetric hypotheses (either H_0 or H_1 is true) and proceed by induction through elimination.

---

2. On the distinction between statistical and substantive hypotheses, see Hager and Westermann (1983) and Meehl (1978).

Fisher (1955) again had second thoughts: "It is a fallacy . . . to conclude from a test of significance that the null hypothesis is thereby established; at most it may be said to be confirmed or strengthened" (p. 73). Thus, although nonsignificant results cannot establish null hypotheses, according to his second thoughts, we can do more than just "ignore" them: We may say that a nonsignificant result "confirms" but does not "establish" the null hypothesis. Now Fisher suggested that a nonsignificant result might indeed support the null hypothesis, but he did not explain how.

Power

In null hypothesis testing, only one kind of error is defined: rejecting the null hypothesis when it is in fact true. In their attempt to supply a logical basis for Fisher's ideas and make them consistent, Neyman and Pearson replaced Fisher's single null hypothesis by a *set* of rival hypotheses. In the simplest case, two hypotheses, H_o and H_1, are specified, and it is assumed that one of them is true. This assumption allows us to determine the probability of both Type I errors and Type II errors, indicated in Neyman–Pearson theory by α and β, respectively. If H_1 is rejected although H_1 is true, a Type II error has occurred. α is also called the *size* of a test, and $1 - \beta$ is called its *power*. The power of a test is the long-run frequency of accepting H_1 if it is true. The concept of power makes explicit what Fisher referred to as "sensitivity."

Fisher (1935) pointed out two ways to make an experiment more sensitive: by enlarging the number of repetitions and by qualitative methods, such as experimental refinements that minimize the error in the measurements (pp. 21–25). Nevertheless, he rejected the concept of Type II error and calculations of power on the grounds that they are inappropriate for scientific induction. In his view, calculations of power, although they look harmless, reflect the "mental confusion" between technology and scientific inference (Fisher, 1955, p. 73). If someone designs a test for acceptance procedures in *quality control*, the goal of which is to minimize costs due to decision errors, calculations of power based on cost-benefit considerations in situations of repetitive tests are quite appropriate. But *scientific inference* and discovery, in Fisher's view, are about gaining knowledge, not saving money.

Fisher always rejected the concept of *power*. Neyman, for his part, pointed out that some of Fisher's tests "are in a mathematical sense 'worse than useless,' " because their power is less than their size (see Hacking, 1965, p. 99). Even in the Tea-Tasting Experiment, used by Fisher to introduce the logic of null hypothesis testing in *The Design*, the power is only a little higher than the level of significance (.05) or cannot be calculated at all, depending on the conditions (see Neyman, 1950).

Random Sampling from Known Populations?

Acceptance procedures involve random sampling from a known population (say, a firm's daily production). They also allow for repeated random sampling (every day a random sample may be taken). Recall that Neyman and Pearson based their theory on the concept of repeated random sampling, which defined the probability of Type I and Type II errors as long-run frequencies of wrong decisions in repeated experiments.

Fisher, in contrast, held that in scientific applications there is no known population from which repeated sampling can be done. There are always many populations to which a sample may belong. "The phrase 'repeated sampling from the same population' does not enable us to determine which population is to be used to define the probability level, for no one of them has objective reality, all being products of the statistician's imagination" (Fisher, 1955, p. 71). Fisher proposed to view any sample (such as the sample of participants in a typical psychological experiment, which is not drawn randomly from a known population) as a random sample from an *unknown hypothetical infinite population*. "The postulate of randomness thus resolves into the question, 'Of what population is this a random sample?' which must frequently be asked by every practical statistician" (Fisher, 1922, p. 313). But how can the practical statistician find out? The concept of an unknown hypothetical infinite population has puzzled many: "This is, to me at all events, a most baffling conception" (Kendall, 1943, p. 17).

Mechanical Scientific Inference

One way of reading *The Design* suggests that null hypothesis testing is a fairly mechanical procedure: Set up a null hypothesis, use a conventional level of significance, calculate a test statistic, and disprove the null hypothesis, if you can. Fisher later made clear that he did not mean it to be so. For instance, he pointed out that the choice of the test statistic and deciding which null hypotheses are worth testing cannot be reduced to a mechanical process. You need constructive imagination and much knowledge based on experience (Fisher, 1933). Statistical inference has two components: informed judgment and mathematical rigor.

Similarly, Neyman and Pearson always emphasized that the *statistical* part has to be supplemented by a *subjective* part. As Pearson (1962) put it: "We left in our mathematical model a gap for the exercise of a more intuitive process of personal judgment in such matters—to use our terminology—as the choice of the most likely class of admissible hypotheses, the appropriate significance level, the magnitude of worthwhile effects and the balance of utilities" (pp. 395–396).

In Neyman and Pearson's theory, once all judgments are made, the decision (reject or accept) results mechanically from the mathematics. In his later writings, Fisher opposed these mechanical accept/reject decisions, which he believed to be inadequate in science, in which one looks forward to further data. Science is concerned with the communication of information, such as exact levels of significance. Again, Fisher saw a broader context, the freedom of the Western world. Communication of information (but not mechanical decisions) recognizes "the right of *other* free minds to utilize them in making *their own* decisions" (Fisher, 1955, p. 77).

But Neyman reproached Fisher with the same sin—mechanical statistical inference. As a statistical behaviorist, Neyman (1957) looked at what Fisher actually did in his own research in genetics, biology, and agriculture, rather than at what he said one should do. He found Fisher using .01 as a conventional level of significance, without giving any thought to the choice of a particular level dependent on the particular problem or the probability of an error of the second kind; he accused Fisher of drawing mechanical conclusions, depending on whether or not the result was significant. Neyman urged a thoughtful choice of the level of significance, *not* using .01 for all problems and contexts.

Both camps in the controversy accused the other party of mechanical, thoughtless statistical inference; thus I conclude that here at least they agreed—statistical inference should not be automatic.

These differences between what Fisher proposed as the logic of significance testing and what Neyman and Pearson proposed as the logic of hypothesis testing suffice for the purpose of this chapter. Both have developed further tools for inductive inference, and so have others, resulting in a large toolbox that contains maximum likelihood, fiducial probability, confidence interval approaches, point estimation, Bayesian statistics, sequential analysis, and exploratory data analysis, to mention only a few. But it is null hypothesis testing and Neyman–Pearson hypothesis-testing theory that have transformed experimental psychology and part of the social sciences.

The Offspring: Hybrid Logic

The conflicting views presented earlier are those of the parents of the hybrid logic. Not everyone can tolerate unresolved conflicts easily and engage in a free market of competing ideas. Some long for the single truth or search for a compromise that could at least suppress the conflicts. Kendall (1949) commented on the desire for peace negotiations among statisticians:

> If some people asserted that the earth rotated from east to west and others that it rotated from west to east, there would always be a few well-meaning citizens to suggest that perhaps there was something to be said for both sides, and maybe it did a little of one and a little of the other; or that the truth probably lay between the extremes and perhaps it did not rotate at all. (p. 115)

The denial of the existing conflicts and the pretense that there is only one statistical solution to inductive inference were carried to an extreme in psychology and several neighboring sciences. This one solution was the *hybrid logic of scientific inference*, the offspring of the shotgun marriage between Fisher and Neyman and Pearson. The hybrid logic became institutionalized in experimental psychology (see Gigerenzer, 1987a), personality research (see Schwartz & Dangleish, 1982), clinical psychology and psychiatry (see Meehl, 1978), education (see Carver, 1978), quantitative sociology (see Morrison & Henkel, 1970), and archaeology (see Cowgill, 1977; Thomas, 1978), among others. Nothing like this happened in physics, chemistry, or molecular biology.

The Hybrid Logic Is Born

Before World War II, psychologists drew their inferences about the validity of hypotheses by many means—ranging from eyeballing to critical ratios. The issue of statistical inference was not of primary importance. Note that this was not because techniques were not yet available. On the contrary: already in 1710, John Arbuthnot proved the existence of God by a kind of significance test, astronomers had used them during the 19th century for rejecting outliers (Swijtink, 1987), and Fechner (1897) wrote a book on statistics including inference techniques, to give just a few examples. Techniques of statistical inference were known and sometimes used, but experimental method was not yet dominated by and almost equated with statistical inference.

Through the work of the statisticians George W. Snedecor at Iowa State College, Harold Hotelling at Columbia University, and Palmer Johnson at the University of Minnesota, Fisher's ideas spread in the United States. Psychologists began to cleanse the Fisherian message of its agricultural odor and its mathematical complexity and to write a new genre of textbooks featuring null hypothesis testing. Guilford's *Fundamental Statistics in Psychology and Education*, first published in 1942, was probably the most widely read textbook in the 1940s and 1950s. In the preface, Guilford credited Fisher for the logic of hypothesis testing taught in a chapter that was "quite new to this type of text" (p. viii). The book does not mention Neyman, E. S. Pearson, or Bayes. What Guilford teaches as the logic of hypothesis testing is Fisher's null hypothesis testing, deeply colored by "Bayesian" thinking: Null hypothesis testing is about the probability that the null hypothesis is true. "If the result comes out one way, the hypothesis is probably correct, if it comes out another way, the hypothesis is probably wrong" (p. 156). Null hypothesis testing is said to give degrees of doubt such as "probable" or "very likely" a "more exact meaning" (p. 156). Its logic is explained via surprising headings such as "Probability of hypotheses estimated from the normal curve" (p. 160).

Guilford's logic is not consistently Fisherian, nor does it consistently use "Bayesian" language of probabilities of hypotheses. It wavers back and forth and beyond. Phrases such as "we obtained directly the probabilities that the null hypothesis was plausible" and "the probability of extreme deviations from chance" are used interchangeably for the same thing: the level of significance. And when he proposed his own "somewhat new terms," his intuitive Bayesian thinking becomes crystal clear. A p value of .015 for a hypothesis of zero difference in the population "gives us the probability that the true difference is a negative one, and the remainder of the area *below* the point, or .985, gives us the probability that the true difference is positive. The odds are therefore

.985 to .015 that the true difference is positive" (p. 166). In Guilford's hands, p values that specify probabilities $p(D|H)$ of some data (or test statistic) D given a hypothesis H turn miraculously into Bayesian posterior probabilities $p(H|D)$ of a hypothesis given data.

Guilford's confusion is not an exception. It marks the beginning of a genre of statistical texts that vacillate between the researcher's "Bayesian" desire for probabilities of hypotheses and what Fisher is willing to give them.

This first phase of teaching Fisher's logic soon ran into a serious complication. In the 1950s and 1960s, the theory of Neyman and E. S. Pearson also became known. How were the textbook writers to cope with two logics of scientific inference? How should the ideological differences and personal insults be dealt with? Their solution to this conflict was striking. The textbook writers did not side with Fisher. That is, they did not go on to present null hypothesis testing as scientific inference and add a chapter on hypothesis testing outside science, introducing the Neyman–Pearson theory as a logic for quality control and related technological problems. Nor did they side with Neyman and Pearson, teaching their logic as a consistent and improved version of Fisher's and dispensing entirely with Fisherian null hypothesis testing.

Instead, textbook writers started to add Neyman–Pearsonian concepts on top of the skeleton of Fisher's logic. But acting as if they feared Fisher's revenge, they did it without mentioning the names of Neyman and Pearson. A *hybrid logic* of statistical inference was created in the 1950s and 1960s. Neither Fisher nor Neyman and Pearson would have accepted this hybrid as a theory of statistical inference. The hybrid logic is inconsistent from both perspectives and burdened with conceptual confusion. Its two most striking features are (a) it hides its hybrid origin and (b) it is presented as *the* monolithic logic of scientific inference. Silence about its origin means that the respective parts of the logic are not identified as part of two competing and partly inconsistent theoretical frameworks. For instance, the idea of testing null hypotheses without specifying alternative hypotheses is not identified as part of the Fisherian framework, and the definition of the level of significance and the power of a test as long-run frequencies of false and correct decisions, respectively, in repeated experiments is not identified as part of the Neyman–Pearson framework. And, as a consequence, there is no mention of the fact that each of these parts of the hybrid logic were rejected by the other party, and why, and what the unresolved controversial issues are.

The Structure of Hybrid Logic

To capture the emotional tensions associated with the hybrid logic, I use a Freudian analogy.[3]

---

3. Here I am elaborating on a metaphor suggested by Acree (1978). In a different context, Devereux (1967) talked about the relation between anxiety and elimination of subjectivity by method.

The Neyman–Pearson logic of hypothesis testing functions as the Superego of the hybrid logic. It demands the specification of precise alternative hypotheses, significance levels, and power in advance to calculate the sample size necessary, and it teaches the doctrine of repeated random sampling. The frequentist Superego forbids epistemic statements about particular outcomes or intervals, and it outlaws the interpretation of levels of significance as the degree of confidence that a particular hypothesis is true or false.

The Fisherian theory of significance testing functions as the Ego. The Ego gets things done in the laboratory and gets papers published. The Ego determines the level of significance after the experiment, and it neither specifies power nor calculates the sample size necessary. The Ego avoids precise predictions from its research hypothesis; that is, it does not specify the exact predictions of the alternative hypothesis but claims support for it by rejecting a null hypothesis. The Ego makes abundant epistemic statements about particular results. But it is left with feelings of guilt and shame for having violated the rules.

Censored by both the frequentist Superego and the pragmatic Ego are statements about probabilities of hypotheses given data. These form the Bayesian Id of the hybrid logic. Some direct measure of the validity of the hypotheses under question—quantitatively or qualitatively—is, after all, what researchers really want.

The Freudian metaphor suggests that the resulting conceptual confusion in the minds of researchers, editors, and textbook writers is not due to limited intelligence. The metaphor brings the anxiety and guilt, the compulsive and ritualistic behavior, and the dogmatic blindness associated with the hybrid logic into the foreground. It is as if the raging personal and intellectual conflicts between Fisher and Neyman and Pearson and between these frequentists and the Bayesians were projected onto an "intrapsychic" conflict in the minds of researchers. And the attempts of textbook writers to solve this conflict by denying it have produced remarkable emotional, behavioral, and cognitive distortions.

Anxiety and Guilt

Editors and textbook writers alike have institutionalized the level of significance as a measure of the quality of research. As mentioned earlier, Melton, after 12 years editing one of the most prestigious journals in psychology, said in print that he was reluctant to publish research with significance levels below .05 but above .01, whereas $p < .01$ made him confident that the results would be repeatable and deserved publication (1962, pp. 553–554). In Nunnally's *Introduction to Statistics for Psychology and Education* (1975), the student is taught similar values and informed that the standard has been raised: "Up until 20 years ago, it was not uncommon to see major research reports in which most of the differences were significant only at the 0.05 level. Now, such results are not taken very seriously, and it is more customary today to see results reported only if they reach the 0.01 or even lower probability levels" (p. 195).

Not accidentally, both Melton and Nunnally show the same weak understanding of the logic of inference and share the same erroneous belief that the level of significance specifies the probability that a result can be replicated (discussed later). The believers in the divinatory power of the level of significance set the standards.

The researcher's Ego knows that these publish-or-perish standards exist in the outside world and knows that the best way to adapt is to round up the obtained p value after the experiment to the nearest conventional level, say to round up the value $p = .006$ and publish $p < .01$. But the Superego has higher moral standards: If you set alpha to 5% before the experiment, then you must report the same finding ($p = .006$) as "significant at the 5% level." Mostly, the Ego gets its way but is left with feelings of dishonesty and of guilt at having violated the rules. Conscientious experimenters have experienced these feelings, and statisticians have taken notice. The following comment was made in a panel discussion among statisticians; Savage remarked on the statisticians' reluctance to take responsibility for once having built up the Superego in the minds of the experimenters:

> I don't imagine that anyone in this room will admit ever having taught that the way to do an experiment is first carefully to record the significance level then do the experiment, see if the significance level is attained, and if so, publish, and otherwise, perish. Yet, at one time we must have taught that; at any rate it has been extremely well learned in some quarters. And there is many a course outside of statistics departments today where the modern statistics of twenty or thirty years ago is taught in that rigid way. People think that's what they're supposed to do and are horribly embarrassed if they do something else, such as do the experiment, see what significance level would have been attained, and let other people know it. They do the better thing out of their good instincts, but think they're sinning. (Barnard, Kiefer, LeCam, & Savage, 1968, p. 147)

Statistics has become more tolerant than its offspring, the hybrid logic.

Denial of the Parents

The hybrid logic attempts to solve the conflict between its parents by denying its parents. It is remarkable that textbooks typically teach hybrid logic without mentioning Neyman, E. S. Pearson, and Fisher—except in the context of technical details, such as specific tables, that are incidental to the logic. In 25 out of 30 textbooks I have examined, Neyman and E. S. Pearson do not appear to exist. For instance, in the introduction to his *Statistical Principles of Experimental Design* (1971), Winer credits Fisher with inspiring the "standard working equipment" (p. 3) in this field, but a few pages later he presents the Neyman–Pearson terminology of Type I error, Type II error, power, two precise statistical hypotheses, cost–benefit considerations, and *rejecting and accepting* hypotheses. Yet nowhere in the book do the names of Neyman and E. S. Pearson appear (except in a "thank you" note to Pearson for permission to reproduce tables), although quite a few other names can be found in the index. No hint is given to the reader that there are different ways to think about the logic of inference. Even in the exceptional case of Hays's textbook (1963), in which all parents are mentioned by their names, the relationship of their ideas is presented (in a single sentence) as one of cumulative progress, from Fisher to Neyman and Pearson (p. 287).[4] Both Winer's and Hays's are among the best texts, without the confusions that abound in Guilford's, Nunnally's, and a mass of other textbooks. Nevertheless, even in these texts the parents' different ways of thinking about statistical inference and the controversial issues are not pointed out.

Denial of Conflicts between Parents

Thus the conflicting views are almost unknown to psychologists. Textbooks are uniformly silent. (Some statistics teachers protest that airing these disputes would only confuse students. I believe that pointing out the conflicting views would make statistics much more interesting to students who enjoy thinking rather than being told what to do next.) As a result of this silence, many a text muddles through the conflicting issues leaving confusion and inconsistency in its wake—at least, among the more intelligent and alert students. For instance, Type I and Type II errors are often defined in terms of long-run frequencies of erroneous decisions in repeated experiments, but the texts typically stop short of Neyman's behavioral interpretation and fall back to epistemic interpretations of the two errors as levels of confidence about the validity of the hypotheses. In fact, the poorer texts overflow with amazing linguistic contortions concerning what a level of significance means. For instance, within three pages of text, Nunnally explained that "level of significance" means all of the following: (1) "If the probability is low, the null hypothesis is improbable" (p. 194); (2) "the *improbability* of observed results being due to error" (p. 195); (3) "the probability that an observed difference is real" (p. 195); (4) "the *statistical confidence* . . . with odds of 95 out of 100 that the observed difference will hold up in investigations" (p. 195); (5) the degree to which experimental results are taken "seriously" (p. 195); (6) "the danger of accepting a statistical result as real when it is actually due only to error" (p. 195); (7) the degree of "faith [that] can be placed in the reality of the finding" (p. 196); (8) "the null hypothesis is rejected at the 0.05 level"; and (9) "the investigator can have 95 percent confidence that the sample mean actually differs from the population mean" (p. 196). And, after the last two versions, the author assured his readers: "All of these are different ways to say the same thing" (Nunnally, 1975, p. 196).

Nunnally did not spell out the differences between the logics of Fisher, Neyman and Pearson, and the Bayesians. He avoided the conflicting interpre-

---

4. In the third edition (1981), however, Hays's otherwise excellent text falls back to common standards: J. Neyman and E. S. Pearson no longer appear in the book.

tations by declaring that everything is the same. The price for this is conceptual confusion, false assertions, and an illusory belief in the omnipotence of the level of significance. Nunnally is a pronounced but not an atypical case.

Obsessive-Compulsive and Mechanical Behavior

As previously mentioned, statisticians have emphasized the indispensable role of personal judgment, although with respect to different parts of their logics. For Fisher, informed judgment was needed for the choice of the statistical model, the test statistics, and a null hypothesis worth investigating. For Neyman and Pearson, personal judgment was needed for the choice of the class of hypotheses (two hypotheses, in the simplest case), and the cost–benefit considerations that lead to the choice of Type I error, power, and sample size. For Bayesians such as de Finetti, finally, "subjectivism" and "relativism" are the very cornerstones of 20th-century probability theory (de Finetti, 1931/1989; Jeffrey, 1989).

The need for these kinds of informed judgments was rarely a topic in the textbooks. Rather, a mass of researchers must have read the textbooks as demanding the mindless, mechanical setting up of null hypotheses and recording of p values. Journals filled with p values, stars, double stars, and triple stars that allegedly established replicable "facts" bear witness to this cookbook mentality.

Guilford's misunderstanding that to set up a null hypothesis means to postulate a *zero* difference or a *zero* correlation was perpetuated. "Null" denotes the hypothesis to be "nullified," not that it is necessary to postulate a zero effect. Rarely were null hypotheses formulated that postulated something other than a zero effect (such as "the difference between the means is 3 scale points"). Rarely were precise alternative hypotheses stated, and even if there were two competing precise hypotheses, as in N. H. Anderson's information integration theory, only one of them was tested as the null hypothesis, sometimes resulting in tests with a power as low as .06 (Gigerenzer & Richter, 1990). Reasons for using a particular level of significance were almost never given, and rarely was a judgment about the desired power made and the sample size calculated. As a result, the power of the tests is typically quite low (below .50 for a medium effect), and pointing this out (Cohen, 1962) has not changed practice. Two-and-a-half decades after Cohen's work, the power of the null hypothesis tests was even slightly worse (Sedlmeier & Gigerenzer, 1989). Rather, null hypotheses are set up and tested in an extremely mechanical way reminiscent of compulsive hand washing. One can feel widespread anxiety surrounding the exercise of informed personal judgment in matters of hypothesis testing. The availability of statistical computer packages seems to have reinforced this mindless, mechanical behavior. A student of mine once tested in his thesis the difference between two means, which were numerically exactly the same, by an F test. Just to say that the means are the same seemed to him not objective enough.

The institutionalization of the hybrid logic as the sine qua non of scientific method is the environment that encourages mechanical hypothesis testing. The *Publication Manual of the American Psychological Association* (APA, 1974) for instance, called "rejecting the null hypothesis" a "basic" assumption (p. 19) and presupposes the hybrid logic. The researcher was explicitly told to make mechanical decisions: "Caution: Do not infer trends from data that fail by a small margin to meet the usual levels of significance. Such results are best interpreted as caused by chance and are best reported as such. Treat the result section like an income tax return. Take what's coming to you, but no more" (p. 19; this passage was deleted in the third edition in 1983). This prescription sounds like a Neyman–Pearson accept–reject logic, by which it matters for a decision only on which side of the criterion the data fall, not how far. Fisher would have rejected such mechanical behavior (e.g., Fisher, 1955, 1956). Nevertheless, the examples in the manual that tell the experimenter how to report results use p values that were obviously determined *after* the experiment and rounded up to the next conventional level, such as $p < .05$, $p < .01$, and $p < .001$ (pp. 39, 43, 48, 49, 70, 96). Neyman and Pearson would have rejected this practice: These p values are not the probability of Type I errors—and determining levels of significance after the experiment prevents determining power and sample size in advance. Fisher (e.g., 1955, 1956) would have preferred that the exact level of significance, say $p = .03$, be reported, not upper limits, such as $p < .05$, which look like probabilities of Type I errors but aren't.

Distorted Statistical Intuitions

Mechanical null hypothesis testing seems to go hand-in-hand with distorted statistical intuitions. I distinguish distorted statistical intuitions from the confusion and inconsistency of the hybrid logic itself. The latter results from mishmashing Fisher and Neyman and Pearson without making the conflation explicit, as I argued earlier. The conceptual confusion of the hybrid logic provided fertile ground for the growth of what I call *distorted statistical intuitions*. The distortions all seem to go in one direction: They exaggerate what can be inferred from a p value.

The network of distorted intuitions makes the obsessive performance of null hypothesis testing seem quite reasonable. Therefore, distorted intuitions serve an indispensable function. These illusions guide the writings of several textbook authors and editors, but they seem to be most pronounced in the users of null hypothesis testing, researchers in psychology and neighboring fields. Some distorted intuitions concern the frequentist part of the hybrid logic, others the Bayesian Id. I give one example of each (there is a larger literature on distorted statistical intuitions taught in statistical textbooks and held by experimenters; see Acree, 1978; Bakan, 1966; Brewer, 1985; Carver, 1978; Guttman, 1977, 1985; Lykken, 1968; Pollard & Richardson, 1987; Rozeboom, 1960; Tversky & Kahneman, 1971).

Replication Fallacy   Suppose α is set as .05 and the null hypothesis is rejected in favor of a given alternative hypothesis. What if we replicate the experiment? In what percentage of exact replications will the result again turn out significant? Although this question arises from the frequentist conception of repeated experiments, the answer is unknown. The α we choose does not tell us, nor does the exact level of significance.

The *replication fallacy* is the belief that the level of significance provides an answer to the question. Here are some examples: In an editorial in the *Journal of Experimental Psychology*, the editor stated that he used the level of significance reported in submitted papers as the measure of the "confidence that the results of the experiment would be repeatable under the conditions described" (Melton, 1962, p. 553). Many textbooks fail to mention that the level of significance does not specify the probability of a replication, and some explicitly teach the replication fallacy. For instance, "The question of statistical significance refers primarily to the extent to which similar results would be expected if an investigation were to be repeated" (Anastasi, 1958, p. 9). Or, "If the statistical significance is at the 0.05 level . . . the investigator can be confident with odds of 95 out of 100 that the observed difference will hold up in future investigations" (Nunnally, 1975, p. 195). Oakes (1986, p. 80) asked 70 university lecturers, research fellows, and postgraduate students with at least two years' research experience what a significant result ($t = 2.7$, $df = 18$, $p = .01$) means. Sixty percent of these academic psychologists erroneously believed that these figures mean that if the experiment is repeated many times, a significant result would be obtained 99% of the time.

In Neyman and Pearson's theory the level of significance (alpha) is defined as the relative frequency of rejections of H_0 if H_0 is true. In the minds of many, $1 - $ alpha erroneously turned into the relative frequency of rejections of H_0, that is, into the probability that significant results could be replicated.

The Bayesian Id's Wishful Thinking   I mentioned earlier that Fisher both rejected the Bayesian cake and wanted to eat it, too: He spoke of the level of significance as a measure of the degree of confidence in a hypothesis. In the minds of many researchers and textbook writers, however, the level of significance virtually turned into a Bayesian posterior probability.

What I call the *Bayesian Id's wishful thinking* is the belief that the level of significance, say .01, is the probability that the null hypothesis is correct, or that $1 - .01$ is the probability that the alternative hypothesis is correct. In various linguistic versions, this wishful thinking was taught in textbooks from the very beginning. Early examples are Anastasi (1958, p. 11), Ferguson (1959, p. 133), Guilford (1942, pp. 156–166), and Lindquist (1940, p. 14). But the belief has persisted over decades of teaching hybrid logic, for instance in Miller and Buckhout (1973; statistical appendix by F. L. Brown, p. 523), Nunnally (1975, pp. 194–196), and the examples collected by Bakan (1966) and Pollard and Richardson (1987). Oakes (1986, p. 82) reported that 96% of academic psychologists erroneously believed that the level of significance specifies the probability that the hypothesis under question is true or false.

The Bayesian Id has its share. Textbook writers have sometimes explicitly taught this misinterpretation but have more often invited it by not specifying the difference between a Bayesian posterior probability, a Neyman–Pearsonian probability of a Type I error, and a Fisherian exact level of significance.

Dogmatism

The institutionalization of *one* way to do hypothesis testing had its benefits. It made the administration of the social science research that had exploded since World War II easier, and it facilitated editors' decisions. And there were more benefits. It reduced the high art of hypothesis construction, of experimental ingenuity, and informed judgment into a fairly mechanical schema that could be taught, learned, and copied by almost anyone. The informed judgments that remain are of a low-level kind: whether to use a one- or a two-tailed significance test. (But even here some believed that there should be no room for judgment, because even this simple choice seemed to threaten the ideal of mechanical rules and invite cheating.) The final, and perhaps most important, benefit of the hybrid logic is that it provides the satisfying illusion of *objectivity:* The statistical logic of analyzing data seemed to eliminate the subjectivity of eyeballing and wishful distortion. To obtain and maintain this illusion of objectivity and impartiality, the hybrid logic had to deny its parents—and their conflicts.

The danger of subjective distortion and selective reading of data exists, to be sure. But it cannot be cured by replacing the distortions of particular experimenters with a collective distortion. Note that the institutionalized practice produces only selective and limited objectivity and hands other parts of scientific practice over to rules of thumb—even parts for which the statistical methods would be applicable. For example, during the 19th century, astronomers used significance tests to reject *data* (so-called outliers), assuming, at least provisionally, that their hypothesis was correct (Swijtink, 1987). Social scientists today, in contrast, use significance tests to reject *hypotheses*, assuming that their data are correct. The mathematics do not dictate which one the scientists should trust and which one they should try to refute. Social scientists seem to have read the statistical textbooks as saying that statistical inference is indispensable in selecting good from bad hypotheses but not for selecting good from bad data. The problem of outliers is dealt with by rules of thumb.[5]

The dogmatism with which the hybrid logic has been imposed on psychology researchers by many textbook writers and editors and by researchers

---

5. So is the problem of how many replications (participants) an experiment should use. Sedlmeier and Gigerenzer (1989) found no use of Neyman–Pearsonian calculations of sample size in published work. Some statistical texts have explicitly encouraged this: "Experienced researchers use a rule of thumb sample size of approximately twenty. Smaller samples often result in low power values while larger samples often result in a waste of time and money" (Bruning & Kintz, 1977, p. 7).

themselves has lasted for half a century. This is far too long. We need a knowledgeable use of statistics, not a collective compulsive obsession. It seems to have gone almost unnoticed that this dogmatism has created a strange double standard. Many researchers believe that their participants must use Bayes's rule to test hypotheses, but the researchers themselves use the hybrid logic to test their hypotheses—and thus themselves ignore base rates. There is the illusion that one kind of statistics normatively defines objectivity in scientific inference and another kind, rationality in everyday inference. The price is a kind of "split brain," where Neyman–Pearson logic is the Superego for experimenters' hypothesis testing and Bayesian statistics is the Superego for participants' hypothesis testing.

Beyond Dogmatism: Toward a Thoughtful Use of Statistics

Here are a few first principles: Do not replace the dogmatism of the hybrid logic of scientific inference with a new, although different one (e.g., Bayesian dogmatism). Remember the obvious: The problem of inductive inference has no universal mathematical solution. Use informed judgment and statistical knowledge. Here are several specific suggestions:

1. *Stop teaching hybrid logic as the sine qua non of scientific inference.* Teach researchers and students alternative theories of statistical inference, give examples of typical applications, and teach the students how to use these theories in a constructive (not mechanical) way. Point out the confused logic of the hybrid, the emotional, behavioral, and cognitive distortions associated with it, and insist on clarity (Cohen, 1990). This will lead to recognizing the second point.

2. *Statistical inference (Fisherian, Neyman–Pearsonian, or Bayesian) is rarely the most important part of data analysis.* Teach researchers and students to look at the data, not just at p values. Computer-aided graphical methods of data display and exploratory data analysis are means toward this end (Diaconis, 1985; Tukey, 1977). The calculation of descriptive statistics such as effect sizes is a part of data analysis that cannot be substituted by statistical inference (Rosnow & Rosenthal, 1989). A good theory predicts particular curves or effect sizes, but not levels of significance.

3. *Good data analysis is pointless without good data.* The measurement error should be controlled and minimized before and during the experiment; instead one tends to control it after the experiment by inserting the error term in the F ratio. Teach researchers and students that the important thing is to have a small real error in the data. Without that, a significant result at any level is, by itself, worthless—as Gosset, who developed the t test in 1908, emphatically emphasized (see Pearson, 1939). Minimizing the real error in measurements may be achieved by an iterative method: First, obtain measurements and look at the error variance, then try methods to minimize the error (e.g., stronger experimental control, investigating each participant carefully

in a single-case study rather than in a classroom), then go back and obtain new measurements and look at the new error variance, and so on, until improvements are no longer possible. Axiomatic measurement theory that focuses on ordinal rather than numerical judgments may help (Krantz, Luce, Suppes, & Tversky, 1971). It is all too rarely used.

4. *Good data need good hypotheses and theories to survive.* We need rich theoretical frameworks that allow for specific predictions in the form of precise research hypotheses. The null hypothesis of zero difference (or zero correlation) is only one version of such a hypothesis—perhaps only rarely appropriate. In particular, it has become a bad habit not to specify the predictions of a research hypothesis but to specify a different hypothesis (the null) and to try to reject it and claim credit for the unspecified research hypothesis. Teach students to derive competing hypotheses from competing theoretical frameworks and to test their ordinal or quantitative predictions *directly*, without using the null as a straw man.

Conclusions

Statistical reasoning is an art and so demands both mathematical knowledge and informed judgment. When it is mechanized, as with the institutionalized hybrid logic, it becomes ritual, not reasoning. Many colleagues have argued that it is not going to be easy to get researchers in psychology and other sociobiomedical sciences to drop this comforting crutch unless one offers an easy-to-use substitute. But this is exactly what I want to avoid—the substitution of one mechanistic dogma for another. It is our duty to inform our students of the many good roads to statistical inference that exist and to teach them how to use informed judgment to decide which one to follow for a particular problem. At the very least, this chapter can serve as a tool in arguments with people who think they have to defend a ritualistic dogma instead of good statistical reasoning. Making and winning such arguments is indispensable to good science.

14

Surrogates for Theories

I enjoy conference dinners. At such a dinner several years ago, I was crammed in with four graduate students and four professors around a table laden with Chinese food. The graduate students were eager to learn first-hand how to complete a dissertation and begin a research career, and the professors were keen to give advice. With authority, one colleague advised them: "Don't think big. Just do four or five experiments, clip them together, and hand them in." The graduate students nodded gratefully. They continued to nod when I added: "Don't follow this advice unless you are mediocre or unimaginative. Try to think in a deep, bold, and precise way. Take risks and be courageous." What a dilemma. How could these students follow these contradictory bits of advice?

Based on an analysis of articles in two major social psychology journals, the *Journal of Personality and Social Psychology* and the *Journal of Experimental Social Psychology*, Wallach and Wallach (1994, 1998) concluded that the theoretical argument in almost half of the studies borders on tautology. If an argument is a "near-tautology," there is no point in spending time and money trying to experimentally confirm it. "Don't think big" seems to be a prescription followed by many professional researchers, not merely conservative advice for graduate students. Complaints about the lack of serious theory in social psychology have been voiced before (e.g., Fiedler, 1991, 1996). Atheoretical research is not specific to social psychology, however, although some parts of psychology do better than others (Brandtstädter, 1987).

In this chapter, I address two questions: What are the surrogates for theory in psychology? and What institutional forces perpetuate reliance on these surrogates? This chapter is not intended to be exhaustive, only illustrative. The examples I use are drawn from the best work in the areas discussed: the psychology of reasoning, judgment, and decision making.

Surrogates

The problem is not that a majority of researchers would say that theory is irrelevant; the problem is that almost anything passes as a theory. I identify four species of surrogates for theory: one-word explanations, redescription, muddy dichotomies, and data fitting. There are other species, such as Wallach and Wallach's near-tautologies (whose banality and lack of imagination are as striking as their circularity). What distinguishes these surrogates from genuine theory is that they are vague, imprecise, and/or practically unfalsifiable, that they often boil down to common sense and lack boldness and surprise.

One-Word Explanations

The first species of theory surrogate is the one-word explanation. Such a word is a noun, broad in its meaning and chosen to relate to the phenomenon. At the same time, it specifies no underlying mechanism or theoretical structure. The one-word explanation is a label with the virtue of a Rorschach inkblot: A researcher can read into it whatever he or she wishes to see.

Examples of one-word explanations are *representativeness, availability*, and *anchoring and adjustment*, which are treated as the cognitive heuristics people use to make judgments and decisions. These terms supposedly explain "cognitive illusions" such as base-rate neglect. These "explanations" figure prominently in current textbooks in cognitive psychology, social psychology, and decision making. It is understandable that when these three terms were first proposed as cognitive processes in the early 1970s, they were only loosely characterized (Tversky & Kahneman, 1974). Yet 30 years and many experiments later, these three "heuristics" remain vague and undefined, unspecified both with respect to the antecedent conditions that elicit (or suppress) them and also to the cognitive processes that underlie them (Gigerenzer, 1996a). I fear that in another 30 years we will still be stuck with plausible yet nebulous proposals of the same type: that judgments of probability or frequency are sometimes influenced by what is similar (representativeness), comes easily to mind (availability), and comes first (anchoring).

The problem with these heuristics is that, post hoc, at least one of them can be fitted to almost any experimental result. For example, base-rate neglect is commonly attributed to representativeness. But the opposite result, over-weighting of base rates ("conservatism"), is just as easily "explained" by invoking anchoring (on the base rate) and adjustment. One-word explanations derive their seductive power from the fact that almost every observation can be called upon as an example.

Even better, one-word explanations can be so parsimonious that a single one can explain both a phenomenon and its opposite (Ayton & Fisher, 1999). For instance, Laplace (1814/1951) had described a phenomenon that is known today as the gambler's fallacy: when in a random sequence a run is observed (e.g., a series of red on the roulette wheel), players tend to believe that the *opposite* result (black) will come up next. Tversky and Kahneman (1974) proposed that this intuition is due to "representativeness," because "the occurrence of black will result in a more representative sequence than the occurrence of an additional red" (p. 1125). Gilovich, Vallone, and Tversky (1985) have described another phenomenon known as the belief in the "hot hand":

when in a random sequence a run is observed (e.g., a series of hits scored by a basketball player), players tend to believe that the *same* result (a hit rather than a miss) will come up next. The hot-hand fallacy has also been attributed to representativeness because "even short random sequences are thought to be highly representative of their generating process" (p. 295). The word "representativeness" can account for observing both *A* and *non-A*—here, the belief that after a run the opposite result will come up (gambler's fallacy) and the belief that after a run the same result will come up (the hot hand). Who could ask for more?

One might think that researchers rely on such one-word explanations because they lack precise models. But this is not always the case. For instance, there are several precise definitions of *similarity,* such as Euclidean distance, the city-block metric, and various measures of feature overlap, including Tversky's (1977) model (Shepard, 1962, 1974). However, attempts to define the word *representativeness* have met with little attention (e.g., Smith & Osherson, 1989). Proponents of one-word explanations continue to defend undefined terms. For instance, it has been argued that representativeness "can be assessed experimentally; hence it need not be defined a priori" (Kahneman & Tversky, 1996, p. 585). The term *availability* is similarly vague. Sometimes it denotes the "number" of instances that come to mind, sometimes the "ease" with which instances come to mind, and at still other times it means something else. Again, some researchers have attempted to pin down the meaning of the term (e.g., Fiedler, 1983, 1991; Wänke, Schwarz, & Bless, 1995) but with little effect on the thinking of others in the field. There is also a long tradition of fairly precise conceptions of *anchoring*, such as in Helson's adaptation level and Parducci's range-frequency theories. But the seductive power of one-word explanations seems to have caused collective amnesia. The strange reluctance of many researchers of reasoning, judgment, and decision making to specify precise and falsifiable process models and to work out the relationship between cognitive heuristics has been pointed out repeatedly (e.g., Einhorn & Hogarth, 1981; Shanteau, 1989; Wallsten, 1983).

But one-word explanations have great advantages. As long as they are plausible and remain unspecified, they are hard to falsify. And if one has three to choose from—such as representativeness, availability, and anchoring and adjustment—at least one of them can "account" post hoc for almost any phenomenon. The near-omnipotence of one-word explanations, however, does not foster theory development.

Redescription

Recall Molière's parody of the Aristotelian doctrine of substantial forms: Why does opium make you sleepy? Because of its dormative properties. Redescription has a long tradition in trait psychology, for instance, when an aggressive behavior is attributed to an aggressive disposition or intelligent behavior to high intelligence. But redescription in psychology is not limited to attributing behaviors to traits and other essences.

Research on thinking and judgment and decision making is another field in which redescription flourishes as a surrogate for theoretical ideas. Hallmarks of redescription in these areas are words such as *transparent, relevant,* and *salient* (which is not to say that every use of these terms implies redescription). For instance, one important issue in problem solving is how the external representation of a problem—whether it is represented in the form of text, figures, probabilities, frequencies, and so on—influences performance. If an effect is found, the question arises: Why does this type of problem representation elicit better performance? Redescription creeps in when researchers propose that the effect was obtained because "the correct answer is made transparent by the representation," because of "a salient cue that makes the correct answer obvious" (Kahneman & Tversky, 1996, p. 586), or because "the problem is now simpler" (for more examples, see Gigerenzer, 1996a; Gigerenzer & Murray, 1987, pp. 159–162; Sahlin, 1991). That a representation makes a problem "simpler" or its answer "transparent" is not an explanation but rather what needs to be explained.

Muddy Dichotomies

Torn between being distressed over and content with the state of research on information processing, Allen Newell (1973) entitled a commentary "You Can't Play 20 Questions with Nature and Win." What distressed Newell was that when behavior is explained in terms of dichotomies—nature versus nurture, serial versus parallel, grammars versus associations, and so on—"clarity is never achieved" and "matters simply become muddier and muddier as we go down through time" (pp. 288–289). There is nothing wrong with making distinctions in terms of dichotomies per se; what concerned Newell were situations in which theoretical thinking gets stuck in binary oppositions beyond which it never seems to move.

Let us consider a case in which false dichotomies have hindered precise theorizing. Some arguments against evolutionary psychology are based on the presumed dichotomy between biology and culture, or genes and environment (Tooby & Cosmides, 1992). One such argument goes: Because cognition is bound to culture, evolution must be irrelevant. But biology and culture are not opposites. For instance, our ability to cooperate with conspecifics to whom we are genetically unrelated—which distinguishes us humans from most other species—is based on mechanisms of both biological and cultural origin. Simply to ask about the relative importance of each in terms of explained variance, such as that 80% of intelligence is genetically inherited, is, however, not always an interesting question. The real theoretical question concerns the mechanism that combines what is termed the "biological" and the "cultural." For biologists, the nature/nurture or biological/cultural dichotomy is a nontarter: Genes are influenced by their environment, which can include other genes, and culture can change gene pools (coevolution).

Cognitive psychology is also muddied by vague dichotomies. For instance, a popular opposition is between associations and rules. Sloman (1996) has linked this dichotomy to Smolensky's distinction between an intuitive processor and a conscious rule interpreter, Hinton's distinction between intuitive and rational processing, Schneider and Schiffrin's distinction between automatic and controlled processing, Evans's distinction between a perceptually based matching process and a linguistic-logical process, and Freud's distinction between primary and secondary processes. The problem is that these distinctions are not all the same (Gigerenzer & Regier, 1996). Collecting more and more binary oppositions—and labeling these "two-process theories"—does not necessarily enhance clarity. Dichotomies can be an important first step, but they cannot substitute for theories of cognitive processes.

Data Fitting

There are other surrogates for theories in psychology, one of which is the use of powerful mathematical tools for data fitting in the absence of theoretical underpinnings. Psychologists have historically embraced such new tools, which they then propose as new theories. When factor analysis became a common tool for data processing in psychological research, humans were modeled as a bundle of personality factors. When multidimensional scaling came along in the 1960s and 1970s, human categorization and other mental processes were proposed to be based on distances between points in multidimensional space. More recently, the advent of the serial computer was followed by that of neural networks as a model of cognitive function. There is nothing wrong with using these mathematical tools per se. The important point with respect to surrogate theories is whether the tool is used for modeling or for data fitting (this is itself a false dichotomy, there being a continuum between these poles). Charles Spearman originally designed factor analysis as a theory of intelligence, but (in the form of principal component analysis) it ended up as a fitting tool for all kinds of psychological phenomena. Likewise, Roger Shepard (e.g., 1962, 1974) interpreted the various Minkowski metrics that can be used in multidimensional scaling as psychological theories of similarity, such as in color perception, but multidimensional scaling ended up as a largely atheoretical tool for fitting any similarity data, with the Euclidean metric as a conventional routine. Similarly, neural networks can be used as constrained or structured networks into which theoretical, domain-specific assumptions are built (e.g., Regier, 1996), but many applications of neural networks to modeling psychological phenomena seem to amount to data fitting with numerous free parameters. Neural networks with hidden units and other free parameters can be too powerful to be meaningful—in the sense that they can fit different types of results that were generated with different process models (Geman, Bienenstock, & Doursat, 1992; Massaro, 1988).

In general, mathematical structures can be used to test theories (with parameters determined by theoretical considerations, e.g., the metric in multidimensional scaling) or as a fitting tool (with parameters chosen post hoc so as to maximize the fit). Fitting per se is not objectionable. The danger is that enthusiasm for a mathematical tool can lead one to get stuck in data fitting and to use a good fit as a surrogate for a theory.

What Institutional Forces Support Surrogates for Theories?

There is one obvious reason why surrogates for theories come to mind more quickly than real theories: demonstrating how a one-word explanation, a redescription, a dichotomy, or an exercise in data fitting "explains" a phenomenon demands less mental strain than developing a bold and precise theory. It takes imagination to conceive the idea that heat is caused by motion, but only little mental effort to propose that heat is caused by specific particles that have the propensity to be hot. In what follows, I identify two institutions that may maintain (rather than cause) the abundant use of surrogates for theories in some areas of psychology.

The Institutionalization of Null Hypothesis Testing

In recent years, more and more scholars have argued against the ritual of null hypothesis testing, which was institutionalized in psychology around 1955. Many other scholars have responded with passionate defenses of it. So far the debate focuses on issues such as whether one should replace significance testing by confidence intervals, effect sizes, or something else. In my view, however, the single most important issue is that institutionalized null hypothesis testing allows surrogates for theories to flourish (Chapter 13). To switch to confidence intervals will not necessarily reverse this trend.

Null hypothesis testing provides researchers with no incentive to specify either their own research hypotheses or competing hypotheses. The ritual is to test one's unspecified hypothesis against "chance," that is, against the null hypothesis that postulates "no difference between the means of two populations" or "zero correlation." As Danziger (1990) has shown, the origin of this practice is in parapsychology and education, where the interest was not in testing positive theories but detecting effects greater than those of chance. The problem lies not in statistical testing per se but in a specific statistical method that became institutionalized. If psychologists had adopted statistical methods that test two or more well-specified hypotheses against one another (such as Neyman–Pearson or Bayesian statistics), then they would have been forced to formulate precise hypotheses.

As long as there is an institutionalized methodology that does not encourage researchers to specify their hypotheses, there is little incentive to think hard and develop theories from which such hypotheses could be derived. Accordingly, the voluminous instruction manual from which graduate students and researchers learn how to write an article, the *APA Publication Manual*, devotes many pages to methodology but not to theory. From this students learn not that hypotheses and theories should be bold, surprising, and precisely stated, but that their business is to test null hypotheses. To perform this ritual, mere surrogates for thinking big are sufficient. The result has been called "null science" (Bower, 1997). It reminds me of a mechanical maxim regarding the critical ratio (the difference between the means divided by the standard deviation of the differences), the predecessor of the significance level: "A critical ratio of three, or no Ph.D."

Disciplinary Isolation

Over the course of the 20th century, academic psychology has become more and more compartmentalized into subdisciplines such as social psychology, cognitive psychology, developmental psychology, and so on. Each subdiscipline has its own journals, reviewers, and grant programs, and one can have a career in one of them without ever reading the journals of neighboring subdisciplines. In addition, job searches are often organized according to these categories. This territorial organization of psychology discourages researchers from engaging with psychological knowledge and colleagues outside of their territory, not to mention with other disciplines. As Jerry Fodor (1995) put it:

> Unfortunately, cognitive psychology as people are trained to practice it, at least in this country, has been traditionally committed to methodological empiricism and to disciplinary isolationism, in which it was, for example, perfectly possible to study language without knowing anything about linguistics. (pp. 85–86)

This isolationism is by no means restricted to the study of language. For instance, the experimental study of logical thinking in arguably the most researched problem, the Wason selection task, has been carried out with little reference to modern logic, and the study of statistical reasoning has been conducted with little attention to the relevant issues in statistics (see Gigerenzer, 1994a; Oaksford & Chater, 1994).

Intellectual inbreeding can block the flow of positive metaphors from one discipline to another. Neither disciplines nor subdisciplines are natural categories. Interdisciplinary exchange has fueled the development of some of the most influential new metaphors and theories in the sciences, such as when Ludwig Boltzmann and James Clerk Maxwell developed statistical mechanics by borrowing from sociology. Bolzmann and Maxwell modeled the behavior of gas molecules on the behavior of humans as Adolphe Quetelet had portrayed it: erratic and unpredictable at the individual level but exhibiting orderly statistical laws at the level of collectives (Gigerenzer et al., 1989, ch. 2). Territorial science, in contrast, blocks the flow of metaphors and the development of new theories. Distrust and disinterest in anything outside one's subdiscipline supports surrogates for theory.

Data without Theory

In this chapter, I have specified four surrogates for theory and two possible institutional reasons why some of these surrogates flourish like weeds. These two reasons certainly cannot explain the whole story.

Several years ago, I spent a day and a night in a library reading through issues of the *Journal of Experimental Psychology* from the 1920s and 1930s. This was professionally a most depressing experience, but not because these articles were methodologically mediocre. On the contrary, many of them make today's research pale in comparison with their diversity of methods and statistics, their detailed reporting of single-case data rather than mere averages, and their careful selection of trained participants. And many topics—such as the influence of the gender of the experimenter on the performance of the participants—were of interest then as now. What depressed me was that almost all of this work is forgotten; it does not seem to have left a trace in the collective memory of our profession. It struck me that most of it involved collecting data without substantive theory. Data without theory are like babies without parents: Their life expectancy is low.

REFERENCES

Aaronson, D., Grupsmith, E., & Aaronson, M. (1976). The impact of computers on cognitive psychology. *Behavioral Research Methods and Instrumentation, 8,* 129–138.

Acree, M. C. (1978). Theories of statistical inference in psychological research: A historicocritical study. *Dissertation Abstracts International, 39* (10), 5037B. (University Microfilms No. H790 H7000.)

Adler, J. E. (1984). Abstraction is uncooperative. *Journal for the Theory of Social Behavior, 14,* 165–181.

Adler, J. E. (1991). An optimist's pessimism: Conversation and conjunction. In E. Eells & T. Maruszewski (Eds.), *Probability and rationality: Studies on L. Jonathan Cohen's philosophy of science* (pp. 251–282). Amsterdam: North-Holland Rodopi.

Ajzen, I. (1977). Intuitive theories of events and the effects of base-rate information on predictions. *Journal of Personality and Social Psychology, 35,* 303–314.

Ajzen, I., & Fishbein, M. (1975). A Bayesian analysis of attribution processes. *Psychological Bulletin, 82,* 261–277.

Alba, J. W., & Marmorstein, H. (1987). The effects of frequency knowledge on consumer decision making. *Journal of Consumer Research, 14,* 14–26.

Alibi des Schornsteinfegers: Unwahrscheinliche Wahrscheinlichkeitsrechnungen in einem Mordprozess [Alibi of a chimney sweep: Improbable probability calculations in a murder trial]. *Rheinischer Merkur,* No. 39.

Allport, D. A. (1975). The state of cognitive psychology. *Quarterly Journal of Experimental Psychology, 27,* 141–152.

Allwood, C. M., & Montgomery, H. (1987). Response selection strategies and realism of confidence judgments. *Organizational Behavior and Human Decision Processes, 39,* 365–383.

American Psychological Association (1974). *Publication Manual of the American Psychological Association* (2nd ed.). Baltimore: Garamond/Pridemark Press.

American Psychological Association (1983). *Publication Manual of the American Psychological Association* (3rd ed.). Menasha, WI: Banta.

Anastasi, A. (1958). *Differential psychology* (3rd ed.) New York: Macmillan.

Anderson, J. R. (1980). *Cognitive psychology and its implications.* San Francisco, CA: Freeman.

Anderson, J. R. (1990). *The adaptive character of thought.* Hillsdale, NJ: Erlbaum.

Anderson, J. R., & Milson, R. (1989). Human memory: An adaptive perspective. *Psychological Review, 96,* 703–719.

Anderson, N. H. (1986). A cognitive theory of judgment and decision. In B. Brehmer, H. Jungermann, P. Lourens, & G. Sevón (Eds.), *New directions in research on decision making* (pp. 63–108). Amsterdam: North-Holland.

Arbib, M. A. (1993). Allen Newell, unified theories of cognition. *Artificial Intelligence, 59,* 265–283.

Arbuthnot, J. (1710). An argument for Divine Providence, taken from the constant regularity observ'd in the births of both sexes. *Philosophical Transactions of the Royal Society, 27,* 186–190.

Arkes, H. R. (1981). Impediments to accurate clinical judgment and possible ways to minimize their impact. *Journal of Consulting and Clinical Psychology, 49,* 323–330.

Arkes, H. R., Christensen, C., Lai, C., & Blumer, C. (1987). Two methods of reducing overconfidence. *Organizational Behavior and Human Decision Processes, 39,* 133–144.

Arkes, H. R., & Hammond, K. R. (Eds.). (1986). *Judgment and decision making: An interdisciplinary reader.* Cambridge, England: Cambridge University Press.

Armelius, B., & Armelius, K. (1974). The use of redundancy in multiple-cue judgments: Data from a suppressor-variable-task. *American Journal of Psychology, 87,* 385–392.

Armelius, K. (1979). Task predictability and performance as determinants of confidence in multiple-cue judgments. *Scandinavian Journal of Psychology, 20,* 19–25.

Ash, M. G. (1987). Psychology and politics in interwar Vienna: The Vienna Psychological Institute, 1922–1942. In M. G. Ash & W. R. Woodward (Eds.), *Psychology in twentieth-century thought and society* (pp. 143–164). Cambridge: Cambridge University Press.

Aspray, W. (1990). *John von Neumann and the origins of modern computing.* Cambridge, MA: MIT Press.

Atran, S. (1990). *Cognitive foundations of natural history: Towards an anthropology of science.* Cambridge: Cambridge University Press.

Axelrod, R. (1984). *The evolution of cooperation.* New York: Basic Books.

Ayton, P., & Fisher, I. (1999). The gambler's fallacy and the hot-hand-fallacy: Two faces of subjective randomness. Manuscript submitted for publication.

Baars, B. J. (1986). *The cognitive revolution in psychology.* New York: Guilford Press.

Babbage, C. (1812–1994). *Passages from the life of a philosopher* (M. Campbell-Kelley, Ed.). Piscataway, NJ: IEEE Press. (Original work published 1812)

Bakan, D. (1966). The test of significance in psychological research. *Psychological Bulletin, 66,* 423–437.

Bar-Hillel, M. (1980). The base-rate fallacy in probability judgments. *Acta Psychologica, 44,* 211–233.

Barnard, G. A. (1979). Discussion of the paper by Professors Lindley and Tversky and Dr. Brown. *Journal of the Royal Statistical Society, Series A, 142,* 171–172.

Barnard, G. A., Kiefer, J. C., LeCam, L. M., & Savage, L. J. (1968). Statistical inference. In D. G. Watts (Ed.), *The future of statistics* (p. 147). New York: Academic Press.

Baron-Cohen, S. (1995). *Mindblindness.* Cambridge, MA: MIT Press.

Barsalou, L. W., & Ross, B. H. (1986). The roles of automatic and strategic processing in sensitivity to superordinate and property frequency. *Journal of Experimental Psychology: Learning, Memory, and Cognition, 12,* 116–134.

Bayes, T. (1763). A essay towards solving a problem in the doctrine of chances. *Philosophical Transactions of the Royal Society of London, 53,* 370–418.

Bazerman, M. H. (1990). *Judgment in managerial decision making.* New York: Wiley.

Bazerman, M. H., & Neale, M. A. (1986). Heuristics in negotiation: Limitations to effective dispute resolution. In H. R. Arkes & R. R. Hammond (Eds.), *Judgment and decision making: An interdisciplinary reader* (pp. 311–321). Cambridge, England: Cambridge University Press.

Becker, G. (1976). *The economic approach to human behavior.* Chicago: University of Chicago Press.

Beretty, P. M., Todd, P. M., & Martignon, L. (1999). Categorization by elimination: Using few cues to choose. In G. Gigerenzer, P. M. Todd, & the ABC Group, *Simple heuristics that make us smart* (pp. 235–254). New York: Oxford University Press.

Binet, A., & Simon, T. (1914). *Mentally defective children.* London: Edward Arnold.

Birnbaum, M. H. (1983). Base rates in Bayesian inference: Signal detection analysis of the cab problem. *American Journal of Psychology, 96,* 85–94.

Björkman, M. (1984). Decision making, risk taking and psychological time: Review of empirical findings and psychological theory. *Scandinavian Journal of Psychology, 25,* 31–49.

Björkman, M. (1987). A note on cue probability learning: What conditioning data reveal about cue contrast. *Scandinavian Journal of Psychology, 28,* 226–232.

Blackwell, R. J. (1983). Scientific discovery: The search for new categories. *New Ideas in Psychology, 1,* 111–115.

Boesch, C., & Boesch, H. (1984). Mental map in wild chimpanzees: An analysis of hammer transports for nut cracking. *Primates, 25,* 160–170.

Boole, G. (1958). *An investigation of the laws of thought on which are founded the mathematical theories of logic and probabilities.* New York: Dover. (Original work published 1854)

Borges, B., Goldstein, D. G., Ortmann, A., & Gigerenzer, G. (1999). Can ignorance beat the stock market? In G. Gigerenzer, P. M. Todd, & the ABC Group, *Simple heuristics that make us smart* (pp. 59–72). New York: Oxford University Press.

Borgida, E., & Brekke, N. (1981). The base rate fallacy in attribution and prediction. In J. H. Harvey, W. J. Ickes, & R. F. Kidd (Eds.), *New directions in attribution research* (Vol. 3, pp. 63–95). Hillsdale, NJ: Erlbaum.

Boring, E. G. (1942). *Sensation and perception in the history of experimental psychology.* New York: Appleton-Century-Crofts.

Boring, E. G. (1957). *A history of experimental psychology.* New York: Appleton-Century-Crofts.

Boring, E. G. (1963). *History, psychology, and science: Selected papers.* New York: Wiley.

Bower, B. (1997). Null science. *Science News, 151,* 356–357.

Brandtstädter, J. (1987). On certainty and universality in human development: Developmental psychology between apriorism and empiricism. In M. Chapman & R. A. Dixon (Eds.), *Meaning and the growth of understanding: Wittgenstein's significance for developmental psychology* (pp. 69–84). Berlin: Springer.

Brase, G. L., Cosmides, L., & Tooby, J. (1998). Individuation, counting, and statistical inference: The role of frequency and whole object representations in judgment under uncertainty. *Journal of Experimental Psychology: General, 127,* 3–21.

Brehmer, A., & Brehmer, B. (1988). What has been learned about human judgment from thirty years of policy capturing? In B. Brehmer & C. R. B. Joyce (Eds.), *Human judgment: The SJT view* (pp. 75–144). Amsterdam: Elsevier.

Brehmer, B. (1988). The development of social judgment theory. In B. Brehmer & C. R. B. Joyce (Eds.), *Human judgment: The SJT view* (pp. 13–40). Amsterdam: Elsevier.

Brehmer, B. (1994). The psychology of linear judgment models. *Acta Psychologica, 87,* 137–154.

Brehmer, B., & Joyce, C. R. B. (Eds.). (1988). *Human judgment: The SJT view.* Amsterdam: Elsevier.

Breiman, L., Friedman, J. H., Olshen, R. A., & Stone, C. J. (1993). *Classification and regression trees.* New York: Chapman & Hall.

Brewer, J. K. (1985). Behavioral statistics textbooks: Source of myths and misconceptions? *Journal of Educational Statistics, 10,* 252–268.

Bröder, A. (in press). Assessing the empirical validity of the "Take The Best" heuristic as a model of human probabilistic inference. *Journal of Experimental Psychology: Learning, Memory and Cognition.*

Brown, N. R., & Siegler, R. S. (1993). Metrics and mappings: A framework for understanding real-world quantitive estimation. *Psychological Review, 100,* 511–534.

Brown, W., & Thomson, G. H. (1921). *The essentials of mental measurement.* Cambridge, England: Cambridge University Press.

Bruning, J. L., & Kintz, B. L. (1977). *Computational handbook of statistics* (2nd ed.). Glenview, IL: Scott, Foresman.

Brunswik, E. (1934). *Wahrnehmung und Gegenstandswelt: Grundlegung einer Psychologie vom Gegenstand her.* Leipzig, Germany: Deutike.

Brunswik, E. (1937). Psychology as a science of objective relations. *Philosophy of Science, 4,* 227–260.

Brunswik, E. (1939). Probability as a determiner of rat behavior. *Journal of Experimental Psychology, 25,* 175–197.

Brunswik, E. (1943). Organismic achievement and environmental probability. *Psychological Review, 50,* 255–272.

Brunswik, E. (1955). Representative design and probabilistic theory in a functional psychology. *Psychological Review, 62,* 193–217.

Brunswik, E. (1956). *Perception and the representative design of psychological experiments.* Los Angeles: University of California Press.

Brunswik, E. (1957). Scope and aspects of the cognitive problem. In H. Gruber,

R. Jessor, & K. R. Hammond (Eds.), *Cognition: The Colorado Symposium* (pp. 5–40). Cambridge, MA: Harvard University Press.

Brunswik, E. (1964). Scope and aspects of the cognitive problem. In J. S. Bruner, E. Brunswik, L. Festinger, F. Heider, K. F. Muenzinger, C. E. Osgood, & D. Rapaport (Eds.), *Contemporary approaches to cognition* (pp. 4–31). Cambridge, MA: Harvard University Press.

Bundeszentrale für gesundheitliche Aufklärung. (1988–1993). *Wissenswertes über den HIV-Test, Issues 1–10*. Cologne: Bundeszentrale für gesundheitliche Aufklärung.

Burke, D. S., Brundage, J. F., Redfield, R. R., Damato, J. J., Schnabel, C. A., Putman, P., Visitine, R., & Kim, H. J. (1988). Measurement of the false positive rate in a screening program for human immunodeficiency virus infection. *New England Journal of Medicine, 319*, 961–964.

Busch, M. P. (1994). HIV testing in blood banks. In G. Schochetman & J. R. George (Eds.), *AIDS testing: A comprehensive guide to technical, medical, social, legal, and management issues* (pp. 224–236). New York: Springer.

Buss, D. M. (1987). Sex differences in human mate selection criteria: An evolutionary perspective. In C. Crawford, M. Smith, & D. Krebs (Eds.), *Sociobiology and psychology: Ideas, issues and applications* (pp. 335–351). Hillsdale, NJ: Erlbaum.

Byrne, R., & Whiten, A. (Eds.). (1988). *Machiavellian intelligence: Social expertise and the evolution of intellect in monkeys, apes and humans*. Oxford, England: Clarendon Press.

Caraco, T., Martindale, S., & Whittam, T. S. (1980). An empirical demonstration of risk-sensitive foraging preferences. *Animal Behavior, 28*, 820–830.

Carnap, R. (1969). *The logical structure of the world* (Trans. R. A. George), Berkeley: University of California Press. (Original work published 1928)

Carpenter, R. G., Gardner, A., McWeeny, P. M., & Emery, J. L. (1977). Multistage scoring system for identifying infants at risk of unexpected death. *Archives of Disease in Childhood, 53*, 606–612.

Carroll, J. B. (1982). The measurement of intelligence. In R. J. Sternberg (Ed.), *Handbook of human intelligence* (pp. 29–120). Cambridge, England: Cambridge University Press.

Carver, R. P. (1978). The case against statistical significance testing. *Harvard Educational Review, 48*, 378–399.

Casscells, W., Schoenberger, A., & Grayboys, T. (1978). Interpretation by physicians of clinical laboratory results. *New England Journal of Medicine, 299*, 999–1000.

Castellan, N. J. (1981). On-line computers in psychology: The last 10 years, the next 10 years—the challenge and the promise. *Behavioral Research Methods and Instrumentation, 13*, 91–96.

Castellan, N. J. (1991). Computers and computing in psychology: Twenty years of progress and still a bright future. *Behavior Research Methods, Instruments, and Computers, 23*, 106–108.

Catalan, J., & Pugh, K. (1995). Suicidal behavior and HIV infection—is there a link? *AIDS Care, 7* (Suppl. 2), 117–121.

Cheng, P. W., & Holyoak, K. J. (1985). Pragmatic reasoning schemas. *Cognitive Psychology, 17*, 391–416.

Cheng, P. W., & Holyoak, K. J. (1989). On the natural selection of reasoning theories. *Cognition, 33*, 285–313.

Christensen-Szalanski, J. J. J., & Beach, L. R. (1982). Experience and the base-rate fallacy. *Organizational Behavior and Human Performance, 29*, 270–278.

Cohen, J. (1962). The statistical power of abnormal-social psychological research: A review. *Journal of Abnormal and Social Psychology, 65*, 145–153.

Cohen, J. (1990). Things I have learned (so far). *American Psychologist, 45*, 1304–1312.

Cohen, L. J. (1981). Can human irrationality be experimentally demonstrated? *Behavioral and Brain Sciences, 4*, 317–370.

Cohen, L. J. (1982). Are people programmed to commit fallacies? Further thoughts about the interpretation of experimental data on probability. *Journal for the Theory of Social Behaviour, 12*, 251–274.

Cohen, L. J. (1986). *The dialogue of reason.* Oxford, England: Clarendon Press.

Cohen, L. J. (1989). *The philosophy of induction and probability.* Oxford, England: Clarendon Press.

Colebrooke, H. (1825). Address on presenting the Gold Medal of the Astronomical Society to Charles Babbage. *Memoirs of the Astronomical Society, 1*, 509–512.

Cooper, W. S. (1989). How evolutionary biology challenges the classical theory of rational choice. *Biology and Philosophy, 4*, 457–481.

Cooper, W. S., & Kaplan, R. (1982). Adaptive "coin-flipping": A decision-theoretic examination of natural selection for random individual variation. *Journal of Theoretical Biology, 94*, 135–151.

Cosmides, L. (1985). Deduction or Darwinian algorithms? An explanation of the "elusive" content effect on the Wason selection task. *Dissertation Abstracts International, 47* (1), 358B. (University Microfilms No. 86-02206.)

Cosmides, L. (1989). The logic of social exchange: Has natural selection shaped how humans reason? Studies with the Wason selection task. *Cognition, 31*, 187–276.

Cosmides, L., & Tooby, J. (1992). Cognitive adaptations for social exchange. In J. Barkow, L. Cosmides, & J. Tooby (Eds.), *The adapted mind: Evolutionary psychology and the generation of culture* (pp. 163–228). New York: Oxford University Press.

Cosmides, L., & Tooby, J. (1994a). Beyond intuition and instinct blindness: Towards an evolutionary rigorous cognitive science. *Cognition, 50*, 41–77.

Cosmides, L., & Tooby, J. (1994b). Origins of domain specificity: The evolution of functional organization. In L. A. Hirschfeld & S. A. Gelman (Eds.), *Mapping the mind: Domain specificity in cognition and culture* (pp. 85–116). Cambridge, England: Cambridge University Press.

Cosmides, L., & Tooby, J. (1996). Are humans good intuitive statisticians after all? Rethinking some conclusions from the literature on judgment under uncertainty. *Cognition, 58*, 1–73.

Cowgill, G. L. (1977). The trouble with significance tests and what we can do about it. *American Antiquity, 42*, 350–368.

Cronbach, L. J. (1957). The two disciplines of scientific psychology. *American Psychologist, 12*, 671–684.

Cummins, D. D. (1998). Social norms and other minds: The evolutionary roots of higher cognition. In D. D. Cummins & C. Allen (Eds.), *The evolution of mind* (pp. 30–50). New York: Oxford University Press.

Curd, M. (1980). The logic of discovery: An analysis of three approaches. In T. Nickles (Ed.), *Scientific discovery, logic, and rationality* (pp. 201–219). Dordrecht, Holland: Reidel.

Daly, M., & Wilson, M. (1988). *Homicide.* New York: Aldine de Gruyter.

Dannenberg, A. L., McNeil, J. G., Brundage, J. F., & Brockmeyer, R. (1996). Suicide and HIV-infection. *Journal of the American Medical Association, 276,* 1743–1746.

Danziger, K. (1985). The methodological imperative in psychology. *Philosophy of the Social Sciences, 15,* 1–13.

Danziger, K. (1987). Statistical method and the historical development of research practice in American psychology. In L. Krüger, G. Gigerenzer, & M. S. Morgan (Eds.), *The probabilistic revolution*: Vol. 2. *Ideas in the sciences* (pp. 35–47). Cambridge, MA: MIT Press.

Danziger, K. (1990). *Constructing the subject: Historical origins of psychological research.* Cambridge, England: Cambridge University Press.

Darwin, C. (1965). *The expressions of the emotions in man and animal.* Chicago: University of Chicago Press. (Original work published 1872)

Dashiell, J. F. (1939). Some rapprochements in contemporary psychology. *Psychological Bulletin, 36,* 1–24.

Daston, L. (1980). Probabilistic expectation and rationality in classical probability theory. *Historia Mathematica, 7,* 234–260.

Daston, L. (1981). Mathematics and the moral sciences: The rise and fall of the probability of judgments, 1785–1840. In H. N. Jahnke & M. Otte (Eds.), *Epistemological and social problems of the sciences in the early nineteenth century* (pp. 287–309). Dordrecht, Holland: Reidel.

Daston, L. (1987). The domestication of risk: Mathematical probability and insurance 1650–1830. In L. Krüger, L. Daston, & M. Heidelberger (Eds.), *The probabilistic revolution*: Vol. 1. *Ideas in history* (pp. 237–260). Cambridge, MA: MIT Press.

Daston, L. (1988). *Classical probability in the Enlightenment.* Princeton, NJ: Princeton University Press.

Daston, L. (1992). The naturalized female intellect. *Science in Context, 5,* 209–235.

Daston, L. (1994). Enlightenment calculations. *Critical Inquiry, 21,* 182–202.

Dawes, R. M. (1979). The robust beauty of improper linear models. *American Psychologist, 34,* 571–582.

Dawes, R. M. (1980). Confidence in intellectual judgments vs. confidence in perceptual judgments. In E. D. Lantermann & H. Feger (Eds.), *Similarity and choice: Papers in honor of Clyde Coombs* (pp. 327–345). Bern, Switzerland: Huber.

Dawkins, R. (1976). *The selfish gene.* Oxford, England: Oxford University Press.

Dehaene, S. (1997). *The number sense: How the mind creates mathematics.* New York: Oxford University Press.

Dershowitz, A. (1996). *Reasonable doubts: The criminal justice system and the O. J. Simpson case.* New York: Simon & Schuster.

Deutscher Bundestag. (1988). *AIDS: Fakten und Konsequenzen.* Progress report of the Enquete Committee of the 11th German Bundestag, 3/88. Bonn, Germany: Bonner Universitäts Buchdruckerei.

Deutscher Bundestag. (1990). *AIDS: Fakten und Konsequenzen.* Final report of the Enquete Committee of the 11th German Bundestag, 13/90. Bonn, Germany: Bonner Universitäts Buchdruckerei.

Devereux, G. (1967). *From anxiety to method in the behavioral sciences.* Paris: Mouton.

de Waal, F. B. M., & Luttrell, L. M. (1988). Mechanisms of social reciprocity in three primate species: Symmetrical relationship characteristics or cognition? *Ethology and Sociobiology, 9,* 101–118.

Diaconis, P. (1985). Theories of data analysis: From magical thinking through classical statistics. In D. C. Hoaglin, F. Mosteller, & J. W. Tukey (Eds.), *Exploring data tables, trends and shapes* (pp. 1–36). New York: Wiley.

Dietz, K., Seydel, J., & Schwartländer, B. (1994). Back-projection of German AIDS data using information on dates of tests. *Statistics in Medicine, 13,* 1991–2008.

DiFonzo, N. (1994). Piggybacked syllogisms for investor behavior: Probabilistic mental modeling in rumor-based stock market trading. Ph.D. diss., Temple University, Philadelphia.

Doherty, M. E., & Kurz, E. M. (1996). Social judgment theory. *Thinking and Reasoning, 2,* 109–140.

Doll, L. S., & Kennedy, M. B. (1994). HIV counseling and testing: What is it and how well does it work? In G. Schochetman & J. R. George (Eds.), *AIDS testing: A comprehensive guide to technical, medical, social, legal, and management issues* (pp. 302–319). New York: Springer.

Dugatkin, L. A. (1996). Interface between culturally based preferences and genetic preferences: Female mate choice in *Poecilia Reticulata. Proceedings of the National Academy of Sciences, 93,* 2770–2773.

Duncker, K. (1945). On problem solving (Trans. T. L. S. Lees). *Psychological Monographs, 58* (5, Whole No. 270). (Original work published 1935.)

Earman, J. (1992). *Bayes or bust? A critical examination of Bayesian confirmation theory.* Cambridge, MA: MIT Press.

Eberle, J. F., Deinhardt, K. O., & Habermehl, M. A. (1988). Die Zuverlässigkeit des HIV-Antikörpertests. *Deutsches Ärzteblatt, 85,* 1512–1514.

Eddy, D. M. (1982). Probabilistic reasoning in clinical medicine: Problems and opportunities. In D. Kahneman, P. Slovic, & A. Tversky (Eds.), *Judgment under uncertainty: Heuristics and biases* (pp. 249–267). Cambridge, England: Cambridge University Press.

Edgington, E. S. (1974). A new tabulation of statistical procedures used in APA journals. *American Psychologist, 29,* 25–26.

Edwards, W. (1954). The theory of decision making. *Psychological Bulletin, 51,* 380–417.

Edwards, W. (1962). Dynamic decision theory and probabilistic information processing. *Human Factors, 4,* 59–73.

Edwards, W. (1966). *Nonconservative information processing systems.* Rep. No. 5893-22-F. Ann Arbor: University of Michigan, Institute of Science and Technology.

Edwards, W. (1968). Conservatism in human information processing. In B. Kleinmuntz (Ed.), *Formal representation of human judgment* (pp. 17–52). New York: Wiley.

Edwards, W., Lindman, H., & Savage, L. J. (1963). Bayesian statistical inference for psychological research. *Psychological Review, 70,* 193–242.

Edwards, W., & von Winterfeldt, D. (1986). On cognitive illusions and their implications. In H. R. Arkes & K. R. Hammond (Eds.), *Judgment and decision making: An interdisciplinary reader* (pp. 642–679). Cambridge, England: Cambridge University Press.

Einhorn, H. J. (1970). The use of nonlinear, noncompensatory models in decision-making. *Psychological Bulletin, 73,* 221–230.

Einhorn, H. J., & Hogarth, R. M. (1975). Unit weighting schemes for decision making. *Organizational Behavior and Human Performance, 13,* 171–192.

Einhorn, H. J., & Hogarth, R. M. (1981). Behavioral decision theory: Processes of judgment and choice. *Annual Review of Psychology, 32,* 53–88.

Elstein, A. S. (1988). Cognitive processes in clinical inference and decision making. In D. C. Turk & P. Salovey (Eds.), *Reasoning, inference and judgment in clinical psychology* (pp. 17–50). New York: Free Press.

Elster, J. (1979). *Ulysses and the sirens: Studies in rationality and irrationality.* Cambridge, England: Cambridge University Press.

Elster, J. (1990). When rationality fails. In K. S. Cook & M. Levi (Eds.), *The limits of rationality* (pp. 19–51). Chicago: University of Chicago Press.

Epstein, J. S. (1994). Regulation of HIV-related tests and procedures. In G. Schochetman & J. R. George (Eds.), *AIDS testing: A comprehensive guide to technical, medical, social, legal, and management issues* (pp. 52–61). New York: Springer.

Ericsson, K. A., & Simon, H. A. (1984). *Protocol analysis: Verbal reports as data.* Cambridge, MA: MIT Press.

Estes, W. K. (1959). The statistical approach to learning theory. In S. Koch (Ed.), *Psychology: A study of science* (Vol. 2, pp. 380–491). New York: McGraw-Hill.

Estes, W. K. (1976). The cognitive side of probability learning. *Psychological Review, 83,* 37–64.

Evans, R. B. (1990). Robert Sessions Woodworth and the "Columbia Bible": How the psychological experiment was redefined. *American Journal of Psychology, 103,* 391–401.

A false HIV test caused 18 months of hell. (1993, March 5). *Chicago Tribune.*

Fechner, G. T. (1897). *Kollektivmasslehre* [The measurement of collectives]. Leipzig, Germany: Engelmann.

Ferguson, L. (1959). *Statistical analysis in psychology and education.* New York: McGraw-Hill.

Feynman, R. (1967). *The character of physical law.* Cambridge, MA: MIT Press.

Fiedler, K. (1983). On the testability of the availability heuristic. In R. W. Scholz (Ed.), *Decision making under uncertainty* (pp. 109–119). Amsterdam: North-Holland.

Fiedler, K. (1988). The dependence of the conjunction fallacy on subtle linguistic factors. *Psychological Research, 50,* 123–129.

Fiedler, K. (1991). Heuristics and biases in theory formation. *Theory and Psychology, 1,* 407–430.

Fiedler, K. (1996). Explaining and simulating judgment biases as an aggregation phenomenon in probabilistic, multiple-cue environments. *Psychological Review, 103,* 193–214.

Fillenbaum, S. (1977). Mind your p's and q's: The role of content and context in some uses of *and, or,* and *if. Psychology of Learning and Motivation, 11,* 41–100.

Finetti, B. de (1989). Probabilism. *Erkenntnis, 31,* 169–223. (Original work published 1931)

Fischer, D. (1990). AIDS-Modellprogramm der Bundesregierung—eine Zwischenbilanz. *Öffentliches Gesundheitswesen, 52*, 425–431.

Fischhoff, B. (1977). Perceived informativeness of facts. *Journal of Experimental Psychology: Human Perception and Performance, 3*, 349–358.

Fischhoff, B. (1982). Debiasing. In D. Kahneman, P. Slovic, & A. Tversky (Eds.), *Judgment under uncertainty: Heuristics and biases* (pp. 422–444). Cambridge, England: Cambridge University Press.

Fischhoff, B. (1988). Judgment and decision making. In R. J. Sternberg & E. E. Smith (Eds.), *The psychology of human thought* (pp. 153–187). Cambridge, England: Cambridge University Press.

Fischhoff, B., & MacGregor, D. (1982). Subjective confidence in forecasts. *Journal of Forecasting, 1*, 155–172.

Fischhoff, B., Slovic, P., & Lichtenstein, S. (1977). Knowing with certainty: The appropriateness of extreme confidence. *Journal of Experimental Psychology, 3*, 552–564.

Fishburn, P. C. (1988). *Nonlinear preference and utility theory.* Baltimore: Johns Hopkins University Press.

Fishburn, P. C. (1991). Nontransitive preferences in decision theory. *Journal of Risk and Uncertainty, 4*, 113–134.

Fisher, R. A. (1922). On the mathematical foundations of theoretical statistics. *Philosophical Transactions of the Royal Society of London, A, 222*, 309–368.

Fisher, R. A. (1925). *Statistical methods for research workers.* Edinburgh, Scotland: Oliver & Boyd.

Fisher, R. A. (1933). The contributions of Rothamsted to the development of the science of statistics. *Annual Report of the Rothamsted Station*, 43–50.

Fisher, R. A. (1935). *The design of experiments.* Edinburgh, Scotland: Oliver & Boyd.

Fisher, R. A. (1955). Statistical methods and scientific induction. *Journal of the Royal Statistical Society, Series B, 17*, 69–78.

Fisher, R. A. (1956). *Statistical methods and scientific inference.* Edinburgh, Scotland: Oliver & Boyd.

Fodor, J. A. (1983). *The modularity of mind.* Cambridge, MA: MIT Press.

Fodor, J. A. (1995). The folly of simulation. In P. Baumgartner & S. Payr (Eds.), *Speaking minds: Interviews with twenty eminent cognitive scientists* (pp. 85–100). Princeton, NJ: Princeton University Press.

Fraisse, P. (1964). *The psychology of time.* London: Eyre & Spottiswoode.

Fretwell, S. D. (1972). *Populations in seasonal environments.* Princeton, NJ: Princeton University Press.

Frey, B. S. (1990). Entscheidungsanomalien: Die Sicht der Ökonomie. *Psychologische Rundschau, 41*, 67–83.

Freyd, J. J. (1983). Shareability: The social psychology of epistemology. *Cognitive Science, 7*, 191–210.

Galison, P. (1987). *How experiments end.* Chicago: University of Chicago Press.

Gallistel, C. R. (1990). *The organization of learning.* Cambridge, MA: MIT Press.

Gallistel, C. R., Brown, A. L., Carey, S., Gelman, R., & Keil, F. C. (1991). Lessons from animal learning for the study of cognitive development. In S. Carey & R. Gelman (Eds.), *The epigenesis of mind: Essays on biology and cognition* (pp. 3–36). Hillsdale, NJ: Erlbaum.

Gallistel, C. R., & Gelman, R. (1992). Preverbal and verbal counting and computation. *Cognition, 44*, 43–74.

Garcia, J., & Koelling, R. A. (1966). The relation of cue to consequence in avoidance learning. *Psychonomic Science, 4*, 123–124.

Garcia y Robertson, R., & Garcia, J. (1985). X-rays and learned taste aversions: Historical and psychological ramifications. In T. G. Burish, S. M. Levy, & B. E. Meyerowitz (Eds.), *Cancer, nutrition and eating behavior: A biobehavioral perspective* (pp. 11–41). Hillsdale, NJ: Erlbaum.

Gardner, H. (1988). Creative lives and creative works: A synthetic scientific approach. In R. J. Sternberg (Ed.), *The nature of creativity* (pp. 298–321). Cambridge, England: Cambridge University Press.

Gavanski, I., & Hui, C. (1992). Natural sample spaces and uncertain belief. *Journal of Personality and Social Psychology, 63* (5), 766–780.

Gavin, E. A. (1972). The causal issue in empirical psychology from Hume to the present with emphasis upon the work of Michotte. *Journal of the History of the Behavorial Sciences, 8*, 302–320.

Geman, S., Bienenstock, E., & Doursat, R. (1992). Neural networks and the bias/ variance dilemma. *Neural Computation, 4*, 1–58.

George, J. R., & Schochetman, G. (1994). Detection of HIV infection using serologic techniques. In G. Schochetman & J. R. George (Eds.), *AIDS testing: A comprehensive guide to technical, medical, social, legal, and management issues* (pp. 62–102). New York: Springer.

Gigerenzer, G. (1981). *Messung und Modellbildung in der Psychologie* [Measurement and modeling in psychology]. Munich: Reinhardt.

Gigerenzer, G. (1984). External validity of laboratory experiments: The frequency-validity relationship. *American Journal of Psychology, 97* (2), 185–195.

Gigerenzer, G. (1987a). Probabilistic thinking and the fight against subjectivity. In L. Krüger, G. Gigerenzer, & M. S. Morgan (Eds.), *The probabilistic revolution:* Vol. 2. *Ideas in the sciences* (pp. 11–33). Cambridge, MA: MIT Press.

Gigerenzer, G. (1987b). Survival of the fittest probabilist: Brunswik, Thurstone, and the two disciplines of psychology. In L. Krüger, G. Gigerenzer, & M. Morgan (Eds.), *The probabilistic revolution:* Vol. 2. *Ideas in the sciences* (pp. 49–72). Cambridge, MA: MIT Press.

Gigerenzer, G. (1990). Strong AI and the problem of "second-order" algorithms. *Behavioral and Brain Sciences, 13* (4), 663–664.

Gigerenzer, G. (1991a). From tools to theories: A heuristic of discovery in cognitive psychology. *Psychological Review, 98*, 254–267.

Gigerenzer, G. (1991b). How to make cognitive illusions disappear: Beyond "heuristics and biases." In W. Stroebe & M. Hewstone (Eds.), *European Review of Social Psychology, 2*, 83–115.

Gigerenzer, G. (1991c). Does the environment have the same structure as Bayes' theorem? *Behavioral and Brain Sciences, 14*, 495.

Gigerenzer, G. (1991d). On cognitive illusions and rationality. In E. Eells & T. Manuszewski (Eds.), *Reasoning and rationality: Essays in honour of L. J. Cohen* (pp. 225–249). Amsterdam: Radop.

Gigerenzer, G. (1993a). The superego, the ego, and the id in statistical reasoning. In G. Keren & G. Lewis (Eds.), *A handbook for data analysis in the behavioral sciences: Methodological issues* (pp. 311–339). Hillsdale, NJ: Erlbaum.

Gigerenzer, G. (1993b). The bounded rationality of probabilistic mental models. In K. I. Manktelow & D. E. Over (Eds.), *Rationality: Psychological and philosophical perspectives* (pp. 284–313). London: Routledge.

Gigerenzer, G. (1994a). Why the distinction between single-event probabilities and frequencies is relevant for psychology (and vice versa). In G. Wright & P. Ayton (Eds.), *Subjective probability* (pp. 129–162). New York: Wiley.

Gigerenzer, G. (1994b). Where do new ideas come from? In M. A. Boden (Ed.), *Dimensions of creativity* (pp. 53–74). Cambridge, MA: MIT Press.

Gigerenzer, G. (1995). The taming of content: Some thoughts about domains and modules. *Thinking and Reasoning, 1*, 324–333.

Gigerenzer, G. (1996a). On narrow norms and vague heuristics: A reply to Kahneman and Tversky. *Psychological Review, 103*, 592–596.

Gigerenzer, G. (1996b). The psychology of good judgment: Frequency formats and simple algorithms. *Journal of Medical Decision Making, 16*, 273–280.

Gigerenzer, G. (1996c). Rationality: Why social context matters. In P. B. Baltes, & U. M. Staudinger (Eds.), *Interactive minds: Life-span perspectives on the social foundation of cognition* (pp. 319–346). Cambridge, England: Cambridge University Press.

Gigerenzer, G. (1997). The modularity of social intelligence. In A. Whiten & R. W. Byrne (Eds.), *Machiavellian intelligence: II* (pp. 264–288). Cambridge, England: Cambridge University Press.

Gigerenzer, G. (1998a). Ecological intelligence: An adaptation for frequencies. In D. D. Cummins & C. Allen (Eds.), *The evolution of mind* (pp. 9–29). New York: Oxford University Press.

Gigerenzer, G. (1998b). Surrogates for theories. *Theory and Psychology, 8*, 195–204.

Gigerenzer, G. (1998c). Psychological challenges for normative models. In D. M. Gabbay & P. Smets (Eds.), *Handbook of defeasible reasoning and uncertainty management systems:* Vol. 1. *Quantified representation of uncertainty and imprecision* (pp. 441–467). Dordrecht: Kluwer.

Gigerenzer, G. (in press). Ideas in exile: The struggles of an upright man. In K. R. Hammond & T. R. Stewart (Eds.), *The essential Brunswik: Beginnings, explications, applications.* New York: Oxford University Press.

Gigerenzer, G., & Goldstein, D. G. (1996a). Reasoning the fast and frugal way: Models of bounded rationality. *Psychological Review, 103*, 650–669.

Gigerenzer, G., & Goldstein, D. G. (1996b). Mind as computer: Birth of a metaphor. *Creativity Research Journal, 9*, 131–144.

Gigerenzer, G., Hell, W., & Blank, H. (1988). Presentation and content: The use of base rates as a continuous variable. *Journal of Experimental Psychology: Human Perception and Performance, 14*, 513–525.

Gigerenzer, G., & Hoffrage, U. (1995). How to improve Bayesian reasoning without instruction: Frequency formats. *Psychological Review, 102*, 684–704.

Gigerenzer, G., & Hoffrage, U. (1999). Overcoming difficulties in Bayesian reasoning: A reply to Lewis & Keren and Mellers & McGraw. *Psychological Review, 106*, 425–430.

Gigerenzer, G., Hoffrage, U., & Ebert, A. (1998). AIDS counseling for low-risk clients. *AIDS Care, 10*, 197–211.

Gigerenzer, G., Hoffrage, U., & Kleinbölting, H. (1991). Probabilistic mental models: A Brunswikian theory of confidence. *Psychological Review, 98*, 506–528.

Gigerenzer, G., & Hug, K. (1992). Domain-specific reasoning: Social contracts, cheating, and perspective change. *Cognition, 43*, 127–171.

Gigerenzer, G., & Kurz, E. M. (in press). Vicarious functioning reconsidered: A fast and frugal lens model. In K. R. Hammond & T. R. Stewart (Eds.), *The essential Brunswik: Beginnings, explications, applications.* New York: Oxford University Press.

Gigerenzer, G., & Murray, D. J. (1987). *Cognition as intuitive statistics.* Hillsdale, NJ: Erlbaum.

Gigerenzer, G., & Regier, T. (1996). How do we tell an association from a rule? Comment on Sloman (1996). *Psychological Bulletin, 119*, 23–26.

Gigerenzer, G., & Richter, H. R. (1990). Context effects and their interaction with development: Area judgments. *Cognitive Development, 5*, 235–264.

Gigerenzer, G., & Selten, R. (Eds.). (2000). *Bounded rationality: The adaptive toolbox.* Cambridge, MA: MIT Press.

Gigerenzer, G., Swijtink, Z., Porter, T., Daston, L., Beatty, J., & Krüger, L. (1989). *The empire of chance: How probability changed science and everyday life.* Cambridge, England: Cambridge University Press.

Gigerenzer, G., & Todd, P. M. (1999). Fast and frugal heuristics: The adaptive toolbox. In G. Gigerenzer, P. M. Todd, & the ABC Research Group, *Simple heuristics that make us smart* (pp. 3–34). New York: Oxford University Press.

Gigerenzer, G., Todd, P. M., & the ABC Research Group (1999). *Simple heuristics that make us smart.* New York: Oxford University Press.

Gillespie, J. H. (1977). Natural selection for variances in offspring numbers: A new evolutionary principle. *American Naturalist, 111*, 1010–1014.

Gilovich, T., Vallone, R., & Tversky, A. (1985). The hot hand in basketball: On the misconception of random sequences. *Cognitive Psychology, 17*, 295–314.

Gilpin, M. E. (1975). Limit cycles in competition communities. *American Naturalist, 109*, 51–60.

Ginossar, Z., & Trope, Y. (1980). The effects of base rates and individuating information on judgments about another person. *Journal of Experimental Social Psychology, 16*, 228–242.

Ginossar, Z., & Trope, Y. (1987). Problem solving in judgment under uncertainty. *Journal of Personality and Social Psychology, 52*, 464–474.

Gleick, J. (1992). *Genius: The life and science of Richard Feynman.* New York: Pantheos.

Glück, D., Vornwald, A., Grossau, E., & Kubanek, B. (1990). HIV prevalence in blood donors in urban and rural areas of the Federal Republic of Germany. *Blut, 60*, 304–307.

Goldstein, D. G. (1994). The less-is-more effect in inference. M.A. thesis, University of Chicago.

Goldstein, D. G., & Gigerenzer, G. (1999). The recognition heuristic: How ignorance makes us smart. In G. Gigerenzer, P. M. Todd, & the ABC Research Group, *Simple heuristics that make us smart* (pp. 37–58). New York: Oxford University Press.

Good, I. J. (1971). 46656 varieties of Bayesians. *American Statistician, 25*, 62–63.

Good, I. J. (1995). When batterer turns murderer. *Nature, 375*, 541.

Gould, S. J. (1992). *Bully for brontosaurus: Further reflections in natural history.* New York: Penguin Books.

Gould, S. J., & Vrba, E. S. (1982). Exaptation—a missing term in the science of form. *Paleobiology, 8*, 4–15.

Gregory, R. L. (1974). *Concepts and mechanisms of perception.* New York: Scribner.

Grether, D. M. (1980). Bayes rule as a descriptive model: The representativeness heuristic. *Quarterly Journal of Economics, 95*, 537–557.

Grice, H. P. (1975). Logic and conversation. In P. Cole & J. L. Morgan (Eds.), *Syntax and semantics:* Vol. 3. *Speech acts* (pp. 41–58). New York: Academic Press.

Griffin, D., & Tversky, A. (1992). The weighing of evidence and the determinants of confidence. *Cognitive Psychology, 24*, 411–435.

Griggs, R. A., & Cox, J. R. (1982). The elusive thematic-materials effect in Wason's selection task. *British Journal of Psychology, 73*, 407–420.

Groner, M., Groner, R., & Bischof, W. F. (1983). Approaches to heuristics: A historical review. In R. Groner, M. Groner, & W. F. Bischof (Eds.), *Methods of heuristics* (pp. 1–18). Hillsdale, NJ: Erlbaum.

Gruber, H. E. (1977). The fortunes of a basic Darwinian idea: Chance. In R. W. Rieber & K. Salzinger (Eds.), *The roots of American psychology: Historical influences and implications for the future* (pp. 233–245). New York: New York Academy of Sciences.

Gruber, H. E. (1981). *Darwin on man: A psychological study of scientific creativity* (2nd ed.). Chicago: University of Chicago Press.

Gruber, H. E., & Vonèche, J. J. (Eds.). (1977). *The essential Piaget.* New York: Basic Books.

Guilford, J. P. (1942). *Fundamental statistics in psychology and education.* New York: McGraw-Hill.

Guilford, J. P. (1954). *Psychometric methods* (2nd ed.). New York: McGraw-Hill.

Guilford, J. P., & Hoepfner, R. (1971). *The analysis of intelligence.* New York: McGraw-Hill.

Guttman, L. (1977). What is not what in statistics. *Statistician, 26*, 81–107.

Guttman, L. (1985). The illogic of statistical inference for cumulative science. *Applied Stochastic Models and Data Analysis, 1*, 3–10.

Hacking, I. (1965). *Logic of statistical inference.* Cambridge, England: Cambridge University Press.

Hacking, I. (1975). *The emergence of probability.* Cambridge, England: Cambridge University Press.

Hacking, I. (1983). *Representing and intervening.* Cambridge, England: Cambridge University Press.

Hackmann, W. D. (1979). The relationship between concept and instrument design in eighteenth-century experimental science. *Annals of Science, 36*, 205–224.

Hager, W., & Westermann, R., (1983). Zur Wahl und Prüfung statistischer Hypothesen in psychologischen Untersuchungen. *Zeitschrift für experimentelle und angewandte Psychologie, 30*, 67–94.

Hamilton, W. D. (1964). The genetic evolution of social behavior: Parts 1 and 2. *Journal of Theoretical Biology, 7*, 1–52.

Hammerton, M. (1973). A case of radical probability estimation. *Journal of Experimental Psychology, 101*, 252–254.

Hammond, K. R. (1966). *The psychology of Egon Brunswik.* New York: Holt, Rinehart & Winston.

Hammond, K. R. (1980). Introduction to Brunswikian theory and methods. *New Directions for Methodology of Social and Behavioral Science, 3*, 1–11.

Hammond, K. R. (1990). Functionalism and illusionism: Can integration be usefully achieved? In R. M. Hogarth (Ed.), *Insights in decision making* (pp. 227–261). Chicago: University of Chicago Press.

Hammond, K. R., Hursch, C. J., & Todd, F. J. (1964). Analyzing the components of clinical inference. *Psychological Review, 71*, 438–456.

Hammond, K. R., Stewart, T. R., Brehmer, B., & Steinmann, D. O. (1975). Social judgment theory. In M. F. Kaplan & S. Schwartz (Eds.), *Human judgment and decision processes* (pp. 271–312). New York: Academic Press.

Hammond, K. R., & Summers, D. A. (1965). Cognitive dependence on linear and nonlinear cues. *Psychological Review, 72*, 215–244.

Hammond, K. R., & Wascoe, N. E. (Eds.). (1980). Realizations of Brunswik's representative design. *New Directions for Methodology of Social and Behavioral Science, 3*, 271–312.

Hansen, R. D., & Donoghue, J. M. (1977). The power of consensus: Information derived from one's own and others' behavior. *Journal of Personality and Social Psychology, 35*, 294–302.

Hanson, N. R. (1958). *Patterns of discovery*. Cambridge, England: Cambridge University Press.

Harcourt, A. H., & de Waal, F. B. M. (Eds.) (1992). *Coalitions and alliances in humans and other animals*. Oxford, England: Oxford University Press.

Harvard University Center for Cognitive Studies. (1963). *Third annual report*. Cambridge, MA: Harvard University, Center for Cognitive Studies.

Harvard University Center for Cognitive Studies. (1964). *Fourth annual report*. Cambridge, MA: Harvard University, Center for Cognitive Studies.

Harvard University Center for Cognitive Studies. (1966). *Sixth annual report*. Cambridge, MA: Harvard University, Center for Cognitive Studies.

Harvard University Center for Cognitive Studies. (1968). *Eighth annual report*. Cambridge, MA: Harvard University, Center for Cognitive Studies.

Harvard University Center for Cognitive Studies. (1969). *Ninth annual report*. Cambridge, MA: Harvard University, Center for Cognitive Studies.

Hasher, L., Goldstein, D., & Toppino, T. (1977). Frequency and the conference of referential validity. *Journal of Verbal Learning and Behavior, 16*, 107–112.

Hasher, L., & Zacks, R. T. (1979). Automatic and effortful processes in memory. *Journal of Experimental Psychology: General, 180*, 356–388.

Hasher, L., & Zacks, R. T. (1984). Automatic processing of fundamental information. *American Psychologist, 39*, 1327–1388.

Hays, W. L. (1963). *Statistics for psychologists* (2nd ed.). New York: Holt, Rinehart & Winston.

Heider, F. (1958). *The psychology of interpersonal relations*. New York: Wiley.

Heider, F., & Simmel, M. (1944). An experimental study of apparent behavior. *American Journal of Psychology, 57*, 243–259.

Herbart, J. F. (1834). *A textbook in psychology* (Trans. M. K. Smith). New York: Appleton-Century-Crofts.

Hertwig, R., & Gigerenzer, G. (1999). The "conjunction fallacy" revisited: How intelligent inferences look like reasoning errors. *Journal of Behavioral Decision Making, 12*, 275–305.

Hertwig, R., Gigerenzer, G., & Hoffrage, U. (1997). The reiteration effect in hindsight bias. *Psychological Review, 104*, 194–202.

Hertwig, R., Hoffrage, U., & Martignon, L. (1999). Quick estimation: Letting the environment do the work. In G. Gigerenzer, P. M. Todd, & the ABC Group, *Simple heuristics that make us smart* (pp. 209–234). New York: Oxford University Press.

Hilgard, E. R. (1955). Discussion of probabilistic functionalism. *Psychological Review, 62,* 226–228.

Hilton, D. J. (1995). The social context of reasoning: Conversational inference and rational judgment. *Psychological Bulletin, 118,* 248–271.

Hintzman, D. L., & Block, R. A. (1972). Repetition and memory: Evidence for multiple trace hypothesis. *Journal of Experimental Psychology, 88,* 297–306.

Hintzman, D. L., Nozawa, G., & Irmscher, M. (1982). Frequency as a nonpropositional attribute of memory. *Journal of Verbal Learning and Verbal Behavior, 21,* 127–141.

Hirschfeld, L. A., & Gelman, S. A. (Eds.). (1994a). *Mapping the mind: Domain specificity in cognition and culture.* Cambridge, England: Cambridge University Press.

Hirschfeld, L. A., & Gelman, S. A. (1994b). Toward a topography of mind: An introduction to domain specificity. In L. A. Hirschfeld & S. A. Gelman (Eds.), *Mapping the mind: Domain specificity in cognition and culture* (pp. 3–35). Cambridge, England: Cambridge University Press.

Hoffman-Valentin, F. (1991). *AIDS: Gefahren, Schutz, Vorsorge, Behandlungsmöglichkeiten.* Landsberg, Germany: Ecomed.

Hoffrage, U. (1994). Zur Angemessenheit subjektiver Sicherheits-Urteile: Eine Exploration der Theorie der probabilistischen mentalen Modelle [On the validity of confidence judgments: A study of the theory of probabilistic mental models]. Ph.D. diss., University of Salzburg.

Hoffrage, U., & Gigerenzer, G. (1996). The impact of information representation on Bayesian reasoning. In G. Cottrell (Ed.), *Proceedings of the Eighteenth Annual Conference of the Cognitive Science Society* (pp. 126–130). Mahwah, NJ: Erlbaum.

Hoffrage, U., & Gigerenzer, G. (1998). Using natural frequencies to improve diagnostic inferences. *Academic Medicine, 73,* 538–540.

Hoffrage, U., & Hertwig, R. (1999). Hindsight bias: A price worth paying for fast and frugal memory. In G. Gigerenzer, P. M. Todd, & the ABC Group. *Simple heuristics that make us smart* (pp. 191–208). New York: Oxford University Press.

Hofstätter, P. R. (1939). Über die Schätzung von Gruppeneigenschaften. *Zeitschrift für Psychologie, 145,* 1–44.

Holland, J. H., Holyoak, K. J., Nisbett, R. E., & Thagard, P. R. (1986). *Induction: Processes of inference, learning and discovery.* Cambridge, MA: MIT Press.

Holton, G. (1988). *Thematic origins of scientific thought* (2nd ed.). Cambridge, MA: Harvard University Press.

Howell, W. C., & Burnett, S. (1978). Uncertainty measurement: A cognitive taxonomy. *Organizational Behavior and Human Performance, 22,* 45–68.

Huber, O. (1989). Information-processing operators in decision making. In H. Montgomery & O. Svenson (Eds.), *Process and structure in human decision making* (pp. 3–21). New York: Wiley.

Hull, C. L. (1943). The uniformity point of view. *Psychological Review, 50,* 203–216.

Humphrey, G. (1951). *Thinking*. New York: Wiley.

Humphrey, N. K. (1988). The social function of intellect. In R. Byrne & A. Whiten (Eds.), *Machiavellian intelligence* (pp. 13–26). Oxford, England: Clarendon Press. (Original work published 1976)

Hutchins, E. (1995). *Cognition in the wild*. Cambridge, MA: MIT Press.

Huttenlocher, J., Hedges, L., & Prohaska, V. (1988). Hierarchical organization in ordered domains: Estimating the dates of events. *Psychological Review, 95*, 471–484.

Inhelder, B., & Piaget, J. (1969). *The early growth of logic in the child*. New York: Norton Library.

Jeffrey, R. (1989). Reading Probabilismo. *Erkenntnis, 31*, 225–237.

John Paul II (1997). The pope's message on evolution and four commentaries. *Quarterly Review of Biology, 72*, 381–406.

Johnson-Laird, P. N. (1983). *Mental models*. Cambridge, England: Cambridge University Press.

Johnstone, D. J. (1987). Tests of significance following R. A. Fisher. *British Journal of the Philosophy of Science, 38*, 481–499.

Jones, E. E., & McGillis, D. (1976). Correspondent inferences and the attribution cube: A comparative reappraisal. In J. H. Harvey, W. J. Ickes, & R. F. Kidd (Eds.), *New directions in attribution research*, Vol. 1 (pp. 389–420). Hillsdale, NJ:Erlbaum.

Jonides, J., & Jones, C. M. (1992). Direct coding for frequency of occurrence. *Journal of Experimental Psychology: Learning, Memory, and Cognition, 18*, 368–378.

Jungermann, H. (1983). The two camps on rationality. In R. W. Scholz (Ed.), *Decision making under uncertainty* (pp. 63–86). Amsterdam: Elsevier.

Juslin, P. (1993). An explanation of the hard-easy effect in studies of realism of confidence in one's general knowledge. *European Journal of Cognitive Psychology, 5*, 55–71.

Juslin, P. (1994). The overconfidence phenomenon as a consequence of informal experimenter-guided selection of almanac items. *Organizational Behavior and Human Decision Processes, 57*, 226–246.

Juslin, P., Olsson, H., & Winman, A. (1998). The calibration issue: Theoretical comments on Suantak, Bolger, and Ferrell (1996). *Organizational Behavior and Human Decision Processes, 73*, 3–26.

Juslin, P., Winman, A., & Persson, T. (1995). Can overconfidence be used as an indicator of reconstructive rather than retrieval processes? *Cognition, 54*, 99–130.

Juslin, P., Winman, A., & Olsson, H. (2000). Naïve empiricism and dogmatism in confidence research: A critical examination of the hard-easy effect. *Psychological Review, 107*, 384–396.

Kadane, J. B., & Lichtenstein, S. (1982). *A subjectivist view of calibration*. Decision Research Rep. No. 82–6. Eugene, OR: Decision Research.

Kahneman, D., & Tversky, A. (1972). Subjective probability: A judgment of representativeness. *Cognitive Psychology, 3*, 430–454.

Kahneman, D., & Tversky, A. (1973). On the psychology of prediction. *Psychological Review, 80*, 237–251.

Kahneman, D., & Tversky, A. (1982). On the study of statistical intuitions. In D. Kahneman, P. Slovic, & A. Tversky (Eds.), *Judgment under uncertainty:*

Heuristics and biases (pp. 493–508). Cambridge, England: Cambridge University Press.

Kahneman, D., & Tversky, A. (1996). On the reality of cognitive illusions. *Psychological Review, 103*, 582–591.

Keeney, R. L., & Raiffa, H. (1993). *Decisions with multiple objectives.* Cambridge, England: Cambridge University Press.

Kelley, H. H. (1967). Attribution theory in social psychology. In D. Levine (Ed.), *Nebraska symposium on motivation* (Vol. 15, pp. 192–238). Lincoln: University of Nebraska Press.

Kelley, H. H., & Michaela, I. L. (1980). Attribution theory and research. *Annual Review of Psychology, 31*, 457–501.

Kendall, M. G. (1942). On the future of statistics. *Journal of the Royal Statistical Society, 105*, 69–80.

Kendall, M. G. (1943). *The advanced theory of statistics* (Vol. 1). New York: Lippincott.

Kendall, M. G. (1949). On the reconciliation of theories of probability. *Biometrika, 36*, 101–116.

Keren, G. (1987). Facing uncertainty in the game of bridge: A calibration study. *Organizational Behavior and Human Decision Processes, 39*, 98–114.

Keren, G. (1988). On the ability of monitoring non-veridical preceptions and uncertain knowledge: Some calibration studies. *Acta Psychologica, 67*, 95–119.

Kita, S. (1993). *Language and thought interface: A study of spontaneous gestures and Japanese mimetics.* Ph.D. diss., University of Chicago.

Klayman, J., & Ha, Y. (1987). Confirmation, disconfirmation, and information in hypothesis testing. *Psychological Review, 94*, 211–228.

Klayman, J., Soll, J., Gonzalez-Vallejo, C., & Barlas, S. (1999). Overconfidence? It depends on how, what, and whom you ask. *Organizational Behavior and Human Decision Processes, 79*, 216–247.

Kleiter, G. D. (1994). Natural sampling: Rationality without base rates. In G. H. Fischer & D. Laming (Eds.), *Contributions to mathematical psychology, psychometrics, and methodology* (pp. 375–388). New York: Springer.

Klix, F. (1993). *Erwachendes Denken: Geistige Leistung aus evolutionspsychologischer Sicht* [Thought coming to life: Cognitive performance from an evolutionary psychological perspective]. Heidelberg, Germany: Spektrum.

Koehler, J. J. (1992). Probabilities in the courtroom: An evaluation of the objections and policies. In D. K. Kagehiro & W. S. Laufer (Eds.), *Handbook of psychology and law* (pp. 167–184). New York: Springer.

Koehler, J. J. (1996). The base rate fallacy reconsidered: Descriptive, normative and methodological challenges. *Behavioral and Brain Sciences, 19*, 1–53.

Koriat, A., Lichtenstein, S., & Fischhoff, B. (1980). Reasons for confidence. *Journal of Experimental Psychology: Human Learning and Memory, 6*, 107–118.

Kosslyn, S. M., & Pomerantz, J. R. (1977). Imagery, propositions, and the form of internal representations. *Cognitive Psychology, 9*, 52–76.

Krantz, D. H., Luce, R. D., Suppes, P., & Tversky, A. (1971). *Foundations of measurement* (Vol. 1). New York: Academic Press.

Krauss, S., Martignon, L., & Hoffrage, U. (1999). Simplifying Bayesian inference: The general case. In L. Magnani, N. Nersessian, & N. Thagard (Eds.),

Model-based reasoning in scientific discovery (Vol. 1, pp. 165–179). New York: Academic Press.

Krebs, J. R., & Davies, N. B. (1987). *An introduction to behavioral ecology* (2nd ed.). Oxford, England: Blackwell.

Krech, D. (1955). Discussion: Theory and reductionism. *Psychological Review, 62*, 229–231.

Kroznick, J. A., Li, F., & Lehman, D. R. (1990). Conversational conventions, order of information acquisition, and the effect of base rates and individuating information on judgments. *Journal of Personality and Social Psychology, 59*, 1140–1152.

Krüger, L., Daston, L., & Heidelberger, M. (Eds.) (1987). *The probabilistic revolution*: Vol. 1. *Ideas in history*. Cambridge, MA: MIT Press.

Krüger, L., Gigerenzer, G., & Morgan, M. S. (Eds.). (1987). *The probabilistic revolution*: Vol. 2. *Ideas in the sciences*. Cambridge, MA.: MIT Press.

Kuhn, T. (1970). *The structure of scientific revolutions* (2nd ed.). Chicago: University of Chicago Press.

Kummer, H. (1988). Tripartite relations in hamadryas baboons. In R. Byrne & A. Whiten (Eds.), *Machiavellian intelligence: Social expertise and the evolution of intellect in monkeys, apes and humans* (pp. 113–121). Oxford, England: Clarendon Press.

Kummer, H., Daston, L., Gigerenzer, G., & Silk, J. (1997). The social intelligence hypothesis. In P. Weingart, P. Richerson, S. D. Mitchell, & S. Maasen (Eds.), *Human by nature: Between biology and the social sciences* (pp. 157–179). Hillsdale, NJ: Erlbaum.

Kyburg, H. E. (1983). Rational belief. *Behavioral and Brain Sciences, 6*, 231–273.

Landman, J., & Manis, M. (1983). Social cognition: Some historical and theoretical perspectives. *Advances in Experimental Social Psychology, 16*, 49–123.

Langley, P., Simon, H. A., Bradshaw, G. L., & Zytkow, J. M. (1987). *Scientific discovery*. Cambridge, MA: MIT Press.

Laplace, P.-S. (1951). *A philosophical essay on probabilities* (Trans. F. W. Truscott & F. L. Emory). New York: Dover. (Original work published 1814)

Larkin, J., & Simon, H. (1987). Why a diagram is (sometimes) worth ten thousand words. *Cognitive Science, 11*, 65–99.

Leary, D. E. (1987). From act psychology to probabilistic functionalism: The place of Egon Brunswik in the history of psychology. In M. G. Ash & W. R. Woodward (Eds.), *Psychology in twentieth-century thought and society* (pp. 115–142). Cambridge, England: Cambridge University Press.

Legendre, G., Raymond, W., & Smolensky, P. (1993). Analytic typology of case marking and grammatical voice. *Proceedings of the Berkeley Linguistics Society, 19*, 464–478.

Legrenzi, P., & Murino, M. (1974). Falsification at the pre-operational level. *Italian Journal of Psychology, 1*, 363–368.

Leibniz, G. W. (1951). The horizon of human doctrine. In P. P. Wiener (Ed.), *Selections* (pp. 73–77). New York: Scribner's. (Original work published 1690)

Leibniz, G. W. (1951). Toward a universal characteristic. In P. P. Wiener (Ed.), *Selections* (pp. 17–25). New York: Scribner's. (Original work published 1677)

Lenoir, T. (1986). Models and instruments in the development of electrophysiology, 1845–1912. *Historical Studies in the Physical and Biological Sciences, 17,* 1–54.

Lenoir, T. (1988). Practice, reason, context: The dialogue between theory and experiment. *Science in Context, 2,* 3–22.

Leslie, A. (1994). ToMM, ToBY, and agency: Core architecture and domain specificity. In L. A. Hirschfeld & S. A. Gelman (Eds.), *Mapping the mind: Domain specificity in cognition and culture* (pp. 119–148). Cambridge, England: Cambridge University Press.

Levelt, W. J. M. (1989). *Speaking: From intention to articulation.* Cambridge, MA: MIT Press.

Levi, I. (1983). Who commits the base rate fallacy? *Behavioral and Brain Sciences, 6,* 502–506.

Levinson, S. (1992). How to think in order to speak Tzeltal. Unpublished manuscript, Max Planck Institute for Psycholinguistics, Cognitive Anthropology Group, Nijmegen, Holland.

Lewontin, R. C. (1968). Evolution of complex genetic systems. In M. Gerstenhaber (Ed.), *Some mathematical questions in biology* (pp. 62–87). Providence, RI: American Mathematical Society.

Lichtenstein, S., & Fischhoff, B. (1977). Do those who know more also know more about how much they know? The calibration of probability judgments. *Organizational Behavior and Human Performance, 20,* 159–183.

Lichtenstein, S., & Fischhoff, B. (1981). *The effects of gender and instruction on calibration.* Tech. Rep. No. PTR-1092-81-7. Eugene, OR: Decision Research.

Lichtenstein, S., Fischhoff, B., & Phillips, L. D. (1982). Calibration of probabilities: The state of the art to 1980. In D. Kahneman, P. Slovic, & A. Tversky (Eds.), *Judgment under uncertainty: Heuristics and biases* (pp. 306–334). Cambridge, England: Cambridge University Press.

Light, P., Girotto, V., & Legrenzi, P. (1990). Children's reasoning on conditional promises and permissions. *Cognitive Development, 5,* 369–383.

Lindquist, E. F. (1940). *Statistical analysis in educational research.* Boston: Houghton Mifflin.

Little, I. M. D. (1949). A reformulation of the theory of consumers' behavior. *Oxford Economic Papers, 1,* 90–99.

Locke, J. (1959). *An essay concerning human understanding* (A. C. Fraser, Ed.). New York: Dover. (Original work published 1690)

Loftus, G. R. (1991). On the tyranny of hypothesis testing in the social sciences. *Contemporary Psychology, 36,* 102–104.

Lopes, L. L. (1981). Decision making in the short run. *Journal of Experimental Psychology: Human Learning and Memory, 7,* 377–385.

Lopes, L. L. (1982). Doing the impossible: A note on induction and the experience of randomness. *Journal of Experimental Psychology: Learning, Memory, and Cognition, 8,* 626–636.

Lopes, L. L. (1991). The rhetoric of irrationality. *Theory and Psychology, 1,* 65–82.

Lopes, L. L. (1992). Three misleading assumptions in the customary rethoric of the bias literature. *Theory and Psychology, 2,* 231–236.

Lopes, L. L. (1994). Psychology and economics: Perspectives on risk, cooperation, and the marketplace. *Annual Review of Psychology, 45,* 197–227.

Lopes, L. L. (1995). Algebra and process in the modeling of risky choice. In J. R. Busemeyer, R. Hastie, & D. Medin (Eds.), *Decision making from the perspec-*

tive of cognitive psychology (pp. 177–220). New York: Academic Press.

Lovie, A. D. (1979). The analysis of variance in experimental psychology: 1934–1945. *British Journal of Mathematical and Statistical Psychology, 32,* 151–178.

Lovie, A. D. (1983). Attention and behaviorism—fact and fiction. *British Journal of Psychology, 74,* 301–310.

Lovie, A. D., & Lovie, P. (1986). The flat maximum effect and linear scoring models for prediction. *Journal of Forecasting, 5,* 159–168.

Lubek, I., & Apfelbaum, E. (1987). Neo-behaviorism and the Garcia effect: A social psychology of science approach to the history of a paradigm clash. In M. Ash & W. Woodward (Eds.), *Psychology in twentieth-century thought and society* (pp. 59–92). Cambridge, England: Cambridge University Press.

Luce, R. D. (1977). Thurstone's discriminal processes fifty years later. *Psychometrika, 42,* 461–489.

Luce, R. D. (1988). The tools-to-theory hypothesis. Review of the book *Cognition as intuitive statistics. Contemporary Psychology, 33,* 582–583.

Luce, R. D. (1989). Autobiography. In G. Lindzey (Ed.), *Psychology in autobiography* (Vol. 8, pp. 245–289). Stanford, CA: Stanford University Press.

Luchins, A. S., & Luchins, E. H. (1994). The water jar experiments and Einstellung effects: I. Early history and surveys of textbook citations. *Gestalt Theory, 16,* 101–121.

Lykken, D. T. (1968). Statistical significance in psychological research. *Psychological Bulletin, 70,* 151–159.

Lyon, D., & Slovic, P. (1976). Dominance of accuracy information and neglect of base rates in probability estimation. *Acta Psychologica, 40,* 287–298.

MacGregor, D., & Slovic, P. (1986). Perceived acceptability of risk analysis as a decision-making approach. *Risk Analysis, 6,* 245–256.

Manktelow, K. I., & Evans, J. St. B. T. (1979). Facilitation of reasoning by realism: Effect or non-effect? *British Journal of Psychology, 70,* 477–488.

Månsson, S. A. (1990). Psycho-social aspects of HIV testing—the Swedish case. *AIDS Care, 2,* 5–16.

Marr, D. (1982). *Vision: A computational investigation into the human representation and processing of visual information.* San Francisco: Freeman.

Martignon, L., & Hoffrage, U. (1999). Why does one-reason decision making work? A case study in ecological rationality. In G. Gigerenzer, P. M. Todd, & the ABC Research Group, *Simple heuristics that make us smart* (pp. 119–140). New York: Oxford University Press.

Martignon, L., & Laskey, K. B. (1999). Bayesian benchmarks for fast and frugal heuristics. In G. Gigerenzer, P. M. Todd, & the ABC Research Group, *Simple heuristics that make us smart* (pp. 169–188). New York: Oxford University Press.

Marzuk, P. M., & Perry, S. W. (1993). Suicide and HIV: Researchers and clinicians beware. *AIDS Care, 5,* 387–390.

Massaro, D. W. (1987). *Speech perception by ear and eye.* Hillsdale, NJ: Erlbaum.

Massaro, D. W. (1988). Some criticisms of connectionist models of human performance. *Journal of Memory and Language, 27,* 213–234.

Massaro, D. W. (1998). *Perceiving talking faces.* Boston: MIT Press.

Maurer, C., Kiehl, W., & Altmann, D. (1993). Zur Prävalenz und HIV-Inzidenz bei Blutspendern in Baden-Württemberg. In V. Kretschmer, W. Stangel, &

R. Eckstein (Eds.), *Transfusionsmedizin 1992/93. Beitrag der Infusions-therapie, 31* (pp. 5–9). Freiburg, Germany: Karger.

May, R. S. (1986). Overconfidence as a result of incomplete and wrong knowledge. In R. W. Scholz (Ed.), *Current issues in West German decision research* (pp. 13–30). Frankfurt am Main, Germany: Lang.

May, R. S. (1987). *Realismus von subjektiven Wahrscheinlichkeiten: Eine kognitionspsychologische Analyse inferentieller Prozesse beim Over-confidence-Phänomen* [Calibration of subjective probabilities: A cognitive analysis of inference processes in overconfidence]. Frankfurt am Main, Germany: Lang.

Mayseless, O., & Kruglanski, A. W. (1987). What makes you so sure? Effects of epistemic motivations on judgmental confidence. *Organizational Behavior and Human Decision Processes, 39*, 162–183.

McArthur, L. A. (1972). The how and what of why: Some determinants and consequences of causal attribution. *Journal of Personality and Social Psychology, 22*, 171–193.

McClelland, A. G. R., & Bolger, F. (1994). The calibration of subjective probabilities: Theories and models 1980–1994. In G. Wright & P. Ayton (Eds.), *Subjective probability* (pp. 453–482). Chichester, England: Wiley.

McClennen, E. F. (1990). *Rationality and dynamic choice.* Cambridge, England: Cambridge University Press.

McCloskey, D. N. (1985). *The rhetoric of economics.* Madison: University of Wisconsin Press.

McCorduck, P. (1979). *Machines who think.* San Francisco: Freeman.

McCulloch, W. S. (1965). *Embodiments of mind.* Cambridge, MA: MIT Press.

McCulloch, W. S., & Pitts, W. (1943). A logical calculus of the ideas immanent in nervous activity. *Bulletin of Mathematical Biophysics, 5*, 115–133.

McKenzie, C. R. (1994). The accuracy of intuitive judgment strategies: Covariation assessment and Bayesian inference. *Cognitive Psychology, 26*, 209–239.

Medin, D. L., Wattenmaker, W. D., & Michalski, R. S. (1987). Constraints and preferences in inductive learning: An experimental study of human and machine performance. *Cognitive Science, 11*, 299–339.

Meehl, P. E. (1978). Theoretical risks and tabular asterisks: Sir Karl, Sir Ronald, and the slow progress of soft psychology. *Journal of Consulting and Clinical Psychology, 46*, 806–834.

Melton, A. W. (1962). [Editorial]. *Journal of Experimental Psychology, 64*, 553–557.

Michotte, A. (1963). *The perception of causality.* London: Methuen. (Original work published 1946)

Miller, G. A., & Buckhout, R. (1973). *Psychology: The science of mental life.* New York: Harper & Row.

Miller, G. A., Galanter, E., & Pribram, K. H. (1960). *Plans and the structure of behavior.* New York: Holt, Rinehart & Winston.

Miller, G. F., & Todd, P. M. (1995). The role of mate choice in biocomputation: Sexual selection as a process of search, optimization, and diversification. In W. Banzhaf & F. H. Eeckman (Eds.), *Evolution and biocomputation: Computational models of evolution* (pp. 169–204). Berlin: Springer.

Miller, G. F., & Todd, P. M. (1998). Mate choice turns cognitive. *Trends in Cognitive Sciences, 2*, 190–198.

Millikan, R. (1984). *Language, thought, and other biological categories*. Cambridge, MA: MIT Press.

Mineka, S., & Cook, M. (1988). Social learning and the acquisition of snake fear in monkeys. In T. R. Zentall & B. G. Galef (Eds.), *Social learning: Psychological and biological perspectives* (pp. 51–73). Hillsdale, NJ: Erlbaum.

Mises, R. von (1957). *Probability, statistics, and truth*. London: Allen & Unwin. (Original work published 1928)

Mitchell, S. D., Daston, L., Gigerenzer, G., Sesardic, N., & Sloep, P. (1997). In the service of pluralism and interdisciplinarity. In P. Weingart, P. Richerson, S. D. Mitchell, & S. Maasen (Eds.), *Human by nature: Between biology and the social sciences* (pp. 103–150). Hillsdale, NJ: Erlbaum.

Morrison, D. E., & Henkel, R. E. (Eds.). (1970). *The significance test controversy*. Chicago: Aldine.

Mueser, P. R., Cowan, N., & Mueser, K. T. (1999). A generalized signal detection model to predict rational variation in base rate use. *Cognition, 69*, 267–312.

Murdock, B. B., Jr. (1982). A theory for the storage and retrieval of item and associative information. *Psychological Review, 89*, 609–626.

Nesse, R. M., & Williams, G. C. (1995). *Why we get sick: The new science of Darwinian medicine*. New York: Vintage Books.

Neumann, J. von (1958). *The computer and the brain*. New Haven, CT: Yale University Press.

Newcombe, R. D., & Rutter, D. R. (1982). Ten reasons why ANOVA theory and research fail to explain attribution processes: I. Conceptual problems. *Current Psychological Reviews, 2*, 95–108.

Newell, A. (1973). You can't play 20 questions with nature and win: Projective comments on the papers of this symposium. In W. G. Chase (Ed.), *Visual information processing* (pp. 283–308). New York: Academic Press.

Newell, A., Shaw, J. C., & Simon, H. A. (1958). Elements of a theory of human problem solving. *Psychological Review, 65*, 151–166.

Newell, A., & Simon, H. A. (1972). *Human problem solving*. Englewood Cliffs, NJ: Prentice-Hall.

Neyman, J. (1937). Outline of a theory of statistical estimation based on the classical theory of probability. *Philosophical Transactions ot the Royal Society of London, Series A, 236*, 333–380.

Neyman, J. (1950). *First course in probability and statistics*. New York: Holt.

Neyman, J. (1957). Inductive behavior as a basic concept of philosophy of science. *International Statistical Review, 25*, 7–22.

Neyman, J. (1977). Frequentist probability and frequentist statistics. *Synthese, 36*, 97–131.

Neyman, J., & Pearson, E. S. (1928). On the use and interpretation of certain test criteria for purposes of statistical inference: Part 1. *Biometrika, 20A*, 175–240.

Nickles, T. (1980). Introductory essay: Scientific discovery and the future of philosophy of science. In T. Nickles (Ed.), *Scientific discovery, logic, and rationality* (pp. 1–59). Dordrecht, Holland: Reidel.

Nisbett, R. E., & Borgida, E. (1975). Attribution and the psychology of prediction. *Journal of Personality and Social Psychology, 32*, 932–943.

Nisbett, R. E., & Ross, L. (1980). *Human inference: Strategies and shortcomings of social judgment*. Englewood Cliffs, NJ: Prentice Hall.

Nisbett, R. E., & Wilson, T. D. (1977). Telling more than we can know: Verbal reports on mental processes. *Psychological Review, 84,* 231–259.

Nunnally, J. C. (1975). *Introduction to statistics for psychology and education.* New York: McGraw-Hill.

Oakes, M. (1986). *Statistical inference: A commentary for the social and the behavioral sciences.* Chichester, England: Wiley.

Oaksford, M., & Chater, N. (1994). A rational analysis of the selection task as optimal data selection. *Psychological Review, 101,* 608–631.

Over, D. E., & Manktelow, K. I. (1993). Rationality, utility and deontic reasoning. In K. I. Manktelow & D. E. Over (Eds.), *Rationality: Psychological and philosophical perspectives* (pp. 231–259). London: Routledge.

Packer, C. (1977). Reciprocal altruism in Papio annubis. *Nature, 265,* 441–443.

Parducci, A. (1965). Category judgment: A range-frequency model. *Psychological Review, 72,* 407–418.

Paulos, J. A. (1988). *Innumeracy: Mathematical illiteracy and its consequences.* New York: Vintage Books.

Payne, J. W., Bettman, J. R., & Johnson, E. J. (1993). *The adaptive decision maker.* New York: Cambridge University Press.

Pearson, E. S. (1939). "Student" as statistician. *Biometrika, 30,* 210–250.

Pearson, E. S. (1962). Some thoughts on statistical inference. *Annals of Mathematical Statistics, 33,* 394–403.

Peichl-Hoffman, G. (1991). Spezifitätsprobleme bei der Testung auf Anti-HIV1 bzw. Anti-HIV2 in der Routineuntersuchung von Blutspendern. *Klinisches Labor, 37,* 320–328.

Peirce, C. S., & Jastrow, J. (1884). On small differences of sensation. *Memoirs of the National Academy of Sciences, 3,* 75–83.

Peterson, C. R., DuCharme, W. M., & Edwards, W. (1968). Sampling distributions and probability revision. *Journal of Experimental Psychology, 76,* 236–243.

Phelps, R. H., & Shanteau, J. (1978). Livestock judges: How much information can an expert use? *Organizational Behavior and Human Performance, 21,* 209–219.

Phillips, L. D., & Edwards, W. (1966). Conservatism in a simple probability model inference task. *Journal of Experimental Psychology, 72,* 346–354.

Piaget, J. (1930). *The child's conception of causality.* London: Kegan Paul, Trench, & Trubner.

Piaget, J., & Inhelder, B. (1975). *The origin of the idea of chance in children.* New York: Norton. (Original work published 1951)

Piattelli-Palmarini, M. (1991, March/April). Probability blindness: Neither rational nor capricious. *Bostonia,* 28–35.

Piattelli-Palmarini, M. (1994). *Inevitable illusions: How mistakes of reason rule our minds.* New York: Wiley.

Pinker, S. (1994). *The language instinct.* London: Penguin Press.

Platt, R., & Griggs, R. (1993). Darwinian algorithms and the Wason selection task: A factorial analysis of social contract selection task problems. *Cognition, 48,* 163–192.

Politzer, G., & Nguyen-Xuan, A. (1992). Reasoning about promises and warnings: Darwinian algorithms, mental models, relevance judgments or pragmatic schemas? *Quarterly Journal of Experimental Psychology, 44A,* 402–421.

Pollard, P. (1982). Human reasoning: Some possible effects of availability. *Cognition, 12*, 65–96.

Pollard, P., & Evans, J. St. B. T. (1983). The role of "representativeness" in statistical inference: A critical appraisal. In J. St. B. T. Evans (Ed.), *Thinking and reasoning: Psychological approaches* (pp. 107–134). London: Routledge & Kegan Paul.

Pollard, P., & Richardson, J. T. E. (1987). On the probability of making Type I errors. *Psychological Bulletin, 102*, 159–163.

Popper, K. R. (1959). *The logic of scientific discovery.* New York: Basic Books. (Original work published 1935)

Porter, T. (1986). *The rise of statistical thinking, 1820–1900.* Princeton, NJ: Princeton University Press.

Premack, D. (1990). The infant's theory of self-propelled objects. *Cognition, 36*, 1–16.

Premack, D., & Premack, A. J. (1994). Moral belief: Form versus content. In L. A. Hirschfeld & S. A. Gelman (Eds.), *Mapping the mind: Domain specificity in cognition and culture* (pp. 149–168). Cambridge, England: Cambridge University Press.

Prince, A., & Smolensky, P. (1991). *Notes on connectionism and harmony theory in linguistics.* Tech. Rep. No. CU-CS-533-91. Boulder: University of Colorado, Department of Computer Science.

Pugh, K., O'Donnell, I., & Catalan, J. (1993). Suicide and HIV disease. *AIDS Care, 5*, 391–400.

Pylyshyn, Z. W. (1973). What the mind's eye tells the mind's brain: A critique of mental imagery. *Psychological Bulletin, 80*, 1–24.

Quetelet, L.A.J. (1969). *A treatise on man and the development of his faculties* (Trans. R. Knox). Gainesville, FL: Scholars' Facsimiles and Reprints. (Original work published 1842)

Regier, T. (1996). *The human semantic potential: Spatial language and constrained connectionism.* Cambridge, MA: MIT Press.

Reichenbach, H. (1938). *Experience and prediction.* Chicago: University of Chicago Press.

Rieskamp, J., & Hoffrage, U. (1999). When do people use simple heuristics and how can we tell? In G. Gigerenzer, P. M. Todd, & the ABC Research Group, *Simple heuristics that make us smart* (pp. 141–167). New York: Oxford University Press.

Ronis, D. L., & Yates, J. F. (1987). Components of probability judgment accuracy: Individual consistency and effects of subject matter and assessment method. *Organizational Behavior and Human Decision Processes, 40*, 193–218.

Rosch, E. (1978). Principles of categorization. In E. Rosch & B. B. Lloyd (Eds.), *Cognition and categorization* (pp. 27–48). Hillsdale, NJ: Erlbaum.

Rosnow, R. L., & Rosenthal, R. (1989). Statistical procedures and the justification of knowledge in psychological science. *American Psychologist, 44*, 1276–1284.

Rouanet, H. (1961). Études de décisions expérimentales et calcul de probabilités [Studies of experimental decision making and the probability calculus]. In *Colloques Internationaux du Centre National de la Recherche Scientifique* (pp. 33–43). Paris: Éditions du Centre National de la Recherche Scientifique.

Rozeboom, W. W. (1960). The fallacy of the null hypothesis significance test. *Psychological Bulletin, 57*, 416–428.

Rucci, A. J., & Tweney, R. D. (1980). Analysis of variance and the "second discipline" of scientific psychology: A historical account. *Psychological Bulletin, 87*, 166–184.

Sahlin, N. (1991). Baconian inductivism in research on human decision-making. *Theory and Psychology, 1*, 431–450.

Sahlin, N. (1993). On higher order beliefs. In J. Dubucs (Ed.), *Philosophy of probability* (pp. 13–34). Dordrecht, Holland: Kluwer.

Saks, M., & Kidd, R. F. (1980). Human information processing and adjudication: Trial by heuristics. *Law and Society Review, 15*, 123–160.

Samuels, R., Stich, S., & Bishop, M. (in press). Ending the rationality wars: How to make disputes about human rationality disappear. In R. Elio (Ed.), *Vancouver studies in cognitive science*: Vol. 11. *Common sense, reasoning and rationality*. New York: Oxford University Press.

Samuelson, P. A. (1938). A note on the pure theory of consumers' behavior. *Economica, 5*, 61–71.

Savage, L. J. (1954). *The foundations of statistics*. New York: Wiley.

Schaefer, R. E. (1976). The evaluation of individual and aggregated subjective probability distributions. *Organizational Behavior and Human Performance, 17*, 199–210.

Schaffer, S. (1992). *Disappearing acts: On Gigerenzer's "Where do new ideas come from?"* Unpublished manuscript.

Schaffer, S. (1994). Babbage's intelligence: Calculating engines and the factory system. *Critical Inquiry, 21*, 203–227.

Schering AG (1992). *AIDS Information*. Berlin: Schering AG.

Scholz, R. W. (Ed.) (1983). *Decision making under uncertainty*. Amsterdam: North-Holland.

Scholz, R. W. (1987). *Cognitive strategies in stochastic thinking*. Dordrecht, Holland: Reidel.

Schönemann, P. H. (1983). Some theory and results for metrics for bounded response scales. *Journal of Mathematical Psychology, 72*, 407–418.

Schrage, G. (n. d.). Schwierigkeiten mit der stochastischen Modellbildung—zwei Beispiele aus der Praxis. [Problems with stochastic models—two examples from real life]. Unpublished manuscript.

Schum, D. A. (1994). *The evidential foundations of probabilistic reasoning*. New York: Wiley.

Schwartz, S., & Dangleish, L. (1982). Statistical inference in personality research. *Journal of Research in Personality, 16*, 290–302.

Schwartz, S., Kinosian, B. P., Pieskalla, W. P., & Lee, H. (1990). Strategies for screening blood for human immunodeficiency virus antibody: Use of a decision support system. *Journal of the American Medical Association, 264*, 1704–1710.

Schwarz, N., Strack, F., Hilton, D., & Naderer, G. (1991). Base rates, representativeness and the logic of conversation: The contextual relevance of "irrelevant" information. *Social Cognition, 9*, 67–84.

Searle, J. (1984). *Minds, brains and science*. Cambridge, MA: Harvard University Press.

Sedlmeier, P. (1997). BasicBayes: A tutor system for simple Bayesian inference. *Behavior Research Methods, Instruments, and Computers, 29*, 328–336.

Sedlmeier, P., & Gigerenzer, G. (1989). Do studies of statistical power have an effect on the power of studies? *Psychological Bulletin, 105,* 309–316.

Sedlmeier, P., & Gigerenzer, G. (in press). Teaching Bayesian reasoning in less than two hours. *Journal of Experimental Psychology: General.*

Sedlmeier, P., Hertwig, R., & Gigerenzer, G. (1998). Are judgments of the positional frequencies of letters systematically biased due to availability? *Journal of Experimental Psychology: Learning, Memory, and Cognition, 24* (3), 754–770.

Seligman, M. E. P., & Hager, J. L. (Eds.). (1972). *Biological boundaries of learning.* New York: Appleton-Century-Crofts.

Sen, A. (1993). Internal consistency of choice. *Econometrica, 61,* 495–521.

Shafer, G. (1976). *A mathematical theory of evidence.* Princeton, NJ: Princeton University Press.

Shafer, G. (1978). Non-additive probabilities in the work of Bernoulli and Lambert. *Archive for the History of Exact Sciences, 19,* 309–370.

Shannon, C. (1940). Symbolic analysis of relay and switching circuits. M.S. thesis, MIT.

Shanteau, J. (1989). Cognitive heuristics and biases in behavioral auditing: Review, comments and observations. *Accounting Organizations and Society, 14,* 165–177.

Shaughnessy, J. M. (1992). Research on probability and statistics: Reflections and directions. In D. A. Grouws (Ed.), *Handbook of research on mathematical teaching and learning* (pp. 465–494). New York: Macmillan.

Shepard, R. N. (1962). The analysis of proximities: Part 2. *Psychometrika, 27,* 219–246.

Shepard, R. N. (1967). On subjectively optimum selections among multiattribute alternatives. In W. Edwards & A. Tversky (Eds.), *Decision making* (pp. 257–283). Baltimore: Penguin Books.

Shepard, R. N. (1974). Representation of structure in similarity data: Problems and prospects. *Psychometrika, 39,* 373–421.

Shepard, R. N. (1990). *Mind sights.* New York: Freeman.

Shepard, R. N. (1992). The perceptual organization of colors: An adaptation to regularities of the terrestrial world? In J. H. Barkow, L. Cosmides, & J. Tooby (Eds.), *The adapted mind: Evolutionary psychology and the generation of culture* (pp. 495–532). New York: Oxford University Press.

Sherman, S. J., Judd, C. M., & Park, B. (1989). Social cognition. *Annual Review of Psychology, 40,* 281–326.

Simon, H. A. (1945). *Administrative behavior: A study of decision-making processes in administrative organization.* New York: Free Press.

Simon, H. A. (1956). Rational choice and the structure of the environment. *Psychological Review, 63,* 129–138.

Simon, H. A. (1957). *Models of man: Social and rational.* New York: Wiley.

Simon, H. A. (1969). *The sciences of the artificial.* Cambridge, MA: MIT Press.

Simon, H. A. (1973). Does scientific discovery have a logic? *Philosophy of Science, 40,* 471–480.

Simon, H. A. (1979). Information processing models of cognition. *Annual Review of Psychology, 30,* 363–396.

Simon, H. A. (1982). *Models of bounded rationality.* Cambridge, MA: MIT Press.

Simon, H. A. (1986). Rationality in psychology and economics. In R. Hogarth

& M. Reder (Eds.), *Rational choice: The contrast between economics and psychology* (pp. 25–40). Chicago: University of Chicago Press.

Simon, H. A. (1987). Bounded rationality. In J. Eatwell, M. Milgate, & P. Newman (Eds.), *The New Palgrave: A dictionary of economics* (pp. 266–268). London: Macmillan.

Simon, H. A. (1990). Invariants of human behavior. *Annual Review of Psychology, 41*, 1–19.

Simon, H. A. (1991). *Models of my life.* New York: Basic Books.

Simon, H. A. (1992a). What is an "explanation" of behavior? *Psychological Science, 3*, 150–161.

Simon, H. A. (1992b). *Economics, bounded rationality, and the cognitive revolution.* Aldershot Hants, England: Elgar.

Simon, H. A., & Kulkarni, D. (1988). The processes of scientific discovery: The strategy of experimentation. *Cognitive Science, 12*, 139–175.

Simon, H. A., & Newell, A. (1986). Information processing language V on the IBM 650. *Annals of the History of Computing, 8*, 47–49.

Sivyer, M., & Finlay, D. (1982). Perceived duration of auditory sequences. *Journal of General Psychology, 107*, 209–217.

Skinner, B. F. (1972). *Cumulative record.* New York: Appleton-Century-Crofts.

Skinner, B. F. (1984). *A matter of consequences.* New York: New York University Press.

Sloman, S. A. (1996). The empirical case for two systems of reasoning. *Psychological Bulletin, 119*, 3–22.

Slovic, P., Fischhoff, B., & Lichtenstein, S. (1976). Cognitive processes and societal risk taking. In J. S. Carroll & J. W. Payne (Eds.), *Cognition and social behavior* (pp. 165–184). Hillsdale, NJ: Erlbaum.

Smith, E. E., & Osherson, D. N. (1989). Similarity and decision making. In S. Vosniadou & A. Ortony (Eds.), *Similarity and analogical reasoning* (pp. 60–75). Cambridge, England: Cambridge University Press.

Smith, L. D. (1986). *Behaviorism and logical positivism.* Stanford, CA: Stanford University Press.

Snell, J. J. S., Supran, E. M., & Tamashiro, H. (1992). WHO international quality assessment scheme for HIV antibody testing: Results from the second distribution of sera. *Bulletin of the World Health Organization, 70*, 605–613.

Sniezek, J. A., & Buckley, T. (1993). Becoming more or less uncertain. In N. J. Castellan (Ed.), *Individual and group decision making* (pp. 87–108). Hillsdale, NJ: Erlbaum.

Sperber, D. (1994). The modularity of thought and the epidemiology of representations. In L. A. Hirschfeld & S. A. Gelman (Eds.), *Mapping the mind: Domain specificity in cognition and culture* (pp. 39–67). Cambridge, England: Cambridge University Press.

Sperber, D., Cara, F., & Girotto, V. (1995). Relevance theory explains the selection task. *Cognition, 57*, 31–95.

Sperber, D., & Wilson, D. (1986). *Relevance: Communication and cognition.* Oxford, England: Blackwell.

Spettell, C. M., & Liebert, R. M. (1986). Training for safety in automated person-machine systems. *American Psychologist, 41*, 545–550.

Spielberg, F., Kabeya, C. M., Ryder, R. W., Kifuani, N. K., Harris, J., Bender, T. R., Heyward, W. L., & Quinn, T. C. (1989). Field testing and comparative evaluation of rapid visually read screening essays for antibody to human immunodeficiency virus. *Lancet, 1*, 580–584.

Statistisches Bundesamt. (1986). *Statistisches Jahrbuch 1986 für die Bundesrepublik Deutschland* [Statistical yearbook 1986 for the Federal Republic of Germany]. Stuttgart, Germany: Kohlhammer.

Statistisches Bundesamt (1994). *Statistisches Jahrbuch 1994 für die Bundesrepublik Deutschland.* Wiesbaden, Germany: Statistisches Bundesamt.

Stephens, D. W., & Krebs, J. R. (1986). *Foraging theory.* Princeton, NJ: Princeton University Press.

Sterling, T. D. (1959). Publication decisions and their possible effects on inferences drawn from tests of significance—or vice versa. *Journal of the American Statistical Association, 54*, 30–34.

Stich, S. P. (1990). *The fragmentation of reason.* Cambridge, MA: MIT Press.

Stigler, J. W. (1984). The effect of abacus training on Chinese children's mental calculation. *Cognitive Psychology, 16*, 145–176.

Stigler, S. M. (1983). Who discovered Bayes's theorem? *American Statistican, 37*, 290–196.

Stine, G. J. (1996). *Acquired immune deficiency syndrome: Biological, medical, social, and legal issues* (2nd ed.). Englewood Cliffs, NJ: Prentice Hall.

Stone, G. O. (1986). An analysis of the delta rule and the learning of statistical associations. In D. Rumelhart, J. McClelland, & the PDP Research Group (Eds.), *Parallel distributed processing: Explorations in the microstructure of cognition* (pp. 444–459). Cambridge, MA: MIT Press.

Strack, F. (1988). Social cognition: Sozialpsychologie innerhalb des Paradigmas der Informationsverarbeitung. *Psychologische Rundschau, 39*, 72–82.

"Student" [W. S. Gosset]. (1908). The probable error of a mean. *Biometrika, 6*, 1–25.

Swets, J. A., Tanner, W. P., Jr., & Birdsall, T. G. (1964). Decision processes in perception. In J. A. Swets (Ed.), *Signal detection and recognition in human observers* (pp. 3–57). New York: Wiley.

Swijtink, Z. G. (1987). The objectification of observation: Measurement and statistical methods in the nineteenth century. In L. Krüger, L. Daston, & M. Heidelberger (Eds.), *The probabalistic revolution:* Vol. 1. *Ideas in history* (pp. 261–285). Cambridge, MA: MIT Press.

Tanner, W. P., Jr. (1965). *Statistical decision processes in detection and recognition* (Technical Report). Ann Arbor: University of Michigan, Sensory Intelligence Laboratory, Department of Psychology.

Tanner, W. P., Jr., & Swets, J. A. (1954). A decision-making theory of visual detection. *Psychological Review, 61*, 401–409.

Teigen, K. H. (1974). Overestimation of subjective probabilities. *Scandinavian Journal of Psychology, 15*, 56–62.

Teigen, K. H. (1983). Studies in subjective probability: IV. Probabilities, confidence, and luck. *Scandinavian Journal of Psychology, 24*, 175–191.

Terman, L. M. (1916). *The measurement of intelligence.* Boston: Houghton Mifflin.

Terman, L. M., & Merrill, M. A. (1937). *Measuring intelligence.* Boston: Houghton Mifflin.

Tetlock, P. E. (1992). The impact of accountability on judgment and choice: Toward a social contingency model. In M. Zanna (Ed.), *Advances in experimental social psychology* (Vol. 25, pp. 331–376). New York: Academic Press.

Thaler, R. H. (1991). *Quasi rational economics*. New York: Russell Sage Foundation.

Thinès, G., Costall, A., & Butterworth, G. (Eds.). (1991). *Michotte's experimental phenomenology of perception*. Hillsdale, NJ: Erlbaum.

Thomas, D. H. (1978). The awful truth about statistics in archaeology. *American Antiquity, 43*, 231–244.

Thorndike, R. L. (1954). The psychological value system of psychologists. *American Psychologist, 9*, 787–789.

Thurstone, L. L. (1927). A law of comparative judgment. *Psychological Review, 34*, 273–286.

Titchener, E. B. (1896). *An outline of psychology*. New York: Macmillan.

Todd, P. M. (2000a). Fast and frugal heuristics for environmentally bounded minds. In G. Gigerenzer & R. Selten (Eds.), *Bounded rationality: The adaptive toolbox* (pp. 51–70). Cambridge, MA: MIT Press.

Todd, P. M. (2000b). The ecological rationality of mechanisms evolved to make up minds. *American Behavioral Scientist, 43*, 940–956.

Tooby, J., & Cosmides, L. (1992). The psychological foundations of culture. In J. Barkow, L. Cosmides, & J. Tooby (Eds.), *The adapted mind: Evolutionary psychology and the generation of culture* (pp. 19–136). New York: Oxford University Press.

Tooby, J., & DeVore, I. (1987). The reconstruction of hominid behavioral evolution through strategic modeling. In W. G. Kinzey (Ed.), *The evolution of human behavior: Primate models* (pp. 183–237). Albany, NY: State University of New York Press.

Toulmin, S., & Leary, D. E. (1985). The cult of empiricism in psychology, and beyond. In S. Koch & D. E. Leary (Eds.), *A century of psychology as science* (pp. 594–617). New York: McGraw-Hill.

Tu, X. T., Litvak, E., & Pagano, M. (1992). Issues in human immunodeficiency virus (HIV) screening programs. *American Journal of Epidemiology, 136*, 244–255.

Tukey, J. W. (1977). *Exploratory data analysis*. Reading, MA: Addison-Wesley.

Turing, A. M. (1950). Computing machinery and intelligence. *Mind, 59*, 433–460.

Turing, A. M. (1969). Intelligent machinery. In B. Meltzer & D. Michie (Eds.), *Machine intelligence* (Vol. 5, pp. 3–23). Edinburgh, Scotland: Edinburgh University Press. (Original work published 1947)

Tversky, A. (1977). Features of similarity. *Psychological Review, 84*, 327–352.

Tversky, A., & Kahneman, D. (1971). Belief in the law of small numbers. *Psychological Bulletin, 76*, 105–110.

Tversky, A., & Kahneman, D. (1973). Availability: A heuristic for judging frequency and probability. *Cognitive Psychology, 5*, 207–232.

Tversky, A., & Kahneman, D. (1974). Judgment under uncertainty: Heuristics and biases. *Science, 185*, 1124–1131.

Tversky, A., & Kahneman, D. (1980). Causal schemata in judgments under uncertainty. In M. Fishbein (Ed.), *Progress in social psychology* (Vol. 1, pp. 49–72). Hillsdale, NJ: Erlbaum.

Tversky, A., & Kahneman, D. (1982a). Judgments of and by representativeness. In D. Kahneman, P. Slovic, & A. Tversky (Eds.), *Judgment under uncertainty: Heuristics and biases* (pp. 84–98). Cambridge, England: Cambridge University Press.

Tversky, A., & Kahneman, D. (1982b). Evidential impact of base rates. In D. Kahneman, P. Slovic, & A. Tversky (Eds.), *Judgment under uncertainty: Heuristics and biases* (pp. 153–160). Cambridge, England: Cambridge University Press.

Tversky, A., & Kahneman, D. (1983). Extensional versus intuitive reasoning: The conjunction fallacy in probability judgment. *Psychological Review, 90*, 293–315.

Tweney, R. D., Doherty, M. E., & Mynatt, C. R. (Eds.). (1981). *On scientific thinking.* New York: Columbia University Press.

Tweney, R. D., & Walker, B. J. (1990). Science education and the cognitive psychology of science. In B. F. Jones & L. Idol (Eds.), *Dimensions of thinking and cognitive instruction* (pp. 291–310). Hillsdale, NJ: Erlbaum.

Wänke, M., Schwarz, N., & Bless, H. (1995). The availability heuristic revisited: Experienced ease of retrieval in mundane frequency estimates. *Acta Psychologica, 89*, 83–90.

Wallach, L., & Wallach, M. A. (1994). Gergen versus the mainstream: Are hypotheses in social psychology subject to empirical test? *Journal of Personality and Social Psychology. 67*, 233–242.

Wallach, M. A., & Wallach, L. (1998). When experiments serve little purpose: Misguided research in mainstream psychology. *Theory and Psychology, 8*, 183–194.

Wallendael, L. R. van, & Hastie, R. (1990). Tracing the footsteps of Sherlock Holmes: Cognitive representations of hypothesis testing. *Memory and Cognition, 18*, 240–250.

Wallsten, T. S. (1983). The theoretical status of judgmental heuristics. In R. W. Scholz (Ed.), *Decision making under uncertainty* (pp. 21–37). Amsterdam: Elsevier.

Ward, J. W. (1994). Testing for human retrovirus infections: Medical indications and ethical considerations. In G. Schochetman & J. R. George (Eds.), *AIDS testing: A comprehensive guide to technical, medical, social, legal, and management issues* (pp. 1–14). New York: Springer.

Wason, P. C. (1966). Reasoning. In B. M. Foss (Ed.), *New horizons in psychology* (pp. 135–151). Harmondsworth, England: Penguin.

Wason, P. C. (1968). Reasoning about a rule. *Quarterly Journal of Experimental Psychology, 20*, 273–281.

Wason, P. C. (1981). The importance of cognitive illusions. *Behavioral and Brain Sciences, 4*, 356.

Wason, P. C., & Johnson-Laird, P. N. (1970). A conflict between selecting and evaluating information in an inferential task. *British Journal of Psychology, 61* (4), 509–515.

Weber, U., Böckenholt, U., Hilton, D. J., & Wallace, B. (1993). Determinants of diagnostic hypothesis generation: Effects of information, base rates, and experience. *Journal of Experimental Psychology: Learning, Memory, and Cognition, 19*, 1151–1164.

Wells, G. L., & Harvey, J. H. (1977). Do people use consensus information in making causal attributions? *Journal of Personality and Social Psychology, 35*, 279–293.

Wells, G. L., & Harvey, J. H. (1978). Naive attributors' attributions and predictions: What is informative and when is an effect an effect? *Journal of Personality and Social Psychology, 36*, 483–490.

Wendt, D. (1966). Versuche zur Erfassung eines subjektiven Verlässlichkeits-niveaus. *Zeitschrift für Psychologie, 172,* 40–81.

Whitehead, A. N., & Russell, B. (1935). *Principia mathematica* (2nd ed., Vol. 1) Cambridge, England: Cambridge University Press.

Whiten, A., & Byrne, R. W. (1988). The Machiavellian intelligence hypotheses [Editorial]. In R. Byrne & A. Whiten (Eds.), *Machiavellian intelligence* (pp. 1–9). Oxford, England: Clarendon Press.

Wickelgren, W. A., & Norman, D. A. (1966). Strength models and serial position in short-term recognition memory. *Journal of Mathematical Psychology, 3,* 316–347.

Wilber, J. C. (1991). New development in diagnosing infections. In P. Volbering & M. A. Jacobson (Eds.), *AIDS clinical review* (pp. 1–15). New York: Dekker.

Wilkinson, G. S. (1990, February). Food sharing in vampire bats. *Scientific American,* 76–82.

Williams, G. C. (1966). *Adaption and natural selection: A critique of some current evolutionary thought.* Princeton, NJ: Princeton University Press.

Wimsatt, W. C. (1976). Reductionism, levels of organization, and the mind-body problem. In G. G. Globus, G. Maxwell, & I. Savodnik (Eds.), *Consciousness and the brain: A scientific and philosophical inquiry* (pp. 199–267). New York: Plenum.

Wimsatt, W. C. (1986). Developmental constraints, generative entrenchment, and the innate-acquired distinction. In P. W. Bechtel (Ed.), *Integrating scientific disciplines* (pp. 185–208). Dordrecht, Holland: Martinus-Nijhoff.

Windeler, J., & Köbberling, J. (1986). Empirische Untersuchung zur Einschätzung diagnostischer Verfahren am Beispiel des Haemoccult-Tests [An empirical study of the judgments about diagnostic procedures using the example of the hemoccult test]. *Klinische Wochenschrift, 64,* 1106–1112.

Winer, B. J. (1971). *Statistical principles in experimental design.* New York: McGraw-Hill.

Winterfeldt, D. von, & Edwards, W. (1982). Costs and payoffs in perceptual research. *Psychological Bulletin, 91,* 609–622.

Winterfeldt, D. von, & Edwards, W. (1986). *Decision analysis and behavioral research.* Cambridge, England: Cambridge University Press.

Wise, M. N. (1988). Mediating machines. *Science in Context, 2,* 77–113.

Wittkowski, K. (1989). Wann ist ein HIV Test indiziert? Schlusswort. *Deutsches Ärzteblatt, 86,* B-138–140.

Woodworth, R. S. (1938). *Experimental psychology.* New York: Holt, Rinehart, & Winston.

Woodworth. R. S., & Schlosberg, H. (1954). *Experimental psychology.* New York: Holt, Rinehart, & Winston.

World Health Organization. (1996). Global AIDS statistics. *AIDS Care, 8,* 501.

Zacks, R. T., Hasher, L., & Sanft, H. (1982). Automatic encoding of event frequency: Further findings. *Journal of Experimental Psychology: Learning, Memory, and Cognition, 8,* 106–116.

Zimmer, A. C. (1983). Verbal vs. numerical processing by subjective probabilities. In R. W. Scholz (Ed.), *Decision making under uncertainty* (pp. 159–182). Amsterdam: North-Holland.

Zimmer, A. C. (1986). What uncertainty judgments can tell about the underlying subjective probabilities. *Uncertainty in Artificial Intelligence,* 249–252.

NAME INDEX

SUBJECT INDEX

acceptance of new theories, 5, 10,
    26, 37–39, 42
accountability, 225
accuracy, 53, 177, 183, 188, 233
achievement, 46, 51, 53, 163
adaptation, 10, 11, 53, 59, 61, 138,
    141, 164, 168, 212, 230, 259,
    260
adaptive
    coin-flipping, 207, 208
    problem, 200, 211, 214, 229
    toolbox, 228
    unpredictability, 233
advertisement, 192
AIDS counseling, 58, 71, 72, 77–91
altruism, 213, 216, 217. *See also*
    cooperation
ambiguity of cues, 44, 46
American Psychological Association,
    12, 212, 284
    Publication Manual, 269, 294
analysis of variance (ANOVA), 6, 8,
    12, 40, 49, 50, 55, 193, 233, 241,
    269
Analytical Engine, 28, 30
anchoring and adjustment, 259, 261,
    290
anthropocentrism, 230
anthropomorphism, 230
anxiety, 280, 281
Archimedian axiom, 174

artificial intelligence, 31, 227, 244,
    260
aspiration level, 167, 193, 259
astronomers, 23, 27, 230, 278,
    286
attribution theory, 8, 9, 40
availability, 51, 216, 217, 220, 242,
    259–261, 290, 291

BACON, 5, 22
base rate, 16, 20, 67, 72, 93, 99, 100,
    106, 151, 255–260, 263
    neglect (fallacy), 16, 20, 51, 52, 57,
    61, 65, 93, 115, 212, 242, 243,
    251–254, 266, 290
    only, 114, 116, 118, 120
battering, 58, 68–71
Bayes's rule, 10, 16, 17, 51, 60–62,
    66–69, 75, 81, 92, 93, 99–110,
    117, 121, 122, 166, 201, 232,
    233, 255, 260, 262, 264, 271,
    287
    physical analog of, 103
Bayesian
    reasoning, 52, 59–61, 63, 64, 70,
    74, 75, 92–123, 167
    statistics, 9, 10, 14, 201, 241, 259,
    277
Bechterev's disease, 67
behaviorism, 6, 31, 37, 212, 228,
    230, 269, 273, 277

337